WHEN BRITAIN SAVED THE WEST

ROBIN PRIOR

WHEN BRITAIN SAVED THE WEST

THE STORY OF 1940

YALE UNIVERSITY PRESS
NEW HAVEN AND LONDON

For information about this and other Yale University Press publications, please contact:
U.S. Office: sales.press@yale.edu   www.yalebooks.com
Europe Office: sales@yaleup.co.uk   www.yalebooks.co.uk

Typeset in Minion Pro by IDSUK (DataConnection) Ltd
Printed in Great Britain by TJ International Ltd, Padstow, Cornwall

Library of Congress Cataloging-in-Publication Data

Prior, Robin.
   When Britain saved the west: the story of 1940/Robin Prior. Pages cm
   ISBN 978-0-300-16662-0 (cl: alk. paper)
1. World War, 1939–1945—Great Britain. 2. Great Britain—Politics and government—1936–1945. 3. Britain, Battle of, Great Britain, 1940. I. Title.
   D759. P75 2015
   940. 53' 41—dc23
                                                                                        2014047024

A catalogue record for this book is available from the British Library.

10 9 8 7 6 5 4 3 2 1

For Patsy Grigg and Heather

CONTENTS

CONTENTS

ILLUSTRATIONS

Plates

Tables

MAPS

ACKNOWLEDGEMENTS

I WISH TO ACKNOWLEDGE both the institutions and the many people who assisted me in the production of this book.

First I would like to thank the University of New South Wales and the Australian Research Council for providing me with initial funding which enabled the research for this project to commence. Without grant money it is becoming increasingly difficult for researchers to travel to major archives overseas for sustained periods. I hope that in current circumstances bodies such as these continue to fund the breadth of research that keeps Australia relevant in modern historical studies.

Conversations with many friends sustained and enlightened me over the years during which this book was written. Gordon Baker suffered through many a long telephone call while I rehearsed my ideas with him. He also proofread the entire manuscript at a vital time. My appreciation for his undertaking this onerous task is immense. Trevor Wilson has been a constant source of encouragement and advice. Special mention must be made of Robert Dare. I shared an office for several years with Robert and ambushed him on many a day to talk about 1940. He can detect an uncertain argument at one hundred paces. I owe him a great debt for helping me hone some of the central themes of this book.

I also owe a debt to my postgraduate students who must have wondered at times whether they actually had signed up to write a thesis on 1940.

Bodie Ashton, Jonathon Endersby, Mel Hampton and Kylie Galbraith listened patiently and forced me to defend my position with more precision than perhaps I was initially inclined to do. Eventually our conversations would drift back to their own topics. Other postgraduates on whom I have inflicted my ideas are Daniel Ashdown and Hilary Locke. I owe a special thanks to Lachlan Coleman who assisted with research in the National Archives at a critical time. If these people are representative of generation Y, we need them to take charge as soon as possible.

For permission to quote from collections in their possession I must thank the Imperial War Museum, Lambeth and Churchill College, Cambridge. For permission to quote from the diary of Lord Halifax I must thank the Borthwick Trust and for permission to quote from the Harold Nicolson diaries I must thank the copyright holders and Balliol College, Oxford for making them available. Material from Mass observation has been reproduced with permission of Curtis Brown Group Ltd, London on behalf of The Trustees of the Mass Observation Archive. The National Archives at Kew continue to amaze. Most of the footnotes in this book will be found to have come from collections in this marvellous and efficient repository. The fish-finger sandwich in their cafe was, however, something else.

I owe a special thanks to two librarians (in particular) in the Barr Smith Library. Margaret Hosking was my point of call for all difficult enquiries. She invariably came up with the books, articles or microfilms that I needed. She was also instrumental in securing the Mass Observation Archive and the Churchill Papers On-line for the library. I made extensive use of both of these invaluable resources. Margaret Galbraith kept me afloat in the library in ways that only she could.

Jo Macleod also kept me afloat in other ways. I am very grateful to her.

Luke Hampton drew the maps for this volume. The clarity and speed with which he was able to do this were remarkable and I owe him a debt of gratitude.

As always, the support I have received from the expert team at Yale University Press London has been exceptional. Rachael Lonsdale has been a model of patience in coaxing out of me details needed for the book. Candida Brazil and Tami Halliday have managed the editorial process deftly and efficiently. It is difficult to express the level of my gratitude to Robert Baldock. He has revived flagging spirits, been a constant source of encouragement and a good friend. His support over a period of years was essential to this project.

My greatest supporter has been my wife, Heather. She has participated in every stage of this book – research, drafting, reading endless chapters, copy-editing, and all round encouragement and patience. It is no truism to say that this book could not have been written without her and that it would have been a much poorer product without her efforts.

My daughter, Megan, has been a constant source of delight, surprise and comfort during the writing of this book. I intend that one day she will read at least one of her father's books. This might be the one.

INTRODUCTION

FROM THE PERSPECTIVE OF the twenty-first century, the Allied victory in the Second World War seems inevitable. It is clear now that the enormous productive capacities of the Soviet and American war economies were bound to overthrow Nazi Germany eventually. And we know now that if there had been significant setbacks in this process the atomic bomb in the hands of the United States would have settled the matter sometime in 1945.

However, none of this was apparent in 1940. In that year Stalin was supplying Hitler with enormous quantities of war materiel, the United States was steadfastly neutral, and the atomic bomb existed only as an equation on the back of an envelope. In 1940 the only major power fighting Germany was Britain. Had Britain collapsed and Europe become Nazified, the future of the West would have been very bleak. This book, then, deals with that period when Allied victory looked anything but inevitable, a period indeed when the war might have been lost.

There are some excellent books on Britain and 1940 but most only deal with one aspect of the war: Stephen Bungay on the Battle of Britain, Juliet Gardiner on the Blitz, John Lukacs on Churchill.[1] There are some more general studies. There is Lawrence Thompson, *1940: Year of Legend, Year of History*.[2] This is an excellent book but it is dated and was written at a time when many official records were not available. There is also the bilious effort by Clive Ponting, *1940: Myth and Reality*, which attempts to destroy myths but manages to mangle realities that were never mythic in the first place.[3] A more modern study by Malcolm Smith, *Britain and 1940: History, Myth and Popular Memory*,[4] is a good social history of the period with an interesting chapter on the influence of '1940' on subsequent British history, but it does not address the military and political issues that are the focus of this book.

In this book I want to approach the period from a slightly different angle. Here I will consider only those crises in 1940 that had the potential to affect the existence of Britain as an independent state. This approach focuses attention on the possibility that if events had played out differently Britain might well have been defeated or reduced to servitude. Many events that happened in 1940 have, with this emphasis, largely been excluded. Some of these events are of minor importance anyway. Nothing much hung on the success or failure of the Dakar expedition in July of that year. The Western Desert, while it was to become significant, had not yet attained that stature by 1940.

Other exclusions require a more detailed explanation. The Norway campaign has found no place here. The chapters were written but then reluctantly discarded. The war in Norway certainly served as a reminder to Britain that the navy would find it difficult to operate without air cover, especially at a distance from British shores. It also exposed some shocking incompetence in military planning and war-making machinery. But the loss of Norway did not affect Britain directly. Its importance to this book and why a little background is given here is that it brought on a debate that ended with the ousting of Neville Chamberlain as Prime Minister. Another important exclusion is the Battle of the Atlantic. It was under way in 1940 and 1941, and Britain was starting to feel the pressure of the cargoes and ships lost to submarines. But the battle had not entered the deadly phase of 1942–3. It is dealt with to the extent necessary in the chapter on Britain and the United States with which the book concludes, because it did affect relations between the two states in our period.

The subjects dealt with here are only those that threatened to end Britain's role in the war, one way or another. These are numerous enough. I start with a depiction of the Chamberlain government, which by the lacklustre way it waged war was in itself a danger to Britain. Then I proceed through the political crises of May 1940 – the replacement of Chamberlain with Churchill and the attack on Churchill's policy by Lord Halifax and (on occasion) Chamberlain. The next crisis concerns the fate of the British Expeditionary Force (BEF). Would it manage the only manoeuvre left to it – a retreat – and would it return to Britain? Then follows the threat of a Nazi invasion and the Battle of Britain, which are in many ways – but not all – interrelated. Finally the ordeal of the Blitz is investigated to examine how close British 'morale' came to collapse and whether the Germans were making serious inroads into Britain's war-making capacity. There are also two large issues regarding Britain's ally – France – and its putative ally – the United States – to be dealt with. Did Britain, despite Dunkirk, make every effort to aid France in the campaign of May–June 1940 or was it merely concerned with its own defence? And how was it that Churchill's pleas for America to enter the war fell on deaf ears? In the course of these chapters the question of whether Britain did fight this period of the Second World War alone will be addressed.

In shaping the book in this fashion I also seek to draw attention to two other issues. The first is the nature of the war had Britain been defeated or withdrawn into a sullen peace with Hitler. Without delving too far into speculation or counter-factual history, I find it difficult to imagine what might have happened. Would Hitler have defeated Russia without Britain to contend with? Would an American reconquest of Europe from the Nazis have occurred without an offshore base? Fortunately, it is not necessary to answer these questions to see how important it was that Britain continued the fight against Hitler.

By taking this approach I also want to highlight the nature of the struggle in 1940. Britain was a class-ridden society with many imperfections. It was also a liberal democracy that stood for the rule of law, representative institutions, tolerance or 'decency' to use George Orwell's word. And Britain was all that stood between Hitler and at the very least the domination of Europe.

On the other side, the Nazis had stamped out the rule of law in Germany, based their policy on racial hatred, wiped out minority dissent, and excluded altogether groups such as Jews, Romani, communists and homosexuals from civil society. If it stood for anything in 1940, Germany stood for war and aggression even against those it had already conquered. And the more it conquered the more it could persecute and spread its vile policies throughout Europe.

The war in the West is not usually portrayed in such black and white terms. It is not that historians have identified any aspects of Nazi Germany that are laudable. It is more that in 1940 the full horror of Nazi policies had not yet revealed itself. But the snuffing out of Poland, Denmark, Norway, Belgium, the Netherlands and most of France was atrocious enough. And the persecution of groups within all those countries was well under way in 1940. This was already not just an old-fashioned war for the acquisition of territory – it was racial war as well.

In 1940 the West stood on the brink of oblivion and perhaps this is the place to say what I mean by the West. It is, in general terms, the group of countries where the state seeks to uphold these values of the Enlightenment – political diversity, freedom of speech, the rule of law, tolerance of minorities. These states are not ruled by religious dogma but are largely secular in outlook. That these states contain many imperfections is beyond question. Some groups within the West have never accepted the values of the Enlightenment. Aspects of the secular state are under attack at present. The West has also made many egregious errors in the fields of foreign, environmental and humanitarian policy, any one of which may yet destroy it. But the West has also been the location of Churchill's 'broad sunlit uplands', the only region in the world where a relatively decent life can be lived free from fear and oppression.

Could it be argued that Germany was still fundamentally part of the West? I reject this view because I believe that it seriously underestimates the almost inconceivable horror lying at the heart of Nazi Germany. Britain was not fighting the land of Goethe, Kant or Beethoven. It was fighting Nazism, and Nazism was not merely a perversion of the Enlightenment like communism; it was its negation. Hitler well understood this. He often referred to 'the West' in entirely oppositional terms. He did not consider Germany to be part of this entity, nor did he want his regime to be thought of as Western.

The sources that underpin the writing of this book represented a considerable challenge. They are immense. The War Cabinet Conclusions and those of its affiliated committees (especially the Defence Committee and the Chiefs of Staff Committee) and the papers that are attached to these committees alone would fill a small room. In addition we have the Admiralty Papers, vital for invasion policy and Dunkirk, the War Office Papers that are also vital for invasion preparations, Dunkirk and the retreat of the BEF, and the papers of Fighter Command which in their detail threaten to overwhelm any study of the Battle of Britain. For the Blitz the papers of the Home Security Department are voluminous but essential, as are the myriad of diaries and letters of those who lived through it. The papers of the Ministry of Information and those of Mass Observation are also essential to gauge at least how public officials and professional snoopers thought 'the people' were coping with the bombing.

In addition to these official or semi-official papers are collections of private papers of individuals. The huge collection in the Churchill Papers is thankfully online but time-consuming to use. There are also large collections of private papers associated with figures such as Eden, Chamberlain, Roosevelt and many others identified in the bibliography.

Nevertheless, despite the overwhelming nature of the sources I can claim that most of this book is based on their solid foundation. Where possible I have used original documents in preference to published collections. An exception is the Roosevelt–Churchill correspondence, which has been so expertly edited by Warren Kimball. This study also owes a debt to the labours of many other historians on whose work I have frequently drawn. Their contribution to this book will, I hope, be obvious from the endnotes.

CHAPTER 1

HALF-HEARTED WAR

THE DAWN OF 1940 GAVE no indication that the year would prove the most critical of the twentieth century – the year when it was possible that liberal democracy in Western Europe and perhaps the world could have vanished from the comity of nations. The 1 January 1940 marked the 123rd day of war, but since the British and French declarations of war on Germany on 3 September 1939 there had been no dramatic events in the west. In the east there had been drama enough. Poland, for which the declarations were made, had been wiped out. The German invasion, launched on 1 September, had been spectacularly successful. The Russian invasion from the east on 17 September saw the end of the Polish state.

But these events had occurred far from the frontiers of France and from the seas around Britain. Nearer to home, on the 123rd day of war, a Swedish trawler had been torpedoed by a German U-boat; the Luftwaffe had made a number of ineffectual raids on RAF bases in Scotland and the Shetlands, during which one enemy aircraft had been shot down. On the Isle of Man an old Handley Page bomber had crashed in bad weather into Mount Snaefill with the loss of three of its four crew. The day had been in fact as bereft of major military events as the preceding 122 days. The war quickly became known as the 'phoney' or 'bore' war.

This is not to deny the drama of events on the civilian front. In the first week of September 1939 over 800,000 unaccompanied children and

500,000 mothers with babies had been evacuated from Britain's industrial cities. Theatres and cinemas had closed, horse-racing ceased, and a blackout had been imposed which had so far killed more people in road traffic accidents than had died in the armed forces.

As for the armed forces, on land there was little to report. The four divisions of the British Expeditionary Force (BEF) had crossed to France and taken up their positions in the line in an area around Lille along the frontier of still neutral Belgium. The troops commenced the tasks of digging trenches, fortifying houses, constructing pillboxes and preparing tank traps. In the air there had been some action. Some RAF bomber squadrons had attacked German naval installations and shipping around Wilhelmshaven. They had been quite unsuccessful. Many aircraft had been lost and no ships sunk. At sea there had been considerably more action. Nine U-boats had been sunk (far fewer than claimed by the navy), but already 420,000 tons of shipping (British, Allied and neutral) had been torpedoed. More alarming for the navy, the *Royal Oak*, a First World War vintage battleship, had been sunk in the supposed safety of Scapa Flow to the north of Scotland, an event that drove the Home Fleet to seek refuge in Loch Ewe on the west coast of Scotland. The great success at sea had been the attack by three small warships on the German pocket battleship, *Admiral Graf Spee*. The British squadron forced it into Montevideo harbour in Uruguay, from which it emerged only to scuttle itself.

The Cabinet that was running or presiding over this war had been formed by Neville Chamberlain on 3 September 1939. His only startling addition had been to bring in Winston Churchill as First Lord of the Admiralty. Lord Hankey was also added but to the lowly position of Minister without Portfolio. If Hankey had visions of running the war through a series of committees of which he was the secretary, he was to be disappointed. In truth he was given no job of any importance. The other members of the War Cabinet were the same men who had presided over the failed appeasement policy throughout the 1930s. Under Chamberlain was Lord Halifax (Secretary of State for Foreign Affairs), Sir John Simon (Chancellor of the Exchequer), Leslie Hore-Belisha (Minister for War), Sir Samuel Hoare (Lord Privy Seal), Sir Kingsley Wood (Secretary of State for Air) and Lord Chatfield (Minister for the Coordination of Defence; formerly Admiral Beatty's Flag Captain at Jutland). Chatfield's position sounded important but there was, as it happened, little defence to coordinate.

The War Cabinet was therefore dominated by appeasers. They had declared war, after some pressure from the House of Commons, but the question remained as to how they would prosecute it.

At a meeting of the War Cabinet on the day after the declaration, Churchill showed that he was keen for immediate action. Britain had gone to war to fulfil its obligations to Poland and he thought that 'every means possible should be employed to relieve the pressure. This could be done by operations against the Siegfried Line, which was at present thinly held. The burden of such operations would fall on the French Army and our Air Force.'[1]

The War Cabinet suddenly realised that they were quite ignorant of what the French intended to do in this situation. General Ironside, the Chief of the Imperial General Staff (CIGS), and Sir Cyril Newall, the Chief of the Air Staff (CAS), were immediately dispatched to France to meet the French commander-in-chief, General Gamelin. He informed them that he intended to concentrate a force of about 80 divisions and begin a slow, methodical advance towards the main French fortifications along the Maginot Line. He would then 'throw out' a reconnaissance force to test the German frontier defences of the Siegfried Line. This phase would not be rushed. It would consist of another slow, methodical advance supported by a heavy concentration of artillery. By 'X' Day, which he could not specify, Gamelin would be ready to commence not a full-scale attack but 'leaning against the Siegfried Line' – whatever that meant. These actions (if they can be so described), as Gamelin made clear, would provide no help for the Poles. He thought Polish resistance would soon be overcome and that the Allies must conserve their forces for the 'main struggle' and 'not be led astray by popular outcry'.[2]

Gamelin's plan essentially rendered inoperative an assurance he had given to the Poles that the Allies would intervene against Germany in the first 14 days of the war. Whenever X Day arrived it was clear that it would lie far outside that period. Germany must be beaten but as it turned out this would have little to do with the fate of Poland.

Back in London it might be thought that this plan would be greeted by the War Cabinet with an outcry of the type that Gamelin feared. Nothing of the kind happened. There was general agreement that nothing could be done for the Poles. When the French were ready, the RAF would be made available to support them. Only Churchill dissented. He urged that Germany be bombed immediately to relieve pressure on the Poles. But his was a lone voice. The decision for inaction won the day.[3]

The sober fact was of course that on land the British in the medium term were dependent on the French. The four divisions already in France would increase only to ten by April 1940 – hardly a match for the 80 to 90 divisions that France had in the field. This was not a case of the British being caught on the hop. It flowed directly from Chamberlain's pre-war policy. In 1935, as Chancellor of the Exchequer, he had vetoed a proposal to equip a force of 17 divisions to be dispatched to Europe on the outbreak of a war on the grounds that the public would not stand for it.[4] When he became Prime Minister he demanded cutbacks in army expenditure that saw it equipped only for the role of imperial policing.[5] This policy defied all logic because it ensured that whatever the situation in Europe, Britain would have no suitable troops to send even to meet demands made by a European ally. After the Munich Agreement of September 1938 those demands were being expressed. Pressure from the French forced a change of policy. A Regular army of six divisions would be equipped for continental war and backed by 11 Territorial divisions.[6] After the incorporation of Czechoslovakia into the Reich in March 1939 the number of Territorial divisions was increased to 26. But these were only divisions on paper, more of which were created by a committee of the Cabinet (the Land Forces Committee) on the outbreak of war. Now an army of 55 divisions, of which 14 would be provided by the Dominions, was mooted, but it would not be ready before 1942.[7] These plans were all too late for Britain to have any influence on French strategy on land, a situation with which Chamberlain was very comfortable.

What of intervention from the air as Churchill had suggested? Only in fighters were the British well placed. The squadrons of Fighter Command were being equipped with modern single-engine Hurricanes and Spitfires, equal to anything the Germans had and superior to the latest French types. But fighters were essentially a defensive weapon. And they could only operate with security in 1939 behind the British radar chain that could give warning of an enemy attack. In France there was no radar. A few squadrons were sent there but only to provide cover for the BEF. Their purpose was hardly to conduct raids into Germany. A small force of light bombers was also sent to operate with the French, but as the French had no intention of bombing Germany these aircraft remained idle.

In terms of strikes against German industry and communications it was the bomber force that was important. On the outbreak of war Bomber Command could muster 272 aircraft. Of these 30 per cent consisted of the Fairey Battle single-engine light bomber, which could carry just 1,000 lbs weight of bombs.[8] Other types, the Hampden, the Whitley and the Wellington, could carry up to 7,000 lbs in bombs, but the Hampdens were old, having first been laid down in 1932, and the Whitleys unstable.[9] All were slow. To some extent this hybrid and obsolescent force was the product of rapid changes in bomber and fighter design in the 1930s.[10] Certainly the air staff realised that their force had many drawbacks. The bomb loads could not crack concreted targets; the force had no long-range fighter capable of protecting the bombers on incursions into Germany; the crews had received little training in navigation, bomb-aiming or even flying; and there were doubts whether the skill existed even to fly in formation, which made a concentrated blow against a target a dubious proposition.

What is striking about the British bomber force is that the War Cabinet considered it to be a fearsome weapon of mass destruction. In their discussions they did not lament that the RAF possessed a bomber force of great feebleness, vulnerability and inaccuracy but instead debated whether the awesome weapon they possessed ought to be unleashed against the Ruhr and other areas of German industrial production.[11] This presented Chamberlain with a dilemma. He was determined, for reasons that will be discussed later, to delay an actual shooting war for as long as possible. Initially he was bailed out by Roosevelt, who just before hostilities commenced issued a plea to all belligerents to refrain from bombing civilian targets.[12] An Anglo-French declaration accepting the restriction was issued the following day and Hitler followed shortly afterwards with a similar statement.[13]

Not everyone on the British side accepted this policy. On 9 September 1939 the Chief of the Air Staff recommended to the War Cabinet that the RAF be used more extensively. He reported that in Poland the Luftwaffe had attacked not just munitions factories but power stations and civilian works of all kinds. Chamberlain's response was to 'consider' these reports and meanwhile to get the Ministry of Information to publicise the type of attacks the Germans were making in Poland. The restrictions on bombing Germany were to remain.[14] Churchill also thought British policy too restrictive and urged that the synthetic oil plants in Germany be attacked. He too was overruled.[15]

One might have thought that the massive German attacks on Warsaw on 24 and 25 September would have altered Chamberlain's perspective on bombing. Surely this meant that Roosevelt's appeal had failed and that a new situation now applied. But Chamberlain demurred. The War Cabinet repeatedly discussed the question of what action by Germany would be 'decisive' enough to warrant the unleashing of the strategic bombers. Clearly Poland did not qualify, but what of an invasion of Belgium? Strangely, although keeping Belgium out of foreign hands had been a cornerstone of British policy since the state had been formed in 1830, Chamberlain doubted that even a German invasion would justify bombing the Ruhr. Even after General Ironside assured him that such an action by Hitler could certainly be regarded as 'decisive', Chamberlain cavilled. Would bombing Germany, he enquired, make the difference between the success and failure of an attack upon Belgium? Hore-Belisha, the Minister for War, came to Chamberlain's aid by stating that from his conversations with Gamelin he had adduced that the French were opposed to bombing the Ruhr in any circumstances, and that in any case they did not view the invasion of Belgium as necessarily constituting a 'decisive' event. This was surely the time to indicate to the French that Britain placed a rather higher value on the integrity of Belgium than Gamelin, but Chamberlain sided with the French. In the upshot the War Cabinet came to the utterly lame conclusion that they should inform the French that they indeed had a plan to bomb the Ruhr but that it would be implemented only if the German invasion 'looked decisive'.[16] In short they would decide not to decide and wait on events.

It would be tedious indeed to follow subsequent discussions on bombing in this detail. Suffice it to say that they all tended to follow the same trajectory. Three months later Chamberlain was still saying that 'an attack on the Ruhr in consequence of Germany's violating Belgian neutrality would be a departure from our previous ideas'.[17] And Lord Halifax was still supporting his leader by asserting that if Britain attacked the Ruhr it would be accused of being the first to 'take the gloves off'.[18] In the light of discussions such as these it is necessary to mention that Chamberlain and Halifax were aware of the bombing of Warsaw and the widespread massacres that had taken place in Poland.[19] The 'gloves', for those who had eyes to see, were well and truly off. But it would take more than widespread massacre in the east to divert Chamberlain from his inflexible resolve to do nothing.

The decision not to drop explosive objects on Germany did not mean that the bomber force would not traverse enemy territory. The bombers would not, however, drop bombs; instead they would drop information leaflets. These leaflets were deemed to serve a dual purpose. Their content, generally urging the German people to overthrow Hitler and make peace without annexations, would 'have an important effect on German public opinion'.[20] Moreover, the demonstration that British warplanes could operate over Germany with impunity would lower enemy morale.[21] The War Cabinet were aware of uneasiness in 'some quarters' about merely dropping leaflets when Poland was being pounded into a pulp, but such hesitations were brushed aside and the leaflet war continued.[22]

The leaflets were dropped by the million, but as early as 16 September Halifax was beginning to doubt their efficacy. Chamberlain, however, considered the programme 'good and useful'.[23] Not surprisingly, the Prime Minister's view prevailed.

The debate over leaflet drops continued in the War Cabinet for months. By 1940 Halifax had been won over. In a long statement he assured members that there was evidence that the Gestapo hated the leaflets and that as the German people were 'natural readers', the leaflet messages were being spread widely throughout the Third Reich.[24] Despite the tendentious, if not ludicrous, nature of these generalisations and the total lack of evidence that the German people, after an intense period of reading, were about to rise up and smite their regime, Halifax's remarks were met with polite silence by the War Cabinet. Leaflets had clearly triumphed over bombs.

A glance at Bomber Command operations between September 1939 and April 1940 confirms that this was so. During the first 250 days of the war not a single bomb fell on German territory, except poorly directed projectiles aimed at ships in port, which hit adjacent areas. The records reveal so many leaflet raids that the historians of Bomber operations felt compelled to group them into periods to avoid constant repetition. Thus between the nights of 4–5 September and 23–24 December 1939 there were 22 leaflet raids; between 4–5 January and 19–20 January 1940 there were probably about the same number, and so on.[25] If, in the 1930s, British policy makers lived 'in the shadow of the bomber', the German people, in the first eight months of the war, lived merely in the shadow of the leaflet.[26]

With an army too small to influence strategy and a bomber force that was in most circumstances not to drop bombs, only the navy remained to Britain as an instrument of war. Here the British were better placed. From 1933–4 to 1937–8, the navy received the highest percentage of the defence vote; only in 1938–9 and 1939–40 was the RAF given more money.[27] On the outbreak of war the Home Fleet (the more modestly named equivalent of the Grand Fleet in the Great War) had in British waters: eight battle-ships, two battlecruisers, four aircraft carriers, three cruiser squadrons, nine destroyer flotillas, and numerous other craft such as submarines, minesweepers and trawlers.[28] In addition, the British had five battleships and six aircraft carriers under construction.[29] Compared with this array, the Germans had four capital ships and two more under construction, five cruisers, 25 destroyers and no aircraft carriers. Only in submarines were the Germans ahead, for the simple fact that the British navy and Merchant Marine provided many more targets for them than did the small number of German ships for the British.[30]

Certainly the navy was a less troublesome weapon of war for Chamberlain than the bomber force. There would be no Cabinet discussions on using the navy to bombard Germany because there were few targets on the short German coastline and its waters were anyway protected by minefields, submarines and destroyers. Churchill's rather madcap idea that the heavy ships of the Home Fleet could be rendered mine, torpedo and bomb proof, and thus dominate the Baltic, had no support either within the Admiralty or outside it. It forever remained in the planning stage.[31]

However, there was a way in which the navy could be used offensively without risking the nightmare of the Chamberlain government – an actual shooting war. The navy could blockade the Third Reich – denying Germany essential war materials and food. In this circumstance those leaf-lets might be read with greater effect. From the outset then, blockade was the one warlike policy adopted by the Prime Minister with something approaching enthusiasm.

Chamberlain was not alone in expecting much from the blockade. There was a school of thought – encompassing military experts from both Britain and Germany – which held that it was the blockade that had brought Germany to its knees in 1918. We now know that this quite misread the situation. Gerd Hardach and others have demonstrated that if the German people were short of food and other consumables at the end of the Great War, it was the usurpation by the military of the greater part of the resources of the country as well as the transportation system that was the root cause.

This is not to say that the blockade had no effect in the Great War or that it was without value in the first eight months of the Second World War. When it was implemented on the first day of the war, it had an immediate effect on some of the 'choke points' in the German economy. One of the most important was the supply of oil. Oil was a constant worry for the Germans during the whole of the Second World War. Germany manufactured 120,000 tons of synthetic oil per month in 1939–40 and had stockpiles of 2.1 million tons. This, they estimated, represented five months' consumption for most of the economy under wartime conditions and just three months for the Luftwaffe.[32] The British had reasonably accurate intelligence on German oil supplies so their attention turned to the one European country that produced oil in quantity – Romania. In one sense both Britain and Germany (and for that matter France) faced the same problem in pursuing Romanian oil supplies – all were short of hard foreign currency with which to pay. In the case of the Allies, what hard currency they had went to the United States, which from November 1939 allowed commodities such as oil to be purchased on a cash-and-carry basis. The Germans were also chronically short of hard currency and were prevented by the blockade from accessing any part of US production. However, they could offer Romania weapons with which to modernise its military. Messerschmitt fighters were therefore exchanged for oil. After the conquest of Poland, the geographic proximity of the German army to Romania induced the government to release more oil.[33] By 1940 Germany was receiving 1.56 million tons of oil per annum from Romania.[34]

This was one leak in the blockade that the Allies were powerless to stop. But there was another that was even more important to Germany. Under a clause of the Nazi–Soviet pact, Stalin had undertaken to supply

Germany with strategic materials of all kinds. In this way shortages of other critical materials such as copper, manganese, chrome and phosphates flowed into Germany from Russia. As Adam Tooze has noted, the Quartermaster General of the German Army considered that it was this pact that allowed the conquests of 1939–40 to be made.[35] The economic blockade was thus neatly circumvented. Chamberlain's main weapon of war was a broken reed.

Britain's armed forces on this reckoning would take some time to play a significant role in the war. But this still left the Chamberlain government much to do. If anything approaching an all-out effort was to be made to win the war, a redirection of industry and labour would be required towards the manufacture of military materiel. And a huge financial effort would then be required to pay for it.

In the event the Chamberlain government did little to put the British economy on a war footing. Before hostilities commenced it set up a system of 'shadow factories' whereby major manufacturers could rapidly convert to war production when the time came.[36] A Ministry of Supply with 'very drastic powers to require supplies to be delivered and work to be done'[37] was also extracted from Chamberlain in March 1939. But the appointment of a nonentity as minister, Leslie Burgin, and Chamberlain's determination that the powers of the Ministry not be used reduced it to a hollow shell.

The passage of a number of Acts (Emergency Powers, Control of Employment, and Conscription) gave the government almost total control of the flow of labour. But yet again it was one matter to acquire powers, quite another to employ them. In the case of the Emergency Powers Act, the government never used the powers that it had made available. Regulations could have been drawn up to direct labour to areas required by war, but no such regulations were passed. The act therefore remained ineffectual.[38] The result was that so far as employment was concerned, labour did not flow with sufficient speed into war industries or, for that matter, into any other industries. In October 1939 the Minister of Labour announced to the War Cabinet the truly alarming fact that since the outbreak of war unemployment had increased from 1 million to 1.3 million.[39]

Nor were the sizes of the three armed forces increasing with sufficient speed. By March 1940 the Conscription Acts had made some difference as evidenced by Table 1.[40]

Table 1: Size of British armed forces, 1939–40.

Date	Navy	Army	Air Force	Totals
Sept. 1939	180,000	900,000	193,000	1,273,000
March 1940	241,000	1,365,000	215,000	1,821,000
Increase	61,000	465,000	22,000	548,000

But an increase of nearly 550,000 in eight months was only a small step towards the War Cabinet's own target of 32 British divisions ready by 1942 or the interim step of having 20 divisions available by September 1941.[41]

Similar situations applied in the air force and the navy. The War Cabinet decided to increase the monthly production of all aircraft from 1,500 to 2,300 and increase the construction of merchant ships from 1 million tons per year to 2 million.[42] These were laudable aims but as two committees (the Wolfe Committee and the Stamp Committee) set up to examine the labour situation reported, there was no hope of any of the targets being reached under the existing arrangements.[43] The response from the Prime Minister was to retain the targets, press on, and hope for the best.[44]

The same lethargy was evident in financial mobilisation. Various White Papers gradually increased war expenditure in 1939–40 from £580 million to £1,000 million.[45] But given that the Chancellor of the Exchequer, Sir John Simon, was well aware that the costs of war had risen greatly since the First World War and that one year's expenditure in that war had amounted to £2,500 million, these steps were patently insufficient.[46]

A number of fiscal measures were proposed by Simon to meet the cost of the war. All were modest. The standard rate of income tax was to be increased from 5s 6d to 7s 6d in the pound after six months.[47] This increase might appear significant but in 1939 only 3.5 million of the 30 million wage earners in Britain paid income tax, meaning that this would only raise £146 million in a full year.

There were also modest rises in taxes on beer, tobacco and sugar, and a small increase in death duties.[48] But in total all indirect tax rises merely produced £75 million. The only new tax was on excess profits (a tax of 60 per cent on any increase in profits over a pre-war standard).[49]

To Simon these amounts seemed bold and dramatic, but an outside observer immediately recognised the inadequacies of the fiscal measures. John Maynard Keynes – not yet employed by the Treasury but still an influential voice – wrote to *The Times* thus: 'I [do not] consider the new burdens [in the budget] excessive. Quite the contrary. What strikes me about the Budget is the utter futility of the old imposts to solve the problem, even when pushed almost to the limits of endurance. Apart from the Excess Profits Tax, the increased taxation comes to less than 5% of our pre-war income.'[50]

Keynes had realised that the indirect taxes (the old imposts) and the modest rises in income tax would not achieve even Simon's limited goals and that only a small fraction of Britain's wealth was being tapped for warlike purposes. He went on to argue that as the war would increase both the numbers employed and the number of hours worked by the employed, the budget would actually leave greater spending power in the hands of the public than they possessed before the war. This was the very opposite of what war finance should achieve. He concluded by describing Simon's proposals as mere 'chicken-feed to the dragons of war'.[51]

In other areas Simon's measures proved equally ineffective. A war loan raised only £200 million of the £300 million expected, but Simon rigidly adhered to the principle that voluntary rather than compulsory means must be used to pay for the war.

Bizarrely, he also attempted to cap the amount that the war would cost, a ludicrous exercise if a country is deemed to be fighting for its existence. Simon's first target was £1,000 million; his second, in April 1940, £2,000 million.[52] But all such targets were futile. If Britain was to wage an effective war no cap on expenditure could be contemplated. Only in one instance did Simon rise above the traditional budget measures of voluntary loans and small indirect tax increases to raise revenue. In his 1940 budget he introduced a point of sale purchase tax on all goods except food, fuel and export goods.[53] But all these measures left a £1,000 million gap between revenue and estimated expenditure. This gap brought censure from Keynes who suggested a scheme for compulsory savings which was utterly rejected.[54] Simon complained that Keynes' approach would 'kill the voluntary method', but he was not willing to accept that this method was already terminally ill.

Simon's first wartime budget in September 1939 had been received by the House of Commons with virtually no debate. Criticism was muted as members focused on how the additional war expenditure would be financed. The budget of April 1940 did not receive the same polite response. Leo Amery, a maverick Conservative, branded the budget as 'limited' and said that the Chancellor was not being honest with the people about the sacrifices the war would require.[55] On the following day Hugh Dalton, for Labour, savaged the budget, pointing out its inadequacies in terms of the effort made in the Great War and demanding a levy on capital.[56] But the outstanding speech on the budget was made by Clement Davies, a prominent Independent Liberal. Davies had been listening with growing exasperation to the dronings of Captain Crookshank, a Tory of no particular distinction. Crookshank was comparing the British war effort favourably with the German one and noting that Britain also had the rightness of its cause, the 'undragooned' beliefs of the people and the support of the Empire.[57] Finally, Davies could take no more. He interjected that the logical conclusion to be drawn from Crookshank was we are so right we need not fight.[58]

Davies had touched a nerve here. Simon's second budget fell far short of the needs of the war that Britain should have been fighting. Even the crushing defeat suffered by Britain in the Norway campaign of April 1940 had not provided a sharp shock to the Chancellor. Still only a fraction of Britain's financial resources were being mobilised. Davies concluded his speech by saying that two wars were being waged in Britain – one against Germany and the other against laissez-faire – and that he regarded the latter as 'pernicious' and 'a foul creed' which should be done away with in time of war.[59]

Davies was right. This was no way to finance a war against as formidable a foe as Nazi Germany. It was bad policy in the phoney war and it was bad policy when the shooting war started in April 1940. A growing chorus of commentators argued that if Britain was going to prosecute the war effectively, Simon's half-hearted laissez-faire approach to war finance would have to go.

The restlessness in the House of Commons was one indication that a growing number of members were becoming convinced that a new approach would only come with a new government.

* * * * *

The period of the war under discussion – from September 1939 to April 1940 – when so far as the Western powers are concerned the shooting war began, presents a puzzle. The Chamberlain government had declared war on Germany but was only waging it on the margins. It would not bomb Germany, it would not put pressure on the French to use their army offensively, and it was blind to the ineffectiveness of the blockade. Moreover, the government was not acting with the urgency required to increase Britain's war-making capacity by directing labour into industries that would address the deficiencies in numbers and equipment of the armed forces, or by mobilising the country's considerable wealth.

The answer to the puzzle is to be found in the personality of the Prime Minister. Chamberlain hated war and in September 1939 found himself in a position he had striven for years to avoid – that of being a war leader. His hatred of war resulted in a perspective on the conflict that ran counter to common sense and, although he certainly did not intend it, posed a real danger to his country. For in the end, Chamberlain convinced himself that the war could be won without serious fighting and that its duration would be short. Let us examine these propositions to see exactly why the half-hearted war came to be waged.

That Chamberlain detested the war he found himself in is not in doubt. His speech to the people on the outbreak of war was depressing in the extreme. He spoke of how *his* world had collapsed in ruins, how *he* had been betrayed by Hitler. Rather than a rallying cry to the nation in time of crisis, this was a cry for sympathy for Neville Chamberlain.[60] Few people that day would have drawn any inspiration from listening to Chamberlain's 'tired sad voice'.[61]

Shortly after the declaration of war Chamberlain confided to the Archbishop of Canterbury that he found his personal position 'hateful'.[62] A few days later he told one of his sisters: 'How I do hate and loathe this war. I was never meant to be a War Minister.' He added that he should hand over his responsibilities to someone else.[63] By December, although he was finding the war 'more hateful than ever', there were no more thoughts about relinquishing office.[64] This change had come about because Chamberlain had arrived at the startling conclusion that the war would soon be over. He 'had a feeling', he told his sister, that 'if Britain kept up the economic pressure and continued to mobilize . . . I reckon we shall have won the war by the Spring.'[65] Considering that the army was minuscule, the RAF was prohibited from bombing, the blockade was having no discernible effect, and the economy was hardly being mobilised, this was an extraordinary forecast. Chamberlain was clearly gambling on a collapse of the German home front. He thought this might be brought about in a number of ways.

Firstly, there was the effect of British propaganda. We have seen how much was made of the leaflet war by Chamberlain in the War Cabinet. He persisted with this most ineffectual of campaigns in the hope that enough Germans would be convinced of the iniquity of the Nazi regime to overthrow it.

Chamberlain's optimism was reinforced by other factors. Hitler's health was a continual preoccupation for the Prime Minister. In November, Chamberlain was claiming that the Führer had fallen into a state of 'abject depression ... owing to his inability to find any opportunity for doing anything'.[66] By early February 1940 he was reporting that Hitler was in the hands of a nerve specialist, on the brink of total collapse.[67]

Then there was the possibility that if Hitler did not collapse the German people would. As early as September, Chamberlain informed the War Cabinet that the long queues of people waiting for food in Germany had been banned because such groups could too easily exchange information on how badly the war was progressing.[68] This view was reinforced by the Romanian Foreign Minister (Viorel Tilea), who reported that the German people were intensely depressed. They could not see how the war could be won and when the first crack appeared, collapse might follow very rapidly.[69] Perhaps this was thought to carry weight because it came from a neutral source. The French also provided evidence in support. The British ambassador in Paris was told that French sources considered 'depression in Germany was growing apace', an item that was immediately passed on to the War Cabinet.[70] Two weeks later Halifax added that 'various sources' within Germany were reporting 'depression and discord existing among the Nazi leadership', and that while it would be 'unwise to pay too much attention to any of these sources . . . they had a cumulative effect'.[71] In other words it *would* be wise to pay attention to them.

The other group that was depressed in Germany was potentially more important – the army. It is certainly true that at times particular generals talked vaguely about overthrowing the Führer, but these murmurings fell well short of the type of disaffection that Halifax and Chamberlain were pedalling to the War Cabinet. On 23 October Halifax announced that a group of generals was extremely discontented with the situation and that a 'considerable' number of army officers had been shot and a larger number arrested. At the same time many naval officers had tendered their resignations.[72] A few days later Halifax stated that peace proposals were being sought from Hitler by some leading generals and that this had caused 'great disagreement' between the Führer and the military.[73] Meanwhile, Chamberlain was telling his sisters that he had information that many army officers 'are disgusted by Hitler's brutality . . . and I guess it takes a lot to shock a German Army Officer'.[74]

There were other reasons, for someone with Chamberlain's cast of mind, to believe that the Nazi regime would be short lived. A continual stream of peace feelers emanated from Germany and other sources in Europe. That many of these feelers were regarded by Chamberlain and Halifax as worthy of consideration is indicated by the regularity with which they were brought to the attention of the War Cabinet. One of the first to arrive came via the British ambassador to Turkey, Sir Hughe Knatchbull-Hugesson, who had been told by the German ambassador (Franz von Papen) that if Hitler could be removed and a provisional government formed led by Hermann Goering, peace would be possible. Chamberlain was quick to characterise Papen as 'hysterical and unreliable', but the War Cabinet proceeded to discuss in great detail what such a peace might involve – an independent Poland in agreement with the Soviet Union, Danzig to remain German, the 're-arrangement' of the frontiers of Eastern Europe by way of a conference of interested powers, autonomy (not defined) for Czechoslovakia and so on.[75] In short, though originating from an unreliable hysteric, the proposal seemed to be taken seriously.

Goering was thought to represent a moderate alternative to Hitler, and a man with whom a peace might be brokered. Berger Dahlerus was a Swedish business acquaintance of Goering and he had made many visits to London in the days before the outbreak of war in an attempt to keep Britain neutral. In early September he held a series of talks with the British Embassy in Stockholm to the effect that Goering was genuine in seeking peace. The result of these talks was a secret visit by Dahlerus to London on

28–30 September. During this time he saw Halifax, his Permanent Secretary, Sir Alexander Cadogan, and Chamberlain. What was said during these conversations remains uncertain. Dahlerus seems to have been told that words were no longer enough and that the Germans must demonstrate that they were serious about peace by actions. However, as Christopher Hill comments, 'The very fact of his access to and apparent intimacy with the highest levels of British decision making must have encouraged him (and his German interlocutors) a good deal.'[76]

Halifax informed the War Cabinet of this visit only after the event and reassured his colleagues that 'our policy should be to hold a stiff attitude in the face of such communications'. But he went on to say that he thought 'that we should not absolutely close the door'.[77] Churchill immediately protested. He told Halifax 'that these German peace feelers might not be sincere and their real object might be to spread division and doubt amongst us . . . [We must] take every step to ensure that we are not deceived.'[78] Chamberlain was unabashed by this intervention. He quickly supported Halifax by saying that indeed every door to peace must remain open.[79]

Hitler made his own grand gesture towards peace on 6 October based on Germany retaining its hegemony in Central and Eastern Europe and arguing that it would be foolish to continue a wasteful war – a bit rich coming from the man who had started it. This so-called 'peace offer' was discussed by the War Cabinet on 9 October. Churchill was first into the discussion, warning that 'our reply must be more definite than had been contemplated a few days previously' and that the Cabinet should 'not attempt to manoeuvre in order to gain time', surely a warning shot across Chamberlain's bow.[80] A long drafting process followed in which Halifax, Cadogan, Chamberlain and the Dominion prime ministers were involved, and into which Churchill managed to insert his views.[81] The result, however, was to some extent at odds with Churchill's preference of outright rejection. Chamberlain told the War Cabinet on 12 October that 'the draft statement left the door open . . . if Herr Hitler was, in fact, sincere in wishing for peace'.[82] In other words, Chamberlain *would* under certain circumstances negotiate with Hitler – a position earlier in the war he had said he would not contemplate.

Hitler's statement was not, however, the last mention of peace. Dahlerus reappeared later in August with an offer from Goering to attend a conference on the European situation convened by the King of Sweden. Halifax seems finally to have had enough of the murky Swede and although Chamberlain argued that he could see no harm in such a conference, on this occasion Halifax won the contest. Dahlerus remained in Sweden and the king's services were not required.[83] Other peace feelers followed. Dahlerus returned to London in early 1940 with an enquiry from Goering about what guarantees Britain would require to end the war. Then the British ambassador to the Vatican relayed a message that top German generals were anxious to conclude peace.[84]

Nothing came of these peace feelers. Their importance, however, lies not in their content or practicability, but in what they tell us about Chamberlain and Halifax. As much as they distrusted Hitler, Papen and the rest, they found themselves unable to dismiss out of hand peace negotiations with Hitler or with one of his gang, or with a group of his generals. In taking this stance they were courting danger. Neither man had ever taken the measure of the Nazi regime or the support that it had within the military and German society. There would be no popular uprising or coup because the majority of the people and of the generals closely identified with the policies of the Nazi regime. Above all, there would be no acceptable peace while Hitler remained at the helm and delivered military successes. The danger with which the British leadership flirted was that some kind of peace might be cobbled up at the expense not just of the Central European states – although they would certainly be its first victims – but of the vital national interests of Britain and France as well. Churchill had grasped this point during the 'peace offensive' in mid-October. He knew that Nazism was not a temporary threat to the West which could be negotiated away at a peace conference; it was a permanent menace which could only be expunged by military victory. This view was some distance from Chamberlain's thinking. He believed that sooner rather than later common sense would prevail in Germany. The Führer would either be overthrown or the Nazi leadership would realise that it made sense to give up their conquests and make peace. It followed that Germany must not be bombed, in case bombing welded the masses more tightly to the leadership or discouraged those Germans on the point of rebellion from acting. It also followed that the full mobilisation of the British economy was not a matter of urgency. Long-term plans had to be put in place in case the expected end to the war (by whatever means) in the spring of 1940 did not eventuate. But there was no need to inject any urgency into mobilisation because the war would probably be over before the measures could take effect. Chamberlain was therefore only waging total war in the sense that his misreading of the German people and the Nazi regime was total. The half-hearted war was in this reading not only pathetic – it was dangerous. By not fully mobilising the vast war potential possessed by Britain in order to fight the deadliest foe that had ever confronted it, by adopting a strategy of 'wait and see' and an economic policy of laissez-faire, the Chamberlain government was conceding to Hitler the military initiative and allowing Germany time to remedy deficiencies in its war economy. The longer the phoney war persisted the greater the danger to Britain. As it happened, the first existential threat to the continuation of the British state as a liberal democracy was the Chamberlain government itself.

CHAPTER 2

THE PARLIAMENTARY CRISIS
CHURCHILL ASCENDANT, 7–10 MAY 1940

FOR THE CHAMBERLAIN GOVERNMENT the shooting war started in the fiords of Norway. Both Britain and Germany had been concerned with Norway from the very beginning of the war. The crucial matter was deemed to be the iron-ore trade which flowed from Sweden through the Norwegian port of Narvik down the coast to the German Baltic ports. This route allowed the Germans a winter supply of Swedish ore when the other route through the Gulf of Bothnia iced over.

To halt this trade the British had a number of plans that ranged from laying a minefield off Narvik to force German shipping into open waters where it could be sunk, to grandiose schemes to entice Sweden and Norway into the war on the Allied side with the consequent halting of the ore trade. The attack on Finland by Russia in December 1939 added an additional dimension to these schemes. The British and French now thought that on the pretence of aiding Finland their troops could occupy the Swedish ore fields *en passant*.

The main problem for the British was that they could not settle on a particular plan and their war machinery, which involved three major committees and the War Cabinet, was cumbersome and inefficient. Chamberlain was possibly not unhappy with this situation. It bolstered his determination to keep the German people in a frame of mind where no irritation from the Allies would deter them from overthrowing the Führer.

In any case the Germans pre-empted the British. Just as a minefield was about to be laid off Narvik, the Germans invaded on 8 April 1940. Before the British could react, 10,000 enemy troops were ashore in Norway supported by several squadrons of bombers and fighters from the Luftwaffe. The British found that in this situation their superior fleet was of limited utility. Around Narvik, which was out of range of German air cover, British destroyer flotillas could take a fearful toll on the German navy, sinking half its entire destroyer fleet. In addition the Germans lost a heavy cruiser to Norwegian guns and two light cruisers to the British. Moreover, every German heavy ship (*Scharnhorst, Gneisenau, Lutzow* and *Hipper*) was damaged.

Central Norway, however, was within range of the German bombers. Here the British attempted landings at Namsos and Aandelasnes, the idea being that they advance pincer-like on Trondheim, Norway's second-largest city. These poorly equipped, hastily thrown together forces were defeated in short order. And in this area the heavy ships of the Home Fleet could provide no support. The danger from German bombers was just too great. Despite Churchill's messages to Admiral Forbes (eerily reminiscent of those sent to Admiral Carden at Gallipoli), urging that he rush Trondheim Fiord, the admiral was not to be persuaded. The heavy ships were withdrawn. Luckily for the British the evacuation of their forces was not opposed by the German navy and hardly a man was lost. At Narvik, a confused command structure, partly inflicted on the force by Churchill, led to Allied paralysis in the one area where they had numerical superiority. The town was finally captured on 28 May, but by then the Allies had greater worries closer to home so the town was destroyed and their forces were withdrawn. A last humiliation was the sinking of the aircraft carrier *Glorious* during the evacuation.

Churchill played an ambiguous role in the Norwegian affair. He was largely responsible for the command shambles at Narvik and, like most of his colleagues, also underestimated the vulnerability of warships to aircraft. But he was not responsible for the overall military fiasco. His only blemish was to be a member of the War Cabinet that had presided over it. Suffice it to say here that the events which were to follow placed him in an interesting, albeit slightly weakened, position.

* * * * *

As a result of the Norway campaign, a debate on the war was called in the House of Commons. Ever after it has been called 'The Norway Debate' but in truth it was about much more than Norway. The debate was in fact entitled in Hansard 'Conduct of the War' and that was a more accurate description. The Norway fiasco itself had served mainly to focus the attention of many Members of Parliament on the supine way in which the government seemed to be conducting the war. We have already noted the disquiet expressed by some members over what they saw as an inadequate response on the financial side and the slow conversion of the economy to a war footing. The setbacks in Norway gave the dissenters a new voice.

We can detect five groups of dissidents at this time. The first was the Eden group that had its origins in the resignation of the Foreign Secretary in February 1938 over differences in approach to Roosevelt and Mussolini. After Anthony Eden's resignation speech, 30 Conservatives abstained on a vote of no confidence moved by Labour.[1] Moreover, 20 of these were younger MPs who had made foreign affairs their area of expertise.[2] However, it was only around the time of the Munich crisis in October 1938 that this group solidified. Their nominal leader was Eden, there were about 20 of them, and they met once a week at the house of the Conservative MP Ronald Tree, in Queen Anne's Gate.[3] Eden's leadership of the group was rather ineffectual as he was always hoping to return to office. Only on the outbreak of war, when Chamberlain included Eden in the government as Dominions Secretary, and Leo Amery took over as chairman, did the group function as an organised body. As well as Amery and Eden the group included General Spears and Duff Cooper, and younger men on the rise such as Richard Law, Harold Macmillan, Harold Nicolson, Lord Cranbourne, Paul Emrys-Evans, Ronald Tree and J. P. C. Thomas.[4] Later adherents included Captain Bower, Captain Gunston, H. J. Duggan, A. P. Herbert, Lord Woolmer, Anthony Crossley and Mark Patrick.[5]

A separate but small group around Winston Churchill – Robert Boothby, Brenden Bracken and Duncan Sandys – held even stronger views about appeasement than the Eden group. They saw Chamberlain's foreign policy as little more than subordination to the whims of Hitler and Mussolini.[6] The problem for this group was that from the outbreak of war its leader occupied a senior position in the government as First Lord of the Admiralty. Criticism from his followers (especially over Norway) was muted.[7]

The third group had its origins in the powerful Cecil family. Lord Salisbury had long been concerned about Chamberlain's leadership in any future war. In July 1939 he wrote to the *Daily Telegraph* and the *Morning Post*, calling for 'all the best men from whatever political party [to be] included in [a] National Government on the outbreak of war'. He deplored the fact that Chamberlain seemed afraid to include Churchill in his administration for fear of offending Hitler.[8] This group, the 'Watching Committee' of 28 original members, did not exist as a formal body until April 1940. Its purpose was not necessarily to seek the overthrow of the Chamberlain government but to monitor the progress of the war. The group consisted of members of both the Commons and Lords, and in line with its charter included some who were generally pro-Chamberlain such as Sir Patrick Spens and Viscount Astor.[9]

From April the committee met regularly and discussed such subjects as the composition of the War Cabinet, strategy, and how better to mobilise the home front.[10] In general the group wanted a small War Cabinet consisting of members without departmental responsibility and a more vigorous prosecution of the war.[11] As a Tory grandee, Salisbury had excellent access to Chamberlain. The day after the German invasion of Norway, he met the Prime Minister and warned him of the consequences of failure. Receiving no satisfactory reply, two weeks later the group sent a deputation to Halifax. He too was unresponsive. A member of the delegation told Lord Cranbourne (Salisbury's son and a member of the House of Commons) that Halifax 'understands the dangers of the position but does not seem to have any solutions for dealing with it'.[12] A further deputation followed when Halifax joined Chamberlain in blaming Norwegian neutrality for the fiasco there. Salisbury bluntly told him that he was 'not satisfied' with this explanation.[13] Clearly, the 'Watching Committee' was starting to do more than watch.

A fourth group formed after the declaration of war. In November Robert Boothby convened an all-party group called the Vigilantes consisting of over 50 MPs (25 Conservative, 16 Labour, 8 Liberal and 4 Independents). Their brief was also to 'monitor the progress of the war'.[14]

Yet a fifth group was formed by government backbenchers who were serving members of the armed forces. By November 1939 there were potentially a hundred Conservatives eligible to sit in this group, although by no means all of them did so. The chairman was Victor Cazalet, an independently minded Chamberlainite who nevertheless had close links with Churchill. Their first foray took place in a Secret Session of the Commons on 13 December 1939, when several members expressed concern about the outdated military equipment provided to them. Chamberlain dismissed their complaints with contempt.[15]

In addition to these five groups, a cluster of Conservatives elected before 1914, called 'The Old Tories', formed an irregular group. They were mostly from a military background and generally supported Chamberlain, but they had joined with Churchill to oppose the India Bill of 1935. A typical 'Old Tory' was Brigadier Henry Page Croft. In his uninformative but nevertheless illuminating memoirs he makes it clear that he supported appeasement only because it bought time for British rearmament.[16] When war came he and his colleagues were appalled by British inaction over Poland. He and Sir John Gretton went so far as to send a letter of apology to the Polish ambassador. Gretton also wrote to Chamberlain begging him to bomb German airfields to relieve pressure on the Poles. When the Prime Minister failed to respond, Gretton told his constituents that Britain might 'have to look elsewhere for leaders in the Great Struggle'. Here then was a group of about 20 to 30 MPs whose support for the Prime Minister was conditional on a more vigorous prosecution of the war and whose long-term support could not be taken for granted.[17]

Estimating the size and influence of the five formal groups is difficult. Boothby, for example, was a member of four of them. Amery was a member both of the Eden and the Salisbury groups, as was Emrys-Evans. Also some members of Lord Salisbury's group were supporters of Chamberlain. Churchill and Eden occasionally attended the meetings of one group or another, although as members of the government their criticisms were necessarily muted. All told, however, it is probably reasonably accurate to suggest that 80 Conservative MPs were by April 1940 looking to replace Chamberlain as Prime Minister.

Then there was the Labour Party. In the early 1930s it had been pacifist or supportive only of collective security through the League of Nations. By 1936 the party had shifted position. Clement Attlee took the lead in convincing members that rearmament was necessary – 'consistent with our country's responsibilities' – a vague enough phrase to allow for many contingencies.[18] As the 1930s progressed and fascism advanced, Labour hardened its position. During the Munich debate Attlee moved a vote of censure against the government. Added to this was the party's abiding hatred of Chamberlain whom they associated with the harsh social policies introduced by the National government after 1931. The party's 167 votes in the House of Commons were usually overwhelmed by the Conservative Party, which had 372 members in its own right, as well as support from National Labour, National Liberal and National splinter groups. Nevertheless, if the Conservative dissidents, of whom Labour was well aware, could be induced to vote against Chamberlain, there was a chance that at least he would be required to broaden his administration. Hugh Dalton was the chief Labour liaison with the Conservative rebels. In his diary on 19 September he noted: 'Government can only be changed if there is a serious breakdown among their supporters, and if as someone says to me privately, "Winston is ready to strike". Not clear that we are there yet.'[19]

The next six months demonstrated that while Winston was not ready to strike, Tory dissidents outside the government were becoming more vocal and the position of the government was weakening. Dalton established regular contact with Harold Macmillan and was slowly persuaded that a major debate on the war might be an occasion to remove 'the old limpet'.[20]

Norway provided that occasion. News of the fiasco was disseminated to MPs through the disgruntled soldiers returning from the campaign and from those inside the Admiralty and the War Office who knew how badly it had been handled. Before the campaign a debate had been scheduled for the adjournment of Parliament on 7 May. These debates are routine parliamentary practice and can be used by members to raise constituency matters or to speak on a specific topic. They do not necessarily end in a formal vote. In this case, however, members made it clear that they wanted an open-ended debate on government policy. The ensuing 'Norway Debate' is possibly the most important in twentieth-century parliamentary history.

On the first day of the debate, 7 May 1940, 14 members spoke – six supported the government and eight opposed it. Worse still for the government, Chamberlain was the only speaker of substance on its side. The remainder, Page Croft, Lewis Jones, Commander Archibald Southby, Arnold Wilson and Oliver Stanley, were either totally obscure or, as in the last case, a very bad speaker indeed. On the other side the speakers were perhaps also not orators of the first rank, but the position in their respective parties of Attlee and Arthur Greenwood for Labour, Archie Sinclair for the Liberals, and Amery, Admiral of the Fleet Sir Roger Keyes and Lord Winterton for the Conservatives, lent a weight to their statements that was absent in the ranks of the Chamberlainites.

In the event, the debate on the 'conduct of the war' opened at 3.45 p.m. with the Chief Whip (Captain Margesson) intoning the words 'that this House do now adjourn'.[21]

Chamberlain led off for the government, amid general turmoil and many cries of 'missed the bus'. This was a reference to a speech made by him just five days before the German invasion of Norway when he told his audience that Hitler had 'missed the bus' by allowing the Allies a seven-month period in which they could catch up with German rearmament. Chamberlain was rattled by the interjections and his speech fell well below the level of events. Even his most ardent supporter ('Chips' Channon) thought he spoke 'haltingly and did not make a good case: in fact he fumbled his words and seemed tired and embarrassed'.[22] The Prime Minister started with the usual praise for the gallantry of the troops and gave a detailed explanation of the reasons for the evacuations around Trondheim and the success of the operation in rescuing almost all British and Allied troops. But MPs were in an unforgiving mood. When Chamberlain admitted that the withdrawal had come as a shock to the country, the following exchange took place:

Mr Benjamin Smith (Rotherhithe): 'And abroad.'
Hon. Member: 'All over the world.'
PM: 'I see Ministers are to be blamed.'
Hon. Members: 'They missed the bus.'[23]

At this point the Speaker intervened to restore order. Chamberlain resumed with a long, rambling explanation for the defeat, which he blamed on the Norwegians for not playing their part, thus depriving the British of useable airfields. This immediately brought renewed cries of 'missed the bus'. Chamberlain then made a tactical mistake by stopping his speech to explain what he had meant by the phrase, which only served to remind members of the ineptitude of the remark in the first place. The Prime

Minister had made a weak beginning but it was about to get worse. Driven totally onto the defensive, Chamberlain quite improperly revealed that he had been advised by the Chiefs of Staff that he should not have allowed debate on a recent military operation on national security grounds. Uproar followed. Chamberlain then dug an even deeper hole for himself by adding that the country had no idea of 'the imminence of the threat which is impending against us'.[24]

A diarist who noted this section of the speech provides evidence that statements such as this helped undermine the standing of the Prime Minister in the country. He wrote:

> His pitiful excuses yesterday, muddled thinking and idiotic saying, 'The people of this country don't realize what they are up against'! Don't we? He most surely doesn't know when Hitler is 10 times more confident of victory and believes Hitler has 'missed the bus'. Blasted rot. What a rotten lot of bottom-warming, chair-polishing humbugs.[25]

Another diarist also commented unfavourably on this section of the Prime Minister's speech:

> It's amazing, the blindness of this man – he seems completely enveloped in the fog of his own complacency out of which he has the effrontery to say that 'the people don't realise the seriousness of the situation'. Don't realise . . . My God![26]

It was typical of Chamberlain that day that the only positive section of his speech concerned Churchill. After noting that the withdrawal from Norway could not be compared in scale to Gallipoli (a snide remark that the First Lord surely noted), he ended by saying that Churchill was to receive more power. He was already the head of the Military Coordination Committee of the Cabinet, but after representations that the system was not working Chamberlain had authorised Churchill to give 'guidance and direction' to the Chiefs of Staff Committee.[27] For all intents and purposes, Churchill would now be First Lord of the Admiralty *and* direct the whole military conduct of the war, an anomalous position that, as far as the war was concerned, would result in the Prime Minister occupying a subordinate position to one of his Cabinet ministers. We may speculate that Chamberlain made this pronouncement as a sign of his willingness to make changes, but all it did was highlight his own incapacity to run the war. If he hoped to end his speech on a high note, he achieved the opposite.

Chamberlain received little help from his supporters that day. The one heavyweight speaker – by dint of his position as Secretary of State for War – was Oliver Stanley. But he had only occupied the position for three months, was a poor speaker, and soon became bogged down in operational detail concerning some small actions around Trondheim. It is a good question whether members could even follow this 'mild and feeble' 'shocking performance'.[28] Perhaps they were shocked into consciousness by Stanley's plea that 'it is not very pleasant to hold office in wartime'[29] – hardly a clarion call from the Secretary of State for War. Eventually, and much to the relief of all, his speech fizzled out with an uninspiring call for greater sacrifice.[30]

Lewis Jones and Commander Southby added precisely nothing to the government's case. Both noted that various cabals were forming among members, both called for national unity – rich coming from supporters of Chamberlain who had on every occasion advised against including the Labour Party in the administration. In addition, Jones managed to insult the public by claiming – on no evidence – that its morale was being sapped by 'barracking' in the House.[31]

When Page Croft got to his feet there was 'a loud groan from the Labour Party . . . and they practically [rose] as a body and left the House'.[32] The old diehard did his best for Chamberlain, but his best was never very good and he ended by saying that 'if you are convinced that you can find a better man then put him there', hardly a ringing endorsement of his leader but in keeping with the conditional support Chamberlain enjoyed from the 'Old Tories'.[33]

The last speaker of the day was Arnold Wilson – an arch appeaser who should have been helpful to Chamberlain. Alas for the Prime Minister he was not. His attack was not primarily directed at the Conservative rebels but at the trade unions for hampering the war effort and at the BBC for broadcasting communist propaganda. In summing up, Wilson actually attacked the government for not mobilising the country sufficiently, for excessive levels of bureaucracy, and for not asking for a greater effort from the people.[34] So ended the case for Chamberlain on the first day of debate.

The poverty of Chamberlain's effort, the droning platitudes of Oliver Stanley, and the modest contributions of other government supporters on 7 May opened the door for the government's opponents.

Attlee led for the opposition. Although Harold Nicolson called his speech 'feeble', this is not the impression gained from Hansard.[35] No doubt Attlee's reedy voice and general lack of presence counted against his speech as a spectacle. However, in substance, Attlee made some telling points. He began by noting the disarray of operations in Norway. There was nothing very original in this, but then he warmed to his task. Attlee complimented Churchill on his great abilities but complained that in his new appointment the First Lord would be placed in an impossible position. He then said:

> I have no doubt whatever in the courage and the constancy of the people of this country, provided they get the right lead, but the Government will be blind and deaf if they do not realize that there is widespread anxiety among the people of this country . . . They are not satisfied that the war is being waged with sufficient energy, intensity, drive and resolution.
>
> It is not Norway alone . . . Norway follows Czecho-Slovakia, and Poland. Everywhere the story is "Too Late" . . . I say that there is a wide-spread feeling in this country, not that we shall lose the war, but that we will win the war, but that to win the war, we want different people at the helm from those who have led us into it.[36]

Whatever Attlee's deficiencies in delivery, this reads quite powerfully. Chamberlain could not have overlooked the reference to 'too late' because it was the same cry that his great enemy, David Lloyd George, had used against Herbert Asquith when he lost the Prime Ministership in 1916. Moreover, while chiding Churchill for his excessive optimism over Norway, Attlee placed the blame for the fiasco squarely on the Prime Minister. The sting in the speech was, however, contained in its conclusion. Attlee might seek a National government but it was clear that Labour would never serve in such an administration while Chamberlain remained at the helm. It would take several days for the old limpet to come to this conclusion himself.

Sinclair as leader of the Liberals followed Attlee. He was a great friend of Churchill, having served under him in the trenches of the Western Front in 1916. Nicolson thought his speech 'good', but Sinclair immediately burrowed into the minutiae of the Norway campaign and stayed there. His only telling points were to criticise Chamberlain for politicising the Chiefs of Staff by making their advice public, to call for the formation of a small War Cabinet, and a rather lame plea for a more vigorous prosecution of the war.[37] His speech was an opportunity missed.

Greenwood – in general not an inspiring speaker – on this day was much sharper than Sinclair. He began by saying that he had never known the House in such a grim mood. He dwelt on Norway, how it had shocked the people and how the only successful British operation there had been the evacuation. But wars, he added, are not won by 'masterly evacuations'.[38] (Was Churchill making notes at this point?) And unlike Sinclair, Greenwood did not confine himself to Norway. He listed failures in mobilisation, supply, shipping and diplomacy. The responsibility for these failures, he concluded, must lie with the Prime Minister and his colleagues. He ended by calling for 'other men to take their place'. And he made an overt appeal to the Conservative rebels by stating that 'the responsibility for any change lies, not with the minority. It lies with the majority whose responsibilities are far and away greater than ours.'[39]

The dissident Conservatives were not to disappoint. Colonel Wedgewood, who had served at Gallipoli, called for a government that 'would take the war seriously'. Captain Bellinger, noting Churchill's great qualities, called for the administration to step aside for different men.[40]

Winterton had also served at Gallipoli. He made a direct comparison between that operation and Norway but insisted that he was exempting from any criticism for either operation 'the First Lord of the Admiralty', who in both cases had been hobbled in his ability to act by lesser men. Thus, strangely, did Gallipoli assist the First Lord 25 years after the event.

These were effective speeches but the main event of the day was to be the appearance of Keyes and Amery. Keyes was an unlikely figure to turn a parliamentary debate. He had a reputation as a war hero, based on the dubious foundations of his insistence that he could have forced the Dardanelles with his destroyer flotilla in 1915 and on his claim that he had blocked the German-held port of Zeebrugge in 1918. (Later investigations demonstrated that neither claim was correct, but somehow Keyes' reputation remained intact.) On 7 May he decided to capitalise on this reputation.

He dressed in the full uniform of an Admiral of the Fleet, complete with gold braid and decorations. This alone was bound to attract the attention of the House. When he began to speak it is a reasonable assumption that members soon found themselves lost in a detailed exposition of why a Keyes-led assault on Trondheim would have turned the tables in Norway. He ended with an encomium to Churchill. The First Lord had been hampered in Norway as he had at Gallipoli, and now 'the whole country . . . is looking to him to help win the war'.[41]

Nevertheless, it was not actually what Keyes said but the spectacle his speech provided that made the impression. Harold Nicolson thought it the most dramatic speech he had ever heard.[42] Dalton commented that it was 'the most striking speech' and even Channon thought Keyes' appearance 'damning'.[43] At the end Keyes sat down to 'thunderous applause'.[44]

More drama was to follow. By May 1940 Leo Amery had emerged as the most energetic Conservative opponent of Chamberlain. His speech reflected the level of despair and anger he felt about the handling of the war and about the lack of leadership provided by the Prime Minister. His words were all the more remarkable in that he had been a long-time friend of Chamberlain and, like the Prime Minister, represented a Birmingham constituency. This is what he said:

> We cannot go on as we are. There must be a change. First and foremost, it must be a change in the system and structure of our government machine . . . Believe me, as long as our present methods prevail, all our valour and all our resources are not going to see us through . . . What we must have and soon, is a supreme war directorate of a handful of men free from administrative routine . . . That is the only way. We learned that in the last war . . . What is no less important today is that the Government shall be able to draw upon the whole abilities of the nation. It must represent all the elements of real political power in the country – whether in the House or not. The time has come when hon. and right hon. Members opposite must definitely take their share of the responsibility. The time has come when the organization, the power and the influence of the Trades Union Congress cannot be left outside . . . The time has come, in other words, for a real National Government.

Somehow or another we must get into the Government men who can match our enemies in fighting spirit, in daring, in resolution and thirst for victory. Some 300 years ago, when this House found its troops being beaten again and again by the dash and daring of the Cavaliers, by Prince Rupert's Cavalry, Oliver Cromwell spoke to John Hampden. In one of his speeches he recounted what he said. It was this: 'I said to him, "Your troops are most of them old, decayed serving men and tapsters and such kind of fellows . . . You must get men of a spirit that are likely to go as far as they will go, or you will be beaten still."' It may not be easy to find these men. They can be found only by trial and by ruthlessly discarding all who fail and have their failings discovered. We are fighting today for our life, for our liberty, for our all; we cannot go on being led as we are. I have quoted certain words of Oliver Cromwell. I will quote certain other words. I do it with great reluctance, because I am speaking of those who are old friends and associates of mine, but they are words which, I think, are applicable to the present situation. This is what Cromwell said to the Long Parliament when he thought it was no longer fit to conduct the affairs of the nation: 'You have sat too long there for any good you have been doing. Depart, I say, and let us have done with you. In the name of God, go.'[45]

As Amery reached the height of his peroration he gestured towards the government front bench. Chamberlain, as it happened, was not present but this did not lessen the effect of Amery's 'terrible words'. The Prime Minister heard about them soon enough. But at this stage that was of lesser importance than the effect on the members of the Labour Party who did hear them. Attlee and Morrison had become increasingly impressed by the number of Conservatives who had spoken out against Chamberlain and by the vehemence of their denunciations. There is some dispute in Labour ranks about exactly who converted the adjournment debate into a vote of no confidence in the government. What is more important is that both Attlee and Morrison at different times decided on this course of action and carried the day with their colleagues. Thus Labour decided that when the debate resumed on 8 May, Morrison would move to divide the House.[46]

At 4.03 p.m. on 8 May, Morrison resumed the debate. He asked a lengthy series of questions on Norway and then turned to Churchill:

Is it the case that the First Lord of the Admiralty is being used as a sort of shield to the Prime Minister when he finds it convenient to do so? I am quite aware that the Prime Minister has great confidence in the First Lord. I have been pleased to note that during recent months. But it appears to me that when the Government are in trouble, when they are open to criticism on grounds of incompetence, they tend to bring the First Lord into the shop window in the belief that will satisfy public criticism. This is not altogether fair. It tends to place on the First Lord responsibilities which he cannot properly carry, and it is doubtful whether, in fact, the Government will allow him to carry.[47]

This was an important statement. Here was a senior Labour figure attempting to separate Churchill from his Cabinet colleagues. It was also an indication that the Labour Party would have no difficulty in working with Churchill.

Morrison then got to the procedural purpose of his speech:

I have a genuine apprehension that if these men remain in office we run the grave risk of losing the war. That would be a fatal and terrible thing for this country and indeed for the freedom of the human race. We are fighting for our lives. Humanity is struggling for its freedom. The issues of the war are too great for us to risk losing by keeping in office men who have been there for a long time and have not shown themselves too well fitted for the task [and because of this] we feel we must divide the House at the end of our Debate tonight . . . I ask hon. Members in all parts of the House to realize to the full the responsibility of the vote which they will give tonight, a vote which will broadly indicate whether they are content with the conduct of affairs or whether they are apprehensive about the conduct of affairs . . . I ask that the vote of the House shall represent the spirit of the country and give a clear indication that we instantly demand that this struggle be carried through to victory.[48]

This laid out the issues with great clarity. Labour had no confidence in Chamberlain, a great deal of confidence in Churchill, and were determined that the war be prosecuted to the bitter end.

Chamberlain was stung by Morrison's speech and immediately intervened:

> I do not seek to evade criticism, but I say to my friends in the House –
> and I have friends in the House. No government can prosecute a war
> effectively unless it has public and Parliamentary support. I accept the
> challenge. I welcome it indeed. At least we shall know who is with us
> and who is against us, and I call on my friends to support us in the
> Lobby tonight.[49]

Chamberlain once again managed to strike the wrong note. His appeal to friendship to see him through seemed petty and hardly fitting in a national emergency. As for accepting Labour's challenge, he hardly had a choice; the House would divide whether Neville Chamberlain wanted it to do so or not. His final statement, that those who are not with us are against us, was perhaps the worst of all. It devalued the patriotism of those who sought a better way to wage war and it was a statement better directed against external enemies than parliamentary colleagues. Whether this unfortunate intervention changed voting intentions is not known but it was a peevish effort that can hardly have enhanced the standing of the Prime Minister in the House.

The other speakers on the government side were as little help to Chamberlain as they had been the day before. Sir Samuel Hoare, who had taken over from Sir Kingsley Wood as Secretary of State for Air, should have made a contribution but failed dismally as he got bogged down in the detail of the doings of a single Gladiator squadron in Norway.[50] George Lambert made the rather startling accusation that the attacks on Chamberlain were doing the work of Hitler and Goebbels. Sir George Couthorpe, hardly a name to conjure with, added that the vast majority of the country had confidence in the leadership, but he was interrupted by shouts of 'No, a thousand times, no', which brought Sir George's intervention to a premature and lame end.[51] Other contributions were mere repetitions of the themes of national unity and supreme confidence in Chamberlain's ability. They were heard in silence by diminishing numbers of MPs.

Once again it was the critics of the government who had the best of it. Duff Cooper, perhaps surprisingly for one who had resigned over Munich, expressed disappointment that Labour had decided to divide the House. But he warned that he would be ignoring the Prime Minister's appeal for support and that the House must discount much of what Churchill would say in the debate because as a minister he was bound to support Chamberlain.[52]

Even lesser lights, such as Commander Bower, made some telling points. He noted that Chamberlain had said that Britain was waging a 'queer war' and added:

It is not being waged in any queer way by the Germans. The German waging of war is not in the least queer; it is ruthless, swift, brilliant in conception and execution, and it has been courageous to the verge of temerity ... We have made it a queer war. The Government has made it a queer war by their acceptance of the fact that apparently we consider the enemy must always have the initiative. By our retreat from one position to another and by our unwillingness to act militarily ourselves.[53]

A number of MPs noted Chamberlain's appeal to his friends. Sir Stafford Cripps stated that this selfish appeal made him 'unfit to carry on the government of this country'.[54] Yet it was Lloyd George who made the most telling intervention on that theme. The animosity between Lloyd George and Chamberlain went back to the First World War when Lloyd George had sacked him from his Ministry because of alleged incompetence. Lloyd George commenced by saying that he was intervening 'reluctantly', which members must have taken with a grain of salt, and then continued:

I was not here when the right Hon. Gentleman made the observation, but he definitely appealed on a question which is a great national, Imperial and world issue. He said, 'I have got my friends.' It is not a question of who are the Prime Minister's friends. It is a far bigger issue. The Prime Minister must remember that he has met this formidable foe of ours in peace and in war. He has always been worsted. He is not in a position to appeal on the grounds of friendship. He has appealed for sacrifice. The nation is prepared for every sacrifice so long as it has leadership, so long as the government show clearly what they are aiming at and so long as the nation is confident that those who are leading it are doing their best. I say solemnly that the Prime Minister should give an example of sacrifice, because there is nothing which can contribute more to victory in this war than that he should sacrifice the seals of office.[55]

Clearly, after such devastating attacks as these, Churchill, who was to wind up for the government, represented the last hope that Chamberlain might emerge unscathed. There was no little irony in this situation. Chamberlain had long complained about the 'overblown' oratory of the First Lord of the Admiralty, yet his fate now to a large extent rested on the power of that oratory. There is no doubt that the speech represented a challenge to Churchill. Many members who had condemned the government had gone out of their way to exempt him. He must have observed that the two-day debate had weakened the Prime Minister. The top job was almost within his grasp. Yet he was a member of the government and must at least seem to give Chamberlain his loyal support. It was a balancing act without precedent in modern British politics.

At 10.11 p.m. Churchill rose to a packed House. They had just listened to a scathing indictment of the Norway campaign from the Labour naval spokesman, A. V. Alexander. Members must have been at least half aware that some of the blows landed by Alexander went to the heart of some of Churchill's own actions during the campaign. How would the First Lord respond?

Harold Nicolson thought that he managed his balancing act well by expressing loyalty to Chamberlain while disclaiming 'that he really had nothing to do with this confused and timid gang'.[56] On the other hand, Chips Channon considered that Churchill had performed a service for the government. He thought Churchill 'made a slashing, vigorous speech . . . trounced the opposition, demolishing Roger Keyes etc'.[57]

In truth, Nicolson summed up Churchill's speech more accurately than Channon. Its tone was set from the beginning. Churchill noted that many members had deplored Britain's lack of initiative in the war. They were correct, he said, and the reason was

Our failure over the last five years to maintain or regain air parity with Germany. That is a long story – a very long story, let me remind the

House – because for the first two years, when I with some friends, was pressing this upon the House, it was not only the Government who objected, but both opposition parties.[58]

Here then was a rebuff for those out of power who had opposed rearmament, but a much sterner one for Chamberlain – who was in power – and also opposed it.

Churchill then launched into a detailed defence of the role of the navy in Norway and turned the debate (rather awkwardly) to the question of whether a battleship or battlecruiser should have been used to support the destroyers at Narvik. There then followed this remarkable passage, which explains why Churchill posed the question in the first place:

> Well then, the question [about the heavy ship] was asked by a very influential person, not a member of the House, Mr. Bevin – who is a friend of mine, working hard for the public cause, and a man who has much gift to help.[59]

The question as to why a capital ship had not been used in the circumstances does not really matter. Here was the First Lord of the Admiralty praising the work of the General Secretary of the Transport and General Workers Union, who happened to be one of the most influential men in the labour movement and in the Labour Party. Churchill was not engaging in a debate on grand strategy with Bevin but reminding the House that he had friends in the labour movement whose 'gift to help' in mobilising the country was being ignored by his government colleagues. The view of the eminent historian Ross McKibbon is that 'it is difficult on reading this not to conclude that Churchill intended to offer Bevin the ministry of Labour in a government he had not yet been asked to form'.[60] Churchill was certainly making an unmistakable plea for Labour support. No doubt he had observed that the debate had gone badly for the government. No doubt he knew that if a broad-based administration was formed it would not be led by Chamberlain, because Labour would refuse to serve under him. No doubt he was aware that he was the main contender for the top job. Why else bring Bevin into the debate? Why else emphasise that he was a good friend? Why else describe him as a very influential person?

The end of Churchill's speech was rather an anticlimax. He got into a slanging match with various members over minor points of order and the whole scene ended in uproar. None of that mattered. The two-day debate had done its damage. It only remained to count the votes.

As members began to move into the Yea or Nay lobby a Tory dissident, General Spears, takes up the story:

> To either side of the opening ahead stood the tellers, one for the Government, the other for the Opposition. As on great occasions, when the Government accepted the Motion as a vote of censure, the Chief Whip [Margesson] was telling for the Government and calling out the new total as every member passed and bowed as he went through the opening according to the ritual. The Chief Whip was an old brother officer, one moreover to whom I was indebted for much kindness. It was very painful. As Duff Cooper passed him and bowed to his front he called 151, and I noted his expression of implacable resentment. '152,' he said as I bowed and went through. 153, 154, the voice was continuing on until I lost it in the general rumour of the House as I regained my seat . . .
>
> No one who was present will ever forget the scene in the House before the figures of the Division were announced. The packed benches were so tense that they seemed to be vibrating like taut wire . . . Then the four tellers appeared, getting themselves into line in front of the table which carries the Mace.
>
> The Government was not beaten, for the Chief Whip was on the right. The four stepped forward, stiffly as usual, making their ordained bows, then Margesson read out the figures. A second's silence whilst their meaning sank in, then a roar from the Socialists. The Government majority was down to 81 from its nominal figure of 200! 'Resign, resign!' they shouted.[61]

How are we to interpret these figures? In terms of brute numbers the government was safe – a majority of 81 was eminently secure in ordinary times. The problem for Chamberlain was that these were hardly ordinary times and that each time a vote of confidence had been called since Munich, his majority had fallen. After Munich it had been 222. It was 200 on the December 1938 vote of no confidence, 167 on the July 1939 no confidence motion, and just 116 on the declaration of war vote.[62] Now it was 81. But even that reduced figure overstates government support. Of the 81, Churchill, Eden and their Parliamentary Private Secretaries, Brenden Bracken and James Thomas, were obliged to vote with Chamberlain while hardly supporting him. This reduces the majority to 73. In addition, as noted, the votes of the 'Old Tories' were probably conditional on a more vigorous prosecution of the war by Chamberlain – something many of them must have thought might not eventuate. If they had cast a vote for the Prime Minister, for at least some of them it might well have been their last show of support.

Why had the government majority fallen so far? There is a consensus that between 38 and 44 Conservatives voted against the government.[63] The number who abstained is much more difficult to establish, the two most detailed studies of the vote even disagreeing on how many Conservatives failed to vote on that day – one (N. Smart) claiming 77 and the other (J. Rasmussen) 88. On abstentions, Rasmussen has identified 36, but Smart puts the figure much lower, at 21 or even 10.[64] Most contemporary observers put the figure at 60.[65] And as Smart notes, it is probably this figure that counted because at the time most people thought it to be true. It was the views of members at the time rather than subsequent analyses that had the effect.

Certainly the voting had an immediate impact on Chamberlain. Channon reported that he appeared 'bowled over by the ominous figures ... he looked grave and thoughtful and sad'.[66] Churchill saw him in his room at the House of Commons soon after the debate. Chamberlain told him he could not go on. There ought to be a National government.[67] Nicolson thought the Prime Minister looked 'pale and angry'. His own view was that Chamberlain can 'scarcely survive'.[68] Even supporters such as Charles Waterhouse (MP for Southeast Leicester), though outraged by the vote, did not 'see that [Chamberlain] has any course but resignation'.[69]

Nevertheless, by the following morning Chamberlain, although hardly anyone else, had decided that it was his duty to continue in office. Perhaps he was encouraged by Churchill's words the night before: 'Do not take this matter to heart. We have a better case about Norway than it has been possible to convey to the House. Strengthen your Government from every quarter, and let us go on until our majority deserts us'.[70]

It seems odd that Churchill of all people would encourage Chamberlain to stay on. But there is not much evidence that this was more than a kind word to a defeated man. Churchill was certainly not of the view that Chamberlain could 'strengthen his Government from every quarter'. Indeed, early on 9 May he had told Eden that 'he thought Neville would not be able to bring in Labour [the only quarter that really counted] and that a national government must be formed'.[71]

For reasons that will become obvious the chronology of events on 9 May is important but difficult to establish. The next significant meeting after the Churchill–Eden encounter was that between Halifax and Chamberlain at 10 a.m. Chamberlain told the Foreign Secretary that the situation could not continue. He thought that Labour would not serve under him and therefore the choice must be Winston or Halifax. Chamberlain then made it clear that he favoured Halifax and that any constitutional problem of a Prime Minister from the Lords could be overcome. But Halifax intervened:

> The conversation and evident drift of his mind left me with such a stomach-ache. I told him again ... that if the Labour people said they would only serve under me I should tell them that I was not prepared to do it, and see whether a definite attitude would make them budge. If I failed then we should all, no doubt, have to boil our broth again. He said that he would like to have a talk with Winston and me together, in the afternoon.[72]

Later, Halifax told his under-secretary, Rab Butler, of this meeting. He said that

> while he felt he could do the job [a view not widely shared] that if he became PM, Churchill's qualities and experience would surely mean that he would be 'running the war anyway' and his own position would quickly turn into a sort of 'honorary Prime Minister'. In this situation he felt that he could at least exert a restraining hand on Churchill as a member of the War Cabinet than as PM.[73]

There is no need to take the Foreign Secretary's main argument against becoming Prime Minister all that seriously. The Prime Minister's power is such that he or she is always in a superior position to restrain a subordinate. What seems clear is that when he spoke to Butler, Halifax was by no means certain that he would be a successful wartime Prime Minister and was already looking for a way out.

Nevertheless, there were many who thought a Halifax premiership a real possibility and a danger. One was the newspaper proprietor Max Beaverbrook, who met Churchill at around mid-morning. Beaverbrook urged Churchill not to serve under Halifax, whom he thought would only continue Chamberlain's policy of appeasement. Churchill refused to agree with his friend, saying that he 'would serve under any Minister capable of prosecuting the war'.[74] In fact Bracken had told the Labour leaders that Churchill would not serve under Halifax, but when this reached Churchill he furiously rebuked Bracken.[75]

News of Churchill's apparent willingness to serve under Halifax was spreading to other members of the Conservative Party. Eden, who had apparently agreed to have lunch with Churchill, arrived at noon to find Kingsley Wood, previously an arch-Chamberlainite, already there. Eden was shocked to hear Wood advise Churchill to refuse to serve under Halifax, although he would be the Prime Minister's candidate. 'Don't agree, and don't say anything,' he told Churchill when apprised of the afternoon meeting between the three men.[76]

Then, probably in the early afternoon, Halifax endured another uncomfortable meeting – this time with Lord Salisbury. On the morning of 9 May the 'Watching Committee' had met. They decided that Chamberlain must resign and that either Halifax or Churchill should construct a Cabinet along National lines. Salisbury was deputed to convey this message to Halifax[77] and reported that Halifax had said that he was too aligned with appeasement and that in any case he could not run the war from the House of Lords. Salisbury made a polite gesture to try to convince Halifax otherwise but left with the distinct feeling that Halifax had already ruled himself out.[78]

Eventually the meeting between Churchill, Halifax and Chamberlain took place at 4.30 p.m. We have three accounts: one from Churchill in his memoirs, one from Halifax in his diary, and a diary entry from Cadogan with whom Halifax discussed the outcome of the meeting soon after the event. All accounts agree on the essentials. Chamberlain spoke first. He had decided that there must be a government of national unity and that it must include the Labour Party. Later in the day he would ask them to join his government. This statement must have come as something of a surprise to both Churchill and Halifax, who had possibly assumed that Chamberlain had grasped the fact that whatever the outcome Labour would not serve under him. He then went on to say, however, that he was doubtful if he could obtain such an agreement. If he was proved correct the choice must lie between Halifax and Churchill. Halifax then spoke, either because Churchill heeded the advice of Kingsley Wood and remained silent, or because – for the third time that day – Halifax wished to rule himself out of the running. He said that although 'the PM said I was the man mentioned as most acceptable [did Chamberlain really say that?] I would be in a hopeless position. If I was not in charge of the war and if I didn't lead in the House, I should be a cypher.'[79] In his diary Halifax observed that his stomach-ache had returned and that he rehearsed the arguments he had been making all day.[80] Then 'Winston, with suitable expressions of regard and humility, said he could not but feel the force of what I had said, and the PM reluctantly, and Winston evidently with much less reluctance, finished by accepting my view.'[81] Only then did Margesson, who had also attended the meeting, note that it seemed that during the day Labour opinion had swung against the idea of a Prime Minister in the Lords.[82]

This meeting therefore settled the Conservative succession but only in the event that Labour refused to serve under Chamberlain. He was to meet Attlee and Greenwood at 6.15 p.m., with Halifax and Churchill in attendance. Churchill's account is of a polite meeting during which the Labour leaders told Chamberlain 'not obscurely' that they would almost certainly refuse to serve in his government but that they must first consult their National Executive which was meeting in Bournemouth. He would receive an answer the following day.[83]

Amery, whose account comes from the Liberal rebel Clem Davies, who was in constant touch with the Labour leadership during this period, suggests that the meeting was the opposite of 'polite'. According to Davies, Attlee was 'flabbergasted' to be asked to serve under Chamberlain:

42

Greenwood then took up the running and explained that the Prime Minister was entirely mistaken and that there was not the slightest prospect of the Opposition joining a government under him, they not only disliked him but regarded him as something evil. Meanwhile Winston delivered himself of an eloquent eulogy of the Prime Minister's efficiency in the dispatch of business and personal charm to work with, to which Greenwood replied that this was perhaps true enough but irrelevant to the main issue which Attlee then flung across the table at Neville in the shape of two questions which he proposed to put to the [Party] Executive at Bournemouth next morning, viz: Are you prepared to support a Government under (a) the present Prime Minister (b) another Prime Minister, adding that there was not a ghost of a chance of the Labour Party Conference or Executive accepting (a).[84]

This discussion, whichever version is accepted, seems to have settled the succession. Unknown to the Labour leadership, the Conservatives had already decided that Churchill would succeed Chamberlain in the almost certain event of Labour vetoing the Prime Minister. That Labour would serve under Churchill also seems certain, given Margesson's view that opinion in the party had turned against Halifax during the course of the day. It also stretches credulity that Labour would have agreed to a cobbled-up constitutional arrangement that allowed Halifax to sit in the Commons.[85]

Nevertheless, the drama had one more act to play. In the early morning of 10 May the Germans launched their great attack in the west. Chamberlain's inclination was that he should now hang on. He managed to contact Attlee before the Labour leader left for Bournemouth. Attlee gave him the dusty answer: 'not at all', resignation should follow immediately.[86] The rumour concerning Chamberlain had reached Clem Davies and he immediately contacted Greenwood who was already at Bournemouth. Greenwood merely repeated Attlee's message and Davies disseminated this to anyone who would listen, including the press.

Finally, at 5 p.m. the Labour Executive telephoned their formal rejection to Chamberlain. He immediately went to Buckingham Palace and advised King George VI to send for Churchill. At 6 p.m. Churchill was summoned to the King and after what passed for light-hearted banter by the monarch, he asked Churchill to form a government. Churchill undertook to contact the Labour and Liberal leadership immediately and to relay the names of the new War Cabinet to the King as soon as possible. At last he was Prime Minister.

CHAPTER 3

THE CABINET CRISIS
CHURCHILL CHALLENGED, 10–28 MAY 1940

THE GERMAN ONSLAUGHT in the west made the formation of a Cabinet by Churchill a matter of the utmost urgency. After returning from Buckingham Palace on the evening of 10 May he summoned Attlee and Greenwood for a discussion about its composition. They indicated that they both expected places in the War Cabinet.[1] During the next forty-eight hours Churchill made various attempts to construct a War Cabinet and an outer ministry. His first efforts listed a War Cabinet of seven – himself as Prime Minister, Attlee as Lord Privy Seal, Greenwood probably as Minister without Portfolio, Sir Andrew Duncan as Minister for Economic Affairs, Halifax as Foreign Secretary, Chamberlain as Leader of the House and Kingsley Wood as Chancellor of the Exchequer.[2]

In a later iteration, Duncan and Greenwood were dropped and Lloyd George was added, but this list may be incomplete or represent musings on Churchill's part because Greenwood had already been offered a post and Lloyd George was problematical because of the mutual antipathy between him and Chamberlain.[3]

The final group of five who were to sit on the War Cabinet was decided early on 11 May. They were Churchill as Prime Minister and Minister of Defence, Chamberlain as Lord President of the Council, Halifax as Foreign Secretary, Attlee as Lord Privy Seal and Greenwood as Minister without Portfolio. An attempt by Churchill to make Chamberlain either

Leader of the House or Chancellor of the Exchequer was vetoed by the Labour members, an indication that their old foe was not to be given too much power.[4]

The outer Cabinet went through many permutations, most of which are recorded in the Churchill Papers. This casts some doubt on the story that the group was selected by Brendan Bracken and Margesson (the Chief Whip) and then shown to Churchill. The final list in many ways reveals Churchill's influence, especially in the posts offered to Eden, Sinclair, Bevin and Beaverbrook. The most important portfolios were as follows:

Secretary of State for War: Anthony Eden
Secretary of State for Air: Archibald Sinclair
First Lord of the Admiralty: A. V. Alexander
Minister of Labour: Ernest Bevin
Home Secretary: Sir John Anderson
Chancellor of the Exchequer: Sir Kingsley Wood
Minister of Economic Warfare: Hugh Dalton
Secretary of State for India: Leo Amery
Minister of Food: Lord Woolton
Minister of Supply: Herbert Morrison
Minister of Transport: Sir John Reith
Minister of Aircraft Production: Lord Beaverbrook
Minister of Information: Duff Cooper

The composition of the Churchill government provoked much comment at the time and continues to do so. In relation to the outer Cabinet it has been claimed that the Conservative rebels were not sufficiently rewarded for their efforts and that there were too many appeasers such as Kingsley Wood and Samuel Hoare left in office. Amery, for example, was furious that these men remained in power and that he was fobbed off with the India Office which he regarded as a fairly minor post. However, if Churchill's list is scrutinised dispassionately, it is probably the best that he could do at the time. Wood had been helpful to Churchill in the last days of the Chamberlain government and even before that they maintained a regular and friendly correspondence. It would not have been politic of Churchill to sweep all the appeasers away in one swoop. And if the posts in the outer Cabinet that he gave them are examined, none of them was crucial. Oddly, the Chancellor of the Exchequer also falls into that category. The demands of war meant that Treasury control of the spending departments was loosened, giving the Chancellor much less hold over ministers than in peacetime. Other posts such as the Woolsack were largely ceremonial and although it was no doubt galling to see Hoare elevated to such a position in the Lords, it hardly affected the running of the war. In contrast Churchill ensured that all three service ministers were anti-appeasers and he gave posts that were of the utmost importance in wartime such as Labour and Aircraft Production to staunch supporters such as Bevin and Beaverbrook.

The composition of the War Cabinet was more controversial. The inclusion in it of both Chamberlain and Halifax caused much adverse comment among the Tory rebels and within Labour circles.[5] The view at the time was that Churchill 'had not been nearly bold enough in his changes and much too afraid of the [Conservative] Party'.[6] Modern scholarship has tended to endorse this view, one authority writing that Churchill was 'a caged animal, prisoner to Chamberlain's majority in the Commons'.[7] Another account states that Chamberlain's position in the War Cabinet was 'pivotal to the existence of the new administration'.[8]

There is something to be said for this view. The vote, while toppling Chamberlain, still left a majority in the House of Commons at least as nominal supporters of the old administration. Chamberlain was also leader of the Conservative Party and any government claiming to be 'all party' would have found it difficult to exclude him.

Halifax is a slightly different case. His move away from appeasement has been much exaggerated by his admirers, as his basic acceptance of the Munich agreement and his hesitations on the declaration of war demonstrate. Nor, as we will see, did the outbreak of war mean that he was entirely weaned from his appeasing ways. Why then did Churchill not replace Halifax with Eden, who was the obvious alternative choice for the Foreign Office? This constellation would have given Churchill a solid bloc of three supporters in the War Cabinet and effectively isolated Chamberlain. Was Churchill so fearful of his position that he felt he could not take this step?

Churchill was certainly solicitous to his former antagonists. On achieving office he immediately wrote to Chamberlain noting that he would need his 'help and council' and that 'to a very large extent I am in your hands'.⁹ He was no less emollient to Halifax, thanking him for the 'chivalry and kindness with which you have treated me' and signing himself 'Your sincere friend Winston Churchill'.¹⁰

There is no need, however, to see these messages as acts of a 'weak' Prime Minister. Churchill soon felt strong enough to attempt to impose Chamberlain's inveterate enemy Lloyd George on him as a Cabinet colleague. Chamberlain, under intense pressure from Churchill, finally agreed to what he regarded as a humiliation and was only spared this fate when Lloyd George eventually refused to serve.¹¹ It must be concluded, therefore, that Churchill's subservience to Chamberlain, if it ever existed, was certainly short lived.

As for Halifax, by his own account, he felt himself tied to Chamberlain's pre-war policies, had no stomach (seemingly literally) for the top job, and was a self-confessed ignoramus on military affairs, as well as having no position in the House of Commons. He was thus hardly in a strong position, especially taking into account the ever-deteriorating military situation in France.

By any measure Chamberlain and Halifax were finished as a political force. Why then did Churchill include them both in his War Cabinet? It seems likely that the Prime Minister took this step, not because he felt desperately weak, but because he was sure of his own ability to manage a War Cabinet in which in most cases he would have the support of Attlee and Greenwood. Moreover, he had strong backing in the press and in the country, something that is often forgotten when the machinations of 'high politics' are all that are taken into account. Furthermore the move was surely a sensible insurance policy. At least if Chamberlain and Halifax were inside the War Cabinet, Churchill could watch their every move. In thinking thus, Churchill may to some extent have miscalculated. The Labour ministers had never held office and had little direct knowledge of foreign affairs. On the other hand, Chamberlain and Halifax had either sat in cabinets or held high office for over a decade. Given this disparity in experience, Churchill was likely to hear much more in Cabinet from his Conservative colleagues than from the Labour men. During the month that followed the creation of his War Cabinet he must at times have wondered whether Amery and the rebels had not been correct in questioning his decision.

The other strand of the 'weak' Prime Minister theory derives from Churchill's first appearance in the House of Commons after taking power and from the chattering of some diehard appeasers.

Churchill first appeared in the House as Prime Minister on 13 May when he made his 'blood, toil, tears and sweat' speech, to which we will return. It is the reception accorded Churchill and Chamberlain that concerns us now. Harold Nicolson recorded the scene in his diary: 'When Chamberlain enters the House, he gets a terrific reception and when Churchill comes in the applause is less.'[12] Later Lord Davidson, a Conservative peer, told Stanley Baldwin that Churchill had been received 'in silence'.[13]

It seems likely that far too much has been made of this incident. The cheers for Chamberlain probably came from some of his diehard supporters – cheers that arose out of embarrassment from those who had failed to support Chamberlain on 8 May, and a last hurrah from some for a long-serving Prime Minister. The seemingly lesser enthusiasm for Churchill (we can dismiss Davidson's 'silence' as an attempt to tell Baldwin what he might want to hear) probably derives from the fact that he was still an unknown quantity, that he had not yet had the opportunity to state his policy, and the sheer curiousness of a Tory leader so heartily endorsed by Labour.

The final strand of the 'weak' Prime Minister theory originates from two incidents involving some still-chattering appeasers. The first concerns John Colville, Rab Butler and Chips Channon. Colville relates a story in his diary about how the three of them gathered at the Foreign Office to drink a toast 'to the King Over the Water' (Chamberlain). He recorded the oily Butler as saying:

> The good clean tradition of English politics, that of Pitt as opposed to Fox, had been sold to the greatest adventurer of modern political history . . . He believed this sudden Coup [!] of Winston and his rabble was serious disaster and an unnecessary one: 'the pass has been sold' by Mr. C[hamberlain], Lord Halifax and Oliver Stanley. They had mildly surrendered to a half-breed American.[14]

The second incident is recorded in a letter from Lord Hankey to Sam Hoare:

I found complete chaos [in government] this morning. No one was gripping the war in the crisis. The Dictator [Churchill] was engaged in a sordid struggle with the politicians of the left about the secondary offices. NC was in a state of despair about it all.

The only hope lies in the solid core of Churchill, Chamberlain and Halifax, but whether the wise old elephants will ever be able to hold the Rogue Elephant [Churchill again], I doubt.[15]

It is surprising that these bilious remarks are still taken seriously. On examination, the line-up of dissidents is not all that impressive. Colville was Chamberlain's private secretary, a position from which he might be expected to show some loyalty to his old chief, but hardly a key post. Channon was Chamberlain's poodle, a sycophant and a backbencher of no political account. Butler was an arch-appeaser, probably a defeatist, who would reveal his true colours later in the year and who was in any case a mere under-secretary. Hankey was yesterday's man, an important figure during the Great War and in the 1930s but much to his chagrin a lightweight in 1940. Even as a collective this group had absolutely no political clout.

Their lack of judgement is even less impressive. It was grotesque of them to claim that Neville Chamberlain represented a 'clean' tradition in British politics. This was a man who did not hesitate to have his opponents' phones illegally tapped or to have derogatory articles about them written by Conservative Party Central Office, and who used threats of de-selection to intimidate them. The chaos described by Hankey can well be imagined. Just before a new administration had taken over and was struggling to come to terms with the German advance in the west while still forming a government. His remarks about sordid struggles with politicians of the left can merely be taken as typical bile from a sclerotic man of the right. But to describe Chamberlain and Halifax as 'wise old elephants' is doing a serious injustice to that animal. Old they might have been, but wise? These were the men after all who had overseen such diplomatic 'triumphs' as the Munich conference, had sat by with insouciant passivity while Poland was overrun, and had conducted the war in such a manner as to cause a widespread revolt within their own party.

Others have suggested that Churchill was in a parlous position because he surrounded himself with 'crooks', 'gangsters' or 'unscrupulous hangers-on and despicable jackals'. These are intemperate words, aimed no doubt at personalities such as Brenden Bracken, Beaverbrook, Boothby, Amery and the like. These remarks should not be taken seriously. They either come from politicians at the time who disliked Churchill or were about to suffer a diminution in their status, or from scholars who have not yet come to terms with the overthrow of their beloved Neville Chamberlain. The men described in such derogatory terms certainly had their share of character flaws but all were to serve their country well in the Second World War. Those who derided them reveal more about themselves than they do about Churchill.[16]

By 13 May Churchill had formed a Cabinet and had staked out his policy position in the House of Commons. He commenced his speech that day by saying 'I have nothing to offer but blood, toil, tears and sweat.' It is these words for which the speech is largely remembered. But of greater importance was this section of it:

> You ask, what is our policy? I can say: It is to wage war, by sea, land and air . . . against a monstrous tyranny, never surpassed in the dark, lamentable catalogue of human crime. That is our policy. You ask, what is our aim? I can answer in one word: It is victory, victory at all costs, victory in spite of all terror, victory, however long and hard the road may be; for without victory, there is no survival. Let that be realized; no survival for the British Empire, no survival for all that the British Empire has stood for, no survival for the urge and impulse of the ages, that mankind will move forward toward its goal.[17]

Some regard this speech as merely windy rhetoric, others as bravado – necessary in the circumstances but bravado nonetheless. These interpretations fundamentally misread Churchill's purpose. At times in 1940 he might use exaggerated language, especially if he was speaking to a foreign audience and especially if that audience was the United States. But when he was speaking to his own people, which is what he was doing here, he spoke the truth. When he spoke of achieving victory *at all costs* and *in spite of all terror*, and of persisting for however long it might take, he meant it literally. And in so speaking he had a dual purpose. He was telling the people that this would be a long and bitter war, with many privations. But he was also telling his Cabinet and parliamentary colleagues that they must come to grips with the policy just laid before them. There would be no hankering after peace deals under Churchill, there would be no half-hearted waging of war, there would be no compromise with the enemy. By saying this just three days after he had assumed office Churchill was also indicating that if any of his colleagues were inclined to oppose him, they would have to argue that victory over Nazi Germany was not a goal for which it was worth risking everything to achieve. They would now have to state why a compromise peace with such a 'monstrous tyranny' would be superior to victory. They would also have to argue against all the evidence of 1938 and 1939 that a bargain struck with Hitler in 1940 would endure while maintaining the British Empire as an independent state. With this speech, Churchill had stolen a march on those who might oppose him. His policy was clear. His opponents, so recently flung from office, had only the failed policy of appeasement to fall back on.

During May and June 1940 the War Cabinet met at least twice a day. Their meetings were attended by the five permanent members, with others such as the Minister for Air, the First Lord of the Admiralty, the Minister for War and the various service chiefs in attendance as required. When matters of the highest secrecy were discussed usually only the permanent five participated.[18]

The critical meetings for this crisis were of course held against the background of the rapidly deteriorating situation in France. Indeed it is likely that the situation at the front was often worse than was realised because of the confusion surrounding the military operations. Nevertheless, just three days after Churchill became Prime Minister, the War Cabinet was discussing 'The Invasion of Great Britain' as an agenda item, so there was no doubt that the five were well informed about the main tendencies of the situation across the Channel.[19]

Meetings dealt with routine matters until 15 May. Then the War Cabinet learned that German armoured columns had broken through the French defences on the River Meuse. In the course of this meeting Halifax made the first tentative steps towards recommending overtures to Mussolini. At first the approach he suggested seemed innocuous. The matter under discussion was contraband control, the method by which British warships prevented warlike goods or armaments reaching hostile or

52

potentially hostile countries. One such country was Italy. Halifax had entered into discussions with the Italian Economic Attaché in London because the Italians were becoming increasingly irritated at the British blockade. Halifax informed the War Cabinet that he had agreed to further discussions with the Italians with the aim of minimising their annoyance and keeping them neutral. He thought a friendly message from Churchill to Mussolini might help.[20] Churchill agreed and a conciliatory message was dispatched on 16 May.[21] Two days later the Italian dictator delivered a stern rebuff to Churchill. The Pact of Steel with Germany was inviolable – it would guide Italian foreign policy.[22]

Meanwhile the War Cabinet was facing the ever-deteriorating situation in France. Chamberlain (temporarily in charge because Churchill was in France trying to stiffen the resolve of Paul Reynaud's government) was asked on 17 May by the Prime Minister to consider two scenarios. What measures might be taken if Paris fell and the BEF had to be evacuated from France? What steps would be necessary if Britain was obliged to continue the war against Germany alone?[23] Chamberlain responded by placing before the War Cabinet a list of demands to be made of the French, including measures to prevent Germany laying hands on their factories and reserves of currency. He also listed the draconian measures (including the total control of labour and property) that Britain would be obliged to institute if it was to fight on alone.[24]

Then on 19 May the War Cabinet was informed that German armoured columns were approaching the Channel, threatening to split the Allied armies and cutting the communications by which the BEF was supplied. The crisis of the war had been reached with alarming speed. On that day Halifax detailed his negotiations with the Italian ambassador. He informed the War Cabinet that he proposed revising contraband controls against Italy and that his proposals went 'very far in the direction of weakening our control [but] if we could hold the position vis-à-vis Italy during the next critical weeks it would be well worth while'.[25] This proposal did not elicit any comment from members; if Italy could be kept neutral, so much the better.

Halifax also mentioned negotiations with Italy at the War Cabinet of 24 May. He read out a telegram from the British ambassador to France, Sir Roland Campbell, to the effect that the French would welcome an approach from President Roosevelt to Mussolini concerning Italian desiderata for remaining neutral. Roosevelt would agree to communicate these demands to the Allies, who would give them every consideration.[26] Again, there was no dissent in the War Cabinet. Roosevelt would be approached.

The next day another line of action with the Italians was suggested. An official at the Italian Embassy met Sir Robert Vansittart, formerly permanent head of the Foreign Office, who suggested that the British make a direct appeal to Mussolini about some kind of mediation between the powers. Halifax told the War Cabinet that he thought the idea worth following up as it might gain time and that it was anyway in tune with French policy.[27]

So far Churchill had not made any extensive comment on the overtures to the Italians. Whether he sensed danger in Halifax's pursuit of Italy is uncertain, but perhaps because of the mention of mediation on the part of Mussolini, he now intervened. He said he had no objection to talking to the Italians but insisted that this be kept secret 'since it might be taken as a confession of weakness'.[28]

At this point Churchill's position, namely that Britain would fight on whatever impact the Italian reply had on the French, had gone unchallenged. Indeed he had restated it with some vigour to the Chiefs of Staff at a meeting of the Defence Committee on 25 May.[29] However, now those same chiefs produced a paper that was decidedly unhelpful to Churchill. They had been working for some time on a document with the ominous title 'British Strategy in a Certain Eventuality', the eventuality that could not speak its name being the fall of France. The conclusions they reached around Britain's ability to fight on in these circumstances were gloomy. The Chiefs of Staff stated that they were unable to say with any certainty whether the Royal Air Force could hold out if the French coast was in hostile hands. They concluded that most of the BEF would be trapped in France and in those circumstances once the German army landed in Britain it would be impossible to drive it out. Even their assessment of the naval position was downbeat. At sea all depended on whether the navy could be protected from aerial attack, and they had no confidence that it could. Finally, the Chiefs of Staff stated that they could see no path that led to the defeat of Germany short of full American military and financial cooperation.[30]

Churchill read this paper on 25 May. It can be imagined that he was appalled by this assessment of Britain's chances. He was also worried that when his War Cabinet colleagues read it the result might be to induce a move to make peace. He would have to deal with this the following day.

That day was to be the most difficult day so far in Churchill's short premiership. He had been informed late on 25 May that Reynaud was coming to London next morning perhaps to discuss a method by which France could leave the war. He had also to manoeuvre the gloomy Chiefs of Staff report through the War Cabinet. Over all this lay the question of whether the BEF could fight its way back to the Channel ports.

Churchill called the first War Cabinet at the early hour of 9 a.m. on 26 May to consider what reply was to be made to Reynaud. He informed his colleagues that the projected French counter-offensive against the German spearheads 'had no chance whatever' of eventuating; that a telegram had been dispatched to General Lord Gort to this effect; and that ships were being collected for the evacuation of the BEF.[31] In addition the War Cabinet should face the fact that Reynaud might tell them the French could not carry on the fight. Churchill then announced that in the light of the above events and in order to meet 'all eventualities' he had given the Chiefs of Staff new terms of reference concerning Britain's ability to fight on alone:

In the event of France being unable to continue in the war and becoming neutral, with the Germans holding their present position, and the Belgian army being forced to capitulate after assisting the British Expeditionary Force to reach the coast; in the event of terms being offered to Britain which would place her entirely at the mercy of Germany through disarmament, cession of naval bases in the Orkneys etc, what are the prospects of our continuing the war alone against Germany and probably Italy. Can the Navy and Air Force hold out reasonable hopes of preventing serious invasion, and could the forces gathered in this Island cope with raids from the air involving detachments not greater than 10,000 men; it being observed that a prolongation of British resistance might be very dangerous for Germany engaged in holding down the greater part of Europe.[32]

In fact the 'eventualities' of which Churchill spoke had been apparent for some time. They were indeed the basis on which the Chiefs of Staff had prepared their gloomy report. Amending the terms of reference to them was simply a manoeuvre designed quite deliberately by the Prime Minister to bring forth a more optimistic assessment. In the new remit Churchill painted the German peace proposals in the bleakest possible light while highlighting the dangers to Germany (which he did not specify) of prolonged British resistance. If Britain was to be placed 'entirely at the mercy of Germany', why not fight on? Churchill was challenging the Chiefs of Staff to dispute this position or declare themselves defeatist.[33]

And surely Churchill was seeing events with greater clarity than the Chiefs of Staff. There was no reason to dismiss the RAF, which would fight the Luftwaffe over Britain behind the immense security of the radar chain. Nor was there any reason to question the effectiveness of the navy in warding off invasion – even without air cover. And the army was not yet 'trapped in France'. It was perhaps a brave prediction to say that most of the BEF could be lifted from French ports, but there was also no reason for the Chiefs of Staff to write off the attempt before it had been made. Finally, the scenario sketched out by Churchill of Germany triumphant was hardly an exaggeration. If Germany were left in control of the economic and financial resources of Western Europe, it would only be a matter of time before Britain *was* entirely at Hitler's mercy. If by some chance Hitler did make a 'moderate' peace proposal, it would only retain its moderation until the Führer was in a position to toughen it. Churchill was surely correct in seeing that any peace with Nazi Germany would not be worth having.

In issuing new terms of reference, Churchill was presumably trying to render the old report obsolete before it could be circulated. Sir Cyril Newall, who was chairing the meetings of the Chiefs of Staff, quickly responded to Churchill's new instructions by saying that although the service chiefs had prepared a paper on the subject they would now examine the question again.

Halifax, the Foreign Secretary, who had been much affected by the impending crisis outlined by Churchill at the beginning of the meeting, now made the first of his substantial interventions. He commented that a dark picture had been presented. 'We now had to face the fact that it was not so much now a question of imposing a complete defeat on Germany but of safeguarding the independence of our Empire and if possible that of France.'[34] He then went on to inform the War Cabinet that he had talked to Signor Giuseppe Bastianini, the Italian ambassador to Britain. This was unremarkable in itself, as the War Cabinet had instructed him to do so. However, it soon became clear that the discussions had ranged more widely than had been intended. Halifax reported:

> The Ambassador had said that Signor Mussolini's principal wish was to secure peace in Europe. The Foreign Secretary had replied that peace and security in Europe were equally our main object, and we should naturally be prepared to consider any such proposals which might lead to this, provided our liberty and independence was assured . . . Signor Bastianini had asked for a further interview that morning, and he might have fresh proposals to put forward.[35]

It is obvious that Halifax had departed from the War Cabinet's instructions to address the Italians *only* on matters concerning Italy and its desiderata for remaining neutral. The Foreign Secretary's introduction of the 'peace and security of Europe' as a whole was merely code. A European-wide settlement would mean that the Germans would have to be involved. Talking to Mussolini in this scenario would soon mean talking to Hitler.

Churchill grasped this point immediately. He replied that 'peace and security might be achieved under a German domination of Europe. That we could never accept . . . He was opposed to any negotiations that might lead to a derogation of our rights and power.'

The War Cabinet left the question of negotiations and turned to an 'Aide-Memoire' prepared by the Chiefs of Staff, 'Arguments to Deter the French from Capitulating', which had been circulated. It pointed out to the French that Germany was not as strong as it looked but that if the French capitulated they should assist the BEF in any evacuation. It also stated that Britain would continue the fight whatever the French decided, the consequences of which might be that the French would find their cities under attack by the RAF and the whole country subject to blockade.[36]

Halifax saw his chance to use the Aide-Memoire to restate his case for negotiations. Apparently he had been flicking through the Chiefs of Staff paper on 'A Certain Eventuality' and argued that while the service chiefs thought that the matter would turn on air superiority, if France collapsed as envisaged by the Aide-Memoire, the Germans would be free to turn the bulk of their war production to aircraft. Although Halifax did not state it directly, the implication was that Britain could not win.[37] Newall once more helpfully intervened. The Chief of the Air Staff noted that the Aide-Memoire did not deal with the matter that Halifax had raised but that this point would be dealt with by the paper to be written on the Prime Minister's new instructions. That for the moment ended the discussion.

Churchill then left his colleagues to meet the French Premier. Churchill had every reason to be apprehensive about this meeting. Ever since Reynaud had awoken him on 15 May to claim that France was beaten, following the German advance across the River Meuse, the state of French morale had concerned the Prime Minister. And since then the situation had grown much more perilous. The French had been unable to mount a counter-offensive against the Germans and the British were occupying only a thin strip of land between Arras and Dunkirk.

In the event, the matter of a separate peace did not arise at their meeting. But Reynaud was insistent that Britain and France approach Mussolini and ask what concessions he would require to remain neutral. Only then would the larger question of a European settlement be discussed.[38] The French stance, if not absolutely defeatist, was bad enough. Reynaud was now taking exactly the same line as Halifax.

Churchill returned to his Cabinet colleagues to give an 'expose' of Reynaud's position. He told them that the new French commander-in-chief, Maxime Weygand, saw no possibility of winning the land war and that 'someone' (surely it was Reynaud) had suggested another approach to Mussolini. France had not been offered any peace terms but Reynaud considered that they 'could get an offer if they wanted one'.[39] Churchill then restated his own position. He said he had told the French leader that Britain was 'not prepared to give in on any account. We would rather go down fighting than be enslaved by Germany.' Churchill then suggested that Halifax leave the meeting and meet Reynaud. However, the Foreign Secretary was not to be fobbed off by such an obvious ploy and proceeded to have his say. He stated that he too favoured an approach to Italy. Mussolini would not want to see Hitler dominating Europe. He was certain that Mussolini would 'persuade Hitler to take a more reasonable line'. For the first time, Churchill seemed rather on the defensive. He replied that he doubted whether anything would come of an approach to Mussolini but that the matter was something the War Cabinet might have to consider. The meeting then broke up.

Later the same day, 26 May (around 5 p.m. according to Cadogan),[40] after Reynaud had departed for France, an 'informal' meeting of the War Cabinet took place at Admiralty House. As the minutes inform us, 'this record does not cover the first quarter of an hour of the discussion, during which the Secretary was not present'.[41] We will never know exactly what was said during those 15 minutes, but it is clear from what followed that an approach to Italy was back on the table. When the Secretary (Sir Edward Bridges) entered, Churchill was making the point that Britain was in a much stronger position than France. Britain could defend itself; this might prove beyond the French. He was opposed to joining France in any negotiations because 'there is no limit to the terms Germany would impose on us if she had her way'. Attlee, the Lord Privy Seal, added rather unhelpfully that if France went out of the war, Hitler would be able to turn on Britain 'the sooner'. Churchill replied that he hoped the French would hang on but that 'we must take care not to be forced into a weak position in which we went to Signor Mussolini and invited him to go to Herr Hitler and ask him to treat us nicely'.

Halifax then spoke. He began by saying that he did not disagree with Churchill's position but,

> He attached perhaps rather more importance than the Prime Minister to the desirability of allowing France to try out the possibilities of European equilibrium. He was not quite convinced that the Prime Minister's diagnosis was correct and that it was not in Herr Hitler's interest to insist on outrageous terms.

He went on to say that Britain should not fear such a prospect. Hitler was well aware of his internal weaknesses and if Britain could save France from being subjected to the Gestapo so much the better. His conclusion made it clear that any talks should include not just terms for France from Hitler but terms for Britain as well:

The Foreign Secretary thought that we might say to Signor Mussolini that if there was any suggestion of terms which affected our independence, we should not look at them for a moment [but] . . . at any rate he could see no harm in trying this line of approach.

The gauntlet had now been thrown down. So far from not disagreeing with the Prime Minister and suggesting that the differences between them were ones of emphasis, Halifax was suggesting a policy diametrically opposed to Churchill. His 'European equilibrium' meant nothing less than a settlement with Germany. Halifax was restating the position of the appeasers – that a deal could be struck with Hitler and that such a deal would last, thus ensuring British independence.

At this point Churchill might have expected that a restatement of Halifax's policy at the Munich conference would elicit strong dissent from the Labour members of the War Cabinet. But on this occasion it did not. Attlee remained silent. Greenwood said that while he was doubtful whether Mussolini had much influence with Hitler, he saw no objection to Halifax's line of approach. Chamberlain also joined the chorus. He referred back to a statement made by Churchill to the effect that Britain might be better off without the French. If Britain could now obtain safeguards on particular points, why not make an overture to Mussolini?

The mention of the Italian dictator and the apparent lack of support for Churchill led Halifax back to the charge. He reminded colleagues of the interview he had had with the Italian ambassador on 25 May. He had told Bastianini that he wished to improve relations with Italy as he had done with some success over contraband control, which tended to suggest that Halifax had been playing a long game when he opened those discussions. He went on to say that he had told Bastianini he wished nothing left undone to 'avoid any misunderstanding or something worse between our two countries'. Bastianini replied that Mussolini thought problems between Italy and any other country should 'be part of a general European settlement', which was now the generally accepted code for saying that the Germans must be included in any talks that might take place. Halifax had concluded his meeting with the Italian ambassador by saying that Mussolini should be informed that the British government did not exclude the possibility of some discussion on the wider problem of European security.[42]

Churchill then intervened. He said that:

> His general comment on the suggested approach to Signor Mussolini
> was that it implied that if we were prepared to give Germany back her
> colonies and to make certain concessions in the Mediterranean, it was
> possible for us to get out of our present difficulties. He thought no such
> option was open to us. For example, the terms offered would certainly
> prevent us from completing our re-armament.[43]

These words have to be read carefully. Some authorities have suggested that
Churchill was making a concession to Halifax – that a colonial deal with
Hitler and Mussolini could extricate Britain from 'its present difficulties'.[44]
But this was not what he was saying. All he was saying was that this was the
implication of the Halifax–Bastianini conversation and that he disagreed
with it. At no time during the Cabinet crisis did Churchill ever consent to
bringing Germany into the discussions. With Italy he also maintained a
consistent line. He was prepared (without enthusiasm) to listen to what
Mussolini required to remain neutral, his lack of enthusiasm reflecting his
view that Mussolini's price would always be too high. Indeed, Churchill
continued in this fashion by concluding that the only way to deal with
Hitler was to 'show him that he could not conquer this country', but 'at the
same time he did not raise objection to some approach being made to
Signor Mussolini'.

Despite pressure from Halifax and the lack of help from Attlee and
Greenwood, Churchill had the situation well in hand. At the end of the
meeting he invited Halifax to circulate a draft communication to Italy but
added that as the matter was so important the leader of the Liberal Party,
Archie Sinclair, should be present when it was discussed. Sinclair was a
firm supporter of Churchill and was bound to agree with the Prime
Minister on the undesirability of peace talks. Moreover, Churchill would by
then have the revised paper from the Chiefs of Staff to discuss and he may
have estimated that it would be far less gloomy than their last effort. Next
day, 27 May, would likely be a difficult one, but Churchill had no reason to
doubt that he could weather the storm.

The War Cabinet reassembled at 11.30 a.m. on 27 May. The news from the
front was grim. The Belgians were wavering and in the last 12 hours just 7,600

troops had been evacuated from Dunkirk. Apart from how to deal with the defeatism of the Australian High Commissioner in London (Stanley Melbourne Bruce), the first business of the day was the original and revised reports from the Chiefs of Staff. Churchill opened the meeting by saying that he did not believe the first report gave 'a true picture of the position' and in particular he challenged the attached tables of British and German air strength.[45] A very long discussion of the merits of the statistics followed. The revised paper, 'British Strategy in the Near Future', which concluded that Britain could indeed hang on if the French capitulated, was not even discussed.[46] Instead, the War Cabinet 'invited the Prime Minister to conduct a searching examination into the strengths of the British and German Air Forces with a view to revising the [Chiefs' figures]', and decided that discussion of the two reports be deferred until that investigation was completed.[47] So by diverting the attention of his colleagues to the detail of the first paper rather than its broad conclusions, Churchill sidelined the entire discussion.

The War Cabinet next met (at 4.30 p.m.) to consider Halifax's draft note on an approach to Mussolini. In part the note read:

> If Signor Mussolini will co-operate with us in securing a settlement . . . we will undertake at once to discuss, with the desire to find solutions, the matters in which Signor Mussolini is primarily interested. We understand that he desires the solution of certain Mediterranean questions: and if he will state in secrecy what these are, France and Great Britain will at once do their best to meet these wishes.[48]

Churchill replied by stating that the tone of the note was very like that suggested to President Roosevelt several days before and it would be better to allow the President to make the approach. Halifax said that since he had circulated the note there had been three developments. First, Roosevelt had approached Mussolini, and second, the French now required that 'geographical precision' (that is, the precise pieces of territory it was proposed to cede to Italy) be added to the note. Third, he had received a telegram from the British ambassador to Italy suggesting that it was too late to make any kind of approach to Mussolini.[49]

Those developments, it might be thought, would spell the end of any approach to Italy. Indeed, Chamberlain seemed to agree. He thought that Mussolini would not state his desiderata until France was beaten and therefore the proposed French approach 'would serve no useful purpose'. However, the French should be allowed to go ahead with an approach in order that there could be no reproaches with Britain if they were beaten.[50]

Churchill had no time for this line. He commented that Chamberlain's argument amounted to this, 'that nothing would come of the approach but that it was worth doing to sweeten relations with a failing ally'.[51] Sinclair agreed. He said 'he was convinced of the futility of an approach to Italy at this time. Being in a tight corner, any weakness on our part would encourage the Germans and Italians, and would tend to undermine morale both in this country and in the Dominions.' Halifax tried to stem the tide by arguing that Mussolini would realise that Roosevelt's approach 'had been prompted by us' and this would in itself be interpreted as showing weakness.

Faced with a definite proposal to approach a fascist dictator for peace terms, the Labour members weighed in. Attlee said 'the suggested approach would be of no practical effect and would be very damaging to us'. Greenwood (reversing himself from the previous day) agreed: 'the approach now suggested would put us in the wrong . . . If it got out that we had sued for terms at the cost of ceding British territory, the consequences would be terrible.'

Churchill now had three members of the War Cabinet opposed to talks with Italy and one (Chamberlain) saying that the French alone should be allowed to make an approach. Halifax was isolated. Now was the time for a conciliatory statement from the Prime Minister to the effect that Britain should be guided by Mussolini's response to Roosevelt. Instead, Churchill, perhaps carried away by the solid support for his position, proceeded to overplay his hand. He started well enough, remarking that 'he was increasingly oppressed by the futility of the suggested approach to Signor Mussolini, which the latter would certainly regard with contempt'. He continued:

The best help we could give to M. Reynaud was to let him feel that, whatever happened to France, we were going to fight it out to the end . . . At the moment our prestige in Europe was very low. The only way

63

to get it back was by showing the world that Germany had not beaten us. If, after two or three months, we could show we were still unbeaten, our prestige would return. *Even if we were beaten, we should be no worse off than we should be if we were to abandon the struggle.* Let us therefore avoid being dragged down the slippery slope with France. The whole of this manoeuvre was intended to get us so deeply involved in negotiations that we would be unable to turn back. We had gone a long way already in our approach to Italy, but let us not allow M. Reynaud to get us involved in a confused situation. The approach proposed was not only futile, but involved us in a deadly danger.[52]

And after an interruption from Chamberlain to the effect that Britain should wait for the Italian response to Roosevelt, Churchill forged ahead:

> France had got to settle this matter [of peace talks] for herself. It was a question of her word and her army's honour. He had heard that there had been some change for the better in the fighting spirit of the French troops. There might be some hope in this. Otherwise everything would rest on us. *If the worst came to the worst, it would be no bad thing for this country to go down fighting for the other countries which had been over-come by the Nazi tyranny.*[53]

To some extent this statement merely repeated Churchill's call for victory at all costs. But there is little doubt that some of what he said had been better omitted, especially that in fighting it out for other countries Britain might go down. In any case this last statement hardly represented Churchill's considered view. He had been scathing about the strategic review of the Chiefs of Staff, and he had a clearer idea than they that Britain had an excellent chance with its air force and navy of preventing a German invasion. Why then did he say it? The impression must be that he was hypnotised by his own rhetoric and he momentarily forgot to whom he was speaking. He was about to receive a nasty reminder.

We can well believe that Churchill's sentiments were anathema to Halifax, the arch-negotiator, who had no doubt entered the meeting expecting that his draft for an approach to Italy would be taken seriously.

Never having grasped the fact that it was impossible to negotiate in good faith with Hitler and there were no conceivable terms regarding British independence to be had from the German dictator, what undoubtedly stuck in his craw was that going down fighting would be 'no bad thing'. This hyperbole from Churchill stung the Foreign Secretary to reply that

> He was conscious of certain rather profound differences of points of view which he would like to make clear . . . He could not recognize any resemblance between the action which he proposed, and the suggestion that we were suing for terms and following a line which would lead us to disaster. In the discussion the previous day he had asked the Prime Minister whether, if he was satisfied that matters vital to the independence of this country were unaffected, he would be prepared to discuss terms. The Prime Minister had said that he would be thankful to get out of our present difficulties on such terms, provided we retained the essentials and the elements of our vital strength, even at the cost of some cession of territory. [As we have seen Churchill had said no such thing. Halifax here is summarising his own position not Churchill's.] On the present occasion, however, the Prime Minister seemed to suggest that under no conditions would we contemplate any course except fighting to a finish. The issue was probably academic, since we were unlikely to receive any offer which would not come up against the fundamental conditions which were essential to us. *If, however, it was possible to obtain a settlement which did not impair those conditions, he, for his part, doubted if he would be able to accept the view now put by the Prime Minister.*[54]

Halifax concluded by saying that if Britain's independence was not at stake, 'he would think it right to accept an offer which would save the country from avoidable disaster'.[55]

Once again, the minutes tone down much of what was said. There is no doubt that Halifax threatened resignation at this point. Immediately after the meeting he told Cadogan 'I can't work with Winston any longer.'[56] And that night Halifax wrote in his diary: 'I thought Winston talked the most frightful rot, also Greenwood, and after bearing it for some time I said exactly what I thought of them, adding that, if that was really their view, and if it came to the point, our ways must separate.'[57]

Actually it had been Halifax who had talked 'rot', in the sense that he still thought it possible to negotiate with Hitler, but Churchill had been unnecessarily belligerent at this meeting. He had isolated Halifax in the War Cabinet and then humiliated him. Threatened resignation was the result. Could Churchill's two-week-old administration have withstood the departure of Halifax? Almost certainly. Halifax had no standing in the country and was in the Lords not the Commons. Moreover, it seems likely that Chamberlain would not have followed Halifax's lead and that this would have been enough to mollify the backbenchers. Finally, the Commons, having voted for war with Churchill, would hardly have reversed themselves over a resignation whose purpose was to institute peace talks. Yet the resignation of a Foreign Secretary at such a critical point in the war was no small matter. The government would be seen as divided and the issue of division would be obvious. The whole position of Britain would be weakened and Churchill had acted foolishly in putting himself in this situation.

The Prime Minister immediately realised that he had gone too far. To keep Halifax in the Cabinet he had to demonstrate that in some circumstances he was willing to negotiate. While insisting on his opinion that no acceptable terms were likely to be on offer, he threw Halifax this bone: 'If Herr Hitler was prepared to make peace on the terms of the restoration of German colonies and the overlordship of Central Europe, that was one thing. But it was quite unlikely that he would make any such offer.'[58]

Too much can be made of this statement.[59] It was clearly a quite unrealistic scenario. Hitler was already overlord of Central Europe and well on his way to becoming overlord of Western Europe as well. Offering him less than he had already conquered plus Tanganyika would hardly have brought him to the negotiating table. On Churchill's part this was a manoeuvre, not a policy. And the person who immediately recognised this was Halifax. He completely ignored Churchill's gesture and brought the discussion back to what he thought *was* a realistic proposition. What would happen, he asked Churchill, if France collapsed and the French insisted on Britain joining them in talks with Germany? Churchill, realising that his first ploy had failed to move the Foreign Secretary, attempted another conciliatory move. He said 'that he would not join France in asking for terms; but if he were told what the terms offered were, he would be prepared to consider them'.[60] This reply also hardly suggested that Churchill was serious about peace offers. All he did was say he would look at terms that had not been formulated. He might have added that after he had considered them he would certainly reject them.

The War Cabinet was finally brought to a definite conclusion by an intervention by Chamberlain. He suggested that Hitler's tactics would be to 'make a definite offer to France, and when the French said that they had allies he would say "I am here, let them send a delegate to Paris"'.[61] But the majority of the War Cabinet were having none of this. They bluntly concluded 'that the answer to such an offer must be "No"'.[62]

The day ended with Halifax being comprehensively outmanoeuvred. He knew that Churchill's conciliatory gestures were essentially meaningless and he was still angry that his suggestions at compromise had been viewed as defeatist or worse. So after the meeting he asked to see Churchill privately in the garden of No. 10. We do not know what was said on this occasion but we have Cadogan's strictures to Halifax that he not do anything foolish and Halifax's diary entry in which he says that Churchill 'was full of apologies and affection'.[63] This was enough to keep the Foreign Secretary on board.

This day, 27 May, has often been portrayed as the rational Halifax wringing concessions from the emotional Churchill. This is hardly the case. Even after the walk in the garden and despite Churchill's 'affection' there was no indication that the Prime Minister had altered his position. His whole stance during that day had been designed to keep Halifax in the Cabinet. He had no more intention of making concessions to Germany or Italy than he had on 26 May. His tactical manoeuvres were just that and recognised by Halifax for what they were. It was the need for unity in a dark hour that kept Halifax from resignation on 27 May. And we must not push the 'rational' Halifax depiction too far. There was nothing 'rational' in trying to arrange what was essentially another Munich conference. Halifax vastly overrated the position of Mussolini, who had absolutely no influence over Hitler. The Führer hardly needed Italy in a war that was virtually won and anyway, if Halifax had not noticed, at Munich the only role played by

Mussolini was to do Hitler's bidding. Nor should we overrate the emotionalism of Churchill. Perhaps his rhetoric had got a little out of hand on 27 May, but he was surely correct in seeing any negotiations as a slippery slope to a humiliating peace. He also knew that Britain's best weapons, the RAF and the navy, had not yet been tested and would be formidable obstacles to an invasion. In this sense it was Churchill who was being rational and Halifax not.

Yet, despite the rejection of negotiations on 27 May, they were back on the table on 28 May. That day was an exceedingly black one for Britain. The Belgians had capitulated, exposing the flank of the BEF, and the number of soldiers evacuated from Dunkirk was again very modest.[64]

The morning Cabinet meeting went well for Churchill. The War Cabinet had been informed by Halifax that Mussolini had at last replied to Roosevelt and that 'the communication had been entirely negative'.[65] Yet at the afternoon session the Foreign Secretary announced that the Chief Diplomatic Advisor to the government, Sir Robert Vansittart, had learned from the Italian Embassy that the Italians would like Britain to give a clear indication that it sought Italian mediation.[66] Halifax then went on to indicate that he still favoured an approach to the Italians. Churchill and Sinclair restated their own positions, Churchill repeating the metaphor of 'the slippery slope'. But after a long discussion an alarming development occurred – Chamberlain wobbled. Until now his position was that whereas it would be advantageous for the French to approach Italy, he thought it futile for Britain to do so. Now, however, he stated:

> It was our duty to look at the situation realistically. He felt bound to say that he was in agreement with the Foreign Secretary in taking the view that if we thought it was possible that we could now get terms which, although grievous, would not threaten our independence, we should be right to consider such terms.[67]

This development, so potentially dangerous, was met by a storm of protest from other members of the War Cabinet. Attlee said it would be a severe shock to public opinion if it was known that terms were being sought and that in that situation it might be 'impossible to rally the morale of the people'. Greenwood added that the industrial centres of the country 'would regard anything like weakening on the part of the Government as a disaster'.[68]

Shortly after this exchange the meeting adjourned and reassembled 45 minutes later. In the interim Churchill had been busy. He had addressed the group of ministers outside the War Cabinet and plainly put the situation facing Britain before them. When he returned he described their reaction to his War Cabinet colleagues:

> They had not expressed alarm at the situation in France, but had expressed the greatest satisfaction when he told them that there was no chance of our giving up the struggle. He did not remember having ever before heard a gathering of persons occupying high places in political life express themselves so emphatically.[69]

In his memoirs Churchill portrayed this incident with more colour:

> Quite a number [of ministers] seemed to jump up from the table and come running to my chair, shouting and patting me on the back. There is no doubt that had I at this juncture faltered at all in the leading of the nation I should have been hurled out of office. I was sure that every Minister was ready to be killed quite soon, and have all his family and possessions destroyed, rather than give in.[70]

Hugh Dalton, who was present, remembered a murmur of assent at Churchill's declaration that Britain would fight on and that after the meeting he clapped Churchill on the back.[71] Leo Amery was also present. He states that Churchill placed the situation squarely before ministers 'in no way minimizing the extent of the disaster [and] . . . that there could be no greater folly than to try at this moment to offer concessions either to Italy or Germany . . . We then had a little question and answering after that and then left all of us tremendously heartened by Winston's resolution.'[72]

There is no doubt that Churchill in his memoirs exaggerated the response of the ministers to his declaration. But there is also no doubt that the ministers, many of whom he had appointed, were entirely in agreement with his decision to fight on. Halifax (and Chamberlain) had now finally been outmanoeuvred. Within the War Cabinet, Attlee, Greenwood and the new addition, Sinclair, were at one with Churchill. Outside the War Cabinet, only a few ministers such as Reith opposed him. For the moment, that was the end of the matter. Churchill drafted a letter to Reynaud which said that whatever the attitude of France, Britain did not deem it appropriate, given 'the firm and resolute' morale of the British people, to approach either dictator at the moment.[73] Churchill had prevailed. There would be no further mention of an approach to Mussolini or Hitler by Halifax or Chamberlain. The war would be fought to a finish.

CHAPTER 4

A CLOSE-RUN THING
THE BEF's RETREAT TO THE COAST, MAY 1940

While Churchill had won the political battle to continue the fight, this would have been a hollow (and probably) temporary victory had the BEF fallen to Hitler's forces in France. When the German attack in the west began on 10 May 1940 the British had about 400,000 men in France. By mid-June approximately 340,000 were back in Britain after a lengthy retreat and then evacuation from Dunkirk and other more westerly French ports. This was nothing less than 'a colossal military disaster'. But the disaster could have been much worse. Although the BEF lost 60,000 casualties (dead and wounded), the return of the bulk of the army to Britain bolstered Churchill's political position. The pressure from the appeasers in the War Cabinet to make some kind of compromise peace with Hitler climaxed as the evacuations from Dunkirk began. Had the great majority of the BEF been captured, leaving Britain without the nucleus of a future army, it is beyond question that the appeasers would have renewed their political attacks with even greater vigour. In these circumstances we cannot know what the outcome might have been, but the return of the army certainly gave Churchill an additional card to play against those who would have made peace. It was therefore vital in political as well as military terms that the army survive.

The army that the British sent to France comprised 10 divisions of infantry, 5 from the Regular Army (1, 2, 3, 4 and 5 Divisions) and 5 from

71

the part-time Territorial Army (42, 44, 48, 50 and 51 Divisions). In April the 12, 23 and 46 Divisions were sent out to dig trenches and maintain the lines of communications stretching back to Rennes in western France. These units had no tanks, no artillery, and were only partly trained.[1] Operating with the BEF was a fighter force of four squadrons of Hurricanes to provide air cover. A second force of aircraft (the Advanced Air Striking Force), comprising 11 squadrons of light or medium bombers and three Hurricane squadrons, were to operate with the French (Map 1).[2]

The commander-in-chief of this force was Lord Gort, who had been Chief of the Imperial General Staff on the outbreak of war. In the Great War he had been one of Field Marshal Haig's liaison officers and had shown considerable moral courage in 1916 during the latter part of the Battle of the Somme in conveying to his chief the appalling conditions under which the troops were fighting. Gort had later commanded a battalion and won the VC. But that was his only experience of commanding troops in the field and his choice as commander-in-chief had raised concerns. One of his Corps commanders thought that Gort was still mired

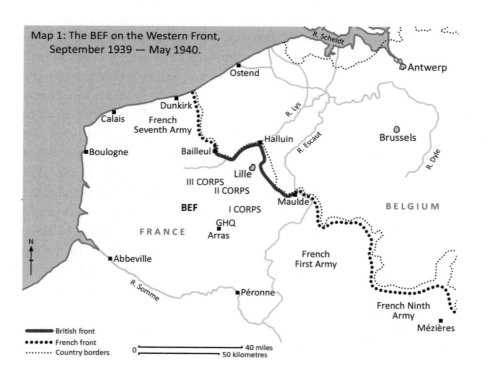

Map 1: The BEF on the Western Front, September 1939 — May 1940.

in detail best left to a battalion commander and was unable to grasp the larger picture.[3] He was, however, well served by General Pownall, his Chief of Staff, who often had to make decisions during Gort's frequent absences from his headquarters.

The Corps commanders of the BEF (Generals John Dill, Alan Brooke and Ronald Adam) were extremely competent and were to have distinguished careers in higher office later in the war. In the weeks to come much would depend on their ability to think and act quickly.

Of the divisional commanders Bernard Montgomery was very skilled but his abrasive personality and often self-serving remarks tended to blind some to his great abilities. General Harold Alexander was also a rising star (in the end perhaps he rose too high) and managed his division with skill. General Michael Barker (Dill's replacement as Corps Commander when he was made CIGS) was less capable. Others, such as Major Generals H. E. Franklyn, R. L. Petre and H. O. Curtis, were much less well known but would rise to the occasion and have good, if brief, campaigns.

When offensive operations began the force was to operate under a number of considerable disadvantages, many not of their making. Because the French had 85 divisions in the line, the BEF was the junior partner and was consequently placed under their unwieldy command structure. In overall charge was General Gamelin. Under him was another Frenchman, General Georges, in command of the armies of the north-east of which the BEF was a part. But the coordination of the armies of four countries (Holland, Belgium, Britain and France) had proved too difficult for Georges and on 12 May another layer of command had been added.[4] General Billotte, a man whose morale would prove highly variable, had been placed in charge of the French First Army, the Belgians and the BEF. Gort was therefore immediately responsible to Billotte, who reported to Georges, who reported to Gamelin, who was ensconced at the Château Vincennes in Paris without a direct telephone line. This sclerotic structure would make it difficult to respond to events with celerity.

The second problem for the BEF (though they failed to recognise it) was the plan developed by Gamelin. If Belgium was attacked by Germany (which seemed highly likely), the French armies of the north-east and the BEF would advance (on invitation) into Belgium – probably to the line of the River Dyle in the case of the British.[5] In addition, in the event of the

Dutch being attacked (also highly likely) the French Seventh Army, on the left of the BEF, would dash to the Dutch city of Breda in order to bolster the Dutch forces.[6] When the British agreed to this plan they failed to notice that the French Seventh Army was the only reserve available to the Allies in the north-east. The so-called 'Breda variation' removed this reserve altogether.

For the British the main problem with this plan was that it played into the hands of the Germans. Initially the Germans had developed a rather unimaginative scheme along the lines of the Schlieffen scheme of 1914 whereby the great mass of their armies would sweep across the Belgian plain. In this scenario they would have met the advancing Franco-British forces head on. But many on the German side were unhappy with this pedestrian plan. In the end, led by General Manstein and others, they persuaded Hitler to change it. Under the new arrangements the Germans would make their main thrust with Army Group A, which contained 37 infantry divisions and 7 of the 10 German Panzer divisions, through the wooded Ardennes country in southern Belgium and Luxembourg.[7] This would have the advantage of outflanking the Maginot Line to its north to strike the Allies at an unexpected point. This point was also vulnerable because the French had rather weak forces in this area (their Second and Ninth Armies).

Belgium and Holland would also be attacked but by a weaker force (Army Group B consisting of 26 infantry and three Panzer divisions). This force would attract the Allied armies advancing into Belgium (the Germans were well aware of this advance because they had broken the French radio codes). The further the Allies advanced the more precarious their position would become, because the southern German armies, after breaking through the French defences, would swing northwards and pin all the north-eastern Allied armies against the Channel. This was Plan Yellow. Then in the second phase of the battle (Plan Red) the German forces would turn south and drive the remaining French armies south-east and pin them against the rear of the Maginot Line.[8] For our purposes, however, it is sufficient to note that should the German plan succeed, the further into Belgium the BEF advanced, the greater their danger of encirclement.

A further disadvantage for the British was that their air component would operate without early-warning radar. The French did not have radar and the British had no intention of building a system that might fall into enemy hands in France. Any attack on the BEF by hostile aircraft was therefore likely to be undetected.

The final disadvantage under which the British would operate was that they would in all probability be squeezed between two Allied armies. Should all go to plan and the Belgians enter the war on the Allied side, they would constitute the force on the left flank of the BEF. On the right flank would be the French First Army. Although the whole force would nominally be controlled by Billotte, immediate contingencies would require close liaison with Belgian and French troops. Who would carry out this function was unclear and it seems certain that the BEF entered battle with little knowledge of the composition and capabilities of the two armies guarding its flanks (Map 2).

* * * * *

The higher echelons of the BEF, including the commander, Lord Gort, first heard of the German offensive in the early hours of 10 May by telegram from the War Office and from its Liaison Mission (led by General Swayne) at French headquarters (GQG). They were informed that the enemy had attacked on a front from Holland to Luxembourg and that the Belgian government (until then neutral) had invited the Allied armies into their country. The Gamelin Plan was therefore implemented. The BEF would advance to the line of the River Dyle where they would join with the Belgian army just east of Brussels on their left. On their right, the French First Army would also advance into Belgium.

Oblivious to the trap into which it was advancing, the BEF, led by the armoured cars of the 12 Lancers, left its pillboxes and trench defences along the Franco-Belgian border and headed for the Dyle. On 11 May the BEF reached the river and commenced digging in between Louvain and Wavre. On the left was II Corps (Brooke) with 3 Division in the front line and 4 Division in close reserve. On the right was I Corps (Barker) with the 1 and 2 Divisions in the line and 48 Division in close reserve. First contact with the enemy came on 14 May. On the left of the British front the Germans penetrated Louvain but were driven out by the 15/19 Hussars from 3 Division.[9]

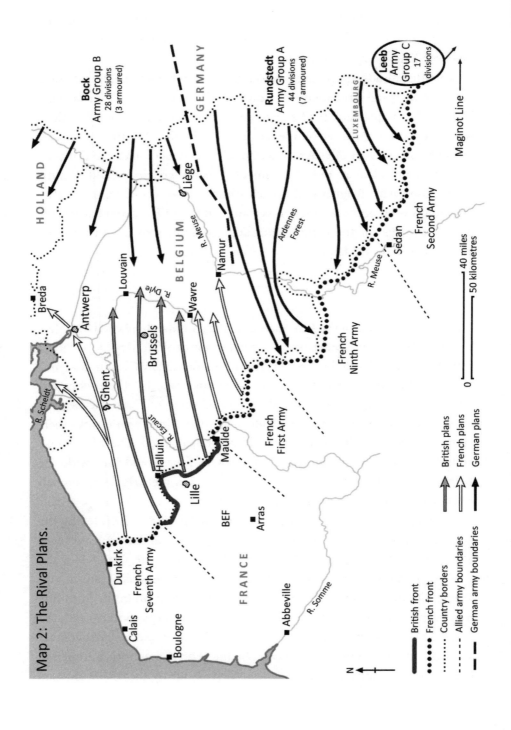

Map 2: The Rival Plans.

Bock
Army Group B
28 divisions
(3 armoured)

GERMANY

Rundstedt
Army Group A
44 divisions
(7 armoured)

Leeb
Army
Group C
17
divisions

Maginot Line

HOLLAND

Breda

Antwerp

R. Scheldt

R. Escaut

Louvain

Ghent

Brussels

BELGIUM

R. Dyle

Wavre

Liège

R. Meuse

Namur

LUXEMBOURG

Ardennes
Forest

R. Meuse

Sedan

French
Second Army

French
Ninth Army

French
First Army

French
Seventh Army

Halluin

Lille

Maulde

BEF

Arras

Dunkirk

Calais

Boulogne

FRANCE

Abbeville

R. Somme

40 miles

50 kilometres

0

N

British front

French front

Country borders

Allied army boundaries

German army boundaries

British plans

French plans

German plans

On 15 May while the BEF was still holding its own along the Dyle, disturbing news arrived from the French. German armoured columns had reportedly penetrated the hilly country of the Ardennes and forced a crossing of the River Meuse at Sedan. They had then fanned out into a gap between the French Second and Ninth Armies. Some reports suggested that the gap was 12 miles wide, others 5 miles. In any event the situation was serious.[10]

The full extent of the debacle in the south became clearer on 16 May. Reports from the French now stated that the Germans had advanced 30 miles westwards from Sedan. The French thought that the southern wing of what was Army Group A was making for the Somme; the northern for Arras, which was where British GHQ was located. The French Ninth Army was in a state of disintegration; the Second Army was in better shape but falling back.[11]

At the same time reports from the left flank of the BEF were causing alarm. The small Dutch army had been attacked in overwhelming force and the inundations on which they had mainly relied for their protection had been rendered useless by German paratroop formations dropped behind them.[12] Further south, the Belgian army was under extreme pressure and was also falling back. The first crisis of the battle had arrived (Map 3).

On 16 May General Billotte called a conference to discuss the implications for his armies of the deteriorating situation. Strangely, Gort did not attend this meeting, dispatching instead a staff officer, Major General T. R. Eastwood. Billotte made the position clear. In the north the Dutch had surrendered on 15 May. In the south, because of the rout of the Ninth and Second Armies, he had no choice but to draw back the First Army to maintain a continuous front. This meant that the BEF and the Belgians must also come back. Billotte's timetable was that on 16–17 May his armies must be on the River Senne, on 17–18 May on the River Dendre, and on 18–19 May on the River Escaut. Eastwood asked that these moves be delayed to allow the BEF time to prepare for the retreat, but Billotte was adamant (and surely correct) that the situation in the south would brook no delay.[13]

The disengagement of the BEF was handled by the Corps commanders. On the left the retreat of II Corps went relatively smoothly. Brooke, though a Francophile, had formed a low opinion of the French army almost from

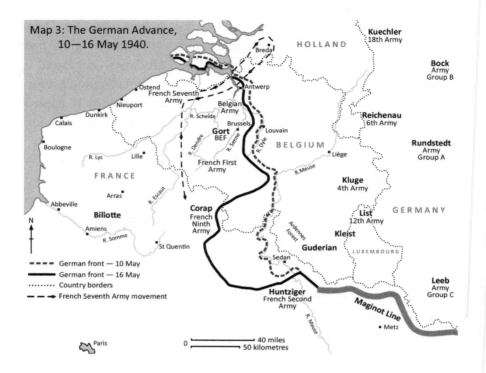

Map 3: The German Advance, 10—16 May 1940.

the day he arrived in France.[14] Perhaps for this reason he had selected a defensive position along the Charleroi Canal, to the rear of the Dyle, and had moved 4 Division forward on 12 May to deploy along it. His other division (50 Division), which he had also ordered forward, was merely turned around and sent back to the Dendre. Then on the night of 17 May, 3 Division withdrew through 4 Division on the canal and by dusk was on the Dendre, the artillery having succeeded in keeping the enemy quiet.[15] The rearguard of 4 Division (15/19 Hussars) was not so fortunate. German motor-cycle units got behind the Hussars and inflicted heavy casualties. In the end only 20 per cent of the unit remained.[16] On the right the orders to withdraw arrived eight hours late. As a result transport could not be provided for all units and at one point it seemed that 48 Division would be overrun by the Germans. However, the 12 Lancers, equipped only with Bren guns mounted on armoured cars, fought off the pursuing Germans who were equipped with some tanks.[17] Over the next two days and without major incident the BEF withdrew behind the Escaut.

In this instance the corps commanders and their divisional generals had saved the day without any intervention from GHQ. Gort, as will be shown, had his virtues as commander-in-chief, but the conduct of orderly procedures was not among them. When hostilities commenced he left GHQ at Arras (in fact it was scattered over an area of 50 square miles in villages around the city) and established a forward command or battle post, thus making him difficult to contact. He compounded these difficulties by frequent moves over the course of the campaign. Between 10 and 28 May the command post had 10 different locations.[18] And at these locations Gort was at the mercy of the French telephone system to relay messages to his commanders. This situation was to prove very frustrating to his Corps commanders. As I Corps War Diary related:

> Lack of good communications with GHQ during the last few days made great difficulties ... Hours were spent trying to get GHQ [which] has also three HQ, 'Advanced', 'Rear' and 'Command Post'. As often as not after a struggle of an hour or so, communication would be established, only to find that the officer or branch required was at one of the other places. It was very exasperating.[19]

Worse still, Gort frequently left his post to visit soldiers near or at the front. On 14 May his Chief of Staff (General Pownall) noted that 'Gort was away for eight hours today – too long in difficult times'.[20] In this sense Brooke's stricture that Gort was nothing more than 'a glorified boy scout' had substance.[21] Gort was soon to show, however, that he was more capable than suggested by these episodes. On 16 May Billotte, who at least demonstrated that there was nothing wrong with his navigational skills, appeared at Gort's command post. He told Gort that he was being attacked by 9 or 10 Panzer divisions, which was a guess but one that happened to be correct as the three Panzers with Army Group B were in the process of joining Army Group A. Billotte then produced a map which indicated that Panzers were already at Cambrai and Peronne, just 22 to 30 miles from GHQ at Arras.[22] Gort realised that the BEF on the Escaut was in grave danger of being enveloped from the south. His response was to create an improvised force consisting of the 127 Brigade from 42 Division, 12 regiments of artillery and an anti-tank battery, and send it to the south-eastern flank of the BEF.

In this area it could guard against a collapse by the French First Army and prevent the BEF itself from being outflanked by the Panzers.[23] This group was entitled Macforce after its commander Brigadier Mason Macfarlane, the Chief of Intelligence at GHQ. At the same time Gort sent the under-trained 'digging' divisions (12, 23, 46) to guard Amiens, the Canal du Nord and Seclin, all to the south-west of the BEF, in case the Panzers turned north when they passed Arras.[24] In addition, on 18 May he established Petreforce (General Petre was commander of 12 Division) to defend Arras in the event that that critical location was attacked. Petreforce consisted of a motley collection of troops from 12 and 23 Divisions with the addition of some GHQ units from around Arras.[25] Then from GHQ reserve Gort sent 50 Division to secure the heights at Vimy Ridge just to the north of Arras.[26]

Gort has been much criticised for the formation of these (and other) improvised 'forces' in the course of the campaign. Certainly, with Macforce he might have sent the entire 42 Division to the south-east but he was unsure of future developments and had precious few units in reserve. The Macforce manoeuvre at least enabled him to retain two brigades from 42 Division for future emergencies. In the event Macforce was not needed. The French First Army remained intact, though considering what was happening to other French units Gort could hardly have anticipated this. The one criticism regarding Macforce which has substance is that in giving the command to Mason Macfarlane, Gort removed his senior intelligence officer from GHQ – a man who would be desperately missed in days to come during Gort's continuing absences. Overall, however, Gort responded appropriately in this period. Billotte's map indicated to him that the Panzers were closing on his southern flank and could at any time move north and take the Regular divisions of the BEF in the rear. By moving some troops to the south and south-west Gort ensured that he had at least some troops in place to oppose them. In fact time would reveal how impor-tant Gort's moves were (Map 4).

After these moves had been completed GHQ made a sober assessment of the position confronting the BEF. On the line of the Escaut (much diminished as an obstacle because of a drought)[27] stood from left to right the 44, 4, 3, 1 Divisions and two brigades from each of the 42, 2 and 48 Divisions. To the south were Macforce, Petreforce and 50 Division. This left in GHQ reserve just two brigades of 5 Division – the third having been

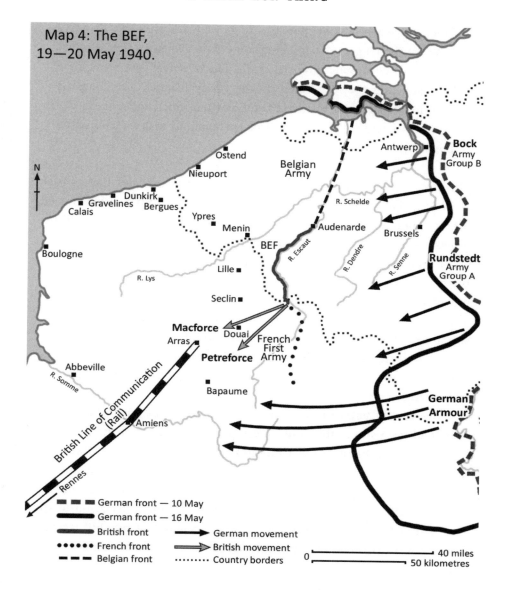

Map 4: The BEF,
19—20 May 1940.

German front — 10 May
German front — 16 May
British front
•••••• French front
— — Belgian front
→ German movement
⇒ British movement
•••••••• Country borders

0 — 40 miles
— 50 kilometres

dispatched to Norway.[28] The conclusions reached were recorded in the GHQ War Diary:

If our right rear now becomes filled with Germans we should be cut off from the French except for the remnants of 3 French Corps [around

81

Lille]. To go S.W. was not possible. To go west almost as bad. By going N.W. we should get the flank protection of the Douai-La Bassée Canal Line. A series of water obstacles on the line of retreat gave some hope of conducting the withdrawal in an orderly manner. The [narrow] corridor would end at the sea at Dunkirk from which hopes of evacuation of personnel with French & of operation[al] material [would be possible].[29]

This note is of the utmost importance because it indicates that as early as 19 May, Gort was contemplating an evacuation from Europe. Indeed, the note implied that it was the only reasonable course on offer. It also shows that GHQ was aware of the defensive possibilities of the canal line which ran north from Douai through La Bassée to Bethune, Aire, Blaringhem to the coast around Gravelines. On the other flank waterways provided similar protection from the Escaut to the Rivers Lys and Yser to the coast at Nieuport. Dunkirk stood squarely in the middle of these two lines of canals and rivers. So important did Gort consider the conclusion reached by GHQ that he had Pownall ring the War Office and inform them, specifically mentioning Dunkirk as a major port of embarkation.[30]

However, the authorities in London were not yet of this mind. Indeed, there had been some strenuous objections to the retreat of the BEF from the Dyle to the Escaut until Churchill crossed to Paris on 16 May and discovered the true position for himself.[31] Nevertheless, a retreat was one thing, evacuation quite another. General Ironside, Chief of the Imperial General Staff, was particularly indignant with Pownall, declaring to the War Cabinet that the proposal was 'unacceptable'. Churchill agreed. Ironside was dispatched to France to 'direct' Gort to attack south-west to link up with the French.[32]

Ironside arrived at GHQ in the morning of 20 May. It was to prove a day of confusion. Gort immediately informed him that as most of his troops were in contact with the enemy any large-scale attack to the south must depend on the French. Gort could provide a few battalions for the operation but that was all. The British leaders accordingly repaired to Billotte's headquarters to see what the French could contribute. What they found shocked them. Billotte was in a state of collapse. He told the British that he had no anti-tank guns and that if any of his infantry were put into the line they would not withstand an attack.[33] According to some accounts Ironside responded by lifting Billotte from the ground by his coat buttons and shaking him.[34] In any event, while something produced a 'calmer attitude' it did not translate into troops. Gort would attack with the small force he could spare.[35]

Meanwhile the French had reconstituted their government with Paul Reynaud appointing himself Minister of National Defence and War as well as Prime Minister. On this day too Gamelin was relieved of his command and replaced by General Weygand, who had been summoned home from the Middle East the day before. One of Weygand's first visitors was General Dill, now Vice Chief of the General Staff. Dill explained to Weygand that if the German advance continued the British might indeed be forced to withdraw to the Channel ports, but that energetic action by Billotte could ensure that the forces in the north linked up with their companions to the south. Weygand immediately rang Billotte (Ironside was still in attendance) and spoke to him in 'energetic' terms. He then spoke to Ironside and assured him that a two-pronged attack from south and north would cut off the German spearheads and restore the situation.[36]

Despite these assurances neither Gort nor Dill expected much from the French. Gort told Anthony Eden, Secretary of State for War, that he was preparing to make a small-scale attack to clear the roads south of Arras from enemy armoured units, and Dill told Churchill that he had no confidence that Billotte would take any action at all.[37]

Meanwhile Gort prepared his small force for action on 21 May. He appointed General Franklyn (5 Division) to command. His force (inevitably named Frankforce) consisted of just two battalions of infantry (6 and 8 Durham Light Infantry), 1 tank battalion and a battery of anti-tank guns.[38] In all Franklyn would have just 58 tanks, of which only 16 were the heavy Matildas capable of withstanding most German anti-tank guns. The French contribution would consist of anything that Franklyn could cajole out of Billotte.[39] Franklyn was soon to find that Billotte had left his headquarters and the senior French commander (General Altmeyer of V Corps) offered no assistance at all. In the end General Prioux contributed some units from his light mechanised division (DLM) for flank protection (Map 5).[40]

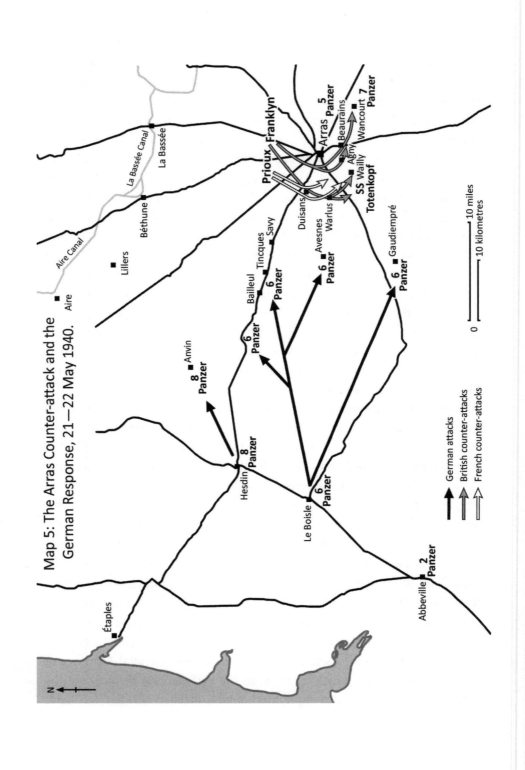

Map 5: The Arras Counter-attack and the German Response, 21–22 May 1940.

Étaples

Aire Canal

Aire

Lillers

Béthune

La Bassée Canal

La Bassée

Bailleul

Tincques

Savy

Duisans

Prioux Franklyn

Arras

Beaurains

Agny

Wancourt

SS Wailly Totenkopf

Warlus

Avesnes

Gaudiempré

5 Panzer

7 Panzer

6 Panzer

6 Panzer

6 Panzer

6 Panzer

Anvin

8 Panzer

Hesdin

8 Panzer

Le Boisle

6 Panzer

Abbeville 2 Panzer

German attacks

British counter-attacks

French counter-attacks

10 miles

10 kilometres

0

N

Gort's orders to Franklyn emphasised the limited nature of the operation. Franklyn was to ensure the safety of Arras by clearing 'advanced guards and light forces' from the roads immediately south of the town.[41] Gort gave Franklyn no intelligence of what enemy forces were lurking south of Arras. In fact, far from being 'advanced guards and light units', elements of no fewer than three Panzer divisions and a mechanised division were in the near vicinity.

After much confusion and delays caused by having to deploy over roads crowded with refugees, Franklyn's two small columns set out at 2 p.m. on 21 May. Initially their progress was unopposed. Then an advanced patrol from the 12 Lancers encountered a column of enemy guns moving to the west of Arras:

A column of German 5.9' How[itzers] were seen approaching down the Duisans road . . . The German column appeared to be entirely lost and as they came straight on C Squadron opened fire on them at nearly point blank range. The enemy never had a chance and were entirely destroyed.[42]

The charred ruins of this column heartened the attackers who then ambushed a group of motorised enemy infantry. These too were completely destroyed by the tanks, the Germans finding to their consternation that shells from their anti-tank guns were bouncing off the British Matildas. Progress continued with the Matildas taking a heavy toll of some German light tanks that had been rushed into action. Next on the scene were some troops from the German 6 Infantry Division, but they turned and fled on the approach of the British armour. By late afternoon the British columns, protected on their right by tanks from Prioux's 3 Division Légère Mécanique (Light Mechanised Division), had swept around to the south of Arras. Warlus, Beaurains, Agny had been captured and Wancourt was in sight.

The British had made these gains at the expense of 7 Panzer Division, commanded by Major General Erwin Rommel. He found the situation on his front 'confused and chaotic' with heavy losses in men and materiel.[43] Nevertheless, he soon brought to bear every gun available (anti-tank and anti-aircraft). He was forced to use the 88mm anti-aircraft gun in an anti-tank role and it proved spectacularly successful, knocking out many of the heavier British tanks. Then Franklyn's men, who were without air cover, were subjected to an intense Stuka attack. By this time the majority of tanks had been knocked out and ammunition was running low. At 3 a.m. on 22 May they were finally forced to withdraw north of Arras.[44]

The Arras counter-attack lasted just a few hours and it failed in all its objectives – it did not clear up the situation to the south of the city, nor did it clear the roads. Yet in some ways the experience heartened the British troops. In the first place the British discovered that not all their equipment was inferior to the Germans' – in particular the enemy had found the Matilda tank difficult to deal with. Further, some German troops were found to be of 'poor fighting quality'.[45]

The most important outcome, however, was that it misled the German commanders about the strength of the British forces. Rommel had witnessed 'panic' and 'confusion' and thought he was being assailed by five British divisions. His impression was confirmed by other accounts. The 6 Panzer Division noted that the situation was tense and confused. They reported strong enemy forces attacking along the Arras–Avesnes road.[46] The XXXIX Corps reported: 'strong enemy motorized columns of all arms are announced underway W to S in Arras'.[47] These reports convinced Army Group A that the situation around Arras was critical. General Gerd von Rundstedt told Hitler that all 'quick troops' should now be deployed on either side of Arras to consolidate the situation before pressing on.[48] At the same time he asked General Gunther von Kluge (4th Army) whether his armour should proceed to Boulogne and Calais as planned or whether they should await 'clarification of the situation around Arras'.[49] But before Kluge could reply Rundstedt had answered his own question:

> The C-in-C of the army group gives decision that <u>first</u> the situation at Arras must be cleared up and only <u>thereafter</u> should [the armour] push towards Calais and Boulogne.[50]

Later General Wilhelm Keitel from Oberkommando der Wehrmacht (OKW; Supreme Command of the Armed Forces) arrived at Rundstedt's headquarters, acquainted himself with the situation and informed the Führer of the decisions made. He then returned to OKW and telephoned

Rundstedt 'to say that the Führer was in full accord with the measures taken by Col-General Von Rundstedt'.[51]

What Rundstedt's decision meant can be seen on Map 5. The 2 Panzer Division remained in place at Abbeville but elements of 6 and 8 Panzer Divisions, which had reached Le Boisle and Hesdin respectively, were turned around and dispatched towards Arras. As Army Group A War Diary stated, 'All quick troops were brought up to the line Arras–Montreuil for the purpose of warding off enemy attempts to break through.'[52]

The Army Group had in fact overreacted. Probably based on Rommel's original reports, they gauged Franklyn's operation as far larger than it had been. Also as we know (but Rundstedt at the time could not) this was not an attempt at a breakthrough. It was merely a minor operation aimed at road-clearing south of Arras. Five Panzer divisions (6, 8, 2, 5 and 7) and one motorised division (SS Totenkopf) were now gathered around Arras to counter a British thrust that they had no intention of making. In short, the *first* halt of the Panzers occurred on 21 May as a direct result of Franklyn's efforts.

But if Gort thought that the counter-attack at Arras had fulfilled his obligation to attack south towards the French, he was mistaken. Churchill still had confidence that the appointment of Weygand might galvanise the French. He told Sir Roger Keyes (then at Belgian HQ) on 21 May that Weygand was 'coming up your way tomorrow [22 May] to concert action of all forces'.[53] Gort was also to be instructed to meet Weygand, but the message never arrived. The meeting therefore went ahead at Ypres with Keyes, the King of the Belgians, his Chief of Staff van Overstraten and Weygand. Nothing much was decided until Billotte arrived. He again emphasised that the French First Army was incapable of offensive action. The only force that could be provided for a southerly thrust must come from the BEF and such a force could only be released if the line was short-ened by the Belgians retreating to the River Yser. Finally, Gort arrived to find that Weygand had left and was heading back to Paris. The Belgians expressed the fear that withdrawing British divisions from the line would leave their army exposed to a major German attack. If forced away from the British they may well surrender. They might also surrender if they were forced to give up most of Belgium by retreating to the Yser. In fact it was becoming difficult to envisage a scenario in which the Belgians would not surrender. Despite this alarming news Gort reluctantly agreed to adopt a form of the plan discussed earlier. He then returned to his command post to plan the necessary moves.[54]

One can imagine that Gort set about this task with the utmost trepidation, for if the Belgians collapsed the Germans could push through to the north and cut the BEF off from the sea. His position did not improve on the next day. Churchill had again crossed to France and met the French leadership at the Supreme War Council. He came away with his confidence in Weygand strengthened. He told Gort that it had been agreed with the French that the Belgians must withdraw to the River Yser to release British and French divisions for the attack. That operation would be made with eight divisions and it must be made 'tomorrow' (that is, on 23 May).[55] This message caused much consternation at GHQ. Pownall fumed at 'impossible' Churchillian orders.[56] However, the determination by the politicians to impose Weygand's Plan on the military got no further. The French command ignored them and made no moves. Gort soon realised that nothing would happen. He therefore ignored Churchill's importunings and got on with the practicalities of the situation facing the BEF. This was dire enough. German armour was now across his lines of communication, which stretched back to Rennes in western France. Supplies of ammunition and food would therefore have to be improvised through the Channel ports and Dunkirk in particular. There was also the matter of the Canal Line on Gort's right flank. The Arras garrison was still intact and Macforce was further north as was 50 Division. But more troops were needed in the certain event that the German armour would recommence its move northwards towards Boulogne and Calais. And the fact was that the British had no troops to block their path.

In ignoring the directives from London and reorganising the BEF to meet the situation it actually faced, Gort played an important role in saving the army. He made a number of crucial decisions between 21 and 23 May. First he drew back the eastern flank of the BEF from the Escaut, where it was under increasing pressure from Army Group B, and directed it to retreat to the frontier defences from which it had commenced the advance into Belgium on 10 May. This allowed Gort to hold this shorter line with four divisions – 42 and 1 Division from I Corps and 3 and 4 Divisions from II Corps. The 2 and 48 Divisions could now be freed to assemble south-west of Lille to defend a section of the Canal Line. The 5 and 50 Divisions would remain around Arras. Even these moves would leave just one division (44) in GHQ reserve (Map 6).[57]

Meanwhile the situation along the Canal Line was rapidly changing. Intelligence told Gort that German armour was on the move and threatened to outflank his recently assembled forces around St Omer. The commander-in-chief therefore created yet more improvised forces, often

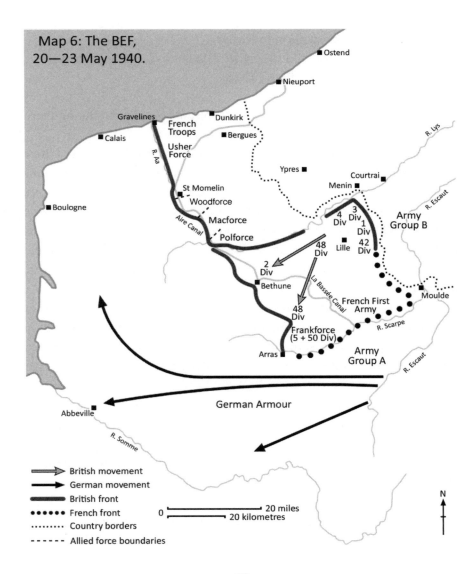

Map 6: The BEF, 20—23 May 1940.

British movement
German movement
British front
French front
Country borders
Allied force boundaries

0   20 miles
0   20 kilometres

N

assembled from line of communication troops, searchlight battalions and any other miscellaneous units available. In short order a ragged but continuous line was established. From north to south along the Canal Line on 23 May were deployed:

Usherforce – a group of miscellaneous troops who held the line from Gravelines to St Momelin.

Woodforce – a similar collection of miscellaneous troops formed around Hazebrouck.

Macforce – redeployed north to Nieppe.

Polforce – formed around 139 Brigade at St Pol and instructed to move forward to defend the La Bassée Canal.

The 2 and 48 Divisions as previously ordered were to defend the southern section of the Canal Line from La Bassée to Arras.[58]

As noted earlier, Gort has been much criticised for the creation of these 'forces'. But in the circumstances it is difficult to see what other options were open to him. On 21 and 22 May the Canal Line north of La Bassée was almost devoid of troops. The small improvised forces could at least be sent there with a minimum of delay. And this line was not as substantial as perhaps is implied by its name. The canals were often narrow and there were many bridges over them.[59] In this situation any defending troops were better than none.

However, this redeployment of forces did put the BEF in a rather curious position. Facing the infantry divisions of Army Group B along the frontier defences stood some of its best divisions, while the improvised forces plus the 2 and 48 Divisions faced the elite Panzer divisions from Army Group A.

The first crisis developed, though, not on the Canal Line or on the frontier defences but at Arras. Here Franklyn's depleted forces had attracted the attention of 7 and 5 Panzer Divisions attacking from the west and east respectively. By 23 May the defensive lines around the city had narrowed to just five miles. Franklyn describes what happened next:

Although during the afternoon [of 23 May], after reporting the situation to G.H.Q., I had been instructed that Arras was to be held at all costs, at 2200 hrs I rang up to explain that unless I withdrew during the course of the night subsequent withdrawal would probably be impossible. I was informed that orders to withdraw were already on the way.

Owing to the late hour . . . the bulk of the infantry had to be moved across the enemy's front along the road Arras-Douai. Arrangements had been made with French Cavalry Corps to cover the withdrawal from Vimy Ridge, but these arrangements miscarried and 17th Infantry brigade had to fight a running rear guard action for some miles. The Arras garrison was successfully extricated and withdrew, but certain detachments ran into parties of the enemy after daylight and suffered casualties.[60]

Despite these mishaps the great majority of troops from Arras were safely withdrawn northward to Lille by the evening of 24 May (Map 7).

Along the Canal Line the situation was far more serious. After the halt on 21 May the Panzer recommenced their advance on the morning of 23 May. The forces they could deploy against the improvised British line were formidable. The XXXIX Corps had the 7 and 5 Panzer Divisions to the north of Arras as well as two motorised divisions (20 and the SS Totenkopf). The SS Verfüngs Motorised Division had two regiments between Aire and Lillers on the Canal Line and a third in close reserve. Further back was 4 Panzer at Avesnes, one day's march from the front. The XXXXI Corps had 6 Panzer across the Canal Line at St Omer and 8 Panzer across it between Aire and Blaringhem. The XIX Corps had 1 and 2 Panzer on the River Canche, 20 miles from the Canal Line and ready to move northwards, 10 Panzer being in close reserve and 9 Panzer not far behind at Doullens.[61] In total Army Group A had nine Panzer divisions and three motorised divisions in the near vicinity of the Canal Line, and elements of two of them (8 and 6) had bridgeheads across the canal at St Omer and around Aire.

These bridgeheads were no more than 30 miles from the units of the BEF along the frontier defences (Map 7). If just three or four of the Panzer divisions and, say, one motorised division had been concentrated for a thrust eastwards, the British would have had only the improvised forces to stop them. Certainly, such a concentration would have taken one or two days to organise, but a force of this size would have been irresistible. And

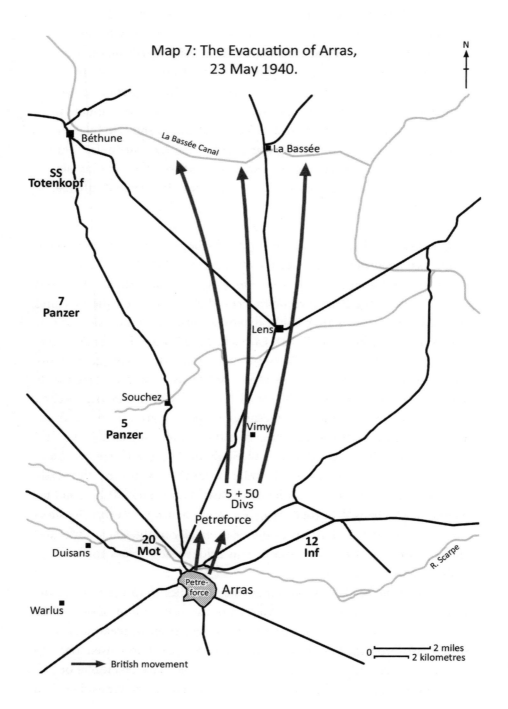

Map 7: The Evacuation of Arras, 23 May 1940.

N

Béthune

La Bassée Canal

La Bassée

SS
Totenkopf

7
Panzer

Lens

Souchez

5
Panzer

Vimy

5 + 50
Divs

Petreforce

Duisans

20
Mot

12
Inf

R. Scarpe

Petre-
force

Arras

Warlus

0   2 miles
     2 kilometres

British movement

if the thrust had been made from St Omer or Blaringhem or Aire and aimed at Ypres or points south, the vast bulk of the BEF would have been cut off from the coast. In this instance surrender must have soon followed because all the ammunition and food required by the British were being delivered through the Channel ports. Without these supplies, no matter what the fighting qualities of the troops, the BEF would have been doomed.

There is no evidence that anyone in Army Group A considered these options. This might seem strange from an army that had brushed aside everything in its path for the past two weeks. However, Rundstedt's attention was elsewhere. He was anticipating a French response against the armoured units that were strung out over a distance of 60 miles. The German southern flank along the Somme was thinly held. A thrust from the south by French units not yet engaged in the battle might place the whole German position in danger. It would be prudent in that circumstance to have at least some Panzer divisions in hand to deal with it.

In fact a thrust eastwards had never been part of Rundstedt's battle plan. That plan called instead for a sweep along the coast to attack Boulogne and Calais and then presumably Dunkirk. A deviation from an established plan is a matter of considerable substance in war. Units have to be reoriented, new orders issued, and the consequences of the change rapidly thought through. Besides the plan had worked well enough until this point, so why change it? Also, Rundstedt was well aware that German tanks had suffered considerable wear and tear in the previous two weeks. The Kleist Group of the German 4th Army reported that tank casualties had reached more than 50 per cent.[62] In an adjoining group it was reported that casualties in 5 and 7 Panzer and 20 Motorised Divisions had reached 30 per cent.[63]

So when Rundstedt met the commander of the 4th Army (Kluge) on 23 May, we can safely speculate that dashing Panzer thrusts across north-eastern France were not on the agenda. Kluge no doubt reiterated the sad state of his divisions. Rundstedt no doubt pointed to the open flank along the Somme and noted that it would take the infantry divisions several days to close it. In any case an order came forth from this meeting to the effect that the 4th Army would 'in the main halt tomorrow [24 May] in order to close up its formations and consolidate'.[64] The Panzers would therefore be halted for a second time.

Back in Berlin there was consternation at this decision, but no clear alternative to it emerged. Field Marshal Walther von Brauchitsch, the commander-in-chief, wanted no pause. He suggested that the armour be transferred to Army Group B in order that one commander could control operations in the increasingly confined spaces in which the two Army Groups were operating.[65] But this plan too would inevitably have led to a pause while the armour was reoriented and General Fedor von Bock from Army Group B reorganised his forces to take the new situation into account. Franz Halder, Chief of Staff to Brauchitsch, disagreed. He wanted Rundstedt's group to retain its armour and press on without pause. This did not meet with the approval of his chief, so Halder passed on Brauchitsch's decision transferring the 4th Army to Army Group B but sourly expressed his disapproval by not signing the order.[66] Enter Hitler, who at this moment happened to be visiting Rundstedt's headquarters. Not surprisingly, he backed the man on the spot. The armour would remain with Army Group A and there would be a pause for consolidation. Hitler had arrived at the same conclusions as Rundstedt but possibly for different reasons. The War Diary of Army Group A recorded him as saying:

There is an all-round need to preserve the armoured forces for the coming operations [against the French] and that a further tightening of the enclosed space would merely result in a most unwelcome curtailment of the effectiveness of the German air force.[67]

Later in the day he expanded these thoughts in Führer Directive No. 13:

1. The next object of our operations is to annihilate the French, English, and Belgian forces which are surrounded in Artois and Flanders, by a concentric attack by our northern flank and by the swift seizure of the Channel coast in this area.
   The task of the Air Force will be to break all enemy resistance on the part of the surrounded forces, to prevent the escape of the English forces across the Channel, and to protect the southern flank of Army Group A.
   The enemy Air force will be engaged whenever opportunity offers.

2. The Army will then prepare to destroy in the shortest possible time the remaining enemy forces in France.

He then went on to give instructions for the three phases of this latter operation in some detail.[68]

Hitler's and Rundstedt's halt order has received much attention from historians but in fact not all the Panzers halted on the evening of the 23rd. The 2 Panzer headed north for Boulogne and the 1 Panzer followed on to Calais. It was deemed essential by the German command to capture these two ports because they lay on the flank of the Canal Line and British reinforcements (there were in fact very few but the Germans were not aware of this) could be sent to France through them. More importantly, it was thought the capture of the ports would deny the British essential supplies. (In fact no supplies were reaching the BEF through Boulogne or Calais but the Germans were also unaware of that.) It might be thought that the Germans were making an error of judgement in sending Panzer divisions to attack fortified cities with mazes of narrow streets in which tanks could not easily operate. But here – perhaps for the first time – the weaknesses in the structure of the German army began to reveal themselves. There were no infantry divisions remotely near the Channel ports on 23 May. The infantry divisions, it must be remembered, were horse drawn and lagging well to the rear. The closest infantry formations were the 12th and 32nd Divisions and they were just north of Arras and designated for operations against the Canal Line. Boulogne and Calais would have to be attacked by Panzers or not at all.

The Panzers therefore headed for the Channel ports. The British were mindful that these ports were important, not because of supply or reinforcement but because their retention might delay any German move on Dunkirk. So late in the day the 20 Guards Brigade was rushed across the Channel from Canterbury to shore up the defences which until that time consisted of a motley force of about 2,500 British, French and a few Belgian troops.[69] When 2 Panzer Division attacked Boulogne the Guards were in place and the Germans met a resolute defence. Moreover, they were now within range of aircraft based in Britain and came under 'violent bombing attacks'. When they attempted to enter the city they soon found that battles degenerated into 'house to house fighting' – hardly the ideal conditions for a Panzer division.[70] Later in the day the Corps reported:

> Corps has impression that the enemy is fighting toughly in and around Boulogne for every inch of ground in order not to let this important harbour fall into German hands. Luftwaffe moves against warships & transports laying before Boulogne (is it a landing or an evacuation?) [are] inadequate 2 Pz Div's attack only progresses therefore slowly.[71]

Eventually the Germans managed to surround Boulogne but not before the 20 Guards Brigade was evacuated. Some French and British troops who could not be rescued held out for another 24 hours and then surrendered.[72] In the end the defence of Boulogne occupied a considerable proportion of the German XIX Corps for the best part of three days.

Attention must now turn to Calais, the last major port in Allied hands before Dunkirk. On 20 May it had been held by just one platoon of troops and two batteries of 1 Searchlight Regiment.[73] On 23 May, 30 Brigade was ordered from England to Calais, its initial task being to reinforce the garrison at Boulogne. In the event the brigade arrived too late to carry out this order. Its actions were confined to Calais where 10 Panzer Division had now taken over the attack on the port from 1 Panzer. The capture of the port again proved more difficult than the Germans had anticipated. After three days, General Heinz Guderian, who was the Corps Commander in charge of the siege, was sufficiently concerned about the 'tenacity' of the defence to order a mass Stuka attack on the port. Even this did not do the trick. It was lack of ammunition that eventually led the British troops to surrender on the afternoon of 26 May.[74]

Were these troops sacrificed to any purpose? Certainly Churchill thought so. He was furious that the War Office had ordered the evacuation of Calais on 24 May and had immediately countermanded it, ordering Brigadier Nicolson to fight to the last and enquiring of Ironside whether there was not 'defeatist opinion in the General Staff'.[75] No doubt this outburst reflected the pressure Churchill was under from

Halifax concerning peace moves, but he was surely correct in his determination that the Channel ports hold out as long as possible. In the end, the defence of Calais and Boulogne occupied three Panzer divisions for three or four days (2 Panzer Division against Boulogne, 10 Panzer Division against Calais and 1 Panzer Division in a blocking position between the two ports). This time gained would prove vital for the Allies in the days to come.[76]

While these operations were proceeding, along the Canal Line there was little action because of the halt order. In the south the British 2 Division arrived and was able to take up its place along the La Bassée Canal unhindered.[77] Opposite them were the German 20 Motorised Division and 5 Panzer Division, which rightly considered that only 'weak' forces opposed them along the Canal and that bridgeheads across it could easily be seized. A request to probe the canal crossings was sent to the higher command but was rejected.[78]

Further north Gort's various 'forces' were having a more difficult time. For example, Pol Force encountered 6 Panzer Division and the SS Verfüngs Motorised Division east of Hazebrouck. Despite hard fighting, during which their artillery managed to take some toll on the enemy tanks, the British were forced back to the outer defences of the town.[79] But then the higher command reminded the Germans of Hitler's halt order and they broke off the attack.[80]

* * * * *

Our attention must now move from these dramatic events along the Canal Line and the Channel ports to a crisis on the Frontier Line to the east. On 24 May an order from the German 6th Army was captured by the British. It indicated that a major attack was being prepared against the Belgians just to the north of the BEF along the frontier positions. This was a matter of the utmost seriousness because if the Belgians gave way it would place the 6th Army between the BEF and the coast.[81]

What could be done to stymie this move? Gort had just two divisions in reserve at this point – 5 and 50 Divisions. The problem was that they were still earmarked for the drive to the south as outlined in the Weygand Plan. A larger problem emerged, however, when the 12 Lancers reported that the

Belgians were already under attack and that a gap between the British and their ally was appearing around Menin.[82]

This was one of the decisive moments of the campaign as far as the British were concerned. As the news came in about the gap between the Belgians and the British, Dill was visiting Gort's headquarters. Discussion between the two men had centred on the timing and the extent of the British contribution to Weygand's scheme. But now with the Belgians apparently disintegrating, Gort, with Dill's approval, abandoned all thought of an attack south. He immediately sought out General Brooke from II Corps and at 1700 hours on 24 May decided that the two reserve divisions must be used to close the Menin gap. One hour later this decision was noted in the War Diary: 'Decision NOT to use 5 and 50 Divs southward'.[83] Although Dill was still informing the Prime Minister that the Weygand Plan might take place on a small scale, this marked the end of any attempt by the BEF to break through to the south.[84] Attention would now shift to the coast.

Next day Gort confirmed this decision with General Maurice Blanchard. They decided that the northern armies should withdraw behind the River Lys and the Canal de Dérivation (Map 8).[85] In London, Anthony Eden confirmed Gort's decision. He suggested that plans for an evacuation be urgently prepared and told Gort that he could expect a maximum effort from the navy and the RAF to cover his movements.[86] Later Eden telegrammed that Churchill had met Premier Reynaud and that all thought of an attack to the south had been abandoned, and that 'you are authorized to operate towards the coast forthwith in conjunction with French and Belgian armies'.[87]

As Gort was aware, however, this was easier said than done. The German attack against the Belgians was making ground and the route to the coast was in peril. He had already ordered Franklyn's 5 Division to move north to the Ypres–Comines Canal and to take under his command 143 Brigade of 48 Division. In addition he now ordered 50 Division to Ypres and arranged for II Corps artillery to move north to assist these forces.[88]

General Brooke immediately motored north to the Ypres–Comines Canal only to find that it was completely dry. The situation was critical. The Germans were attacking the 'canal' and 5 Division were only beginning to arrive. Brooke therefore began adding to Franklyn's force any other units he could find. During the next few days three battalions of infantry and two machine-gun battalions arrived from 1 Division, the field artillery from 48 Division and the I Corps heavy artillery. Later 10 and 11 Brigades from 4 Division were added to Franklyn's command.[89]

The fighting that ensued between the Germans and this improvised force was some of the fiercest faced by the BEF in the entire campaign. Between 25 and 28 May no fewer than six enemy infantry divisions attacked Franklyn's force along the canal. Some ground was lost on the British right but the position was stabilised by intense artillery fire. The I Corps heavy artillery alone fired 5,000 rounds in 36 hours.[90] A 'last attempt' by the Germans to gain ground was stopped by 'the accurate shooting of our medium artillery and this together with good infantry shooting not only stopped the attack making any progress but caused the enemy to vacate some of his more advanced positions'.[91]

There were similar tales from all along the front. On 26 May some crucial ground on the far bank of the canal was gained by the Germans, but an attack by 150 Brigade assisted by some French troops restored the situation.[92] By these means, the British were still clinging to the canal on 28 May.

These were useful days gained, but the eventual collapse of the Belgians was inevitable. Their battle-worn and under-equipped army was gradually forced away from the British. As early as 26 May, Gort considered them on the brink of collapse.[93] So did Brooke, and in order to shore up the position between the extreme left of the British line and the sea, he ordered Montgomery's 3 Division to execute a side-step which would help fill the gap. This was no easy matter. The manoeuvre had to be carried out by night along roads congested with refugees, parallel to and only 5,000 yards distant from the front held by the composite 5 Division group. Brooke, who carried this move through largely on his own initiative, admitted that he 'had some bad moments wondering whether Montgomery would complete his move before daylight [but by then] . . . the 3rd Division was through'.[94] The British front had now edged to within 20 miles of the sea (Map 8).

However, news from the Belgians indicated that this might not be enough to save the BEF. Gort, through Keyes at Belgian GHQ, heard on the morning of 27 May that the government was considering a surrender to

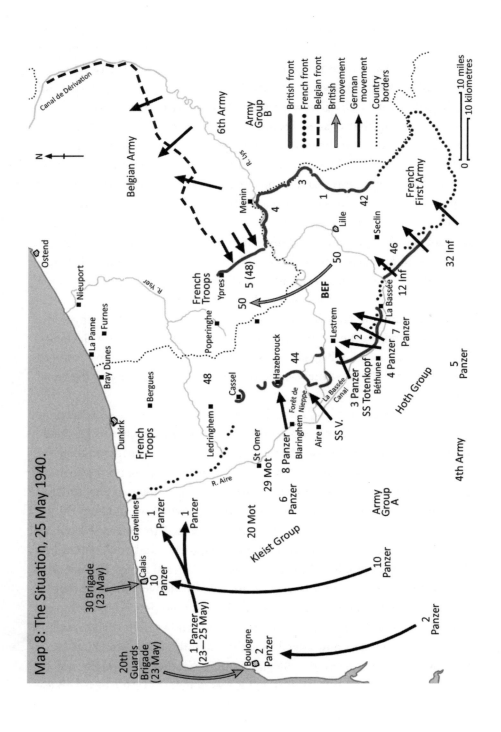

Map 8: The Situation, 25 May 1940.

avoid a debacle.[95] By evening it was clear that this was no rumour – the Belgians had decided to seek an armistice.[96] The King ordered his commander-in-chief to send a plenipotentiary to the Germans. The diarist at Army Group A recorded the scene:

> At 2030 hours Col-Gen V. Reichenau reports that a Belgian general has presented himself at XI Army Corps headquarters with a message from the King of the Belgians, asking for the terms for an armistice.

The bearer of the flag of truce had been given the following reply:

> The hostilities should cease only after the acceptance of German conditions. Unconditional surrender. At 2100 the Führer's decision is reached: Only unconditional surrender, no further assurances or supplications.[97]

That was the end of the Belgians. Their army had fought well against impossible odds. Nevertheless their surrender came at an awkward moment for the British. There were no Allied troops in the 20-mile gap between 3 Division and the sea. If the gap could not be filled it might be the German army rather than the BEF that arrived at Dunkirk first.

It was the swift reaction, first by Montgomery and then by Brooke, that ensured the gap would be filled. As early as 27 May, Montgomery (whose 3 Division would hold the extreme left of the British position) met the commander of the 12 Lancers and ordered him to destroy all the bridges over the Yser Canal between 3 Division and the sea. This was accomplished with some difficulty and many casualties the next day. News then arrived that substantial German reinforcements were heading for Nieuport, where the last remaining bridges between the enemy and the Dunkirk perimeter were still intact. One was blown, but the 12 Lancers had run out of explosives. The desperate expedient of trying to destroy the remaining bridge, using hand grenades brought forward by a detachment of Royal artillerymen, failed. As the town was now under air attack and heavy bombardment by German guns, the 12 Lancers had little alternative but to withdraw under cover of darkness. The bridge therefore fell into German hands.[98]

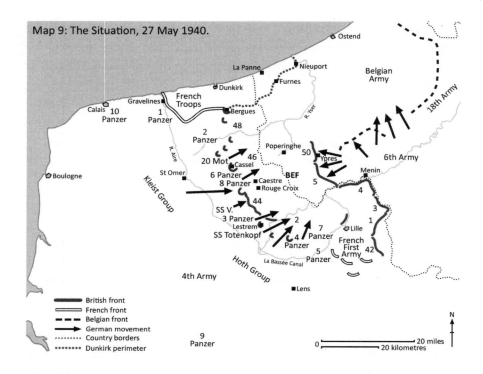

Map 9: The Situation, 27 May 1940.

This situation was potentially disastrous because if the Germans could force their way along the coast the BEF might yet be trapped. But Brooke had already seen the danger. He sent orders for a brigade of 4 Division (it was 12 Brigade) to proceed to Nieuport at once to block any German move west.[99] This the brigade was able to do. Its plans to recapture the bridge had been overtaken by events – there were now too many German infantry formations across it for any such action to be possible. But the brigade was able to block the Germans as they attempted to move across the bridge towards the Dunkirk perimeter, which brought at least a semblance of order to that flank of the BEF.[100]

* * * * *

While these actions were taking place in the east, two events of great importance were occurring on the southern flank of the Allied forces and along the Canal Line.

On the night of 26–27 May the German halt order was lifted and the Panzers began to move. In the south, under pressure from 5 and 7 Panzer Divisions the British withdrew to the line of the River Lys. But the bulk of the French First Army, which had been fighting with the British around Lille, did not move. Its III Corps and part of its cavalry had followed the British to the Lys. But Blanchard had not been told of the order to retreat to Dunkirk and despite the pleadings of Gort and Pownall he refused to move the remainder of his force. It soon became trapped by the rapid moves of 5 and 7 Panzers. Although surrounded, the remaining French troops fought hard and until 30 May continued to engage the attention of the Panzers. The final surrender of these troops did not take place until 31 May and 1 June. They therefore performed the valuable task of keeping many German divisions away from the Dunkirk area during several vital days.

While the French fought around Lille the British had managed to improve their defences along the La Bassée Canal. The 2 Division had arrived and was well dug in along it. To its north it was supported by 44 Division. From there to the coast there were elements of 46 and 48 Divisions with the French 68 Division completing the line from Bergues to Gravelines. Facing them from south to north were 7 Panzer, 4 Panzer, SS Totenkopf, 3 Panzer, SS Verfüngs, 8 Panzer, 6 Panzer, 20 Motorised Division, 2 Panzer and 1 Panzer. The inequality in the two forces is obvious. The British and French had no armoured division north of the Somme and what tanks they had were scattered among the infantry formations.

The first British unit to feel the force of the renewed Panzer attack on 27 May was 2 Division. Assaulted by three Panzer divisions and two motorised SS divisions, the result could not be in doubt. Although the canal crossings were 'stubbornly defended', the British were gradually forced back.[101] The fighting was so fierce that neither the divisional nor the brigade commanders could exert much control.[102] The sole action taken that day by the commander of 2 Division was to commit his only reserve (25 Brigade) at mid-morning (Map 10).[103] At the front, this action made little difference. His troops were being attacked by Panzers accompanied by Stuka dive-bombers. There was no air cover because the RAF back in Britain had no idea of exactly which units were under fire. By the evening, orders had finally got through to the front for the remnants of the three brigades to withdraw to Poperinghe some 20 miles to the north. The 'surprising news' was that their next destination would be Dunkirk and after that England.[104]

This attack by massed Panzers is a demonstration of what the Germans could have achieved on the Canal Line had they put their minds to it. The British Regulars fought well but they were no more able to withstand this type of attack than the French earlier in the campaign. There also seems little doubt that the Germans could have made life even more difficult for the British had they attacked three days earlier, before 2 Division joined the line. Yet they did not take this course, and what is even more surprising is that this attack by massed armour would be the only one of its type to be carried out against the defenders of the Canal Line for the remainder of the campaign.

Further north the 8 Panzer and the 20 Motorised Division attacked the very weak 44 Division, which could only manage to place two battalions in the front line. Yet the Germans made little progress. They reported that they had encountered 'an enemy who fought obstinately and who were holding a line of fortified emplacements east of [the Rouge Croix–Caestre] road. Rouge Croix could not be taken during the day. 8 Pz Divs losses during the house-to-house fighting in Rouge Croix were considerable.'[105] The 4 and 5 Royal Sussex Divisions would no doubt have been bemused to see the roadside ditches they occupied described as 'fortified emplacements', but there is no question that their defence was spirited. They knocked out six German tanks and captured their crews. Nevertheless, there was something half-hearted about the German attack. Perhaps the units involved had not yet met stiff resistance; perhaps they were tiring because of the efforts of the previous two weeks. We do know that Field Marshal Paul von Kleist was concerned about the condition of his Panzers and on this day, 27 May, he made no intervention to insist that the attack be pushed. Yet, there is something odd about the actions of XXXIX Corps on this day. Why, for example, did they engage in house-to-house fighting in a village as small as Rouge Croix? This tiny strongpoint could have been bypassed with ease, as the Panzers had bypassed so many similar positions in their journey west.

There is a similar tale to be told of the attack on the town of Cassel just to the north of this battle. Cassel was attacked by the 6 Panzer and elements

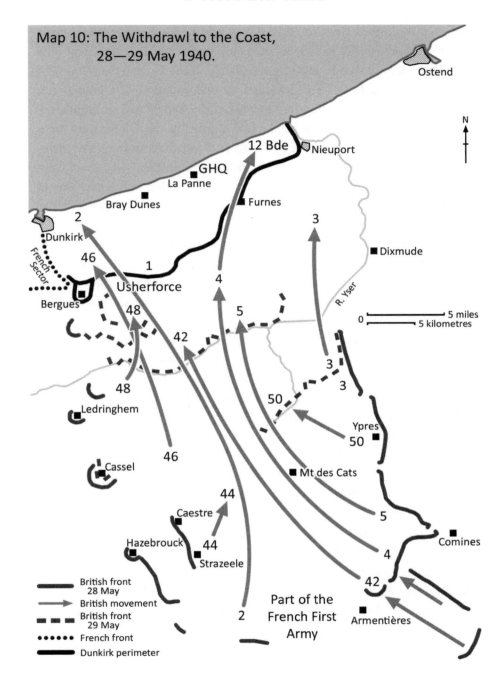

Map 10: The Withdrawl to the Coast,
          28—29 May 1940.

Ostend

N

12 Bde   Nieuport

GHQ
La Panne

Bray Dunes   Furnes

2   3
Dunkirk   Dixmude

French Sector
46   1
Usherforce   4

48   5   R. Yser

42   0   5 miles
                                           5 kilometres
48
Ledringhem   50   3
                                             3
46   50
                              Ypres
Cassel   50

                    Mt des Cats
44
Caestre   5
Hazebrouck 44   4   Comines
            Strazeele
                                     42
British front   Armentières
    28 May
British movement   2   Part of the
British front   French First
    29 May   Army
French front
Dunkirk perimeter

of the 20 Motorised Division. Cassel was, however, a much stronger position than Rouge Croix, the town being atop one of the few prominent hills in the area. Cassel stands out from the plain and can be seen for miles. The town and its outskirts were defended by one battalion (2 Gloucesters). During the day these few hundred men were attacked by tanks and infantry and shelled by mortars and artillery.[106] Gradually the Gloucesters were forced to give up their outpost positions and withdraw towards the town. Their artillery, which consisted mainly of 18-pounders, was practically useless because the field guns did not have the elevation to fire over Cassel hill. Enemy tanks started to assemble at the foot of the hill to deliver what they must have imagined to be the *coup de grâce*. But at this moment they were subjected to a bayonet charge by Captain Cholmondeley and six men. The infantry protecting the tanks fled as did two of the armoured vehicles. In the end just one enemy tank remained but it made no attempt to advance. By early evening the Gloucesters in the front defences could report that the enemy was withdrawing. The shelling, which had been constant all day, slackened. There were several more infantry encounters, but the Gloucesters fought them off and by nightfall they were still in control of Cassel.[107] Once again the German actions seem inexplicable. They attacked frontally several hundred men well dug in on the top of a hill when they might have bypassed the town leaving the Gloucesters to wither on the vine. Once again, poor tactics by the Panzers gave the British an unexpected respite and another precious day was gained.

Further north the Allied position was not so secure. The 48 Division and the French units between the British and the coast had been driven back. Gravelines, which was actually on the coast, had fallen. There were now German formations within four miles of Dunkirk.

Because of the disintegration of 2 Division and the collapse along the coast, 28 May was just as crucial in the west as it was in the east. In fact, as the day progressed fewer distinctions could be made between east and west. From all directions British units were streaming back towards the perimeter defences around Dunkirk (about which more later). But this day was as important for the actions taken by the Germans as it was for any stalwart defence put up by the British.

By 28 May the Germans were certainly aware of British intentions to evacuate. Army Group A reported the day before that 'in Dunkirk and in the Flanders ports the enemy are embarking'.[108] This was even more obvious to commanders closer to the front. As early as 23 May, Guderian had identified Dunkirk as the last major port available to the British and observed that if it fell into German hands the encirclement of the BEF would be complete.[109] On 26 May he reported that transports were 'with certainty' evacuating British forces from Dunkirk.[110] The following day similar views were expressed by XXXXI Corps.[111] Yet despite clearly recognising what was occurring at Dunkirk, on 28 May the Germans did not undertake an armoured thrust to the coast. Instead, at various levels, German commanders chose to emphasise the difficult conditions under which they were operating. For example, the XXXXI Corps noted:

> Fighting is severe at every position and . . . at every village – indeed at every house – so that the Corps cannot gain ground to any extent . . . Casualties in personnel and equipment are considerable. The enemy fights tenaciously and stays at his post until the last man; if he is shelled out of one position he appears in another a short time later and resumes the fight. The enemy artillery is firing with apparent good observation.[112]

The Corps Commander (Reinhardt) reported to Army Group A that damage to his tanks had been considerable. He advised that his Corps should not 'rush in head-on, but rather preserve itself . . . for fighting in the greater tasks which were ahead'.[113]

Heinz Guderian of XIX Corps agreed. He noted the 'severe casualties' suffered by the SS Adolf Hitler Regiment and concluded that he could see no point in continuing his assault, which would only lead to 'useless sacrifice'.[114] Later he added:

> Attack in the marshy terrain with tanks is considered futile. Useless sacrifice of our best soldiers. Speedy restoration of the attacking panzers of the regiments will become more and more difficult. It appears more fitting to hold the positions reached [and] to let 18 Army [Army Group B's infantry divisions] attack from the east to take effect.

Later he sent a message to the Army Group as follows:

(1) After the capitulation of the Belgians, continuation of operations is not desired here, because the continuation of the battle costs unnecessary sacrifice. The Panzer Divisions have only 50% of their armoured strength. There is an urgent need of reserves if the Corps is to be again ready, in a short time, for other operations.

(2) A tank attack is pointless in the ... country which has been considerably soaked by the rain. The troops are on the high ground south of Dunkirk and on the Cassel-Dunkirk Road, and they have favourable positions on the high ground of Crochte and Pitzen where they can fire on Dunkirk. Moreover, approaching [Kleist] Group from the East [is] 18 Army which, with its infantry forces, is more adapted to fighting in marshy country than are tanks and to which therefore the closing of the gap can be left.[115]

Army Group A was already in possession of a report from XXXXI Corps entitled 'Unsuitability of tanks against well-defended field positions'. It read:

From the fighting of the last few days, which has cost severe losses in personnel and equipment, as already stressed ... the following brief conclusions can be drawn: the Panzer Division is little suited for fighting against an enemy who obstinately defends himself in a partially fortified field position, especially in barricaded villages because it has too small an infantry force under command and because the tanks afford too good targets for the numerous A/T weapons dug in.[116]

On 28 May a major realignment of German forces took place. In the north Kleist asked for his Panzer divisions (2, 10 and 1) to be pulled out and in the terse words of the XXXIX Corps War Diary: 'Group agreed. All 3 Panzer Divisions were withdrawn.'[117] A glance at a map will show the import of this decision. The 1 Panzer Division had captured Gravelines and was approaching the French 68 Division, the only unit between the Germans and Dunkirk. The 2 Panzer Division was slightly to the south and approaching Bergues, the hinge between the French and British force holding the Dunkirk perimeter. Between this division and Dunkirk were the remnants of 48 and 46 Divisions, between which German armoured columns had already penetrated. Many of the battalions of these British divisions had been reduced to the strength of weak companies. And yet on 29 May they would not be required to fight off Panzer divisions – with one exception – but the infantry divisions of Army Group B.

On 29 May similar decisions were made concerning the Panzers of XXXXI Corps. The 8 and 6 Panzers, which were still fighting around Caestre and Cassel, found it disagreeable, noting that all enemy defensive positions were 'strongly organized ... with skill and with up-to-date means'. Even the SS Verfüngs Division had 'to fight through here step by step in the strictest sense of the phrase'.[118] The end result was that the decision was taken to withdraw 8 Panzer Division on 30 May and to rest 6 Panzers and replace it with the SS motorised division.[119] Meanwhile on 29 May the 4, 5 and 7 Panzer Divisions were still engaged in the fighting around Lille and the 3 Panzers was in reserve.

A comparison of the situation on 28 and 29 May reveals that instead of six Panzer divisions being in the front line there was now just one – 9 Panzer Division, brought up from reserve to just south of Gravelines. The Panzer commanders and the Group clearly had no appetite for inflicting further wear and tear on their armour, across what they regarded as difficult terrain against an enemy that was fighting hard. And were their decisions not in line with Hitler's wishes expressed on 24 May? He had emphasised saving the armour for the coming battle with the French south of the Somme. He had also implied that the Luftwaffe could to a large extent deal with the encircled armies and prevent their evacuation. In any case a plethora of German infantry divisions were closing on Dunkirk. These two forces would fight the battle of 'annihilation' on the coast while the armour moved south. It remained to be seen whether Hitler and his commanders had made the right moves.

CHAPTER 5

THE GREAT ESCAPE
THE BEF, MAY–JUNE 1940

AFTER GORT, AS commander-in-chief of the BEF, ordered the retreat to the Channel on 26 May, the army began its final series of withdrawals. Dunkirk was its destination but if it was to be the major evacuation port for the force, a defensive perimeter would have to be established to prevent German attacks during embarkation. Late that evening Gort held a conference at GHQ to discuss this. At the conference he relieved General Adam from command of III Corps and instructed him to liaise with the French in establishing a perimeter defence. Adam, accompanied by a few staff officers, left immediately. He directed his staff to set up headquarters at La Panne on the Belgian coast while he proceeded to Cassel to consult the French. There he found assembled General Blanchard, Commander of the French First Army, Admiral Abrail, Naval Commander at Dunkirk, and General Fagalde, Military Commander at Dunkirk. An agreement was soon reached, although the purpose of the perimeter does not seem to have been discussed. The French zone would be to the west of the port and extend just past the port itself. The British would occupy the ground from there to Nieuport in the east.[1]

The location of the perimeter line was relatively straightforward. A series of canals ran from just west of Dunkirk, through Bergues to Furnes and then to Nieuport, and provided the best protection from a German thrust from the south. The Canal Line gave a perimeter of some 30 miles long and 8 miles deep, a depth sufficient to keep all but German heavy artillery from shelling the beaches. The centre of the perimeter could also be flooded and steps were taken to prepare the sluices for letting in the sea when this became necessary.

General Adam's main problem was to find troops to man the perimeter. He gave the task to Brigadier Lawson, commanding 48 Division artillery, some units of which happened to have made their way to Dunkirk. Lawson found a group of gunners and infantry under Lieutenant Colonel Usher (Usherforce) and moved them into the line around Bergues. To their left a motley assortment of infantry from III Corps occupied the Canal Line to Furnes, and yet another improvised force of gunners and engineers moved in between Furnes and Nieuport.[2] Future movements would see III Corps occupy the western section of the British perimeter, II Corps the eastern section near Nieuport, and I Corps the centre near Bray.

Some evacuations from Dunkirk had taken place before the perimeter had been established. As early as 20 May, Colonel Whitfield had been ordered to Dunkirk to arrange for the evacuation of 'unwanted mouths' already in the area. The men rather unflatteringly referred to were some headquarters staff moved from Arras, administrative and line-of-communication staff and other non-combatant soldiers who happened to be near the port. Whitfield found his task challenging. Many of the officers and men had been cut off from their units for some time and their morale, not improved according to Whitfield by being described as 'unwanted mouths', was low. An attempt at an orderly evacuation broke down. Officers left their men and rushed the boats; groups of men also panicked. Military police sent to restore order took the first opportunity to embark for England.[3] The 'miracle' in this period was that anyone got off at all, but from 20 to 25 May, Whitfield managed to send about 28,000 men to England. Nevertheless, such a shambles could hardly continue if large numbers of the BEF were to be saved. Fortunately for the British, planning for a major evacuation had been under way in London for some time.

It was General Pownall's phone call on 19 May that provided the trigger. Churchill immediately alerted the Admiralty that Gort might retreat to the sea and that they should make provisions against a necessity that 'seemed far away'.[4] Next day the prospect of an evacuation seemed not far away at all and Churchill instructed the Admiralty 'as a precautionary measure' to 'assemble a large number of small vessels in readiness to proceed to ports and inlets on the French coast'.[5] Later that day a committee of representatives from the War Office and the Admiralty met with Admiral Ramsay, Naval Commander, Dover, to arrange for the assembly of as many ships as possible to meet the War Cabinet's demand. The number of ships at Dover available for such an operation was listed, though at the end of the minutes the following note was appended: 'It will be realised that these notes provide for an emergency which may arise only in certain circumstances.'[6] Nevertheless, they hastened with their preparations for these circumstances. Ramsay immediately consulted other naval bases around the coast about additional craft and was alarmed to find that he would have at his disposal no more than 40 destroyers. To these he added requisitioned passenger vessels and ferries, 50 Dutch motor vessels, and a host of smaller privately owned pleasure vessels, fishing boats and yachts.[7] Would they be sufficient? Ramsay hardly had time to contemplate. The evacuation – codenamed Operation Dynamo – was to begin on 26 May.

Ramsay made two decisions on receipt of the evacuation order. He immediately dispatched what passenger vessels he could muster to Dunkirk and sent Captain Tennant to act as Senior Naval Officer there along with 160 naval ratings (sailors) to help him organise the evacuation.[8]

Tennant set sail from Dover on the destroyer *Wolfhound* in the afternoon of 27 May and arrived at Dunkirk at 6 p.m., after suffering a series of attacks from Stukas.[9] What he found appalled him. Dunkirk town and harbour had been under attack by the Luftwaffe for most of the day. Tennant saw a town ablaze from end to end, 'the streets being littered with wreckage of all kinds, and every window . . . smashed. Great palls of smoke from the oil depots and refineries enveloped the docks and town itself.'[10] After a quick reconnaissance Tennant signalled Ramsay that embarkation was impossible from the docks and that ships should be sent to the beaches east of the harbour.[11] The naval ratings were ordered to spread out along the 10 miles of coastline to act as guides to troops making their way towards the sea.

The destruction of Dunkirk port on 27 May raises questions about the effectiveness of the RAF. For the first time since the shooting war began they should have been operating at some advantage. Until Dunkirk the air force had found it difficult to give direct support to the troops. The position of British units was often not known with certainty and the numerical superiority of the Luftwaffe usually made support a hazardous undertaking anyway. Now, however, the exact position of British troops would be known. And the bulk of the Luftwaffe would be operating at the outer limits of its range. The Germans had brought a few forward airfields into operation, but most of the fighters and all the bombers would have further to fly than the RAF squadrons based in south-eastern England. In particular the Me 109 fighters would have less time over Dunkirk than the British squadrons.[12]

But the potential advantages favouring the British were not really exploited by Air Chief Marshall Sir Hugh Dowding, the commander-in-chief of Fighter Command. With a force of some 40 squadrons of 16 aircraft, he allowed Air Vice Marshall Sir Keith Park, the commander of 11 Group based in the south-east of England, just 16 squadrons for operations over Dunkirk.[13] No doubt Dowding was concerned with the heavy losses that the Germans had inflicted on his fighter forces during the French campaign. Since 10 May, 290 Hurricanes had been destroyed, the equivalent of 18 squadrons.[14] This left Dowding well short of the 60 squadrons he deemed necessary for home defence. Yet 60 squadrons may well have been an excessive estimate, especially considering that such numbers were never deployed during the Battle of Britain. And his Dunkirk policy was parsimonious to the point of danger. With only 16 squadrons, Park could not maintain standing patrols over Dunkirk during daylight hours, giving the enemy free rein over the beaches and port. If the Luftwaffe could wreak enough havoc on troops, ships and port facilities to prevent the evacuation of the BEF, then what good would Dowding's anti-invasion force of fighters be? A government that had just lost its army might well have made peace rather than face invasion. By his policy Dowding had elevated Fighter Command to the front rank of Britain's defences – ahead of both the BEF and the navy. This was not only a risky decision, it was not Dowding's to make. However, the political leadership seemed unaware of what he was doing. The troops and sailors at Dunkirk would have a greater awareness in the days that followed.

So on 27 May, while Dunkirk was being destroyed as a port, Park flew single-squadron patrols over it with lengthy intervals between each patrol. Even when the Hurricanes and Spitfires encountered German aircraft they were often so heavily outnumbered as to be unable to inflict serious damage on the enemy. Moreover, as well as destroying the port, the Luftwaffe mounted 12 attacks against the few ships sent from Dover that day, in some cases forcing them back to Britain before they arrived on the French coast.[15] As a consequence, at the end of the day just 7,669 men had been evacuated.[16]

Given the damage done to the port, most ships that sailed from England on 28 May assembled off the beaches, mainly at Malo, Bray and La Panne. Two passenger ships did attempt to enter Dunkirk harbour but one was sunk and the other so badly damaged that it had to limp back to Dover. Ramsay made an immediate decision to confine embarkation from Dunkirk during daylight to warships. Meanwhile the difficulty of evacuating troops from the beaches was making itself apparent. The gentle slope of the shore along the beaches to the east of Dunkirk meant that heavy craft such as destroyers and passenger ships had to anchor at least half a mile offshore. As few of the little boats had yet arrived from England, these ships had to row their own boats to the shoreline, fill them with soldiers, and then row them back. Not surprisingly, the crews soon became exhausted and the intervals between trips became longer and longer as the day progressed. Moreover, on this day a 'lop' was running inshore, that is a choppy sea with waves at short intervals. This meant that many boats had difficulty in maintaining direction and finished broadside on to the beach. The waiting soldiers had little understanding that the small ships' boats had to be pointed directly out to sea and attempted to clamber into them as they found them. The result was that the boats often capsized but even when they did not, the sailors found it impossible to get them in the correct position to row. Furthermore, given the exhaustion of the naval crews, the inexperienced soldiers often took over the rowing, which made the journeys to the big ships even slower. Finally, if soldiers successfully rowed to a destroyer, they often cut the boats adrift as they hauled themselves on board. As the day wore on, therefore, there were fewer and fewer boats available for evacuation but a great many drifting up and down the coast well out to sea.[17]

The air cover provided by Fighter Command on 28 May was no better than the day before, but in the afternoon low cloud descended along the coast, reducing the frequency of the enemy attacks. Indeed, the RAF reported no combats at all during the afternoon and early evening.[18] Nevertheless seven ships were lost or damaged this day and the total number of troops evacuated, while an improvement on the previous day, only amounted to 17,000.[19] In two days only one tenth of the BEF had reached the safety of home soil.

A significant problem which added to the slow progress of the evacuation was the long, indirect route that some ships were forced to sail. Because of the treacherous sand banks off the coasts of southern England, Belgium and France, and the uncertainty concerning the whereabouts of German minefields, ships were forced to sail from Dover via Route Y. This took them due north and then due east across the North Sea until they approached Ostend where they performed a sharp right turn to navigate between the sandbars off the Belgian coast to Dunkirk. All told this route was 97 miles long, about three times the direct distance between Dover and Dunkirk. At its eastern end this route also left vessels potentially vulnerable to German U-boat or motor-torpedo-boat attack. The alternative was Route Z, which was much more direct – just 39 miles. From Dover it led to the French coast off Calais where the ships turned left and travelled parallel to the French coast to Dunkirk. The problem with this route was that after the fall of Calais the Germans mounted heavy artillery along the coast which placed ships sailing this route in great danger, especially during the daylight hours. Yet for the first days of Operation Dynamo these were the only routes to Dunkirk available to the Royal Navy.[20]

Despite these setbacks, 28 May was in some ways *the* vital day for the success of Operation Dynamo. Captain Tennant had discovered that the eastern protective pier outside Dunkirk harbour might be suitable for embarkation. The pier, or the Mole as it was soon to be called, was not constructed to be used by ships. It was nothing more than a lattice-work concrete breakwater with a wooden walkway on top. A heavy ship might well smash the wooden planking, making it impassable for troops. The walkway was also narrow. It could take no more than three or four men abreast. It did have some advantages, however. It was 1,600 feet long, which meant that a number of ships could tie up to it together and even while narrow the walkway could accommodate several thousand men at once.[21] It was true that the stationary ships and the long queues of men might present enviable targets for dive bombers, but given the difficulty of lifting men from the beaches, Tennant considered this a risk worth running. The next day, 29 May, would test whether he was right.

Of course the evacuation of troops could only proceed if the perimeter held. On 27 and 28 May it was held only by Lawson's improvised forces, with the addition of some stragglers from various units of III Corps. On 29 May this situation improved. Brooke's II Corps consisting of 3, 4 and 50 Divisions began to arrive around Furnes. And at the other end of the perimeter 42 and 46 Divisions began to improve the defences at Bergues. Attacks were mounted by the Germans against both these positions but they were in general penny-packet operations that were easily seen off by the British. Indeed, the Germans showed a surprising lack of coordination and energy in this phase of the campaign. They allowed the British forces to disengage at night without making the slightest attempt to interfere with the withdrawals, and they seemed incapable of mounting attacks across a reasonable proportion of the front. Perhaps two weeks of hard campaigning were starting to tell on forces that had so far proved unstoppable.

So, untroubled by close German pursuit, by the end of 29 May the perimeter was defended by elements of 4 Division around Nieuport, 3 Division on either side of Furnes, by 50 Division around Bulscamp, and by various units of 42 and 46 Divisions around Bergues. And the Canal Line they were defending was in some ways a more formidable position than their original position along the Dyle. The Bergues–Furnes Canal was on average 15 to 20 metres wide and in most places had steep banks. Bergues was an easily defended old town. The weakest point was Furnes where the southern bank of the canal was in general higher than the bank occupied by the British. Moreover, the enormous piles of destroyed trucks and other detritus allowed the Germans to occupy some excellent sniping positions, which made movement in the town hazardous.[22]

In many ways the picture sketched above of the movement of British troops inside the perimeter is far too neat. Most units struggled along roads crowded with refugees, blocked by burning and disabled trucks, tanks and equipment of all kinds. Attacks on these columns by the Luftwaffe seemed incessant and the appearance of the RAF was an event rare enough to be noted in most accounts of the retreat.[23] The British official history displays an unusual vividness in describing the scene:

> The roads to the coast presented an astonishing spectacle in those
> days when motor and horse-drawn transport of two armies, refugees on

foot, stragglers and the fragments of units, and the withdrawing divisions all sought to find a way northwards. In the roadside fields burning equipment and abandoned stores heightened the appearance of disintegration.[24]

The path to the coast was often tortuous. Ken Anderson was an RAF meteorological officer travelling with a small group of men from an artillery survey team. They had retreated from Poperinghe, 'throwing all wrecked instruments, clothing, the ashes of documents, gas cylinders – anything that could be abandoned – into the roadside ditches'. They arrived in Hoogstade where they wrecked any remaining small vehicles and embussed for Bulscamp, which they reached late on 28 May. There they joined with other men, were split into parties of 25, and force-marched to Tétegham. They then set out for the sea, losing their way on numerous occasions and at one point making directly towards the enemy until they were turned around by an officer from the RASC. At Tétegham they rested for 30 minutes, had a rudimentary meal, and headed towards the flames of Dunkirk. Over the last mile they stumbled forward, 'a cursing, motley crew, calling on our ebbing physical and mental strength to push one foot in front of the other . . . So we came to the dunes, where we halted, to fall asleep in the sand and the coarse grass.'[25]

Some divisions had great difficulty in maintaining cohesion. The 44 Division was one of the last to withdraw from the south. It was then involved in bitter fighting at Mont des Cats where it was dive-bombed and attacked by enemy tanks. The command had received orders on 28 May to retreat on Dunkirk, but next day the division was scattered over the following locations: HQ 131 Brigade, en route to Dunkirk; remainder 131 Brigade and 5 Queens, Mont des Cats; 6 Queens, en route to Dunkirk; Buffs, some at Mont des Cats, remainder unknown; HQ 133 Brigade, Mont des Cats; remainder 133 Brigade and 2 Sussex, on road Bailleul to Poperinghe; 4 and 5 Sussex, Mont des Cats; 132 Brigade and attached troops, on road Bailleul to Poperinghe; Engineers, Mont des Cats; Field Ambulance, en route to Dunkirk; 57 Battery Royal Artillery (no guns), unknown; 58 Battery Royal Artillery (no guns), on road Bailleul to Poperinghe; 65 Battery Royal Artillery (16 guns, no ammunition), Mont des Cats; anti-tank guns, with 132 Brigade.[26] In the event the division was never entirely reunited.

One section of it made its way to the Dunkirk Mole while the other ended up at Bray.[27]

So chaos there certainly was, but perhaps too much has been made of it. For within the chaotic scenes described above there was some kind of order. At most roads that led into the perimeter, Adam had placed officers to direct men in the general direction of their Corps. Thus men from I Corps were directed to Bray, II Corps to La Panne and III Corps to Malo.[28] Further reordering in these locations ensured that eventually most brigades and battalions were more or less united. In addition not all units retreated in disorder. The 1, 3, 4 and 50 Divisions in particular retired together in good order. Despite complaints from the British about being intermingled with French soldiers, most Frenchmen eventually found their way to the west of the perimeter, except for General Benoit Laurencie's 12 and 32 Divisions, the remnants of which chose to remain with the British around Nieuport. So the men on the beaches were, despite appearances, in units cohesive enough to be embarked under the control of their commanding officers.

The Canal Line was better defended on 29 May than the day before, but the increased strength was soon needed as German infantry divisions finally made contact with this last line of Allied defence. And the British suffered from one considerable disadvantage. Only one of the 16 regiments of medium and heavy artillery was still operational – the remainder, too cumbersome to retreat at speed – had been destroyed. The regiments of field artillery were largely intact but they often lacked reliable supplies of ammunition.[29]

The 3 Division was the first to notice the disparity in firepower on 29 May. They were shelled heavily all day in their positions around Furnes. Then the enemy attacked and penetrated the front in several places. Counter-attacks drove them back, but German shelling continued and Allied casualties mounted. Only night saved the division from further harassment.[30] The major attack that day, however, came at the western section of the British front. At Bergues and points south and west, the motley force from 42 and 48 Divisions was attacked by 20 Motorised Division and regiments from the SS Adolf Hitler and Grossdeutschland Regiments. Tanks and artillery were employed and those British positions guarding the south of the canal were soon lost. But once more, nightfall saw hostilities cease. The British were now entirely behind the Canal Line, but it was still intact. It would clearly take more than these uncoordinated attacks to break it.

The defence of the perimeter saw a remarkable change in Luftwaffe tactics. As the French could attest, at the Meuse the Stuka dive-bombers could bomb with great accuracy (especially when unopposed), confident even when their own troops were nearby. But very few such attacks took place on the troops defending the perimeter. Apparently the Germans adopted a policy of concentrating their air effort against the port of Dunkirk, ships offshore and troops on the beaches. Indeed, at times the priority seems to have been to bomb ships at sea in order to avoid hitting friendly troops advancing on Dunkirk. Why the Luftwaffe changed policy at Dunkirk is hard to fathom. Perhaps it arose from the fact that they were now liaising with Army Group B, which had little experience with dive-bombers, instead of Army Group A, which had directed the bombing along the Meuse.[31]

These rather ineffectual German attacks against the perimeter gave the British a chance to improve the rate of evacuation. At first, conditions did not seem promising. A moderate surf was running along the beaches from Bray to La Panne, hampering the efforts to row the soldiers out to the larger ships offshore.[32] But Captain Tennant at Dunkirk had been informed about these conditions by Commander Ellwood at Bray,[33] and Tennant had also observed that the Mole was working well as an embarkation point. Just after 7.00 a.m. he signalled Ramsay: 'No enemy interference at present. Embarkation going at 2000 an hour. This can be kept up provided supply transport is maintained. Swell prevents use of beach. All ships to Dunkirk.'[34] Ramsay was not, however, willing to go this far. He held it 'essential to maintain lifts off the beaches as well as Dunkirk harbour', which certainly underestimated the difficulties caused by the 'lop' at Bray and La Panne. It also ignored the experience of those on the spot.[35] Ramsay therefore continued to dispatch some ships to the beaches. But there would be a delay in sending some of the most useful vessels, the passenger ships, to any destination that day. Ramsay discovered that in 'certain vessels' the 'crews were unwilling to sail when ordered'. Consequently he had to send to the Nore Command for officers and naval ratings to take over.[36] These useful ships that could load several thousand soldiers would not, to the chagrin of Tennant and others at Dunkirk, appear for some time off the French coast.

Meanwhile Tennant had increased the embarkation rate from the Mole to 4,000 men per hour. He was impressed with the greater discipline of the fighting troops, which made this speed possible compared to that of the straggling 'non-combatant' troops who had been lifted in previous days.[37] All proceeded smoothly until noon. Then Tennant was forced to cable Ramsay:

> Bombing of beaches and Dunkirk pier [the Mole] has now commenced without opposition from fighters. If they hit Dunkirk pier embarkation will become very jammed. Beach at La Panne covered with troops congregating in large numbers. Very slow embarkation taking place from Eastern Beach.[38]

In fact the RAF had increased its effort during 29 May, flying patrols of two squadrons instead of one. Nevertheless, because of Dowding's policy, the beaches and harbour remained uncovered during the following hours: 6.10 a.m.–7.20 a.m.; 9.25 a.m.–10.30 a.m.; 12.00–1.00 p.m.; 2.00 p.m.–2.50 p.m.; 4.20 p.m.–5.00 p.m.; 6.00 p.m.–7.30 p.m.; 8.30 p.m.–9.10 p.m.[39]

In short, for nearly seven hours of daylight there were no Spitfires or Hurricanes over Dunkirk or the beaches. And the Luftwaffe engaged in more or less continuous attacks from noon until 8.00 p.m. The results of these attacks were disastrous for the navy. Between 4.00 and 6.00 p.m. the destroyers *Jaguar* and *Canterbury* were so badly damaged that *Jaguar* had to be towed to Dover and *Canterbury* was not used in Operation Dynamo again. Then the passenger ship *Fenella* was hit alongside the Mole as was the destroyer *Grenade*. Both threatened to flounder in the fairway, but quick work saw them towed away to sink in less critical waters. In addition, two more passenger ships, two paddle minesweepers and four other miscellaneous ships were also sunk.[40] These disasters were all inflicted by the Luftwaffe, but there were other causes of loss that day. A passenger vessel (the *Mona's Queen*) was sunk by a mine as it neared Dunkirk. And earlier the destroyer *Wakeful* had been torpedoed by a German motor-torpedo boat. Almost all troops went down with the ship. Chaos quickly ensued after this incident. The nearby *Grafton* – another destroyer – was torpedoed by the same German boat. The escorting warships then saw a craft loom out of the murk and opened fire. It was another British destroyer, the *Comfort*, which they sank in a few minutes.[41]

All told on 29 May, 12 ships were sunk, including two valuable destroyers and four passenger vessels, all capable of carrying substantial numbers of soldiers. In addition eight other craft were damaged, some so badly that they could not be used again. The Admiralty took fright at these losses and told Ramsay that he must sail the modern destroyers (H, I and J class) to safer ports. There were now just 15 destroyers available for Dynamo.[42]

There was yet more confusion ashore. A signal from the beaches at La Panne reached Dover to the effect that Dunkirk harbour was blocked and all evacuation should proceed during the night from the beaches. As a result Ramsay directed ships away from the Mole and during the whole of the night of 29–30 May just four trawlers and a yacht entered the harbour. Had there been a regular flow of ships it is likely that 10,000 additional troops could have been lifted from the Mole, which was largely free from air attack during those hours.[43]

Nevertheless, despite the sinkings and confusion the Mole had proved its worth on 29 May. While just 13,700 men were lifted from the beaches, 33,500 were taken from the Mole, making a total for the day of 47,200, more than the preceding two days combined: 73,000 men from the BEF were now back in England.[44]

One of the factors that helped speed up evacuations on this day was the opening of a new sailing route by the navy. Minesweepers had cleared a new passage (Route X), which went almost direct to Dunkirk from just north of the Goodwin Sands. It had the advantage of being much shorter (55 miles) than Route Y and much safer than Route Z, being out of range of any enemy artillery.[45]

What of the Germans? We have seen that on 29 May only small probing attacks were made on the Dunkirk perimeter around Bergues and Furnes. The next day a more serious attack was launched on Furnes. However, the brigadier in charge of the defence soon established that the Germans invariably advanced along the area's roads to avoid a more arduous trek across country with its many irrigation ditches. To counter these moves he placed patrols of infantry and anti-tank guns in areas covering all approaches to Furnes by road. These tactics worked. The Germans advanced along the roads and were wiped out on them. Soon they ceased their attacks. They would make no more attempts to cross the Canal Line at Furnes until the British had left the area.[46] At Bergues there was a small probing attack from a few tanks that quickly withdrew when shelled. On the British side this lack of action was particularly welcome. In this area were the exhausted remnants of 2, 23 and 44 Divisions plus the improvised Usherforce. So dire was their situation that when the weakened 'digging' divisions were withdrawn, Usherforce had to remain in the line until I Corps could take over the whole area from III Corps. Any large-scale attack in this area would have been disastrous. But the small attacks at either end of the perimeter constituted the only action that day by the Germans.

To seek an explanation for this surprising lack of resolve we have to identify those elements of the German army approaching Dunkirk on 30 May (Map 11). On the left there were elements from the 4th Army (including Panzer Group Kleist), within Army Group A; in the centre the 6th Army and on the right the 18th Army, both from Army Group B. For the Germans the main problems were that the three armies were converging on a relatively small area and that the attention of Army Group A increasingly turned to its realignment to deal with those French forces south of the River Somme.

This last matter especially was of concern to Panzer Group Kleist. Around midday the Chief of Staff of Army Group A, Colonel Sodenstern, enquired of Kleist Group whether an attack was to be made on Dunkirk, because 'the impression exists that nothing is happening today, that no one is any longer interested in Dunkirk'. He urged General Kleist at least to fire on the harbour and town to hinder the evacuation and create panic.[47] Roth Wuthmann, the Chief of Staff of the 4th Army (of which Kleist's Group was a part), resisted. If mobile troops were used against Dunkirk it would cost considerable casualties, and artillery fire might endanger units of the 6th Army that were understood to be advancing on Dunkirk.[48] Nothing happened for three hours. But then the 4th Army Commander (General Kluge) returned from visiting the southern front at Abbeville. This visit had given him a different perspective from Wuthmann's. He was concerned that a French drive from the south was imminent and that it was 'necessary to finish off the operation [at Dunkirk] rapidly' so that the armour could

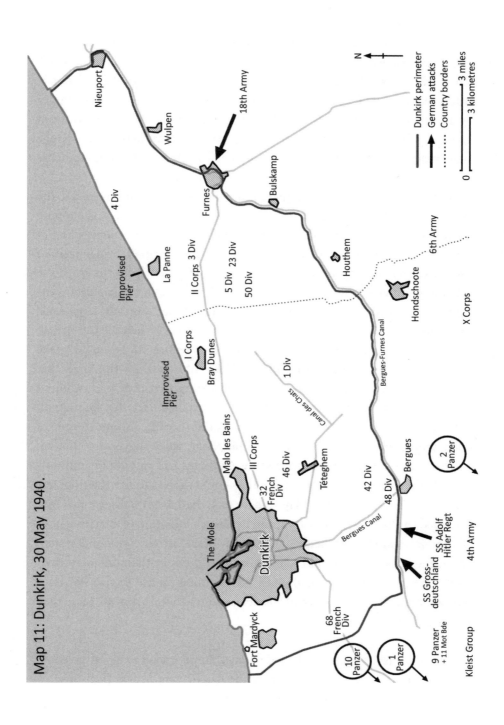

Map 11: Dunkirk, 30 May 1940.

be reoriented against the French.[49] Kluge therefore ordered Wuthmann to propel the group of armour nearest Dunkirk (Kleist Group) against the perimeter. Kleist replied that his armoured troops were not suitable for such an attack. Wuthmann, now falling into line with Kluge, curtly informed him that this fact was known, but on orders from a 'higher authority an end must be made of the evacuation in progress from Dunkirk. Therefore a thrust is to be made past Dunkirk to the coast.' Kluge personally reinforced this order stating that 'the Divisional Commander is to say that he unquestionably stands on the coast today'.[50]

But this seemingly imperative command by no means resolved the matter. Kleist Group replied at 4.15 p.m. (note how the day was slipping away) that they were attacking towards Bray to cut off the enemy's line of retreat, but that their left was held up by 'the fortified bridgehead of Dunkirk' and that to get forward it was essential that X Corps from the adjoining 6th Army advance on their right. This message was pure invention. There is no evidence that Kleist Group carried out any large-scale operations against the perimeter on 30 May. Certainly neither the British nor the French recorded such an attack. But before Kluge could make further enquiries about Kleist's 'attack', Kleist informed the 4th Army that he had received a message from X Corps stating that they had captured Dunkirk.[51] Wuthmann was incredulous. He signalled back that he thought X Corps were much further back and that Kleist should continue in spite of such reports.[52] But Kleist remained stationary, now suggesting that no further moves were possible because the Germans had run out of ammunition for the heavier-calibre guns. All they could do was to fire their lightest calibres at the port.[53] The day ended as it had begun. Kleist had not intended to attack in the morning and he had no intention of attacking now.

Recriminations travelled right through the German command system regarding these non-events. Army Group B thought their infantry divisions inferior to armour for the task of rounding up the British. When it was apparent that there would be no armoured attack on 30 May, they commented:

They [Army Group A] are halted because they are soon to be extracted from the front in compliance with the deployment orders [for] 'Rot' [Red]. This is a matter of the deepest regret to the army group command because thereby the attack against Dunkirk from the <u>West</u>, the importance of which is of a decisive nature, is abandoned once again.[54]

But so far from upbraiding Army Group A for their failure to act, at OKH in Berlin, Halder issued instructions for Army Group B's 18th Army, which consisted only of infantry divisions, to take over the entire operation against the Dunkirk perimeter commencing on 31 May. As a concession some additional infantry divisions from X Corps of the 6th Army were added to this force, but Army Group A, which contained all the Panzer and mobile forces near Dunkirk, was to be directed away from the perimeter, against the French to the south of the Somme.[55]

Apart from General Bock at Army Group B there was little dissent from this decision. As noted, Guderian had decided as early as 28 May that Dunkirk was not for him, Kleist clearly had no stomach for the operation, and Kluge, who seemed momentarily to favour it, made no comment. As for Hitler, he played no conspicuous part in this series of decisions, although it is known from his earlier remarks that he was worried about the French acting against the so-called open flank along the Somme.

We can never know what an attack by the elements of the Kleist Group (9 Panzer, the 20 Motorised, and the motorised brigades of the Grossdeutschland and SS Adolf Hitler regiments) might have accomplished had they attacked the perimeter. While some of the land between Bergues and Furnes was being flooded by the Allies, an attack parallel to the coast from west to east would have found some good going. Certainly such an attack would have tested in particular the improvised units from mainly Territorial divisions that were concentrated around Bergues. Had that citadel fallen or been bypassed, the perimeter defences would have been outflanked with disastrous consequences for the BEF and the French. It is true that the German mobile units might have become mired in the low land and the attack brought to a sudden halt. What seems so extraordinary about German decision-making on this day is that no one on the ground or in Berlin thought the attack a chance worth taking. The risk of incurring casualties in three or four motorised units was not deemed worth the prize of eliminating the BEF from the war.

* * * * *

One of the continuing problems faced by the British in the evacuation was the difficulty of communicating from the beach embarkation points at La Panne and Bray and the Mole at Dunkirk. It was also difficult to communicate from the beaches to ships offshore. In the haste of evacuation planning, insufficient signal lamps and radios had been dispatched to Dunkirk.[56] Partly to remedy the communication problem Ramsay sent Rear Admiral Wake-Walker to Dunkirk on the night of 29 May. He was not to land but remain offshore on a destroyer from where it was hoped by travelling up and down the coast he could communicate both with Tennant at Dunkirk and Ramsay, and keep them up to date with the situation on the various beaches.[57] This was vitally necessary as the following example demonstrates. In the early morning of 30 May (3.00 a.m.) Tennant signalled to Ramsay that he had no destroyers.[58] In fact 15 destroyers were either on the way to Dunkirk, off the beaches, or at Dover discharging troops. If the troops on the Mole were to be readied for embarkation, Tennant desperately needed to know when he might expect large ships to arrive. In the days that followed Wake-Walker was to prove an invaluable conduit for such information.

As it stood, Ramsay was aware by 6.00 a.m. that Dunkirk harbour was not blocked and that passenger ships and destroyers could use it. But considering the carnage of the previous day, Ramsay and Tennant decided that only one destroyer at a time would enter the harbour, though no limit would be placed on the passenger ships.[59] Meanwhile Tennant was receiving reports about a huge build-up of troops on the beaches at La Panne and Bray. He telegraphed Ramsay this news and asked him to direct ships accordingly. As a result Ramsay sent most destroyers to the beaches. This was undoubtedly a mistake. Destroyers off a beach, given the continuing shortage of small boats, could embark about 600 men in 12 hours, whereas in good conditions at the Mole this number could embark in 20 minutes.[60] But Ramsay was doing the best he could with the limited knowledge available to him, and Tennant had asked him to direct the ships. The result was, however, that few destroyers entered Dunkirk harbour on the morning of 30 May.

Meanwhile at Bray, Commander Richardson had had an idea that would at least mean that the destroyers approaching the beaches might take more men than hitherto. He went to the headquarters of 1 Brigade and suggested that what trucks there were in the vicinity of Bray be assembled and driven onto the beaches at low tide to form a rudimentary pier. This the engineers from the brigade did. The trucks were run out onto the beach, head to tail, with a plank footbridge connecting them. Then heavy objects (blocks of concrete, old engines from unusable trucks) were placed in the vehicles to give them some kind of stability. When the tide came in, small craft could moor at the end of the pier in a reasonable depth of water and ferry the troops on the footbridge out to the larger ships. In this way a continuous procession of men was embarked until the tide went out too far. On 30 May elements of 1, 50 and 42 Divisions were lifted to safety.[61] In due course a similar structure was erected at La Panne.

This was a timely move because there was a distinct shortage of heavy craft at the Mole. This was partly offset by the efforts of one man. The normal rate of loading troops was about 3,000 per hour, but at Dunkirk, Commander Ellwood, one of Tennant's right-hand men, decided that in the absence of air attack the rate could be improved. In his words:

> I therefore went down to the Eastern Arm [the Mole] and rigged up a loud speaker and addressed the troops in the following terms 'Remember your Pals, Boys. The quicker you get on board the more of them will be saved.' This worked like a miracle. The thousands of troops, tired, depressed, and without food or water for days, broke into a double and kept it up for the whole length of the Eastern Arm for more than two hours. During that period I estimate that more than 15,000 troops were embarked.[62]

The work at the Mole and the pier at Bray boosted the figures that day. A total of 24,000 men were taken from the Mole, and with the pier at Bray 29,500 were taken from the beaches, the only day of the evacuation where beach embarkations exceeded those from the Mole. In all then, about 54,000 men escaped that day, bringing the running total to just over 125,000 men.[63]

One factor that helped boost these numbers was the increased effort made by the RAF. On 30 May they flew patrols in three- or four-squadron strength. There still remained periods when there were no aircraft over the beaches, but now when the stronger RAF patrols clashed with the Luftwaffe they found accurate bombing impossible. The weather also played a part. In the early morning visibility was poor – 10/10ths cloud being reported between 300 and 3,000 feet. In the afternoon the cloud lifted a little but visibility was still limited.[64] Just two destroyers were damaged that day, but these were more than compensated for by the Admiralty reversing their decision and returning the modern craft to Ramsay's command. All told, 30 May was the best day yet for the British.

The following day was to be fraught with difficulty mainly because political factors entered the operation and threatened to disrupt it. In a sense this was bound to happen sooner or later. The British were leaving; the French until this point were not. And the command structure at Dunkirk was complicated. In nominal control was the French Admiral Abrail, but he commanded few ships and the majority of troops in his area of control were British. Lord Gort was nominally under his command but he had the escape clause of every British commander who fought overseas in the twentieth century – he could appeal to his own government if he thought decisions by his ally imperilled his force. In the perimeter were also General Blanchard, commander-in-chief of the remains of the French First Army, and General Fagalde, commander of X Corps, the main French force protecting Dunkirk. Above all these men were, for the British, General Dill who had replaced Ironside on 27 May as Chief of the Imperial General Staff, Anthony Eden, Minister for War, and Winston Churchill; and for the French, General Weygand, commander-in-chief of all French forces, and Paul Reynaud as Prime Minister. In general terms the further from the action the participants were, the less they understood of the day-to-day position inside the perimeter.

Tensions arose on 31 May because of differing French and British perceptions of the operation. When General Adam set up the perimeter, some on the French side thought that the position was to be held indefinitely. As late as 30 May, Admiral Abrail still held that view, despite the fact that 125,000 British troops had left for England.[65] Others on the French side considered that the entire BEF was indeed going, leaving French troops the ignominious tasks of first covering the British evacuation and then themselves surrendering. General Fagalde was one who held this view and a few days earlier had threatened to use force to prevent the British from embarking.[66] Yet others thought that the evacuation should be shared and that any capitulation that followed should also be shared. Churchill was of this opinion and as early as 29 May had suggested to the Chiefs of Staff via General Hastings Ismay that to maintain alliance harmony this might be the best solution.[67] Gort, sensing trouble, sought written confirmation from London of his instructions.[68] He then proceeded to Dunkirk where he arranged with Admiral Abrail that the British would play a considerable role in holding the perimeter while as many French troops as possible embarked for Britain.

But whatever Gort's intentions expressed to Abrail, he soon issued another set of instructions to General Alexander, who was to take control of the bridgehead when the commander-in-chief sailed for England.[69] In these orders Gort emphasised that while he was to 'assist' the French, his prime responsibility was to the BEF, and if any order of Abrail's imperilled that force he was to appeal to his home government. The allotment of facilities for evacuation between the French and the British would be made 'by the authorities at home'.[70]

Armed with these instructions Alexander made his way to see Abrail at the Bastion, his fortified headquarters. They soon clashed over Alexander's plans to proceed with the evacuation of the BEF as rapidly as possible. The position was now delicate, for if Abrail closed the port to prevent any further embarkation, Operation Dynamo would grind to a halt with over 100,000 of the BEF still on French soil. Alexander announced that he must consult higher authority in London and left for La Panne.[71]

That same day, 31 May, Churchill had flown to Paris for a meeting of the Supreme War Council. At the meeting it was decided that French troops would join the evacuation. Churchill agreed that the British would keep three divisions in the line for as long as possible and that the evacuation would proceed on equal terms between the British and the French, *bras dessus bras dessus* (arm in arm).[72]

This did not dissuade Alexander from reiterating to Abrail that the BEF was his first priority, to which Abrail retorted that this would dishonour England.[73] In the event, the perimeter held at least three days longer than had been foreseen, which allowed the numbers evacuated to be approximately 50:50, British and French.[74]

Meanwhile the situation at the perimeter grew steadily worse. The main German offensive took place against the eastern section of the line. Near

Nieuport, 4 Division were subjected to attacks for most of the day. They were forced back along the dunes and the situation appeared serious until a unit of the East Surreys counter-attacked and stabilised the line.[75] Later in the day a renewed attack was broken up by some Blenheim and Albacore bombers that happened to be in the area, one of the few instances where the RAF was able to support ground troops.[76] Just to the left of this a heavy German attack developed against the junction of the 50 and 3 Divisions near Bulscamp. The troops were forced back, but later in the day machine guns were sent forward and undercover of a barrage fired by them the British were able to reoccupy most of the lost territory.[77] The best opportunity for the Germans lay around Bergues, which had only 500 defenders. But although shelling was heavy, the German infantry did not press the attack and the defenders were able to hang on for another day.[78]

Nevertheless, it was clear to the commanders on the ground that the defences could not hold for much longer. They therefore decided to evacuate the eastern end of the perimeter on the night of 31 May and abandon La Panne the following day. However, choppy conditions in the early part of the evening raised doubts that any troops could be evacuated from the beaches. Admiral Wake-Walker, offshore on the *Keith*, certainly thought they could not and signalled Ramsay that 'Dunkirk our only real hope'.[79] This seemed to be confirmed by the experiences of at least some of the boats. The minesweeper HMS *Sutton* operated off La Panne for most of the day and night and managed to evacuate just 120 soldiers.[80] But at the same time Ramsay was receiving reports that Dunkirk was under heavy air attack and that accurate artillery fire was beginning to land around the Mole.[81] He decided to hold passenger ships off the coast until the situation improved and asked for additional flotillas of small boats to proceed to the beaches. The last move proved important because in the afternoon the swell subsided and many men were embarked from La Panne and Bray with the assistance of these flotillas. The improvised pier of trucks at La Panne that had been hastily thrown up on 30 May proved useful and by the end of the day no fewer than 5,000 soldiers (mainly from 4 Division) had been embarked.[82] In addition, despite the air raids and shelling, the Mole and the Western Pier (from which French troops were embarked) continued to be used throughout the day and night, and in the end 46,000 troops were lifted from the port. Added to that were 23,000 from the beaches, making a total of 69,000 men, the most successful day so far at Dunkirk.[83]

On the morning of 1 June the situation at Dunkirk was this: 195,000 troops had been embarked of which about 160,000 were British. This left about 40,000 British troops in the perimeter and an unknown number of French but possibly in the region of 100,000. On the British side those evacuated consisted of a few men from 1 Division, all the remaining men of 2 Division, the whole of 3 and 4 Divisions, the very few soldiers left in 12 and 23 Divisions, and more substantial numbers from 44 and 48 Divisions. Remaining were most of 1 Division, a few men from 5 Division, 42 and 46 Divisions, and some from 50 Division.[84] In addition most of the senior commanders were now also in Britain: Brooke, Adam, Montgomery, Franklyn, Petre, Osborne, Thorne, Martel and many of the brigadiers. Here was the nucleus around which a future British army might be built.

However, about three divisions of British and six divisions of French troops still remained to be evacuated. And the area left to them had shrunk. On the night of 31 May–1 June in the east, Nieuport, Furnes, La Panne and the intervening territory had been given up. The perimeter was now no more than 9 miles long and 6 miles deep.

But once more German attempts to liquidate the perimeter seemed half-hearted. Army Group B War Diary records the constant lament that its infantry divisions were required to attack when the job could have been much more easily accomplished by the armour in Army Group A.[85] Thus although there were attacks of one kind or another along the entire front, they were uncoordinated, and while much was made of the ground gained on 1 June, most of this had been abandoned by the British the previous night.[86] Overall, four German divisions attacked the Canal Line this day, which was defended by no more than six battalions of British troops with significant help from the French 12 Division covering the Franco-Belgian border defences. The main German attacks came against Bergues. The troops there were driven back but later re-established their position on the Canal Line. Further east, however, the canal could not be held. Despite heroic efforts by the East Lancashires the British were driven back to the Canal des Chats, only a few miles from the beaches.[87]

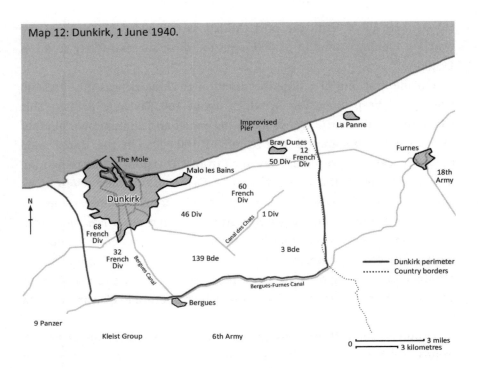

Map 12: Dunkirk, 1 June 1940.

This defence allowed the navy to have another successful day, albeit with heavy losses that were having a depressing effect on many ships' captains. In some cases drastic action was needed:

> There was an increasing unwillingness to sail [on the part of passenger ships] so steps were taken to place on board each a Naval Lieutenant-Commander or Commander, with 10 seamen acting as a moral stiffening, the officer acting as adviser and persuader to the Master of the Ship, and the seamen for handling the wires and going alongside under fire.[88]

These methods not only persuaded the ships' crews to sail but ensured that they entered Dunkirk harbour and embarked troops instead of lurking around outside the harbour and then sailing for home empty.[89]

By now most troops had been evacuated from the Mole or the beaches near Malo. Even so morale was deteriorating. Rear Admiral Wake-Walker offshore on the *Keith* had to have a gun trained on a tug to force it to rescue a minesweeper that had breached near Bray.[90] Nevertheless, a maximum effort was made at Dunkirk this day, 1 June. At one moment in Dunkirk harbour were seven passenger ships, eight destroyers, and nine drifters and special power boats.[91] By these means 64,500 men – about half of whom were French – reached safety in England.[92]

The cost in terms of ships lost was high. Although the RAF flew eight patrols of three or four squadrons, for considerable periods they did not coincide with the main Luftwaffe attacks.[93] The losses for the day amounted to three destroyers, one passenger vessel, one gunboat, one corvette, one yacht and one minesweeper sunk, and three destroyers, three passenger vessels, two minesweepers, one trawler and one harbour defence craft damaged – in total eight vessels sunk and ten damaged.[94] As a result of these losses Ramsay decided to abandon daylight evacuations. Any remaining troops would have to be evacuated by night.[95]

The remainder of the Dunkirk story can soon be told. The perimeter, which was increasingly defended by French troops, was held 'with undiminished tenacity' through 2 to 4 June.[96] During each of these nights about 25,000 men were embarked – most of them French. The British rearguard got away on 3 June when Alexander and Tennant sailed for England. As it happened, the British during the period 30 May to 4 June fulfilled their promise of 50:50 to the French – some 139,335 British troops were evacuated in this period and 139,097 Allied troops, the vast majority of whom were French.[97] Probably about 40,000 French troops, many of whom bravely defended the perimeter in the final days, surrendered.[98]

This was not quite the end of the affair, however. The British had considerable forces south of the Somme, including their only armoured division. There was also 51 Highland Division, which had been serving with the French along the Maginot Line when the Germans attacked and which had never been able to reunite with the main BEF. In addition there was a large number of lines of communication troops who had staffed the main British supply bases at Rouen and Rennes. It is not intended to describe the actions fought by these troops. Overwhelmingly the German operations were directed against the remaining French armies. The 51 Division suffered the saddest fate of all, being trapped at St Valery.

A rescue mission by the navy had to be abandoned because of thick fog and in the end about 8,000 Highlanders surrendered.

A half-baked plan was then developed whereby the west of France and especially Brittany might become a permanent redoubt from where a counter-offensive could be launched against the Germans. General Brooke was dispatched on 12 June to investigate this possibility. It soon became clear to Brooke that the French intended to surrender come what may and that the Breton Redoubt was impossible to defend, no more than a pipe-dream. He telephoned Eden to say that all British forces must be evacuated immediately. Churchill then came on the line, accused him of having 'cold feet' and stated categorically that he must continue to fight. Brooke, after 30 minutes of exhaustive argument, convinced Churchill that he (Brooke) was right. All British forces south of the Somme were to be brought home.[99] The numbers were considerable. All told 140,000 British troops and 46,500 Allies (the majority were Polish forces serving with the French army) were evacuated from various western French ports.[100]

Taking these men into account, the total number of troops removed from France and Belgium was about 560,000. Of these about 370,000 were British, the nucleus of the armies that were to fight in later years in the Middle East, Italy, the Far East and north-western Europe. Most of the French troops were immediately returned to France only to find that the Vichy government had surrendered. They would take no further part in the main land battles of the Second World War.

The cost to the British of the campaign in France and Flanders was considerable. About 70,000 troops were lost, either killed wounded or taken prisoner. In addition the BEF lost almost all of its equipment. Of the 2,294 guns dispatched to France, just 322 returned to England. For vehicles the figures were 68,618 and 4,739 respectively. Only a fraction of the supplies, stores and petrol sent across could be returned.[101] In terms of ships, approximately 200 vessels took part in the evacuation, along with a host of small craft. Of the larger vessels the most important were the destroyers, passenger vessels and minesweepers. Of the 39 destroyers that took part, 6 were sunk and 24 damaged; for passenger vessels the figures were respectively 29, 6 and 8. Thirty-six minesweepers took part. Five were sunk and six damaged. As for the RAF, they downed 132 enemy aircraft for a loss of 106 of their own fighters.[102] But considering that the Germans were operating further from their bases than the British, it hardly amounts to the overwhelming success claimed at the time. Nor do the figures support the wisdom of Dowding's policy of husbanding his forces. Had more aircraft been used then the casualty rates between the British and the Germans might have been more in favour of the British, and perhaps the totals of British ships lost (37) and damaged (50) might have been lower.

Nevertheless, Dunkirk was at least some kind of success. The vast bulk of the BEF had retreated in good order and had been rescued from the beaches in the teeth of German military superiority. The BEF had fought hard, and when it was opposed by German infantry divisions, had often fought them to a standstill. German armour was another matter. The BEF was fortunate only to suffer sporadic attacks from concentrated German Panzer divisions. On each of these occasions it had been beaten, but due to confused German orders and an ambiguity in German aims in the last days of the campaign, the German Panzers had not greatly affected the evacuation. The navy had also proved effective in operating during periods when there was only sporadic British air cover. When better cover was provided the Germans had very little success in sinking or damaging even unarmed ships. As for the RAF, it could have been used more effectively, but the presence of the Spitfire demonstrated to the Germans that daylight operations over Britain would be bitterly opposed by first-class machines. The greatest result to flow from Dunkirk was probably political. Churchill had been under pressure from the appeasers (especially Halifax) to make peace. The presence even of an unarmed army in Britain strengthened his position, and the actions of the navy and the RAF gave encouragement that an attempted Nazi invasion might be fought off. In any case there was no question that after Dunkirk, Germany would be fought to the end.

CHAPTER 6

ALONE
THE COLLAPSE OF THE FRENCH
ALLIANCE, MAY–JULY 1940

BY 4 JUNE THE bulk of the BEF had been evacuated, but that still left significant numbers of French forces (some 60 divisions) and a few British divisions (about three) south of the Somme where they would face an attack by the entire German army. Attention now turned to what additional help the British could provide. Churchill, an ardent Francophile, was eager to do all he could. But that eagerness had been tempered by his encounters with the French leadership dating back to the early days of the German invasion.

On 15 May he had been rung by Reynaud in 'a very excited' mood. The French Premier told him that the Germans had broken through south of Sedan and that the 'battle was lost'.[1] Churchill was so shaken by Reynaud's apparent concession of defeat that he felt it necessary to stress that 'whatever the French did, we would continue to fight to the last'.[2]

Soon after this call Churchill summoned the Chiefs of Staff to discuss Reynaud's request for additional British resources, both troops and fighter aircraft. Before he detailed the Premier's request he told the service chiefs that Britain would fight on whatever happened to the French, 'if necessary alone'. There were no troops immediately available in Britain, so the discussion turned on sending more fighters. Hugh Dowding, head of Fighter Command, who had by then joined the meeting, emphasised his absolute opposition to 'parting with a single additional Hurricane'. It is perhaps a sign of their concern over France's resolve (even at this early stage) that no one suggested a single Spitfire, Fighter Command's best aircraft, be sent to aid the French. Churchill closed the meeting by saying that the issue of assistance to the French was so important that he wanted the War Cabinet to consider the matter.[3]

The War Cabinet met later that day. It initially decided to send nothing to Reynaud on the grounds that his reaction was 'alarmist'.[4] But this attitude did not survive 24 hours. The next day, 16 May, as the width of the breach made in the French front became obvious, the Chiefs of Staff decided that six additional squadrons of fighters should be sent and the War Cabinet agreed. Four would be sent immediately and two more if required. The French, however, were only to be told about the first four; the availability of two additional squadrons was for the moment kept from them.[5]

These early meetings about the crisis in France reveal that as early as 16 May Britain was preparing for its own defence and Churchill was warning those elements in Britain – be they servicemen or politicians – not to link the fate of Britain with that of France. This stance would define British policy from this point. Churchill would do everything he could to support the French – short of endangering the defence of Britain. And he would do everything he could to support those politicians in France who would fight, but he would have no truck with defeatism wherever it appeared.

The War Cabinet had decided on 15 May that Churchill should go to Paris accompanied by General Dill, Vice Chief of the Imperial General Staff, and General Ismay, to see for himself whether the situation in France was as bad as Premier Reynaud had portrayed. The delegation assembled at the Quai d'Orsay where they met the 'dejected' Reynaud, Edouard Daladier, Minister of National Defence and War, and the French military commander-in-chief, General Gamelin.[6] The discussion was notable for its gloom. Gamelin asked for more fighters as the French had only 100 in working order – a gross underestimate. He told Churchill that the entire French army was engaged, that there were no more reserves, that Paris lay exposed to the Nazis, and that its fall would mean the war would be lost.[7] Ismay and Churchill were hardly cheered when they saw from the window that the courtyard garden at the Quai d'Orsay was now covered in burning documents as the French archives were consigned to the flames.[8]

Clearly action was required and quickly if the French were to remain in the war. From Paris, Churchill telegraphed to the War Cabinet that the situation was 'grave in the last degree'. In this circumstance the policy decided just the day before was scrapped. The Prime Minister urged that six squadrons of fighters should be sent 'tomorrow', *in addition to* the four already allocated.[9] Churchill was finding that the need to keep the French in line was rapidly outweighing any theoretical decisions made in London. The War Cabinet watered down his request. Six of the squadrons offered would only operate from France during daylight hours and they would operate in shifts – three squadrons deployed in the morning and three in the afternoon.[10] This gave the French a little more than they originally requested, but not much.

The promise of additional help improved Reynaud's mood, but over discussions during the next few days Churchill decided that no more fighters could be sent to France.[11] Then the sacking of Gamelin and his replacement with General Weygand was announced. (Did no one in Britain note that Marshal Pétain was also added to the Cabinet this day, 18 May?) Churchill's spirits rose and on his next visit to France he was assured by the new commander-in-chief that a pincer movement was being planned that would cut off the advanced German armoured spearheads and restore the situation. In this circumstance his decision to send no more fighters was modified. He now offered relays of fighters flying from Britain to participate in this battle.[12]

This offer rapidly became redundant. Weygand's pincer movement failed to eventuate and soon Churchill was 'demanding' that he fulfil his promise.[13] General Dill, who had just returned from visiting the French, warned Churchill that any major movement by their armies was almost certainly chimerical. It was hoped that Reynaud's visit to London on 26 May would yield definite information on the timing of the Weygand Plan, but in the event the French leader offered only vague reassurances that an attack would eventually take place. His more definite news was thoroughly alarming. He told Churchill that he was sure terms would be forthcoming from Germany if he asked for them.[14] Churchill successfully diverted Reynaud from this path as he had done with Halifax earlier in the day, but that was the only concrete outcome of the visit.

By the end of the week it was clear that Churchill would have to meet the French yet again to try to shore up their nerve. He flew to Paris on

31 May, but much of the discussion involved the evacuation from Dunkirk then in full swing. On the matter of additional help, the British promised to re-examine the whole question and report back to the French at the earliest possible moment.[15]

Back in London Churchill put the issue to the Chiefs of Staff. He informed them that he would like to tell the French that Britain would send three divisions and asked for them to consider the entire matter of aid to France.[16] The Chiefs of Staff reported the next day that the most that could be done was to send two divisions to the French immediately, followed by an additional one in ten days' time. As for aircraft, it was only possible to bring up to strength the six bomber and three fighter squadrons already operating with the Advanced Air Striking Force in France. Anything more would threaten the air defence of Great Britain.[17]

The admittedly modest British offer of aircraft was not sufficient for General Vuillemin, commander-in-chief of the French Air Force. In a note that the British received on 1 June he said:

> The enemy is in position to launch at short notice a fresh attack on our front, prepared and assisted by their bombers; interception of these bombers by a powerful force of Fighter aircraft is bound to have a decisive influence on the result of the battle.
>
> French Fighter aircraft, of which at the present only 350 are available, would soon be overwhelmed, if they are not heavily reinforced right from the start of the enemy attack by British Fighter aircraft. Such reinforcements, although provided tardily and in insufficient numbers at the time of the battle which started on 10th May, proved however to be of value . . . It is necessary that the British High Command should take every necessary measure so that at least half, and if possible all, the Fighter aircraft based in England (620 aircraft) could intervene in this eventuality . . . [and that] 320 aircraft from the 620 in England should be able to operate from bases situated in France . . . for both countries [it is] a question of life and death.[18]

It might be thought that accusing the British of tardiness and insufficiency of effort would not be the best tactic to induce them to commit more aircraft. But the issue went beyond verbal niceties. The French had

now asked the British for more aircraft on 14, 15, 16, 20 and 31 May –
five requests in two weeks. It might seem from these requests that the
French were chronically short of fighters and indeed that has been the
accepted story for many years. The actual situation was in fact more
complicated.

On 10 May the French had a total of 67 fighter squadrons with a further
21 in reserve.[19] In all that amounted to about 1,800 aircraft, about three
times the number the British had. However, of these only 583 were
deployed against the Germans, leaving the French outnumbered on the
battlefront. This deplorable situation came about partly because their
squadrons were scattered throughout France and in North Africa. Partly
it came about because so many aircraft never got beyond the holding
depots. The commander of the air force depots, General Redempt, had
pointed this out, yet in mid-June air force officers found the depot at
Toulouse full of aircraft – Potez 175 and Bloch 150 – the most modern
French types.[20]

Those aircraft that did make it to the battlefront performed very well
indeed against the Germans. The Dewoitine 52s, American Curtis 75A and
the Bloch 150 were all modern types roughly comparable in speed and
armament to the Me 109, and in fact these three types shot down more
German aircraft than they lost themselves. However, the involvement of
these French planes was limited to about one third of their total force as
revealed in a census conducted in July 1940 that counted 1,739 modern
French aircraft, the vast majority being fighters.

How did this situation come about? To some extent it was through inept
leadership in the frontline squadrons. For every sortie flown by a French
plane the Germans managed to fly four, magnifying the numerical superiority they already had. And partly it was defeatism, which rapidly took
hold among the top French air leaders once it became clear that the battle
had turned against them. Instead of bringing into battle some of their
many aircraft held in reserve, from 15 June they actually sent planes to
North Africa. In all, before the Armistice was signed, at least 20 fighter
squadrons of the better types were there, along with older fighters and
some bomber units. It was not technical or overall numerical superiority
that led the French to ask for more and more of the RAF. It was a combina-
tion of ineptitude at all levels of command, disorganisation and, in the end

defeatism.[21] In fact it has been suggested that the early retirement of the fighter squadrons to North Africa was a ploy by the Air Force Chiefs to preserve their 'precious capital' as a bargaining chip in the talks they anticipated with the Germans.[22]

Churchill responded to Vuillemin's 'altogether unreasonable' telegram on 5 June. He told Reynaud and Weygand that Vuillemin's demands could not possibly be met.[23] But he was now in possession of intelligence from Sir Roland Campbell, the British ambassador to France, that Pétain had told Reynaud that if no more British help was forthcoming, Reynaud should hand power over to him and he would make peace.[24] Under this pressure Churchill modified British policy yet again. He told the French that an additional four squadrons of bombers and two of Hurricanes would be available for operations that day and that this commitment would be maintained for as long as possible.[25] Once more the shaky resolve of the French had forced the commitment of yet more British aircraft.

Meanwhile Reynaud had reshuffled his Cabinet. Some defeatists were dropped, as was Daladier. This last move might not be thought such a disaster except that he was replaced at Pétain's behest as Under-Secretary for Foreign Affairs by the slippery Paul Baudouin. One positive step was the addition of Charles de Gaulle as Under-Secretary for National Defence, but overall Reynaud's new Cabinet was less resolute than the one it replaced.[26]

As the reshuffle took place so did the start of the German offensive across the Somme. This brought forth immediate French requests for yet more British aid. Once more, circumstances forced Churchill to respond. Two more fighter squadrons were dispatched to France to operate during daylight hours and the number of bombing sorties was increased.[27] The French considered this additional effort insufficient for the situation and they asked Churchill yet again to cross to France to discuss what further resources could be provided. Churchill clearly thought that the crisis was at hand to the extent that he asked President Roosevelt to intervene: 'Anything you can say or do to help them now may make the difference.'[28] As it happened, before Churchill could leave, Roosevelt made a blistering attack on Italy for declaring war on France. He proposed that all material aid be given to the Allies to prosecute the war. Churchill listened to this speech and was emboldened to write to Roosevelt again:

Everything must be done to keep France in the fight and to prevent any idea of the fall of Paris, should it occur, becoming the occasion of any kind of parley. The hope with which you inspire them may give them the strength to persevere.[29]

Later that day, 11 June, Churchill caught a flight for France, escorted by 12 Hurricanes because of the proximity of the Luftwaffe. He was accompanied by Eden, Dill, Ismay, the Director of Operations at the War Office, Ismay's assistant and General Spears, whom Churchill had appointed his personal liaison with Reynaud.[30] This time they were not heading for Paris. The French government considered the danger to Paris so great that they had decamped to Briare, a small town on the eastern Loire.

There they were met by Reynaud, Pétain, Generals Georges and De Gaulle, and Admiral Darlan. Churchill began by detailing the help that was on its way – in fact it only amounted to one regular division with another two Territorial divisions to arrive shortly. In addition six to eight squadrons of fighters were in action every day and he would examine whether more could be done in the air. Could the French not hold on a little longer as they had in 1918? This cut little ice with the French. The battle was going badly, with German armour penetrations in several places. Pétain pointed out that he had had 20 divisions available to plug gaps in 1918; now he had none. Weygand was quick to agree. 'I am helpless,' he said, 'I cannot intervene for I have no reserves, there are no reserves. C'est la dislocation – the break up.'[31] He then demanded that Britain commit its entire fighter force. The dramatic moment is well captured by Ismay:

'Here,' Weygand exclaimed, 'is the decisive point. Now is the decisive moment. The British ought not to keep a single fighter in England. They should all be sent to France.' There was an awful pause, and my heart stood still . . . It was a terrible position for a man like Churchill – generous, warm-hearted, courageous and with a pronounced streak of optimism, and I was terrified lest he might be so moved as to promise that he would ask the Government to send some additional air support. Thank God my fears were groundless. After a pause, and speaking very slowly, he said, 'This is not the decisive point. This is not the decisive moment. The decisive moment will come when Hitler hurls his

Luftwaffe against Britain. If we can keep command of the air over our own island – that is all I ask – we will win it all back for you.'[32]

Ismay's account might be thought too dramatic.[33] Churchill had repeatedly said that the air defence of Great Britain would always come first. But since 20 May, when the decision to send no more aircraft to France had been made, the RAF had committed around 10 more squadrons to the fight, admittedly flying from bases in England but still suffering casualties and thus reducing the strength of Fighter Command. The help that Britain could give France on land was derisory. Now there were to be no more aircraft. The French must fight the battle with what they had. It is highly probable that both sides realised that the battle was lost. If there was a precise moment when France ceased to be a great power, it occurred on 11 June at the unlikely location of Briare.

The meeting that resumed the next day, 12 June, was a reprise of the issues discussed the day before. Churchill detailed the help given to the French in the air (50–60 fighters and 70–80 bombers per day) and the French declared it inadequate. The meeting ended with a Churchillian declaration that whatever happened Britain would fight to the end. The Prime Minister promised to make a further appeal to Roosevelt and he specifically requested from Reynaud a promise that 'if there was any change in the situation' (barely concealed code for the French leaving the war), the British government would be consulted. Reynaud agreed, although what store Churchill placed in French promises by this time is dubious.[34]

Nevertheless, Churchill had not quite given up. In London he promised Reynaud and Weygand that the RAF would make a further effort by directing 10 squadrons of fighters over the battlefield (a slight increase on what he had detailed at Briare) and by additional bombing sorties. In effect, though, the British knew that the game was up. At the War Cabinet later that day they conceded that this chapter of the war was closing. The French might continue the fight from their colonies but their resistance on land was almost over.[35] Churchill also fulfilled his promise to Reynaud to intercede with Roosevelt. He told the President that now 'is the moment for you to strengthen Reynaud the utmost you can, and try to tip the balance in favour of the best and longest possible French resistance'.[36] Given Roosevelt's silence so far, however, he could have had very little expectation of a positive response.

Churchill in any case had no time to wait for a reply. The French had summoned him back, this time to Tours, well west of Briare, an indication in itself of the deteriorating circumstances at the front. The situation seemed worse than the day before. There was no one at the airport to meet the British Prime Minister. When a taxi was summoned, he was whisked into Tours and after some detours finally located the French. Ostensibly French resolve was firm. Investigations were being made into the viability of the so-called Breton Redoubt as a last refuge; preparations were under way to transfer forces to North Africa if required.[37] The Supreme War Council, however, gave a truer indication of French thinking. Two items dominated the agenda. The first was that without immediate American aid or an American declaration of war the French felt they could not continue. The second was: how would Britain act in 'a certain contingency', that is if France asked for terms? Churchill promised to contact Roosevelt yet again and asked the French to delay their decision until then. Whatever happened Britain would fight on, but France as well as the rest of Europe would then be subjected to blockade. This provoked a furious exchange between the delegations, but very little was actually resolved at Tours.[38]

When Churchill returned to London he received a copy of Roosevelt's reply to Reynaud, sent three days before. It stressed that Roosevelt was 'moved' by the message and 'impressed' with Reynaud's determination to fight on from North Africa and the Atlantic. Roosevelt declared that efforts to send material assistance to the Allies were being redoubled because 'of our faith in and our support of the ideals for which the Allies are fighting'.[39]

Churchill became extremely excited about this message, which he momentarily took as a virtual declaration of war. He proposed to the War Cabinet that he tell Reynaud the message 'fulfilled every hope and could only mean that the United States meant to enter the war on our side'. Clement Attlee then intervened. He thought the message from Roosevelt might be strengthened by 'a statement in dramatic terms' to the people of France. After discussion it was decided to proclaim 'the indissoluble union of our two peoples and of our two Empires', the statement to be given the widest possible publicity. The other matter that was also to be given the widest publicity was Roosevelt's response to Reynaud. But that of course required the President's approval.[40]

The first action taken by Churchill after this meeting was to write to Roosevelt and ask that he publish his message to the French. He told the President that in his view the French were on the verge of seeking an armistice and continued:

Mr. President I must tell you that it seems to me absolutely vital that this message should be published tomorrow June 14 in order that it may play a part in turning the course of world history. It will I am sure decide the French to deny Hitler a patched-up peace with France.[41]

Roosevelt's answer was extremely dusty. After the usual platitudes about the magnificent courage of the French and British nations, he absolutely forbade the publication of his letter, noting that it 'was in no sense intended to commit and did not commit the Government to Military participation', adding for Churchill's edification that only Congress could declare war.[42]

The letter was handed to Churchill by Ambassador Joseph Kennedy, who asked Churchill to pass on its contents to the French Premier. This infuriated Churchill who clearly thought that Roosevelt should do his own dirty work. He told the War Cabinet that he had declined this request and had stressed to Kennedy that if President Roosevelt appeared now to be holding back, this would have a 'disastrous' effect on French resistance.[43] This would not be the last time that Churchill would misinterpret a strong statement by Roosevelt as an indication of future commitment.

In the end appeals to the Americans were to no avail. Two more letters flowed from Churchill to Roosevelt with essentially the same message – the US must act or the French would leave the war. The answers were also the same. Roosevelt would not intervene to save the French.[44]

Meanwhile, unknown to the British, the Vice President of the French Council, Camille Chautemps, had suggested that the government should approach the Germans 'unofficially' through a third party to ascertain what terms would be on offer. If these were too stiff they could be rejected and in any case an unofficial approach could not be construed as breaking their word with Britain.[45] Reynaud opposed this manoeuvre but was outvoted 13 to 6. The only concession he could win was to postpone a decision until the British were made aware of the proposal and their reaction to it was gauged.[46]

When the Chautemps proposal was submitted to Britain, Churchill realised that the end game was fast approaching. The last British troops were being evacuated from France and the War Cabinet decided in these circumstances reluctantly to allow the French to make the approach, provided the French Fleet sailed for British ports before the question was raised.[47]

At this moment the matter of Anglo-French union, first mentioned by Attlee on 13 June, gained some traction. Since that meeting various parties – of whom the most important were Amery, Sir Robert Vansittart, the Chief Diplomatic Adviser to the government, Desmond Morton, Churchill's Chief Economic Adviser, and on the French side Jean Monnet, René Pleven and later De Gaulle – had held a series of informal meetings to discuss a possible union. By the time the War Cabinet met on the afternoon of 16 June a draft declaration had been produced. Churchill then read it to the Cabinet. He said that he had at first been sceptical about it but that he now favoured some such proposal. This was not the time to be accused of a lack of imagination. After some redrafting, the declaration was ready to be dispatched to the French. And to encourage its acceptance, Churchill would tell Campbell, the British ambassador to Paris, to hold up the telegram regarding armistice terms and the fate of the French Fleet.

In its final draft the declaration read as follows:

At this most fateful moment in the history of the modern world the Governments of the United Kingdom and the French Republic make this declaration of indisoluble union and unyielding resolution in their common defence of justice and freedom against subjection to a system which reduces mankind to the life of robots and slaves.

The two Governments declare that France and Great Britain shall no longer be two nations, but one Franco-British Union.

The constitution of the Union will provide for joint organs of defence, foreign, financial and economic policies.

Every citizen of France will enjoy immediately citizenship of Great Britain, every British subject will become a citizen of France.

Both countries will share responsibility for the repair of the devastation of war, wherever it occurs in their territories, and the resources of both shall be equally, and as one, applied to that purpose.

During the war there shall be a single War Cabinet, and all the forces of Britain and France, whether on land, sea or in the air, will be placed under its direction. It will govern from wherever best it can. The two Parliaments will be formally associated. The nations of the British Empire are already forming new armies. France will keep her available forces in the field, on the sea, and in the air. The Union appeals to the United States to fortify the economic resources of the Allies, and to bring her powerful material aid to the common cause.

The Union will concentrate its whole energy against the power of the enemy, no matter where the battle may be.

And thus we shall conquer.[48]

This startling document has received scant attention from historians. It is generally discounted as merely a last-minute attempt by the British to keep the French in the war – operating from North Africa or London. No doubt that was one purpose. But the declaration deserves to be taken more seriously than that. It was also an attempt to gather together what resources remained to the West (including the economic resources of the United States) to resist the tide of barbarism engulfing Europe. The British were indeed deadly serious about saving themselves from the evils inherent in this tide. But they were also serious about including the French in the system of resistance. If this meant merging the two nations, so be it. In an age when the nation state was supreme there could be no more serious move than sweeping away previous forms of citizenship, long-evolved institutions and customs. There would be no more Britain, no more France, but Franco-Britannia or Anglo-Franconia. The single War Cabinet would certainly have included Reynaud and De Gaulle. The question of leadership was left open. Reynaud thought he might have been given the task, but it is difficult to see Churchill being supplanted. In that case Reynaud would certainly have been his deputy. How long the union would have lasted is moot. Perhaps it would not have survived the war. But that is not the point here. The point is that the offer was made and could well have been accepted. The British, De Gaulle and other Frenchmen certainly thought it might sway Reynaud and his colleagues. In the sense that the French could have accepted it, the declaration *might not* have amounted to an empty gesture. No nation offers to surrender sovereignty on a whim.

As soon as the offer had been drafted by the War Cabinet it was handed to De Gaulle, who had been waiting outside the Cabinet room. He immediately telephoned Reynaud in Bordeaux, the last resting place of the Third Republic. Reynaud was at that moment engaged with Spears and Campbell on the fate of the French Fleet.[49] Reynaud heard the message with mounting excitement and hastily scribbled it down as De Gaulle read it. At the end Reynaud asked whether Churchill approved and the Prime Minister was put on the phone to assure him that it was a Cabinet decision.[50] Reynaud was enthusiastic and thought it might turn the defeatist tide. So did Spears. Campbell was less certain.

The last French Cabinet assembled in the next room. Meanwhile Reynaud informed the President (Albert Le Brun) of the news. He took the news calmly but Baudouin, the Under-Secretary for Foreign Affairs, and another minister were more negative. Later the Council of Ministers confirmed the views of these two men. Chautemps thought it would reduce France to the status of a British Dominion, not a bad option considering what else was on offer, but at least one other minister exclaimed 'better to be a Nazi province'.[51] Pétain rejected 'fusion with a corpse'. In fact only Reynaud, Le Brun and Mandel were enthusiasts of the plan. A few others were lukewarm; the remainder hostile.[52] Reynaud left the meeting and later resigned. Whether it would have been more sensible to stay to try to persuade some waverers or to leave for England and join De Gaulle is outside the scope of this book. Pétain was now Premier, Chautemps his Deputy; Weygand was Minister for National Defence (an ironic title considering that there was now no nation to defend) and Darlan was Minister for the Navy; Baudouin was Foreign Minister.[53]

Churchill made one last effort to ensure that the French Fleet would not be used against Britain. He sent the First Lord of the Admiralty (A. V. Alexander) and the First Sea Lord (Sir Dudley Pound) to Bordeaux to obtain assurances. The question arose in discussion with Darlan about whether the Fleet would sail to British ports. This suggestion was brushed aside by Darlan, but he assured the British that on no account would he surrender the French navy. If the armistice terms turned out to be dishonourable (the idea of getting honourable terms from Hitler is an interesting construct), he would destroy the Fleet or sail what could be got away to a friendly country.[54]

This was the best that the British delegation could obtain, but then came the armistice terms. When it came to the French Fleet the clause read:

> The French war Fleet – with the exception of that part left at the disposal of the French Government for the protection of French interests in its colonial empire – will be assembled in ports to be specified and there demobilised and disarmed under German or Italian control.[55]

In the days that followed the French government tried to assure the British that they would keep as much of their fleet as possible in North African ports to subject as little of it as possible to German or Italian 'control' (actually 'administrative supervision' was a more accurate translation of that word in the armistice document).[56]

But it was too late for such assurances. The French Fleet was the second largest in Europe and if added to the Italian or German fleets would represent a mortal peril to Britain. And if the British offer of surrender of sovereignty was met with the seeking of an armistice from Nazi Germany, then what trust could be placed in any French assurances? As Churchill told the War Cabinet, once France had been occupied by Germany it would be entirely at the mercy of the conquerors.[57]

Indeed, the armistice meant that Churchill ran out of patience with the Pétain regime. He would never trust it because while the French Fleet remained in being he could not afford to. He quickly put it to the War Cabinet that they should recognise De Gaulle's Council of Liberation as being the true representatives of France and arrange for De Gaulle to broadcast to France as the head of that organisation.[58] Churchill made his views public on 25 June when he read out the armistice article concerning the French Fleet to the House of Commons and continued:

> From this text it is clear that the French war vessels under this Armistice pass into German or Italian control while fully armed. We note, of course, in the same Article the solemn declaration of the German Government that they have no intention of using them for their own purposes during the war. What is the value of that? Ask half a dozen countries what is the value of such assurances . . . Finally, the Armistice

can at any time be voided on any pretext of non-observance, and the terms of the Armistice explicitly provide for further German claims when any peace between Germany and France comes to be signed.[59]

And ominously Churchill added that he hoped the House of Commons would have confidence that the government would not lack the resolution to take any measures 'they may think it right to take for the safety of the Empire'.[60]

Not surprisingly, the main topic on the agenda of the War Cabinet for the next few days was how to deal with the French Fleet. From the tenor of the discussions it is clear that Churchill favoured one of two options – that the French scuttle their heavy ships or that they be sunk by British naval action. Two other options were always on the table – that the French sail their heavy ships to a British port or that they sail them to a neutral or American port well away from European waters.[61]

Churchill's resolute stand was determined by two factors. One, already discussed, was the imbalance of naval power should the Germans take over all or some of the French ships. The second was political. At the same time that decisions were being made about the French ships the oleaginous Rab Butler had re-entered the scene in a most disagreeable manner. On 17 June he had met the Swedish ambassador, Bjorn Prytz, 'by chance', and invited him back to the Foreign Office.[62] In the course of the meeting Butler was called out by Halifax, who told him to tell Prytz that British policy would be dictated by 'common sense and not emotion', a direct slap at Churchill. Prytz relayed this message to his government and it was perhaps via an intercept of this telegram that Churchill got wind of these conversations. He felt it necessary to remind Halifax that 'the present Government and all its Members were resolved to fight on to the death' and that the 'odd language' used by Butler to the Swedes was taken by them as defeatism and that he must find out what actually was said.[63] This was as much a warning to Halifax as to Butler and the Foreign Secretary moved quickly to reassure Churchill that the matter had been settled. Churchill did not follow up on the affair, but Butler would not last long at the Foreign Office.[64] Here, then, was another reason for firm action. Churchill again needed to demonstrate that he would take any measures necessary to keep Britain secure. Not even a hint of parley, especially at a time when the French were talking to the Germans, would be tolerated.

There was a potential glitch in British policy towards the French. In a paper presented to the Chiefs of Staff by the Joint Planning Committee on 29 June the Planners worried about the implications of taking hostile action against the French Fleet. They thought a declaration of war by France might follow and concluded that 'we do not consider that the destruction of these French ships by force would be justified'.[65] These objections were swept aside by the Chiefs of Staff themselves. In their view the danger of the ships falling into German hands outweighed all other considerations. They also pointed out that any contemplated action taken would have to be swift to enable the forces in the Mediterranean to return to home waters to counter a German invasion threat.[66]

The French and British naval forces now began to gather. The new, yet to be finished, battleship *Richelieu* was at Dakar in West Africa from where it had attempted a breakout to home waters on 25 June but was shadowed by British ships and promptly returned to its base. The other super-modern battleship (the *Jean Bart*) was at Casablanca where it was also under watch by British cruisers. There were about 200 craft, including two old battleships, some cruisers, destroyers and submarines in British home waters, and finally there was a squadron of ships (one battleship, four cruisers, two destroyers and a number of smaller ships) at Alexandria watched by a powerful squadron under Admiral Cunningham. The most dangerous concentration of ships from the British point of view lay at Mers-el-Kabir near Oran in Algeria. These included two modern battlecruisers, *Dunkerque* and *Strasbourg*, two old battleships, *Bretagne* and *Provence*, a seaplane carrier, six large destroyers, seven smaller destroyers and four submarines. Unlike the *Richelieu* and *Jean Bart*, all these units were battleworthy and the speed of the modern battlecruisers made them potentially a deadly weapon against British commerce.[67]

In addition to the 'watching forces' in home waters, Dakar, Casablanca and Alexandria, the British began to concentrate Force H at Gibraltar, commanded by Admiral Somerville. It consisted of the battlecruiser *Hood*, the battleships *Valiant* and *Resolution*, the aircraft carrier *Ark Royal*, two cruisers, 11 destroyers and some submarines. The battleship *Nelson* was on standby in home waters to join Force H if required.[68]

On 30 June the War Cabinet decided that the operation should take place on 3 July and to keep the *Nelson* at home because of the threat of invasion.[69] The next day the Admiralty gave Somerville his instructions – the French Fleet should fight with the British, demilitarise in a British port, scuttle itself or scuttle the ships in situ to British satisfaction.[70] Somerville begged to differ. He put forward some alternatives whereby the French would emerge from the harbour and be 'captured' by Force H, insisting that hostilities between the fleets must be avoided at all costs.[71]

This communication was not greeted kindly by their Lordships who in any case were acting under War Cabinet direction. They told Somerville in the bluntest of terms that force remained an option and that his proposals were not acceptable. However, they did modify the four options to include internment in a neutral harbour, possibly in Martinique.[72]

With these instructions Somerville sailed for Mers-el-Kabir where he arrived at 3 a.m. on 3 July. Captain Holland, the former British Naval Attaché in Paris, was sent in a destroyer to put the alternatives to Admiral Gensoul, the French commander-in-chief at Mers. The day played out as high farce. Gensoul refused to see Holland, who refused to hand his instructions to a French underling. Finally, late in the afternoon, Gensoul changed his mind. Holland showed him the proposals, which Gensoul rejected, emphasising that his orders were to sink his fleet rather than hand it over to the Germans. Holland reiterated that action must be taken immediately. Gensoul then contacted the French Admiralty with the gist of the proposals but omitted the option to sail to Martinique. Meanwhile the Admiralty had intercepted the message from Gensoul to the French authorities, which contained a hint that French reinforcements might be on the way. In other words Somerville might soon have an actual naval battle on his hands. He was therefore ordered to end the affair. Even then Somerville waited for 25 minutes after the ultimatum to Gensoul had expired. He finally opened fire at 5.54 p.m., very late in the day. By the time fire ceased at 6.06 p.m., 1,250 French sailors were dead. The *Bretagne* had blown up, the *Dunkerque* was damaged but not destroyed, the *Provence* had to beach, and other small craft were caught up in the fires that broke out. The *Strasbourg*, however, escaped. Belated and feeble attempts by the British to catch it failed and it arrived safely at Toulon. Elsewhere the *Richelieu* was put out of action for a year by Swordfish torpedo bombers; the *Jean Bart* at Casablanca was discovered to have no ammunition for its main armament; in England most French ships were taken over without bloodshed; and at Alexandria, by a remarkable piece of diplomacy, Cunningham secured the demobilisation of the French squadron without loss of life.[73]

In the event, the main operation had been rather botched, the gunnery had been poor, and the escape of one of the main French units was hardly to Somerville's credit. Much sympathy has been showered on Somerville for what was indeed a most odious task. However, the decision lay with the civilian leadership. It was Somerville's job to carry out its instructions or resign. There has also been much gnashing of teeth and wringing of hands about whether a bloodless compromise could have been reached. Given Gensoul's slavish adherence to Darlan's orders, this is doubtful.

Most of this hand wringing is beside the point. The British could not trust Darlan or indeed any member of the Vichy government, however well intentioned they might have been. In fact most were not at all well intentioned towards Britain and some were looking forward to what they regarded as an imminent British collapse. Churchill could not take naval or any other sensibilities into account in these circumstances. It was his job to secure the survival of Great Britain, which with its dominions and Empire was all that stood between Hitler and European supremacy. So far the United States had talked tough but carried a bundle of twigs, hardly a stance likely to bolster or strike terror into anyone. If sinking the French Fleet furthered those ends, so be it. Moreover, from Churchill's reception in the House of Commons when he announced the news, the House was resolute for action of this kind as well. So, as we will see, were the British people. The scene played out at Mers-el-Kabir was a tragedy, but with the world to play for it was hardly extravagant.

So it was that from 10 May to Mers, Churchill, the War Cabinet and their military advisers did everything they could to keep France in the war. They sent valuable aircraft from home bases to France when requested and eventually sent far more than they had initially considered safe. Even as the French armies behind the Somme began to disintegrate, British fighters and bombers attempted to stem the tide.

Churchill's reaction, had he known of the many uncommitted French fighters, can only be imagined. It is certainly true that Britain could offer little in the way of additional troops. But even if they had been available, the lamentable performance of sections of the French army might well have prevented their commitment as Churchill and other British leaders' confidence in the French suffered one blow after another. Reynaud's decla-ration that the battle was lost on 15 May, Weygand's repeated failure to mount any kind of resolute offensive, and the infiltration of defeatists such as Baudouin and Pétain into the government, all eroded confidence. Nevertheless, Churchill never ceased to encourage and cajole the French into staying in the war, even if that be from one of their colonial outposts. He did this for three reasons. First, he was a great Francophile and hated to see what was happening to the French. Second, he saw the French as a vital part of what he sometimes called Western Christendom and sometimes called simply the West. Third, he realised that it was in Britain's interest to have a major ally still in the fight. The Dominions and Empire could provide some help, but the extensive Empire of the French with what remained of their armed forces could provide more.

Only when Churchill realised that at least some of those forces might be turned on Britain did he determine on a hard line against the Pétain regime. He would blockade the country and sink their fleet. But at the same time he supported De Gaulle and if that partnership went through some turbulent times in the years ahead, Churchill in the end stuck to the leader of the Free French when the Americans were urging that he be ditched. At the end of the war French participation at the Nuremberg trials and the grant of a French occupation zone in Germany owed everything to Churchill. If he could not save the French in 1940, his promise that all would be restored to them came about in 1945, something that De Gaulle never forgot.

CHAPTER 7

HITLER AT THE DOOR
THE INVASION THREAT,
JUNE–OCTOBER 1940

BY MID-JUNE 1940 Hitler had overrun six European countries – Poland, Denmark, Norway, Belgium, the Netherlands and Luxembourg. Only the details of the so-called armistice with France remained before he added the better part of a seventh. Britain stood against him as the only European power of any consequence. Hitler had developed a plan for Poland, a plan for Norway, and two for his sweep across Western Europe. Surely he would have a plan for Britain.

The British certainly thought so. The day before the Dunkirk evacuation commenced the Chiefs of Staff warned that a German invasion from Norway, from Eire, or across the Channel could not be ruled out, and that air patrols of the east and south coasts should be instituted immediately.[1]

It would have surprised the British to learn that in June the Germans were yet to develop an invasion plan. But events in the west had moved in ways not anticipated by Hitler or the German high command. They considered, not without reason, that if the Allied armies were overwhelmed, armistices all round would follow. But the BEF had not been overwhelmed. At times it had been comprehensively outmanoeuvred and at times comprehensively outfought, but it had maintained cohesion and had been evacuated more or less intact, albeit without most of its equipment. With the Channel, the nucleus of an army, the navy and the RAF for protection, with Halifax neutered and Churchill firmly in control, there was no sign from the British that they wished to join the French in coming to terms with Hitler. A rather bemused Führer realised that a plan to subdue Britain would indeed be required but not until France had been conquered.

Only the most rudimentary planning for an invasion of Britain had been undertaken by the Germans by June 1940. In the late autumn of 1939 Admiral Raeder, the head of the German navy, had ordered the naval staff to investigate the problem in case Hitler decided to invade Britain. A special section of the naval staff set to work and came up with plan 'Northwest'. They thought a landing 'possible' but only if the Royal Navy and the RAF had been largely eliminated.[2] This paper was not circulated and the navy soon had other matters on its mind, such as the preparations for the Norway expedition. Nothing more was heard of the plan.

Raeder raised the question of an invasion of Britain with Hitler on 21 May, pointing out the 'exceptional difficulties of such an operation'. Hitler agreed that an invasion would be difficult but made no further comment and issued no instructions.[3] There the matter rested until just before the signing of the armistice with the French. Then on 20 June Raeder again raised the matter with the Führer but again got no response.[4]

Either Raeder's promptings finally had an effect or Hitler got tired of waiting for British peace overtures, for on 2 July the OKW issued a directive from the Führer's headquarters entitled 'Warfare against England'. The directive stated that a landing in England was 'possible' if air superiority and 'certain other necessary conditions' were fulfilled. The three services were asked for their opinions, keeping in mind that the landing would probably take place on a broad front by a force of 25 to 40 divisions.[5]

The period – May–June 1940 – in which no plan against Britain was developed has been seen by some as evidence of Hitler's lack of interest in the whole idea and in any case a period when valuable time was lost. Neither of these interpretations is accurate. Hitler first had to defeat the French armies and establish a safe base along the French coast from which a crucial part of any invasion fleet must sail. This could not be assured until after the armistice with France. Then there was the matter of the French ports. There was never a possibility that an invasion could have been launched immediately after Dunkirk, because all the northern French and Belgian ports had been wrecked. The damage done to Calais, Boulogne,

Dunkirk, Nieuport and Ostend was almost total. Docks had to be rebuilt, harbours cleared of sunken ships, cranes brought in to handle cargo, approach roads repaired. This work could not commence before the fighting stopped. In addition, minefields off the ports had to be swept and a myriad of other tasks undertaken to prepare these places for the vast quantity of shipping that would make up an invasion fleet. Even had Hitler possessed a plan to invade Britain straight after Dunkirk he would have been prevented by these factors from carrying it through.

The OKW directive seems to have caught the navy by surprise. Although Raeder had made what little running there had been, he was perhaps trying to alert Hitler to the dangers of the operation rather than hasten its approval. Now he was being required to undertake detailed planning for it. What is evident in these early discussions amongst the naval staff are the difficulties they foresaw in such an operation. They were quick to point out to the other services that invasion was largely a problem of transportation and that the navy could only guarantee the security of the army if the invasion fleet was confined to a fairly narrow front – identified as being between 1.30° west longitude to 1.30 east. They also emphasised the necessity of obtaining absolute control of the air before the operation was launched.[6]

But with Hitler finally engaged in invasion planning the navy found that many matters passed beyond their control. For example, Hitler insisted that a large number of heavy batteries of guns be placed in the Cape Gris-Nez, Calais and Boulogne area to seal off the flanks of the armada from British naval attack.[7] The naval staff indicated that such batteries would be of limited utility. The guns would not possess the accuracy to hit distant, fast-moving ships. Nor would they be able to fire with sufficient rapidity to 'seal' a flank.[8] On the Führer's orders work on them went ahead anyway.

Nevertheless, Raeder continued to hammer home the difficulties of invasion to Hitler. At a meeting on 11 July he told the Führer that he regarded invasion as a last resort or perhaps a threat that would push Britain into suing for peace. He concluded by saying that he could not himself advocate the landing.[9] Hitler was quick to agree about the difficulty of the operation. He too thought of invasion as a 'last resort'. In any case, before it could be attempted air superiority must be obtained.[10]

In fact Hitler with one exception accepted all Raeders' premises but not his conclusion. The operation would be difficult but the question of whether it would prove too difficult would be decided by Hitler. In the meantime planning for it would go ahead. To ensure that planning started promptly, on 16 July Hitler issued Führer Directive No. 16, 'Preparations for a landing against Britain'. It commenced with the usual Hitlerian rhetoric: 'Since Britain, despite her hopeless military situation, still shows no indications or desire to come to terms with us, I have decided to prepare an invasion, and, if necessary, to carry it out.'[11] What followed had more substance. It was the first detailed exposition of an invasion plan. The landing would take place on a broad front from Ramsgate in the east to Lyme Bay in the west. No time was to be wasted. Preparations were to be completed by mid-August. There were the usual preconditions – the operation was to be launched when air superiority had been obtained, when mine-free channels had been cleared, and when the flanks of the invasion could be secured by minefields and coastal artillery. The three services were to draw up plans for their contributions to the invasion and their commanders would relocate their headquarters to be in close proximity to advanced Führer headquarters. The operation was to be called Seelöwe (Sea Lion).[12]

Joint planning meetings began on the next day but the navy entered them with the greatest trepidation. The naval staff had read the Führer's directive and commented that 'the Army regard the whole operation as entirely practicable, undoubtedly lacking knowledge of the difficulties in regard to sea transport and its protection and the exceptional danger to the whole Army'.[13]

This apprehension only increased when the navy read the army's draft plan. The army intended to land in three main groups – the first between Ramsgate and Dover, the second between Dover and the Isle of Wight, and the third to the west of the Isle of Wight around Lyme Bay.[14] Raeder immediately protested that the navy could not guarantee a crossing on such a broad front. He warned the army that they might lose their entire force and that in any case preparations could not be completed until the end of August or early September. He returned to the question of keeping channels clear of mines and the fact that air superiority was not yet in sight.[15]

The meeting broke up without any clear direction but Raeder now thought it necessary to produce a detailed appreciation from the navy's point of view. The paper was decidedly downbeat. He began by noting that the navy was being given a task 'out of all proportion to its forces'. Raeder then went on to list the difficulties:

- The limited capacity and damaged condition of the Channel ports
- The uncertainty of weather conditions in the Channel
- The fact that as the enemy harbours were defended the troops would have to be landed on open beaches
- Beach landings would require shallow draft ships which would have to be modified to suit these conditions
- The difficulty of sweeping enemy minefields in the Channel and keeping channels swept in the face of enemy naval superiority
- The impossibility, even with minefields and defensive gun fire, of keeping units of the Royal Navy from entering the Channel
- The difficulty of re-supply given the above circumstance.[16]

Raeder's gloomy prognosis was well founded. The German navy had been shattered by the campaign in Norway. In July 1940 it had no serviceable heavy units at all. The *Scharnhorst* and *Gneisenau* had been damaged in Norway and would take some months to repair. The *Bismarck* and *Tirpitz* were still under construction and the two Great War vintage battleships were not thought sufficiently strong to fight even the cruisers of the British Home Fleet. Just two cruisers and 13 destroyers were available to escort the invasion fleet. Raeder knew that the British would have at least a dozen cruisers and 40 or 50 destroyers to deploy against him in the first instance, and even greater numbers in the days that followed.[17]

A meeting between Hitler and Raeder took place to discuss the naval appreciation. Hitler took Raeder's paper seriously. A recent paper on invasion by Alfred Jodl from OKW had described the operation as being in the nature of an 'opposed river crossing'.[18] Hitler was having none of this. He described the operation as 'an exceptionally daring undertaking . . . *not just a river crossing* but the crossing of a sea which is dominated by the enemy'.[19] A force of 40 divisions would be required, as would the subjection of the enemy air force. The Führer accepted Raeder's point that September would be the earliest possible date for invasion and he asked the navy to work towards that date. Hitler was also worried about the broad front of attack and he asked Raeder to what extent he could guard the crossings to the landing areas suggested in the army plan and when the coastal guns would be ready to protect the flanks.[20]

Despite Hitler's misgivings, the navy now knew that it was committed to detailed planning for Sea Lion. The staff met on 22 July and came to the following conclusions. Due to the lack of specialist craft, coastal and river barges by the thousand would need to be assembled to ferry troops across the Channel. Inspections would have to be made of all invasion ports to assess the repairs required to make them functional. The suggested landing places would have to be reconnoitred. Channels in the minefields protecting the British coast would have to be swept. All this would take time.[21]

Before any of these matters could be resolved the navy was rocked by receiving for the first time the detailed number of troops the army considered would be required for the invasion. The army envisaged an operation in three phases. The first phase would involve the transportation of an initial force of 100,000 men, with appropriate equipment, including artillery and tanks. This force would rapidly be followed by a second wave of 90,000 men, also with heavy equipment. Finally, there would be a third wave of 160,000 men with appropriate equipment.[22] In all about 350,000 men plus equipment would have to be landed along the British coast from Ramsgate to Lyme Bay in a period of three days.[23]

An analysis by the naval staff of these requirements revealed the following: a total of 1,722 coastal or river barges, 471 tugs, 1,161 motor boats and 155 transport ships would be required – in all 2 million tons of shipping. Such a mass of shipping could not be assembled in the invasion ports at the same time because of their limited size. Troops and equipment would have to be brought in relays to the Channel ports from as far away as northern Germany. The distances to be travelled and the necessity for a shuttle service to and from the invasion ports would take time. For practical reasons the waves of troops could not be dispatched daily but would need to be separated into four or five echelons at intervals of two days.[24] The army wanted the troops transported in three days; the navy thought more in terms of three weeks for the first wave to six weeks for all three.

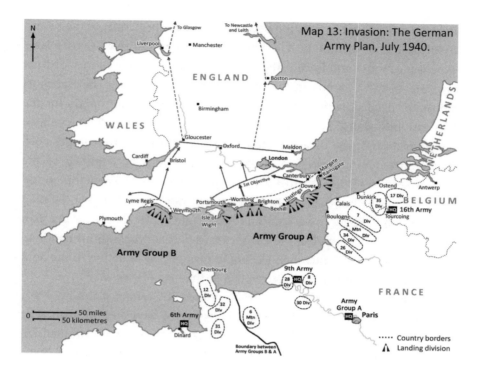

Map 13: Invasion: The German Army Plan, July 1940.

The navy also pointed out that the gathering of this enormous amount of shipping would have important implications for the German war economy. It would disrupt inland and coastal shipping to the extent that vital raw materials such as coal might not be available for steel manufacture.[25] Twenty-four thousand naval personnel would be required to man the invasion fleet. These could only be found by decommissioning some old battleships and ceasing work on the *Tirpitz*, and reducing the crews from the *Scharnhorst* and *Gneisenau* now in dry-dock.[26]

Notwithstanding these difficulties, Hitler ordered preparations to continue and on 31 July Raeder could report that invasion plans were in 'full swing'. The conversion of river and coastal barges for a sea crossing would be completed by the end of August; the conversion of merchant shipping for the invasion fleet was proving 'difficult', but progress was being made and the entire fleet should be ready for a landing in mid-September.[27]

However, after this rather optimistic assessment, Raeder went on to enter some severe caveats about the feasibility of the army plan. A landing in Lyme was out of the question because of its close proximity to the British naval base at Portsmouth. The barges would be required to cross large expanses of water and for this the seas had to be absolutely calm, a distinct problem in the Channel in the second half of September. The transport ships also needed calm weather to transfer their load onto barges for the final run into shore. The small resources at the disposal of the navy made the protection of the invasion force across such a wide front impossible. Raeder strongly suggested to Hitler that operations be confined to the narrow section of the Channel despite the difficulties he knew this would cause for the army, because, after all, the first essential was to get the men ashore safely.[28] Raeder's advice should have told Hitler that the army plan was totally impractical, but the Führer insisted that preparations continue for a landing on 15 September. He would reassess the situation in the light of what the Luftwaffe could accomplish in the next few weeks.[29]

Hitler's last point raises one of the oddities of German planning. Most discussions about Sea Lion took place between the navy and the army. The Luftwaffe, in the person of Hermann Goering or any senior air commander, was absent. The air force plan will be discussed in some detail in later chapters but it is necessary to note here that it was never integrated with the planning of the other two services. The Luftwaffe was in essence fighting its own war without relation to invasion. Certainly, the elimination of the RAF was thought to be an essential precondition for invasion by both the army and the navy, but they had other targets they also thought essential to success – the denial of certain ports to enemy warships, the elimination of as many of those warships as possible, the destruction of communications behind the invasion beaches and so on. The Luftwaffe paid very little attention to these requirements. It attacked its own selected targets without reference to the other services. The explanation for this situation is not difficult to find. It seems certain that Hitler and Goering thought that the Luftwaffe alone might bring Britain to its knees. An invasion force would then only be required to sail across the Channel and occupy a defeated country. In this sense the Luftwaffe might solve all the difficulties that were starting to emerge between the army and the navy in their planning sessions.

Essentially their differences boiled down to the broad front versus the narrow front approach. The navy kept insisting that it did not have the craft to protect the flanks of a landing on such a broad front. The army replied that only by landing on a wide front could its divisions deploy for an effective advance after the landing. In the coming weeks many meetings between the services were held without a resolution of these issues. A particularly acrimonious exchange took place on 7 August. Franz Halder stated that the navy's plan to land only on a narrow front each side of Dover was unacceptable. The army must land at least as far west as Brighton because of the difficulty in deploying in the low ground inland from the Dover–Folkestone area. He concluded by saying: 'I utterly reject the Navy's proposal from the point of view of the Army I regard the proposal as complete suicide.'[30]

Only Hitler could resolve these differences, but he preferred to keep his options open. While telling the navy that he understood the difficulties of protecting a landing on a broad front, the Führer ordered preparations to continue for just such an operation.[31] The day after this decision and in response to a desperate plea from the navy for a definite plan to be developed, a compromise was put forward by Jodl at OKW. The operation would be on a narrow front with the addition of two forces to outflank the British divisions between Dover and London. On the left a force of 4,000–5,000 men would be transported from Le Havre to Brighton while on the right a force of 5,000 paratroopers would be dropped in the Deal–Ramsgate area. In preparation for the landings an all-out assault would be made by the Luftwaffe on London to panic the population and block the roads the British intended to use to bring up reserves (Map 14).[32]

Despite some minor adjustments, this was the basis of the final plan. On the right, elements of six divisions from the 16th Army would land between Folkestone and Beachy Head. They would then spread out and seize an initial bridgehead between Hadlow and Canterbury. At the same time, on the left, a force of three divisions from the 9th Army at Le Havre would seize a line from Cuckmere to Brighton and push inland to extend the bridgehead. The paratroopers were eventually given the tasks of landing north of Dover. The initial force with suitable reinforcements would then advance to a line running from Gravesend to west of Portsmouth. Mobile forces would then move to the west of London to isolate the capital and then advance to a line north-east of London, from Maldon in Suffolk to the Severn Estuary in the west.[33] The troops would be landed in four waves. In

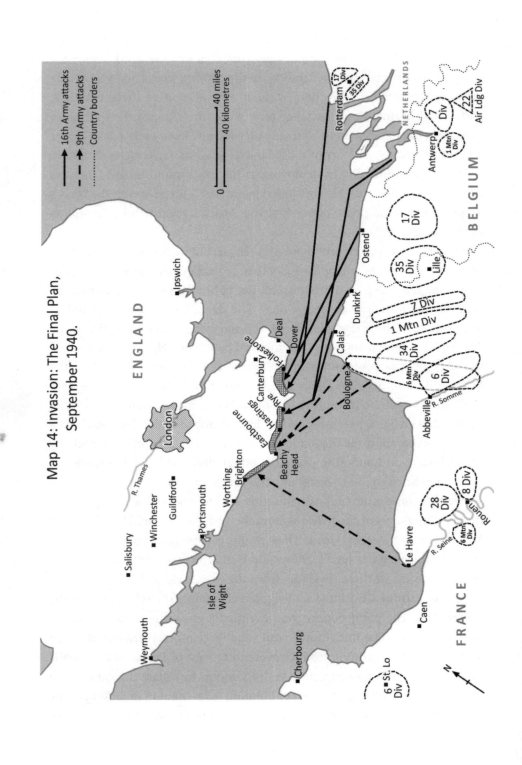

Map 14: Invasion: The Final Plan, September 1940.

the first wave 50,000 men from the nine assault divisions would be landed in the first two hours. The remainder of these divisions (75,000 men) would follow two hours later. After that the plan was to land an additional two divisions every four days so that within four weeks a total of 16 divisions would be ashore. A further nine divisions would constitute the remainder of the third and fourth waves and be ashore by S-Day plus six weeks.[34]

Further discussions and meetings between the Führer, the navy and the army took place in September and October, but this remained the final plan. This raises the question: on the evidence we have, was Hitler serious about Sea Lion or was he, as some historians have suggested, just using the preparations for invasion as a means of exerting pressure on Britain to make peace?

The scale of preparations for Sea Lion makes it extremely unlikely that the operation was merely a giant bluff. It was noted earlier that the collection of shipping placed sections of the German war economy under great strain – hardly an indication that Hitler was bluffing. Moreover, consider the number and scale of the meetings held to thrash out the final plan for Sea Lion: between 25 May and 19 September no fewer than 44 meetings concerning Sea Lion were held – about one meeting every two and a half days. And these meetings often tied up the naval staff, OKH, OKW and the Führer himself. In fact Hitler attended 12 of the 44 meetings. The Führer would not have wasted his time if he was merely intending to deceive. The acrimony resulting between the navy and the army as they fought for their respective plans at these meetings was surely hardly the result of mere posturing. Furthermore, the level of detail contained in the plans – the consignment of particular divisions to particular beaches, the precise assembling of craft at the appropriate ports, the difficulties of landing armour over open beaches and a myriad of other matters discussed – does not suggest that the staffs were merely going through the motions. There are many other indications that Hitler was indeed serious about an invasion. The instruction to the SS to compile a handbook on Britain for the invasion forces looks serious enough. So does the list of persons to be immediately arrested by the Gestapo, with which the handbook concludes.[35]

Much of the myth of Hitler's invasion 'bluff' can be traced back to those who have suggested that the Führer thought well of the British and had no wish to conquer them. This is nonsense. Hitler hated the British and there is little question that had he succeeded in his plans, Great Britain would have been subjected to the reign of the Gestapo, the SS and his other instruments of oppression – as had happened in Western Europe. Indeed, this occupation might in some ways have been harsher than that imposed upon the French, for of all his contemporary enemies Hitler feared the British the most. In this scenario it is impossible to imagine that he would have allowed even the pseudo-autonomy that the Vichy-controlled section of France was granted. Once Britain was in Hitler's grip he would surely have crushed it out of existence.

* * * * *

How well would the British have withstood a German invasion had it been launched? What anti-invasion plans had the three services made and what progress had been achieved from June to September in implementing these plans?

Let us start with a discussion of the state of the army after Dunkirk. It was desperate. After the evacuations from Dunkirk and western France there were just over 500,000 fighting men in Britain, but they lacked equipment of all kinds.[36] The divisions possessed just 295 of the 25-pounder guns as against the establishment figure of 1,368.[37] For Matilda tanks (the only tank of proven worth against the Germans) the establishment figure of 1,480 compared starkly with the actual number of 140.[38] All other equipment was in short supply. There were several score of Great War vintage 18-pounder guns and some 4.5-inch howitzers, but there were few anti-tank guns, armoured cars and mortars. There was not even a rifle for every infantryman.[39] The Army Council noted that in the crucial invasion area between the Wash and the Isle of Wight just five divisions were spread along the coast and there were only three in GHQ Reserve. These under-equipped units would surely have been brushed aside had the Germans got ashore in numbers in this period.

The commander-in-chief of this force was General Ironside, replaced by General Dill as Chief of the Imperial General Staff but perhaps now in a more appropriate role. In these early days he had few resources to work with and his anti-invasion plan reflected that situation. Ironside issued a paper on 'Preparations for Defence' on 4 June. Some 50,000 anti-tank mines were to be placed opposite the most likely landing beaches along the south and eastern coasts. Another 200,000 of these were ordered to cover *all* beaches in the area from the Wash to Portsmouth. Work commenced on rendering useless any potential drop zones for parachutists and glider-borne troops. Road bridges near ports were prepared for demolition and roadblocks were established to slow the progress of enemy armour. A total of 47 batteries of 6-inch guns were installed near likely landing places as were some batteries of anti-tank guns. Guns were also fitted to lorries to provide at least some mobile artillery.[40] Most of these units were in place by mid-June.

Meanwhile, inland, what became known as the GHQ Line was developed. This position stretched from south of London to the Midlands and followed defensive positions such as waterways, canals or the reverse slopes of hills. Essentially it consisted of an array of anti-tank obstacles placed to intercept any German armour that broke through the coastal crust into the interior. The 'line' was supplemented by a number of forward positions consisting of anti-tank guns, machine guns and infantry that were designed to confine, break up and delay enemy forces advancing from the coast before they reached the GHQ Line. This would give Ironside time to deploy mobile columns, consisting of what few armoured cars, tanks and truck-borne infantry he had in GHQ Reserve, against any German lodgement areas.[41]

On paper, the manpower at Ironside's disposal looked adequate. The number of fighting men had increased from 500,000 at the end of May to 1,270,000 by mid-June. But over half of these were still in training. This left just 595,000 trained troops and of these 275,000 had just returned from France and were almost entirely without equipment.[42]

Despite Ironside's efforts the whole defensive position of the British army was very weak. The roadblocks could easily have been circumvented by armoured vehicles as could the stop lines. Many of the anti-tank positions in the GHQ Line existed largely on paper. The mobile columns were few in number and deficient in armour. Yet it is hard to see what other dispositions Ironside could have made given the state of training of his force and its lack of equipment.

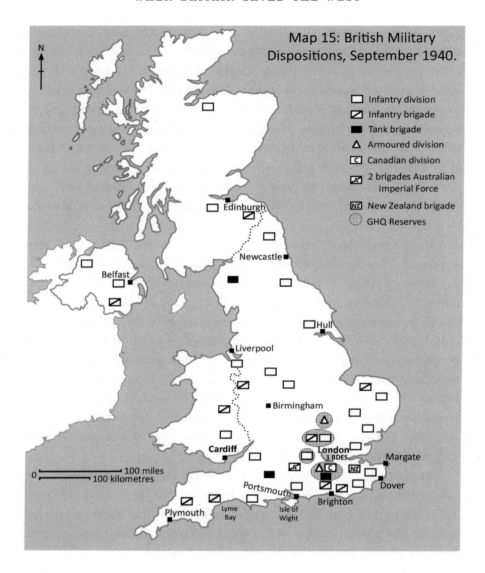

Map 15: British Military Dispositions, September 1940.

Infantry division
Infantry brigade
Tank brigade
Armoured division
Canadian division
2 brigades Australian Imperial Force
New Zealand brigade
GHQ Reserves

Churchill soon tired of what he considered Ironside's conservative approach and on 20 July replaced him with General Brooke. This was a harsh judgement given the little with which Ironside had to work. However, there is no doubt that Brooke was a good choice and a better leader if an invasion was to take place.[43] He embarked on a lightning tour of his forces, finding them, as a whole, not very impressive.[44]

Brooke was also unhappy with the static nature of the defences and was no doubt relieved to receive a note from Churchill assuring him that the navy now had sufficient vessels at sea at any given time to rule out a surprise attack on a large scale. In this circumstance he thought Brooke could withdraw some of his forces back from the coast for training.[45] Brooke, who envisaged only a light defence on the beaches, was only too happy to comply.

With the army growing to just over 900,000 reasonably well-trained men (including one Canadian division and two Australian brigades), the main constraint continued to be equipment.[46] The number of 25-pounder guns in the country had only increased from the 295 in June to 368 in August.[47] Matilda tank numbers had only increased from 140 to 216. The 200 lighter cruiser tanks were also well short of the numbers required.[48]

Gradually, though, the state of the army improved. In early September the five divisions that in June had held the coast between the Wash and the Isle of Wight had increased to eight, and in addition there were two brigades and one brigade group in the area. And in the close vicinity of London were another three divisions, two armoured divisions and two brigade groups. Included in these forces were the 1 Canadian Division, the New Zealand Division and the Australian Brigade group, so an invasion would have involved a Commonwealth response.[49]

Brooke, however, still took a pessimistic view of the situation, regarding only 50 per cent of his divisions as fit for any form of mobile combat.[50] The responsibility of command weighed heavily upon him and he had been seared by his experiences against the German army in France. On the positive side his dispositions were well placed to oppose the most likely German lodgement areas and by September the nucleus of the old BEF was reasonably well equipped. For example, by then each of its 12 infantry divisions had 80 guns of all types, well below the establishment figure but at least able to put down a reasonable volume of fire.[51] And each month that passed saw the munitions factories produce another 220 field-artillery pieces.[52]

However, in the event of a major invasion there is no doubt that Brooke's pessimism would have been well founded. Had the Germans managed to land their projected number of 100,000 troops plus armour along the southern English coast in the first few hours of an invasion, the British forces would have had a difficult time dislodging them. But the vital question was whether the Germans would have been able to land such a force in the light of British naval superiority.

The Dunkirk operations had taken their toll on the navy. Of the main anti-invasion craft, nine destroyers and five minesweepers had been sunk, and 19 destroyers, one anti-aircraft cruiser and seven minesweepers damaged.[53] In addition, over the next few months some powerful naval craft had been diverted from home waters for other purposes. In July, after the French had concluded their armistice with Germany, concerns had arisen in the War Cabinet about the strong French Fleet in the Mediterranean. The naval action that eliminated much of the French Fleet has already been dealt with, but here it is important to note its effect on the Home Fleet. To build up a force at Gibraltar strong enough to deal with the French, first the aircraft carrier *Ark Royal* and then the battlecruiser *Hood* followed by the battleship *Valiant* had been dispatched from the Home Fleet to the Mediterranean.[54] So for some weeks in July the commander-in-chief of the Home Fleet, Admiral Forbes, was deprived of three of his best capital ships.

Another diversion occurred in September when an expedition sailed to West Africa to assist the Free French in claiming the colony of Senegal and its capital and naval base, Dakar. A successful action, so it was thought, might rally the entire French Empire to the Allied cause and consolidate the position of General de Gaulle. It was also feared by the Admiralty that enemy forces might use Dakar as a base from which to interrupt British convoys, though this seemed to overlook the difficulty that enemy ships would have had in reaching them across waters dominated by the Royal Navy. In fact there was never an attempt by the Germans to hazard such a move. Nevertheless two battleships, an aircraft carrier, three cruisers and 10 destroyers accompanied the expedition and were therefore absent from Gibraltar from 7 September until early October.[55] In the event the expedition was a total failure. French forces at Dakar, including the battleship *Richelieu*, put up such a stiff fight that the expedition was forced to withdraw. In retrospect the decision that deprived the Home Fleet of reinforcement by such a powerful squadron seems bizarre. The fact that the danger was noted by the Assistant Chief of the Naval Staff before it sailed cut no ice.[56] The operation was approved by Churchill. He was perhaps fortunate that the failure at Dakar was swift and came at a time when Hitler was reconsidering the whole question of invasion.

In the meantime the navy honed its anti-invasion strategy. This process was not without some friction. Admiral Forbes had strong views on the use of his heavy vessels in the event of an invasion. He thought that they should remain at Scapa Flow to counter an enemy attempt to break out into the Atlantic or invade Eire.[57] The Admiralty staff thought that at least some heavy units should be placed further south for anti-invasion duties.[58] After an acrimonious exchange of telegrams the naval staff won. Forbes would base a force of battlecruisers at Rosyth 'as soon as possible'.[59]

There was further dissent from Forbes. When told about the plans of the army and the RAF to counter invasion, he seized on the strength of the RAF to conclude that an invasion was extremely unlikely.[60] As it happened, Forbes was probably correct, but such a conclusion was not his to make. It took a minute from the Vice Chief of the Naval Staff to pull Forbes into line. He was told that his ships should be optimally disposed to meet a seaborne attack[61] and to act on the basis that an invasion was likely.[62]

This was the end of that matter but another soon arose. Forbes, it was now revealed, regarded German warships as his main target should an encounter occur in the south, rather than any transports carrying the German army towards the English coast. This time it took just a single acerbic minute to redirect his policy. The Admiralty informed him that '*in case of invasion repetition in case of invasion* . . . attack on enemy transports and landing craft becomes primary object, enemy warships being dealt with only in so far as they interfere'.[63]

Despite these distractions, the navy plan was rapidly developed. Warships would attack the German invasion fleet before it departed, on the way across and at the point or points of arrival. In the first phase the navy assumed they would have some advance intelligence of the gathering enemy force from aerial reconnaissance and observation from patrolling ships. They would attack these forces with naval craft where possible and call on Bomber Command to assist.

When the force was under way the navy would rely on four flotillas of destroyers (about 40 ships) assembled between the Humber and Portsmouth. These could be reinforced by battleships based at Plymouth and cruiser squadrons in the Thames Estuary and the Humber, minesweepers, corvettes and any other small craft with offensive capability. Any enemy force that effected a landing would be attacked by small inshore craft while the main strike force would attempt to interdict any enemy reinforcements in the Channel or the east coast.[64] And once the Admiralty had won out over Forbes, the heavy units of the Home Fleet would be in close attendance as reinforcements where required.

The other aspect of planning that concerned the navy was the seizure of a port by the Germans. Only at a port, it was considered, would the enemy be able to land tanks in any number and considering what had happened in France it was imperative to keep this number to a minimum. During June naval officers were dispatched to all major ports between Aberdeen and Swansea. Their main task was to develop a plan to immobilise those sections of the ports useful for offloading tanks and other vehicles for a period of 7 to 10 days, by which time it was thought that the army would have dealt with the invaders. Then the ports could resume their normal duties. These plans were well in hand by the end of the month, but the fine-tuning of the planned demolition works was problematic. To close certain sections of a port temporarily would have been difficult to calibrate – putting the entire port out of action was much easier. Clearly some ports would have been totally demolished on invasion and out of action for much longer than a week or so. But on the positive side it is very doubtful whether a usable port could have been seized by the invaders. In all likeli-hood they would have been forced to land tanks, trucks and other vehicles over open beaches.[65]

To make ports even more difficult for an enemy to use, blockships were to be sunk at the entrance to harbours, making it hard for enemy follow-up forces to enter. These too were supposed to be temporary arrangements, with the ships being lifted out of the channels when the threat was over. As with demolition, it is doubtful whether this would have worked as smoothly as anticipated. Clearly many English harbours would have been out of action for some time, but the main purpose of denying the ports to the enemy had an excellent chance of success.[66]

This basic plan remained in force throughout the invasion period. By August a truly formidable array of anti-invasion craft was in place. At Scapa Flow were two battleships, two aircraft carriers and a battlecruiser, with attendant cruiser, destroyer and minesweeping squadrons. Further south were elements of 18th Cruiser Squadron at Rosyth where there were also 13 anti-aircraft destroyers. On the Humber were six destroyers, while

1 Chamberlain and Halifax with the Italians at Munich, 1938. This was the group that Halifax wanted to meet in 1940 to discuss peace terms.

2 The key players in the Cabinet Crisis of May 1940, apart from Churchill are Attlee, Greenwood, Halifax and Chamberlain, with Archie Sinclair having a walk-on part. Note the absence of Chamberlain and Halifax.

3 Bren Gun Carriers of the 13/18 Hussars near Arras.

4 Matilda Tanks of the 4th Royal Tank Regiment. This unit would shock the German command in the Arras counter-attack on 21 May.

5 British Tanks cross into Belgium, 10 May 1940 thus implementing the first phase of the disastrous Plan D.

6 Lord Gort and his nominal superior, General Georges inspect British troops. Gort soon found the French command structure chaotic and ineffectual.

7 Devastation at Dunkirk. Nevertheless, the bulk of the BEF escaped capture.

8 Officers of the Royal Ulster Rifles awaiting evacuation from an improvised pier at Bray Dunes.

9 British troops boarding a destroyer at the Mole, Dunkirk.

10 Paul Reynaud in 1940. The French Premier was overwhelmed by the crisis that destroyed the Third Republic.

11 The destruction of the French Fleet at Mers-el-Kebir.

12 Concrete blocks at a bridge on the GHQ Line.

13 Britain's answer to a Panzer Division, June 1940.

14 How British ships were guarded whilst in port.

15 Winston Churchill meets infantrymen manning coast defences, July 1940. No aspect of invasion planning escaped the eye of the Prime Minister.

16 Invasion Planning Conference at the Berghof, July 1940. Hitler and Admiral Raeder in discussion with Field Marshal Brauchitsch and General Jodl.

17 Troops of the Australian 6th Division cross Westminster Bridge, June 1940. Troops from Australia, Canada and New Zealand were given key roles in British invasion planning.

18 Sea Lion: a chilling photograph of German invasion barges at Boulogne.

19 Hurricanes of 85 Squadron. Note the three plane 'Vic' or 'V' formations.

20 Spitfires of 65 Squadron taking off from a grass strip at Hornchurch, August 1940.

21 Sir Keith Park. His tactical genius ensured that his pilots won the Battle of Britain.

22 Sir Hugh Dowding. His cautious strategy meant that the Battle of Britain could not have been lost.

23 After the raid on Coventry, 14/15 November 1940.

24 Defiance in the London Blitz.

25 Normal services will be resumed. Men of the London Electric Supply Corporation at an air raid site.

26 A defused parachute mine in Glasgow, March 1941. Its great size made this one of the most feared German bombs.

27 Herman Goering addresses German pilots during the Battle of Britain. The head of the Luftwaffe failed to develop a plan to defeat the RAF.

28 Henry Morgenthau Jr. Roosevelt's treasurer demanded all aid for Britain but at a price.

29 Harold Ickes. Roosevelt's Minister for Labor was shocked at his chief's supine attitude towards aid to Britain.

30 Not yet a Special Relationship. Roosevelt talked tough but did little to aid Britain in this period.

at Harwich there were 10 destroyers, three corvettes and 13 motor torpedo boats. On the Thames estuary at Sheerness were seven destroyers. Along the south coast were three more destroyer flotillas (just over 20 ships), a collection of motor torpedo boats, an aircraft carrier, and a miscellaneous collection of other warships. There was also a strong force of destroyers based at Liverpool and the Clyde, and more fighting ships at Chatham, Portland, Hull, Greenock and other ports. Nearby were several flotillas of submarines and the armed merchant vessels of the northern patrol. This is not to mention hundreds of armed sloops and patrol vessels scattered around the coast but concentrated mainly along the eastern and southern coasts. Moreover, at Gibraltar just 36 hours away were the two battleships, two battlecruisers and an aircraft carrier from Force H.[67] There were some weaknesses. There was still only cruisers based at Rosyth and the attentions of the Luftwaffe had forced the destroyer flotilla at Dover to redeploy to Harwich or Portsmouth and be replaced with a few motor torpedo boats.[68] But despite these weaknesses this was a mighty force, especially at a time when the Germans had not a single heavy ship available, just one heavy cruiser, 13 destroyers and a few motor torpedo boats.

In the event this force was never required to thwart an invasion, but there were some alarms. On 13 August (Eagle Day for the Luftwaffe) the increased aerial activity and a German feint with a collection of merchant vessels towards the northern coast brought the Home Fleet to two hours' notice.[69] Then, on 7 September, the code word for invasion, *Cromwell*, was issued. The heavy ships of the Home Fleet put to sea, raising steam for 24 knots. An invasion was expected imminently and the force with its attendant cruisers and destroyers headed into the North Sea. The Admiralty advised Forbes that the scheme to immobilise the ports should be brought to the shortest possible notice.[70] But it was a false alarm based on the movement of German barges towards the Channel.[71] The last major alarm occurred on 13 September. The Admiralty signalled Forbes:

All evidence points to attempted invasion on a large scale and we must expect that Germany will throw everything into it including every capital ship they can make available. Taking everything into consideration following dispositions of capital ships is considered necessary: (i) *Nelson, Rodney* and *Hood* at Rosyth; (ii) *Repulse* and 8-inch cruisers at

Scapa; (iii) *Revenge* at Plymouth. It is realised that this disposition is weaker than present one for dealing with operations against Iceland or Ireland, but this is accepted . . . Request you move *Nelson* and *Hood* to Rosyth as soon as possible.[72]

Nothing came of this, but it provides evidence that in an emergency the deployment of Forbes' heavy ships would be decided by the Admiralty.

The air force plan was developed with just one hitch. The Admiralty and the RAF seemed to have different priorities for fighter aircraft during an invasion. At an inter-service meeting Admiral Drax, commander-in-chief of Nore Command, asked the RAF what role Fighter Command would play in the invasion. Group Captain Lawson, the RAF liaison officer, replied that its primary object would be 'the destruction of the invading enemy aircraft'.[73] This alarmed Drax. It seemed that the RAF would attack the enemy warplanes and leave his warships unprotected. In the end it was agreed that Drax would contact Hugh Dowding of Fighter Command to clarify the position.[74] Drax lost no time, writing to Dowding at the end of the meeting. He told him that the anti-invasion forces would be mainly destroyer flotillas which would be very vulnerable to air attack and that 'they will be defeated by the enemy bombers if our fighters are not on the spot to attack them'.[75] Dowding replied that he considered the whole issue of such importance that it must be discussed by the Chiefs of Staff Committee, but his own opinion was that the fighters would indeed cover the navy's warships while the bombers attacked their transports.[76] Not surprisingly, when the issue came before the Chiefs of Staff they agreed with Dowding. The navy would be protected by Fighter Command.[77]

With that issue decided, the air force developed its plan. Its first duty was to fly regular reconnaissance flights to give early warning of concentrations of enemy shipping in ports from the Baltic to Cherbourg. This task fell to Coastal Command. Should such concentrations be discovered, Bomber Command was to bomb them while continuing to bomb communications between Germany and the invasion ports. When the invasion commenced, bombers escorted by fighters would attack the enemy transports. The majority of fighters would provide protection for the navy against attack by enemy aircraft. Enemy troops would be attacked on the beaches and any counter-attack forces be given fighter protection. If the enemy should land, the priorities established by Fighter Command were:

1. attack dive-bombing aircraft operating against naval forces
2. attack tank-carrying aircraft (in fact the Germans had none of these)
3. attack troop-carrying aircraft
4. attack enemy bombers
5. attack enemy fighters

On 8 July 1940 Britain had 720 serviceable modern single-engine fighters and about 500 bombers with which to carry out these duties.

That the British armed forces would be kept up to the mark and that their chiefs would undergo constant prodding on almost every critical issue regarding invasion was the self-imposed task of the Prime Minister and Minister of Defence. Churchill kept the closest possible oversight of invasion preparations. So ubiquitous were his demands that General Brooke feared that should the invasion come, the Prime Minister would use his position as Minister of Defence to assume supreme command of all the armed forces.[78]

Churchill demanded information on all aspects of invasion planning. In just one memorandum he asked the Chiefs of Staff to provide him with statistics on enemy tank-carrying barges, urged Ironside to hold more troops in reserve, sought assurances that the destroyer forces would attack the barges 'with gusto', and came to the sensible conclusion that 'the power of the Navy remains decisive against any serious invasion'.[79]

One of his abiding obsessions was to establish batteries of heavy guns near Dover to strike at an invasion fleet and to strike back at the enemy batteries erected at Hitler's insistence around Boulogne and Calais. In fact such guns were not very useful. At these distances they would have to be fortunate to hit stationary targets more than twice in a hundred shots, by which time the barrels of the guns would have been worn down to such an extent as to require replacement. Nevertheless, Churchill insisted that they be installed. He wrote to Ismay on 21 June asking for a report and followed this up with requests as to progress on 7 July, 15 July and 5 August.[80] On 8 August he was pleased to hear that a 14-inch gun had been mounted but then fretted because there seemed to be no plan to attack the German guns systematically.[81] On 1 September he was 'deeply concerned' that the German guns could not be engaged until 16 September and he demanded a more rapid response.[82] In fact firing began the day before and continued sporadically throughout the invasion period. Little damage was done in these long-range duels, either to shipping in the Channel or to the enemy batteries. Air power was now the key to controlling the Straits of Dover.[83]

Other interventions by Churchill were more useful. He decried the many papers produced by various services suggesting that the Germans might strike at England through an invasion of Eire. In response to one such paper he informed Ismay that 'it is not at all likely that a naval descent will be effected there'. He thought it might be possible for the Germans to transport some paratroopers to southern Island but that in any case 'nothing that can happen in Ireland can be immediately decisive'.[84]

Churchill's views on Ireland, as well as calming the Chiefs of Staff, had strategic consequences. In June the military had decided that two fully equipped divisions should be sent to Northern Ireland to counter any German moves against the south. Churchill deplored this action. At the time fully equipped divisions were rare and he wanted them to remain near the shores most threatened with invasion.[85] Nevertheless, the Chiefs of Staff decided to send Montgomery's 3 Division to Belfast. Somehow Chamberlain got wind of this scheme and brought it to Churchill's attention. The matter was discussed in Cabinet on 2 July. Representing the Chiefs, the Chief of the Air Staff said the movement of the division had been 'carefully weighed up' and that they had decided to send it because 'the threat to this country resulting from a German invasion of Ireland is a very serious one'.[86] Churchill strongly disagreed and in the end the War Cabinet 'agreed that the Third Division should not be sent to Northern Ireland'.[87]

A second intervention by Churchill prevented 2 Canadian Division being deployed to Iceland. Three battalions of this first-rate formation had already been dispatched when Churchill found out and he ordered Anthony Eden to stop the whole process as the troops were needed in England. Needless to say the Canadians remained.[88]

Even after Brooke's appointment as commander-in-chief of Home Forces, Churchill was not content just to read reports on the progress of re-equipping the army. He constantly toured divisions and interrogated commanders about their requirements. One such visit paid dividends. Montgomery's 3 Division was occupying a key sector of the southern coast but it was strung out along the beaches and had no transport for those reserves held back to intervene at the invasion points. Montgomery asked Churchill for civilian buses to be supplied for this purpose. The following day Churchill minuted Eden to request the buses. They were delivered with all speed.[89]

Indeed, there was hardly an aspect of the invasion problem that Churchill did not investigate. He was concerned that desperately needed rifles coming from the US were adequately convoyed, that the anti-invasion destroyers had sufficient ammunition, that tank production was lagging, or that fog might prevent the navy from responding to an invasion with appropriate vigour.[90]

One matter that was to cause much controversy later was Churchill's position on the use of poison gas on an invading army. As early as June he asked Ismay to report on what stocks of mustard gas and other variants Britain held and whether the substances could be delivered by guns, air bombs or by aerial spraying. He asked for output by month and concluded that 'there would be no need to wait for the enemy to adopt such methods. He will certainly adopt them if he thinks it will pay.'[91] In other words Britain would in the event of an invasion use what gas it had on the German army the minute it touched ground. The fact was, however, that there would have been little gas available. There were few gas shells, so the main method of delivery would have been to spray the gas (which was in the main mustard gas) from the air.[92]

The modern outcry about this decision takes little account of the situation facing the British in 1940. Certainly they could be confident in the superiority of their navy and in the prowess of the RAF, but their army was outnumbered and out-munitioned by the Germans and in general was of inferior skill. If the enemy army gained a foothold in Britain the situation might rapidly become desperate. If poison gas appeared necessary to keep the Nazi army at bay, then there was no doubt that it would have been used. When Churchill spoke of victory at all costs he meant it.

To sum up, by September the British army was well short of its establishment of guns and tanks but was in reasonable shape and was well led. The RAF was also well led and had first-rate fighters available to attack an invasion force. The navy was well led at the lower levels (e.g. destroyer flotillas) that would have played a key role in thwarting an invasion, and in numbers was far superior to the Germans.

The question remains whether the German invasion plan as finally developed could have succeeded. The answer surely must be a resounding no. There has been much futile debate in Britain in recent years about whether the navy or the air force actually thwarted Hitler's designs. There is in fact no need to designate any service as being the vital factor in preventing the German fleet from sailing. Had it sailed, the navy, with more than adequate means of reconnaissance, would have had sufficient warning that the enemy was coming. The arrival of the destroyer flotillas, protected by Fighter Command, could only have had one result. Most of the German barges and their tugs would have been sunk. One calculation suggests that the bow of a destroyer in close proximity to a barge would have created a wave large enough to sink it. Therefore, many destroyers could have performed their anti-invasion role without firing a shot. And in addition to the destroyers the navy also had available cruisers, armed trawlers, corvettes and many other craft. Behind this force stood the heavy units of the Home Fleet, which Churchill would certainly have ordered into action if an invasion was under way. The merchant ships, transferring their cargoes to barges in the Channel, would have been the easiest of targets. It is doubtful whether any could have survived a sustained naval attack. And then there was the matter of the six weeks that the Germans calculated they would require to reinforce the initial waves of attacks. It seems beyond doubt that if any of the second, third or fourth waves had left port, they would have been sunk at some stage during the crossing. In fact, because of the almost certain destruction of the first wave, it is highly unlikely that they would have ventured out. It is of course true that the Luftwaffe would have exacted some toll on the British ships. Some destroyers and other ships would have been sunk by the Germans. But the fact remains that there were just too many British ships for the Germans to forestall the carnage that would have followed.

The inescapable conclusion must be that the German command was well aware of these scenarios. The forces available to them were indeed formidable but not appropriate for an invasion of Britain. The failure to capture the BEF, the failure to subdue the RAF, and the woeful German inferiority at sea were the factors that led Hitler to call off the operation. He would finally turn to the only expedient remaining to him, an attack on the British people. If he could not invade, if Churchill would not see reason, then perhaps a terrified and cowed population would decide the issue.

CHAPTER 8

THE BATTLE OF BRITAIN
THE ANTAGONISTS

ANY ACCOUNT OF THE Battle of Britain must note from the outset the strange nature of the encounter. Consider these points:

- There is no agreement on when the battle started or when it ended.
- For most of the battle a maximum of 50 per cent of the Luftwaffe engaged a maximum of 40 per cent of Fighter Command and usually the numbers were much smaller than that.
- Although almost all the action was in south-east England, for the entire battle 25 per cent of Fighter Command's single-engine fighters were in Scotland.
- Neither side knew the strength of the other. Nor did they establish with any accuracy what damage they were inflicting on each other.
- The Germans had no overall plan to defeat the RAF.
- For any given day of the battle, it is not known with any certainty the number of German aircraft over Britain, nor is it known exactly how many British planes were sent against them.

We will return to many of these matters as the battle is described.

In 1940 the air defence of Great Britain depended on two factors. The first was the performance of two types of single-engine fighters, the Hurricane and the Spitfire, and the skill of the pilots who flew them. The aircraft were outstanding and the pilots who survived their first encounters showed increasing skill as the battle progressed. However, it is doubtful whether Fighter Command could have prevailed had it not been for the second factor. Britain possessed the most sophisticated air-defence weapons system in the world. There were three keys to this system – the gathering of information about incoming raids, the rapid dissemination of this intelligence to the fighting squadrons, and the direction of those squadrons onto the enemy aircraft.

Intelligence of raids was gathered from two sources – radio waves and human observation. In 1935 R. W. Watson-Watt discovered that aircraft passing through radio waves interrupted them and produced a 'blip' on a small cathode-ray screen. This blip could be read with sufficient accuracy to obtain a rough idea of the distance of the aircraft from the screen.[1] In further developments, the direction and the height of the incoming aircraft could be determined, although these measurements were very crude in the initial period.

The practical application of radar began in 1936 when a series of stations (called Chain Home) was built around the British coast. The stations consisted of eight lattice towers standing from 250 to 350 feet high. They looked out to sea and gave the stations a range of 70 to 140 miles (Map 16).[2] At the beginning of the Battle of Britain there were 34 Chain Home stations between Scapa Flow and Pembrokeshire in Wales. To account for low-flying aircraft, a second series of stations called Chain Home Low was constructed along the same stretch of coastline.[3]

The radar stations worked thus. The staff continually scanned the small screens (approximately 5 × 3 inches) for blips that indicated incoming aircraft. After allowing for friendly aircraft that were equipped with an electronic identification device (pip-squeak), they conveyed the information by buried cable to Fighter Command headquarters at Bentley Priory.[4]

The radar chain pointed out to sea where there were no hills and valleys to interrupt the radar signal. Once the raiders had crossed the coast, the Observer Corps would plot their course. This corps consisted of 30,000 men grouped in small dugouts that dotted the country. They were equipped with an aircraft identification chart, binoculars and a telephone. They would telephone information regarding type of aircraft, numbers and course to Bentley Priory or to the nearest Group or Sector airfield.

So Bentley Priory received a huge volume of plots from the Observers and from the radar chain. On the suggestion of Sir Keith Park in his capacity as Dowding's Senior Air Staff Officer (SASO), all these plots were sent to a special operations room to be sorted out or 'filtered'.[5] This was necessary because different radar stations and Observer Corps posts might be plotting the same raid, and the filter room attempted to remove any duplication and sort the plots into discrete raids. It was only 'filtered' information that was sent to the central operations room and displayed.

This display consisted of a huge horizontal gridded map of the United Kingdom. Each raid was assigned a number and a tentative strength, both of which were written on small wooden blocks. The blocks were then placed on the map and pushed across it by members of the Women's Auxiliary Air Force (WAAFs) armed with long croupier-like poles as further information came in. The blocks were also colour coded against a large clock divided into coloured five-minute segments so that it could be seen at a glance when the plot had last been updated.[6]

In a gallery above the map sat a group of men who made decisions based on the plot. The most important was of course Dowding, but it was his Senior Controller who made most of the operational decisions including what plot references would be sent to each of the headquarters of the four fighter Groups into which Britain was divided. Alongside the Senior Controller sat the heads of Anti-Aircraft Command and Balloon Command so that AA batteries and barrage balloon concentrations could also be warned of raiders.

When the plot information reached Group headquarters the first operational decisions were taken, because in Dowding's decentralised system it was the Group that dispatched fighters against particular raids. When Group HQ received the intelligence they would plot it on a gridded map of their own area in the same way that it had been first put on the large map at Fighter Command HQ. The Senior Group Controller would then decide which squadrons from their main or 'Sector' airfields would be most appropriate to intercept the raid. In selecting these squadrons Group HQ was aided by a large display called a Tote Board on the wall of its operation room. This board indicated by a series of coloured lights the state of readiness of the squadrons or whether they had already been dispatched for battle.

Once he had received the signal from Group, the Sector airfield commander would 'scramble' a squadron or squadrons from his airfield or dispatch a force from one of the satellite airfields attached to his sector. Once aloft the fighter force would be directed or 'vectored' onto the incoming raid by the Sector Controller. 'Tally-ho' was the signal from the squadron commander that his aircraft had made contact with the enemy.

The whole system was designed for rapid response to emerging and ever-changing situations. Fighter Command HQ aimed to update plots to Groups every minute and Groups aimed for the same order of speed to Sectors. Once a squadron had been selected to scramble it took several minutes (reduced to 90 seconds later in the battle) to get it airborne. Ideally, then, from the first plot being received at Bentley Priory to 'squadron airborne' would take less than five minutes. In practice, with inexperienced plotters and controllers, it often took longer than that, but as an Me 109 could cross the Channel in two or three minutes, speed was of the essence.

This system had many advantages but undoubtedly the most important was the reduction in the number of standing patrols that had to be flown by Fighter Command. These patrols could consume valuable fuel, tire pilots, and produce wear and tear on the planes without necessarily finding the enemy or bringing them to battle. In 1940 most British squadrons were only dispatched to meet significant threats.

In many accounts the system is described as a near perfect air-defence arrangement. However, despite its relative sophistication it did have some imperfections. The radar chain was a very recent innovation and more stations were being added as the battle commenced. Many of its operators were new to the job and their estimates of the height of a raid or the numbers of aircraft it contained could be wildly inaccurate. Moreover, a large number of hostile aircraft could clutter the small screens aggregating the blips to such an extent as to make the size of a raid a matter of guesswork. At the beginning of the Battle of Britain one to three aircraft could be estimated accurately, four to nine with some degree of accuracy, and 10 and above only very approximately according to the skill of the operator.[7] The estimates of the operators improved as experience was gained but it remained something of a matter of chance until the end of the battle.

Estimates of the height of incoming aircraft were even more inexact than those of numbers. Operators consistently underestimated height, which often led to the intercepting fighters being jumped by their opponents.

The Observer Corps also had its difficulties. In the early days there were many mistakes in aircraft identification and there was the perennial problem of cloud, a common phenomenon over southern England at any time of year. Cloud could also muffle the sound of an enemy formation and allow it to reach its target undetected.

The system had one surprising vulnerability. Sector operations rooms were situated on the airfields in relatively flimsy wooden or brick buildings.[8] It should have been obvious to Fighter Command that at some point in the battle the airfields would be prime targets for the Luftwaffe and that if the sector operations rooms were destroyed a vital link in the intelligence chain would be gone. The obvious solution was to fortify these rooms or put them underground, or to locate them away from airfields where they could still operate quite satisfactorily. Indeed, at the height of the battle some Sector airfields were forced into this expediency without a serious loss of efficiency.

A comment is necessary on the organisation of Groups and Sectors into which Fighter Command was divided. The north of England and Scotland were defended by 13 Group with its headquarters near Newcastle. It had six Sector airfields and guarded the north-east, Scottish industrial zones and Scapa Flow, the base of the Home Fleet. To its south was 12 Group with its headquarters near Nottingham. It too had six Sector airfields, which were placed to defend the industrial Midlands and East Anglia. In the south-west was the newest and smallest of the Groups, No. 10. It had just three Sector airfields (to become four when Middle Wallop was transferred to it once the battle started) and covered the West Country, South Wales, and was always on call to defend such vital targets as Southampton (where the Supermarine works were located) and the ports of Portland and Portsmouth. Its headquarters was at Box, 10 miles east of Bristol.

The most important of all the Groups was No. 11, under the command of Air Vice Marshal Park, which covered south-east England and was closest to the enemy squadrons based in the Pas de Calais. It had seven Sector airfields. It protected the most likely invasion area from Harwich to Portsmouth. Above all, it defended London, which was surrounded by a great circle of Sector airfields – Kenley, Biggin Hill, Hornchurch, North Weald and Northolt. Its headquarters was at Uxbridge (Map 16).

Of the Group commanders, Air Vice Marshal Saul of 13 Group had a reputation as a thorough trainer and an efficient and capable officer. In the west Air Vice Marshal Brand was also thought to be thoroughly professional. His ability to work easily with Park in the neighbouring 11 Group was one of the features of the battle. In contrast was the inability of the

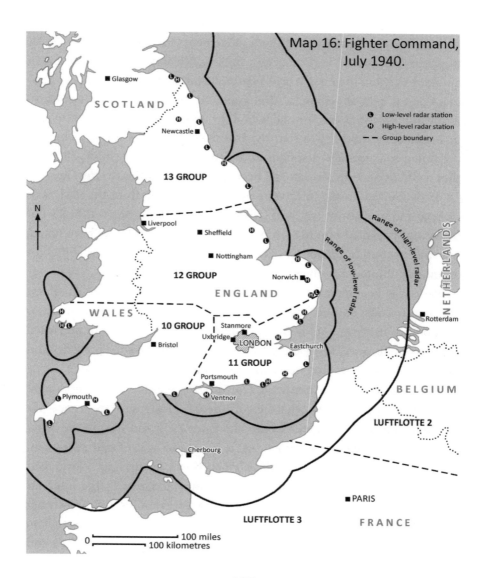

commander of 12 Group, Air Vice Marshal Trafford Leigh Mallory, to work easily with Park. Indeed, as the Battle of Britain wore on, his disagreements with Park gained him a certain notoriety. Whether that reputation was deserved or not will be investigated later.

Air Vice Marshal Park was the key figure in the Battle of Britain. His was the strongest Group, in the most dangerous place and guarding the most important targets. On most days of the battle, 11 Group fought the overwhelming number of combats. It was on Park's judgement that Dowding relied about which squadrons to dispatch and when. It is not an overstatement of the case to say that if these judgements had been poor, the battle might have been lost. Park was born in New Zealand. He tried his hand as a sailor but when the First World War broke out he joined an artillery regiment and fought at Gallipoli. After Gallipoli he transferred to the British Army and served at the Somme, where he was wounded. As he recovered in England, he decided to join the Royal Flying Corps. In 1917 he was promoted to command a squadron. By the time of the Armistice he had shot down five enemy aircraft and been awarded the Military Cross and the Croix de Guerre. In the interwar period he graduated from the RAF Staff College and was Senior Air Staff Officer to Dowding. When war broke out Dowding appointed him to command 11 Group, which, as we have noted, saw much action in France and Flanders. Park demonstrated his ability for optimising limited resources during the evacuation at Dunkirk.

Park was a complex man. He neither drank nor smoked, had few personal friends, and his memoranda and instructions could be blunt to the point of rudeness. Yet he was popular with his pilots whom he visited regularly in his own Hurricane. At the same time he shunned publicity and this remoteness prevented him from becoming a household name.[9]

We have already encountered Dowding as an implacable opponent of dispatching fighters to what he considered a lost cause in France. He had been the head of Fighter Command since 1936 and was on the brink of retirement when war commenced in 1939, and again faced retirement on the eve of the Battle of Britain. He had flown in the First World War and was then sent home to improve training standards. In the interwar years he had served in Iraq, been Director of Training and a member of the Air Council for Supply and Research. He was among the first to grasp the operational implications of radar and oversaw the growth and development of the British fighter defensive system. In the end this was identified so closely with him that it became known as the 'Dowding System'.

Dowding was an intensely private man, with few friends and no small talk. He could be difficult and opinionated and by 1940 had alienated almost all his superiors on the Air Council. In addition, he failed to mediate the conflicts between the Group Commanders Park and Leigh Mallory, most importantly the dispute over the merits of large versus small fighter formations. Ultimately, the situation was resolved, not by Dowding, but by the practicalities of the situation. He had, however, defenders in powerful places including Beaverbrook, the Minister for Aircraft Production, and Winston Churchill.

On the German side, the most outstanding fact was their almost total ignorance of the defensive system just described and which Hitler required them to defeat. In the pre-war period German blimps had observed and photographed the radar towers, and as German scientists were working on radar themselves they had a reasonable idea of what they were. However, they had no understanding of the importance of the radar chain for rapidly disseminating intelligence on raids to the British squadrons. The radar towers, which were anyway difficult to bomb, never became a priority target for the Luftwaffe and were never systematically attacked.

The Germans did know that the enemy squadrons were controlled by radio from the ground. However, they considered this a negative for the RAF as they thought it tied squadrons to very specific areas and thereby hampered their mobility.

The Germans did not understand the relationship between Fighter Command HQ, the Groups and the Sectors. The location of Fighter Command headquarters at Bentley Priory was quite unknown to them, as were the locations of the Group headquarters. As for the vital Sector airfields, apart from recognising that locations such as Biggin Hill, Kenley and others were important fighter bases and therefore worthy of attention, they failed to grasp their role as receivers and disseminators of raid intelligence. As a result they were unaware of the function or even the existence of the control rooms. This intelligence failure explains why there was no systematic attempt to destroy these rooms and to ensure that they remained destroyed.

Even the function of many airfields in Britain remained a mystery to the Luftwaffe. When they attacked an airfield they were often unsure about whether it was part of Fighter Command or whether it belonged to Bomber Command or Coastal Command. As it happened, the airfield that received most attacks during the Battle of Britain belonged to Coastal Command and formed no part of the system the Germans were aiming to destroy.

Lack of intelligence was not the Germans' only problem. There was a huge gap in their communications arrangements. Once aircraft were aloft, ground control could not speak to the pilots because of a lack of ground-to-air radio. This meant that once orders were given, a raid could not be recalled or redirected.

Were the men in command of the Luftwaffe of a type and flexibility of mind to overcome these formidable disadvantages? The answer is no. Goering had little grasp of detail nor the enquiring mind to probe for any weaknesses that his force might possess. Anyway, a considerable amount of his energy was devoted not to developing a coherent strategy against Britain but to maintaining his position in the Nazi hierarchy, a perennial problem for many of those who led the country. Moreover, Goering's relatively easy victories against the Poles and the French seemed to confirm that his air force was invincible. The air battles over Dunkirk, which saw the introduction of the Spitfire, might have provided valuable lessons, but there is no evidence that Goering was paying attention.

Nor was Goering good at appointing competent subordinates. General Udet of the production department actually thought that the Spitfire and Hurricane were poor-quality machines. His head of Intelligence, Major Josef Schmid, spoke no foreign languages, had never flown, and while identifying Britain as Germany's 'most dangerous enemy', had no quality target information about the British defensive system, overlooked the importance of the radar chain, and rated the Spitfire as little better than the Me 110 fighter bomber.[10]

Under Goering were the commanders of the three Luftflotte that were to operate against Britain. The leader of Luftflotte 5, which was based in Norway, was Generaloberst Hans-Jürgen Stumpff. He was to play a minor role in the battle and his one contribution will be discussed in due course.

More important were the commanders of the Luftflotte based in the Low Countries and France. In command of Luftflotte 2 was General

Kesselring. In the interwar period he had been involved in the establishment and growth of the Luftwaffe, and was influential in selecting the Me 109 as its principal fighter. However, Kesselring had no battle experience and if he had a view of the role of air power it was that it should operate in tactical support of the army. This was of course not the role it needed to play against Britain. Despite his rather high post-war reputation, there is little to suggest that Kesselring thought deeply or incisively about the task before him. In the absence of clear direction from above he had an opportunity to impose a strategy on the Battle of Britain, but he conspicuously failed to do so. There is much evidence that he thought the unprecedented numbers of aircraft in his hands could accomplish anything. That they had an unprecedented task to perform never seems to have occurred to him. The traits he was to develop as an army commander later in the war, namely fixity of purpose and the relentless pursuit of an objective, were not evident in his conduct during the battle in the skies.

Hugo Sperrle, in charge of the smaller Luftflotte 3, lacked Kesselring's charm (or any charm at all for that matter) but had the advantage of being a professional airman with experience in Spain with the Condor Legion. As will become apparent, his ideas on how to win the battle differed from Kesselring's, thus preventing the Luftflotte commanders from presenting a united front to Goering. How these ideas fared will be discussed later.

The organisation of the Luftwaffe differed little from the RAF. Under the Luftflotte was the *Geschwader* (Group), which had three *Gruppen* (wings), which in turn had 3 *Staffelen* (squadrons). Bombers and fighters were ordered in the same way. Most Me 109s and the dive-bombers were in Kesselring's Luftflotte 2 and were arrayed near the Channel coast because of their short range. Bombers were placed further back and it was usually the manoeuvring of these aircraft to assemble into attack formations that was first picked up by the British radar chain.

The aircraft available to each side have often been described and only features that affected the battle will be mentioned here. The only single-engine German fighter to participate in the battle was the Me 109. It had a maximum speed of about 350 mph, which put it on a par with the Spitfire but gave it at least a 30 mph advantage over the Hurricane. It was equipped with 2 x 20mm cannon in its wings and two machine guns that fired through the propeller. This weaponry gave it a greater punch than the

8 x .303 machine guns of the British fighters but required greater accuracy to score a hit. The engine was fuel injected, which meant that the plane could climb faster than its British equivalents and could dive in the sure knowledge that it would not cut out – something that could not be said about the carburettor-supplied British engine. The Me 109 had some disadvantages. It was difficult to fly and with its narrow undercarriage had more crashes on takeoff and landing than either the Spitfire or the Hurricane. More importantly, both of its British opponents could turn inside it, often a matter of life and death in a dogfight. Another factor that greatly hampered the effectiveness of the aircraft in the Battle of Britain was its short range. Its cruising range was just over 400 miles with no combat allowance. In practice, combat limited its range to London and only gave it a few minutes over the city before it had to turn for home. An oversight in this regard was the German failure to consider fitting the fighter with drop tanks to increase its range.

Mention has been made of the British fighters, the Hawker Hurricane and the Supermarine Spitfire. It only needs to be added that the wood and cloth construction of the Hurricane made it difficult to shoot down, while its sturdy build made it a more stable gun platform than the Spitfire or the Me 109. Both the Hurricane and Spitfire also had a short range (the Spitfire's was 575 miles non-combat flying), but this was less of a factor because in the main they were operating over home territory. The Spitfire was probably the better fighter, but two-thirds of the planes that took part in the Battle of Britain were Hurricanes.

The only other British fighters to take part in the battle were the Blenheim and the Defiant. Both were obsolete and sitting ducks for the Me 109. It is a wonder that any at all survived combat.

Most German bombers came from an earlier era than the fighters. Of the two main German types, the Dornier 17 had been flying since 1934 and the Heinkel 111 since 1935. These planes only averaged around 250 mph and carried relatively light bomb loads – between 1,750 and 4,000lbs These characteristics were no great disadvantage when used in close support of the army, but British fighters could easily catch them and their bombs could not penetrate hardened military targets – as against civil buildings. Nevertheless, both bombers could withstand a great deal of punishment from .303 bullets before being brought down.

The newest German bomber was the Junkers 88. It could carry up to 5,000lbs of bombs at 285 mph. However, it was under-gunned, having just three machine guns compared with four for the Dornier and Heinkel. It was difficult to fly and much prone to accident at takeoff and landing.

Much was expected but little delivered by two other aircraft in the Luftwaffe. The twin-engine Me 110 was a fighter-bomber that proved to be too light to deliver a substantial bomb load and too heavy to be an effective fighter. Originally it had been designed to escort bombers but soon required a fighter escort of its own. It was a liability during the Battle of Britain and was withdrawn at the end of August.

The other aircraft with a high reputation at the beginning of the battle was the JU 87 dive-bomber (the Stuka). This aircraft had terrorised the Poles, the French and British troops at various times during the battle in the west and civilian columns trekking away from the fighting. It was the most accurate of the German bombers but only carried a 1,100lb bomb load and had a maximum speed of just 230 mph. It had rear firing guns and was very vulnerable to first-class fighters as it pulled out of a dive when its speed might drop to 110 mph. As the Germans were about to find out, the Stuka could not survive against Hurricanes or Spitfires.[11]

Overall, then, the Luftwaffe's aircraft were ill equipped to fight the Battle of Britain. Its bombers carried very light bomb loads and were too slow. Its fighter-bomber and dive-bomber were not fit for purpose. Its single-engine fighter was first class but lacked range. These planes did not amount to a strategic air force or anything like it.

The Germans did possess one advantage at the beginning of the Battle of Britain. This was the experience of many of their pilots, gained in combat in Spain, Poland and in the west. However, the losses inflicted by the Allies in 1939, although often overlooked, were considerable. Many Luftwaffe pilots would therefore fly for the first time against Britain.

On the other side, British fighter pilots possessed limited experience. Some of them had combat experience in the west, but there they had fought at a tremendous disadvantage in trying to support a retreating army from ever shifting airfields. To a great extent they would learn on the job between July and October 1940 – or they would not survive.

What of numbers? On 13 July (near enough to the British date for the commencement of the battle) the Germans possessed:[12]

Table 2: German Aircraft, July 1940.

Type	Total	Serviceable	
		Number	Per cent
S E Fighters (Me 109)	1,077	899	83
T E Fighters (Me 110)	382	280	73
Bombers	1,347	943	70
Dive-bombers	436	340	78
Totals	3,242	2,462	76

Not all these aircraft would have been available against Britain. During the battle approximately 10 per cent of the single-engine fighters and between 10 and 20 per cent of the twin-engine fighters would have been held back to defend Germany.[13]

The German figures look impressive but on analysis reveal some weaknesses. On the reasonable assumption that it would take more than one fighter to protect a bomber, on any given day the Germans would only be able to offer protection to a small fraction of their bomber force. At the rate of two fighters to one bomber, if the Luftwaffe could field, say, 700 serviceable fighters, this would have limited the number of bombers the Germans could have deployed on a single raid to 300 – that is, only around 30 per cent of their available force. And the fact is that on most days the number of single-engine fighters available to the Luftwaffe was fewer than 700. In this way the limited availability of Me 109s constrained the bombing capacity of the Germans throughout the daytime offensive.

For Britain, only figures for fighters will be given because only they could oppose the assault of the Luftwaffe; and only serviceable fighters are given because as the Luftwaffe could strike at any time, only those could take to the sky immediately. The figures for 8 July are as follows:[14]

Table 3: British Fighters, July 1940.

Type	Serviceable
Hurricanes	469
Spitfires	283
Total	752

In addition, there were about 100 serviceable Blenheims and Defiants available, but as will be seen there is good reason to discount these aircraft.[15] For practical purposes then, Britain had 750 serviceable fighters to oppose 2,500 serviceable German planes of all types. Fighter Command was outnumbered by 3.5 to 1.

What did the opposing sides know of each other's strength? On the German side Major Josef (Beppo) Schmid, the Chief of Intelligence for the Luftwaffe, produced a report on the RAF on 16 July 1940. This report contained many errors, but as far as numbers were concerned Schmid was not that wide of the mark in his estimate of 675 serviceable frontline fighters. However, he did underestimate British serviceability rates.[16]

The RAF's estimates of Luftwaffe strength were much wider of the mark. The Air Intelligence (AI) section of the Air Ministry estimated in June 1940 that the total German frontline strength was 5,000 aircraft, of which 2,500 were bombers.[17] These figures were only accurate if reconnaissance, ground attack and transport aircraft were included. The actual figures, including these types, was in fact 5,005 on 8 June.[18] Yet if these largely non-strategic types of aircraft were eliminated, the AI section of the Air Ministry's estimate was far too high. In particular they overestimated the number of bombers possessed by the Germans by about 100 per cent.

The Air Ministry figures were soon questioned. Professor Lindemann, Churchill's scientific adviser, had been subjecting the figures to careful scrutiny and comparing them with the emerging order of battle that was being built up for the Luftwaffe from the Enigma decrypts. These indicated that in the case of bombers the Germans possessed no more than 1,250, which was remarkably close to the mark.[19] These new estimates were sent to the Air Ministry as coming from 'an apparently sure' source.[20] However, there is some doubt whether the air staff or Dowding (if he saw them) believed Lindemann's estimates, because in August 1940 the air staff produced a paper that estimated the German bomber force at 2,000 – a paper which Dowding did see.[21] The serviceability rate of this force was estimated at 80 per cent, which gave the Luftwaffe 1,600 serviceable bombers when the true figure was 876.[22]

Why the air chiefs chose to ignore Lindemann's estimates is a mystery. Perhaps they were unaware of his source and regarded him as a rank amateur, meddling in areas where he had no expertise. And the higher figures would have suited Dowding's cautious cast of mind. Whatever the reason, it seems that the head of Fighter Command and his superiors thought they were fighting a battle against double the numbers of German bombers that the Luftwaffe actually possessed.

There were some other factors that would affect the Battle of Britain. It is clear that the British had one obvious advantage. They would be fighting over home soil. They could therefore recover damaged aircraft and pilots who managed to parachute out of disintegrating planes and who might therefore fight another day. Damaged German planes and pilots and crew who bailed out would be a dead loss. This factor is particularly noticeable in pilot strengths for single-engine fighters. Despite some bad moments the British figures rose from about 1,200 at the beginning of the battle to 1,800 at the end. At the same time the German figures dropped from 850 to 650.[23]

Fighting over home soil also gave the British an advantage in aircraft maintenance. The British had a sophisticated series of Aircraft Storage Units in reasonable proximity to their fighter airfields. In France and Belgium the Germans were not as well placed. In 1940 many workshops were located in Germany, meaning damaged aircraft had to be transported back by road or rail, repaired, and then flown back. The Luftwaffe maintenance organisation was quite efficient but this process took time and meant that for the entire battle the serviceability rates were much lower than the British.[24] Between July and December 1940 British serviceability rates remained virtually constant at 90 per cent, while the rates for the Luftwaffe fell from 80 per cent in July to 70 per cent in December.[25]

The Germans had two advantages. As the aggressors, they could choose their targets. The radar chain would give warning of their approach but the British could never be sure where the bombers would proceed once they crossed the coast. Especially baffling was a common German tactic of splitting into small groups and attacking multiple targets.

The other German advantage is a cause for some surprise. The Luftwaffe had developed an efficient sea-rescue service for pilots who ditched or bailed out in the Channel. German pilots were equipped with flares to attract a small group of Heinkel 59 rescue planes. On the other side the British had nothing. Their pilots had to rely on sharp-eyed observers along the coast who might alert nearby ships. For a maritime nation this was an important and surprising omission.

CHAPTER 9

THE BATTLE OF BRITAIN
OVERTURE

IN THE LAST DAYS of June 1940 the destiny of Britain seemed to hang in the balance and Germany had every reason to be confident of victory in the ensuing battle. Their forces had expelled the British army from Europe and crushed all its major allies. The Dominions still stood with Britain but their armies were too small and too distant to be of significant consequence. Britain's own army that had escaped from France was a shattered remnant in a state of hasty reorganisation. Most of its equipment was strewn across the beaches around Dunkirk. Once Hitler's soldiers landed in Britain they expected to make short work of it. Military defeat would most likely lead to the overthrow of the Churchill government. All Europe would then be at Hitler's mercy. The United States would be isolated, though not splendidly.

All that stood between Germany and the realisation of this ambition, so the Luftwaffe chiefs thought, were the 750 aircraft of Fighter Command. Goering was quick to assure his colleagues that he had the means to destroy this force. After all, the Luftwaffe had 900 fighters, 1,000 bombers, 350 fighter bombers and 300 of the Stuka dive-bombers that had proved so destructive to morale during the campaign in the west. He would soon bring Britain to its knees or its senses.

This appealed to Hitler. If the RAF could be defeated, some welcome political changes in Britain might take place. A British Pétain might come to power and seek to make whatever peace he could. This would mean victory without invasion. And without Britain to contend with, the Wehrmacht could single-mindedly turn against other foes in the east.

In a memorandum on 30 June, Goering laid down the strategy that he would employ to defeat Fighter Command. The battle would be fought in several phases. The first phase, as he later described, amounted to a 'recon-naissance in force',[1] involving flights over the Channel designed specifically to lure Dowding's Hurricanes and Spitfires into engagements over water. This would exploit the RAF's weakness in sea rescue, which rendered its losses in aircraft and pilots over water irredeemable. During the first phase the Luftwaffe would also be able to gauge the strength and grouping of the enemy air force. For the second phase, Goering listed a whole raft of targets to be destroyed. They included the remainder of the RAF and its ground organisation, the aircraft industry, importing harbours, merchant ships and warships. Within this plethora of objectives, however, Goering made it clear that the destruction of the RAF was paramount: 'As long as the enemy air force is not defeated the prime requirement of the air war is to attack the enemy air force on every possible opportunity by day or by night, in the air, or on the ground, *without consideration to other tasks*.'[2] This was how the battle was supposed to be fought. It was not, and as we will see Goering did not seem to notice.

How had Dowding disposed Fighter Command to meet the coming onslaught? The number of serviceable Hurricanes and Spitfires in each group on 10 July (conventionally taken as the first day of the battle)[3] was as follows:[4]

Table 4: Serviceable Aircraft, 10 July 1940.

Group	Squadrons	Hurricanes	Spitfires	Total fighters
10	8	59	51	110
11	19	223	70	293
12	10	68	74	142
13	14	119	88	207
Totals	51	469	283	752

In addition there were about 20 Defiants and 70 Blenheims serviceable on that day but these obsolete aircraft were to play little role in the battle and none at all in deciding the outcome.[5]

Dowding's dispositions call for some comment. The relatively large number of aircraft in 13 Group, which covered Scotland and the north of England, can be explained by a number of factors. Some of the Group's 14 squadrons had recently fought in France and were resting. Others were present to counter the frequent appearance of German bombers in the area in the early months of 1940. Their targets were divided between the main fleet base at Scapa Flow and Scottish industrial towns such as Glasgow, Edinburgh and Aberdeen. On 6 April six bombers attacked Scapa Flow and there were raids on the north-east and Scotland on 18, 20, 21, 24, 25 and 26 June and 2 July.[6]

The relatively high number of Spitfires in 12 Group (covering the Midlands and the east coast) reflected the fact that some squadrons in this Group (especially those at Duxford) were close to London and had to be available for its defence. Other aircraft were needed to patrol east-coast convoys, which brought coal and coke to London. This duty was unwelcome to Dowding but nevertheless was imposed on him by the Admiralty.[7]

The comparative weakness of 10 Group requires little comment. It had only just been formed to provide air defences for the west of England to prevent Fighter Command from being outflanked by the German occupation of western France. For the purposes of the battle the most important stations in the Group were at Westhampnett and the wonderfully named Middle Wallop, where they flanked 11 Group and assisted in defending such vital ports as Portsmouth and Portland.

That 11 Group was by far the strongest of the four was not surprising. The Group covered south-eastern England and London. What is surprising is that just 54 per cent of Fighter Command's Spitfires and Hurricanes were concentrated in it, whereas 46 per cent were north of London. Perhaps more strikingly, just 43 per cent of Britain's most modern fighters, the Spitfires, were in the south, whereas 57 per cent of them were in the north. These dispositions might have been sensible before the intentions of the Germans became clear but they would require close scrutiny as the battle progressed.

As the dispositions stood, 11 Group was destined to be the major player. Three factors imposed upon it the tactics that it would use in the Battle of Britain. The first was the number of fighters at Sir Keith Park's disposal. He had 293 first-line fighters and could call on about 50 from 10 Group to assist in the defence of the south coast. This relatively small number of aircraft made it imperative that he commit his force to battle in limited numbers because if he scrambled a large number of squadrons at the first sign of attack, subsequent German formations might reach their destinations unimpeded or catch his initial contingent of fighters on the ground refuelling or rearming (Map 17).

The second factor was time. The radar chain could give him 30 to 40 minutes' warning of an impending attack. But it was not until the Germans formed up and headed for Britain that their direction of attack became clear, and that might cut the warning time to little more than 15 minutes. Moreover, a Spitfire required nearly six minutes to reach 18,000 feet while the more numerous Hurricanes took seven minutes to reach 15,000 feet.[8] The British aircraft then had to be gathered into formation and vectored on to the incoming Germans. If extra squadrons were sent to fight in larger formations, the additional assembly time meant they risked being too late to forestall the German bombers or they surrendered the advantage of height, or both.

The third and final factor was the requirement by the Admiralty to fly standing patrols over coastal convoys, potentially reducing the number of aircraft available to respond to radar sightings. For all these reasons, therefore, Park had little choice but to send single squadrons into battle, holding back others until the German targets, the weight of attack, and the movements of other German formations had been identified. This meant that on most occasions where the enemy was encountered the British would be outnumbered.

This modus operandi was evident from the very first day of battle, 10 July. It will be useful to discuss that day in detail as it reveals both the strategy employed by the Germans in the first phase and the tactics used in particular by 11 Group for the entire battle. The day dawned fair but it soon became showery in the south and over the Channel, while continuous and heavy rain fell elsewhere.[9] The first encounter of the battle took place after radar operators identified a single German bomber off Yarmouth, and

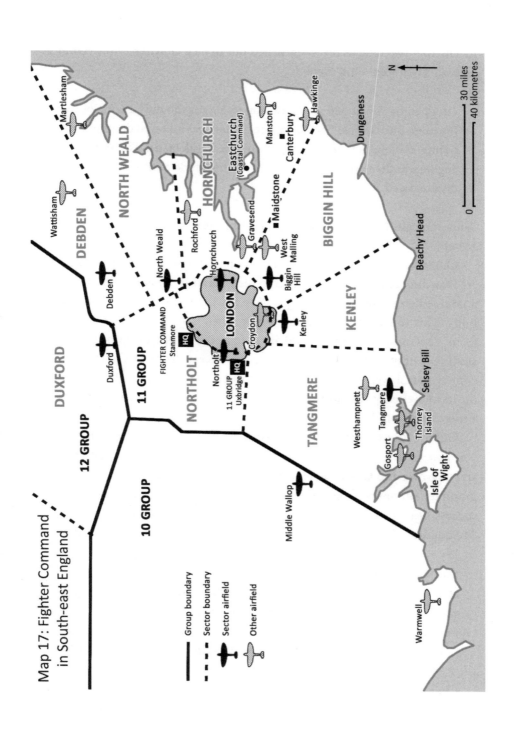

Map 17: Fighter Command in South-east England

Group boundary
Sector boundary
Sector airfield
Other airfield

N

0 — 30 miles
0 — 40 kilometres

12 GROUP
DUXFORD
Duxford

10 GROUP
11 GROUP
NORTHOLT
Northolt
11 GROUP Uxbridge HQ
FIGHTER COMMAND Stanmore HQ

DEBDEN
Wattisham
Debden
Martlesham

NORTH WEALD
North Weald
Rochford
Hornchurch

HORNCHURCH
Eastchurch (Coastal Command)
Gravesend
West Malling
Manston
Canterbury
Hawkinge
Maidstone
Dungeness

LONDON
Croydon
Kenley
Biggin Hill
KENLEY
BIGGIN HILL
Beachy Head

TANGMERE
Westhampnett
Tangmere
Gosport
Thorney Island
Selsey Bill
Isle of Wight

Middle Wallop
Warmwell

a section (three planes) from 66 Squadron at Duxford was sent to intercept it. The first two attacks on what turned out to be a Dornier 17 proved ineffectual. Then Red 3 intervened:

> On opening fire at 300 yards, closing to 50 yds the port engine of the E/a burst into flames. The E/a lost height but was followed down and on noting e/a leveling out another stern attack was made. The starboard engine was then on fire and about 4 minutes later e/a struck the sea and disintegrated.[10]

Thus Sergeant F. W. Robertson could claim the first victory in the Battle of Britain.

One duty that had to be undertaken on 10 July was convoy protection. As Dowding had anticipated, forcing his aircraft to fly at a set altitude, on a course determined by the ships, gave his fighter formations little flexibility. This was evident early in the day when a section of 242 Squadron from 12 Group was just too distant to prevent enemy bombers from sinking a straggling 2,000-ton ship. Later, aircraft from 11 Group also on convoy patrol were jumped by a superior number of Me 109s. They shot down four enemy aircraft but at a cost of three of their own and the loss of a merchant ship.[11]

Other actions were more successful. In these instances the radar chain was able to give timely warning of small formations of German aircraft arriving over the Channel. This allowed Park to dispatch relatively parsimonious numbers from Fighter Command to intercept them.[12] The success of this strategy is illustrated by the following combat report from 74 Squadron detailing the experiences of eight Spitfires on the first day:

> 8 a/c 74 Sqdn. left Manston 1345 hours [to] patrol Dover-Deal. Patrolling at 9,000 ft. with cloud base at 12,000 ft. a large 3 layered formation of e/a were sighted. This appeared to consist of about 20 Do. 17's at 4,000 ft. attacking a convoy, approx. 40 Me 110's at 8,000 ft. circled above the Do. 17's and on top at 12,000ft approx. 40 Me 109's circled above the Me 110's.[13]

> A general dogfight developed against superior numbers. Red 1 ['Sailor' Malan, one of the best shots in the RAF] climbed above the circling e/a and started a spiral dive down the centre of the encircling e/

as. Red 1 attacked 1 Me. 110 observing smoke coming from his port engine and his De Wilde hitting the fuselage of a Do. 17.[14] [This caused an Me 109] to collide with a Do. 17 or Me 110. The Me 109 was completely destroyed and the twin-engined aircraft went down in a slow spiral.

Blue 1 ordered his section line astern and attacked 3 Do. 17's. Blue 1 opened fire at 400 yds. and observed e/a starboard engine on fire. Blue 2 fired a burst of 10 secs. into 1 Me 110, the rear gunner appeared to be hit. Blue 2 then attacked another Me 110 using the remainder of his ammunition, but observed no apparent damage. Yellow 1 picked out a straggler from the Do. 17's and attacked astern with full deflection shots. Thick black smoke poured from the starboard engine. Making a second attack Yellow 1's a/c was hit in the radiator by e/a fire and Yellow 1 successfully broke away, used extra burst and force landed at Lympne.

Yellow 2 fired a short burst at 1 Me 109 which immediately half rolled and dived. After climbing away from several e/a Yellow 2 attacked another e/a from above, without apparent damage. Yellow 2 attacked a second Do. 17 in a 60° dive putting in a 4 sec. burst, e/a emitted smoke from starboard engine. Three parachutes were seen descending.[15]

This report shows that a force of only eight Spitfires was able to attack at least 80 German aircraft, destroy two Dorniers, damage three other aircraft, destroy a Me 109 and damage another for a toll to themselves of just one fighter damaged. Overall, on that first day, just 66 British aircraft were sent into combat, less than one tenth of Fighter Command's force.[16] At the end of the day the Germans had lost 11 aircraft (two fighters, four Me 110s and five bombers) and in addition had five bombers and two fighters damaged. The British had five fighters destroyed and four damaged.[17]

Despite British difficulties over convoy protection it is hard to see how Goering thought he could possibly wear down Fighter Command by these methods, which allowed Park to adhere to his strategy of minimum engagement. Indeed, the calling of a conference by Goering on 21 July perhaps indicated that he was uneasy with the tactics so far employed by the Luftwaffe. He asked his Luftflotte commanders to comment on the general situation and give detailed proposals for future action. Nothing substantial followed. Hugo Sperrle of Luftflotte 3 seemed quite happy with continuing the attack on convoys and ports but he wanted the Luftwaffe's effort to be greatly increased. Kesselring agreed that a more vigorous offensive should be conducted, but against London, not shipping and ports. He thought that in the defence of the capital Fighter Command would have to deploy a large force, which could then be overwhelmed by the superior numbers of the Luftwaffe.[18]

In the short term neither of these views affected operations. Goering was not ready for a maximum effort and an attack on London was a decision that he knew would not be made by the Luftwaffe command but by Hitler. Operations therefore would continue as before.

What was the pattern of attack against British targets in the first phase of the battle, from 10 July to 7 August? An analysis of targets indicates that most combats occurred along the south-eastern coast of England, with a smaller number along the east coast of Scotland, south Wales and Cornwall.[19] It must be kept in mind that the numbers represent *combat* locations. They do not therefore necessarily indicate the targets for which the Germans aimed. Nevertheless, in this period, we may surmise that the combat area and the target were closely correlated, the German policy being to attack convoys and ports.

One factor is very clear. The German effort was dispersed along the entire length of the coast of the UK. In all we can identify 45 major attacks. But apart from Dover, which was attacked on 12 days and often more than once per day, and the attacks around Portsmouth and Portland, each of which was attacked seven times, there were no other concentrated efforts against other targets. Plymouth was attacked twice, Folkestone three times, Harwich once, Newcastle once and so on.[20] Of course convoys were attacked where found and as they generally moved along the coast from east to west, this could account for some of the apparent dispersion.

What did the Germans achieve by this effort? The short answer is very little. Through attacks on convoys they sank just 24,000 tons of shipping, a tiny fraction of the total tonnage sailing through the Channel and significantly less than the 38,000 tons they sank, for almost no loss, in their night-time mine-laying operations.[21]

As for attacks against harbours, the main inconvenience was caused at Dover. After two destroyers were sunk there on 19 July, the Admiralty relocated the Dover flotillas to Harwich. But an increase in anti-aircraft batteries, balloon defences at Dover and an instruction to Fighter Command to make the defence of the port a priority, kept the harbour facilities intact, ready to receive the Harwich force in the event of an invasion.[22]

One aspect of these German operations did represent a danger to Fighter Command. Many encounters, especially by aircraft escorting convoys, took place over the sea. Any British fighter shot down over water represented a dead loss, as too often did the pilot, in the absence of a decent sea-rescue service. As early as 19 July, Park was forced to remind his pilots to attack only within 'gliding distance of the coast'.[23]

In other ways the period proved to be of advantage to Fighter Command. Firstly, the relatively low intensity of the German effort did not overextend the squadrons. For the entire period the Luftwaffe committed no more than 340 aircraft from Luftflotte 2 and 240 from Luftflotte 3 – only 16 per cent of the forces available. As a result, the number of British aircraft in combat on any one day could be kept quite low, reaching a maximum of just 140 on 25 July.[24] So Park never had to commit more than 50 per cent of his serviceable Hurricanes and Spitfires on any day of this first period.[25]

What this relatively low-intensity warfare amounted to for an individual pilot can be seen from the diary of Pilot Officer Wissler. He was based at Debden and at Martlesham Heath (Debden's satellite airfield) in 11 Group. From 12 July to 7 August, Wissler flew patrols on eight days, most of them over east coast convoys. He saw action just once. On 29 July his section encountered an He 111 bomber. They attacked it head on and from astern (it is worth noting that some squadrons were already departing from the attack formations laid down by Fighter Command). Wissler then followed the bomber down and carried out another head-on attack until 'it went in to the water'.[26]

On six other days Wissler carried out practice attacks, noting of the first that it was 'not very good as the leaders had never led attacks before and the C.O. had never done them'.[27] Nor did practice seem to help. On the 28 July he recorded that scores were 'awful' and that 'I failed to hit anything at all'. On the last practice attack for this period the squadron lost its C.O. in the dark.[28]

The remainder of Wissler's time was taken up with such activities as formation flying for photographers from Life Magazine, ferrying mid-ranking officers from one airfield to another, resting at a stately home, and being duty pilot ('of all the God forsaken jobs this is the worst'). In addition he attended two drunken parties ('everyone got plastered'), had two days leave, and was grounded on one day because of the weather. He witnessed two aircraft written off in accidents and one death 'because of a botched landing', and heard of another death in the squadron due to a further landing accident. He mentions fatigue just once, after four and a half hours flying on 25 July ('God we were tired this evening'), and on various other days he was on standby but did not fly. Not one of his squadron was lost to enemy action.[29]

For Wissler and other pilots in similar situations, the Luftwaffe's tactics allowed many inexperienced British pilots to be eased into battle without excessive strain or heavy casualties. This is not to underestimate the nervous energy expended in flying standing patrols or the risks involved in merely taking off and landing relatively fragile fighters. Nevertheless, Wissler got in quite a few hours of practice fighting and despite his self-deprecating remarks he was skilled enough to down a German bomber when the moment came. In this way the Luftwaffe in this period gave many in Fighter Command a month to hone their skills.

Pilots based near the south coast no doubt saw more action than Wissler. However, when we examine the combat statistics for the period as a whole, they provide further evidence that the British won this opening skirmish. During the period 10 July to 7 August, Dowding's force lost 220 Hurricanes and Spitfires, shot down, written off or damaged. Comparative figures for the Luftwaffe for the period are 344 aircraft (88 Me 109s, 189 bombers, 36 dive-bombers, 31 twin-engine fighters). If just the aircraft destroyed are examined, the figures are even less flattering to the Germans. Some 85 Hurricanes and Spitfires were destroyed as against 258 enemy aircraft – 46 Me 109s, 164 bombers, 17 dive-bombers and 31 twin-engine fighters.[30] The ratio of aircraft destroyed, therefore, is almost exactly 3:1 in favour of Fighter Command.

Two aspects of these figures need to be noted. The British had destroyed 17 per cent of the German serviceable bomber force. If damaged bombers are included, that number increases to 20 per cent. This represents a significant attrition rate on a force that had been committed in small numbers and had been heavily protected by fighters. On the other hand the figures for fighters lost indicate that the Germans destroyed about twice the number they lost. This might have been a serious matter for Fighter Command had it not been for the aircraft production effort. During this period Dowding's force gained 400 fighters.[31] By contrast the Germans added just 140.[32] Early in the battle the British were winning the numbers game.

The figures for loss ratios are even more remarkable when other factors are taken into account. Firstly, as noted, in this period German bombers were heavily escorted by fighters, making interception for the British very perilous. Second, Fighter Command had to fly a large number of standing patrols over convoys. This limited the combat time available to the escorting fighters and often conceded the advantage of height and sun to the enemy. Third, the inexperience of the radar operators meant that they often underestimated the numbers or height of the German raiders, in these instances also conceding these advantages to the enemy. Fourth, the guns of British fighters were harmonised to 450 yards. Experienced pilots such as Sailor Malan (74 Squadron) realised that the stopping power of a fighter's eight machine guns was much greater at closer range because of the higher velocity of the bullets and that in any case it was easier to hit the target from close in. He therefore harmonised his own guns at 250 yards. Others in his squadron and no doubt adjacent squadrons followed suit. However, most pilots in this period kept to the Air Ministry standard of 450 yards, thus depriving themselves of this advantage.[33] Moreover, Malan and others realised that the German bombers were particularly vulnerable to a head-on attack because few of their guns fired forward. He and others in his squadron adopted this form of attack to break up enemy formations and pick the stragglers off when they separated from the main group. This method gradually became standard in those squadrons close enough to Malan's to pick up on what he was doing. But neither the Air Ministry nor Dowding nor Park saw fit to inform the entire command of this method, which went unused by many squadrons during the battle.

A fifth factor, that of flying and attack formations, deserves more detailed consideration because it is often claimed that Fighter Command entered the battle with formations and tactics that were markedly inferior to those employed by the Luftwaffe. The standard flying formation used by Fighter Command was a 'vic' or v of three planes with a squadron deploying into four vics, one per section. In a vic formation No. 1 is the section leader and Nos 2 and 3 are his support. It was the task of the leader to scan the air for the enemy, the task of the support pilots to keep their eyes on the leader. This scheme had an obvious weakness. Only one aircraft in three was actually looking for the enemy, which meant that Nos 2 and 3 could be 'jumped' by an enemy flying directly behind them.

Some in Fighter Command (Saul in 13 Group and the commander of 19 Squadron at Duxford) wanted to adopt something like the German 'finger 4' formation – which was essentially two groups of two planes slightly staggered in distance and height like the four fingers of a hand.[34] This formation was much looser and meant that each pilot searched ahead and astern, thus providing each other with mutual support. It also allowed for greater flexibility. If the four aircraft were separated into two groups of two, there would still be some support available. The Germans had developed this formation after experience in Spain and it was undoubtedly a better grouping than the vic. Indeed, it was implemented by Fighter Command after the Battle of Britain and was used for the remainder of the war. Its one disadvantage for the relatively inexperienced pilots of Fighter Command was that the spread of four planes took skill to maintain and a slight divergence off course could cause a single fighter (flying, it must be remembered, at over 300 miles an hour) to lose touch with the formation. In the hands of unskilled pilots a formation of four could rapidly fracture into four single aircraft.

Nevertheless, it is a mark against Dowding and the Air Ministry that they did not draw to the attention of the Groups the benefits of either the head-on attack, the finger-4 formation, or the harmonisation of guns at a shorter distance. Squadrons that did not adopt any of these methods of attack could occasionally pay a heavy price. To take just two examples, between 9 and 21 August, 266 Squadron from 11 Group had 12 aircraft destroyed and 11 damaged. It was immediately withdrawn to 12 Group. Similarly, between 22 August and 1 September when it was withdrawn, 616 Squadron from 13 Group had 13 aircraft destroyed and eight damaged.[35] Fortunately for Dowding, most squadrons survived the battle without suffering these horrific casualties. It is strange, however, that Dowding never saw the dissemination of information about the latest fighting methods as one of his tasks. Had such tactics been adopted more widely there is little doubt that the kill rate of Fighter Command would have gone up and the accuracy rate of German bombing gone down.

So in the first period of the battle, the British had a force with little training, some with experience in France, directed by a radar system that was still learning its business, flying planes in the wrong formations, with guns harmonised at too great a distance and using obsolete methods in moving to attack. Moreover, few pilots had mastered the skill of deflection shooting – that is aiming not directly at the enemy aircraft but at a position where that aircraft would be when the bullets arrived. Yet during this first month the Luftwaffe did not put this inexperienced force to the test. Probably the most aircraft sent over by Kesselring and Sperrle was 200. Why the Germans adopted this tentative approach has never been satisfactorily explained. The widespread German view that this period should not be designated as part of the Battle of Britain at all misses the important point that during this time the Luftwaffes tactics allowed Dowding's men to learn on the job without being overwhelmed. When the Germans increased the tempo from 8 August, they were to find a much more experienced force lying in wait for them.

CHAPTER 10

THE BATTLE OF BRITAIN
THE CRISIS

THE DESULTORY NATURE OF the air war being waged against Britain in July was ended by Hitler. He had been mulling over future grand strategy with his generals and advisers, and on 30 July he came to a decision. The Soviet Union would be invaded in the spring of 1941. 'England' had to be eliminated well before then. The Führer's problem was that this window for an invasion was very short. Bad weather in the Channel could be anticipated to be endemic from October. This left fewer than eight weeks to accomplish the main precondition for invasion – the establishment of air superiority over Britain. Clearly, the air war would require a greater effort and a new plan.

Consequently, on 1 August Hitler issued Führer Directive No. 17, which in part detailed a new direction for the Luftwaffe. The RAF must be eliminated as well as its ground installations and the aircraft industry. Ports, which provided shelter for the Royal Navy or through which food and raw materials were imported, must be destroyed. Any decision to bomb the civilian population as a deliberate act he reserved for himself. Hitler's military staff, the OKW, added that the RAF must be dealt with in the same way as the Polish and French air forces – that is destroyed on the ground, and that the radar chain should be attacked as a first priority.

Goering, who had largely left the operational conduct of the air battle to Kesselring of Luftflotte 2 and Sperrle of Luftflotte 3, responded immediately to the Führer directive. On 2 August he outlined his second plan against Britain. It was to open on 5 August with an all-out attack (grandiloquently called Adler Tag – Eagle Day) against a wide list of targets – the RAF, ports, merchant ships and warships. And in line with the OKW paper, the British early-warning system, the radar chain, was to be attacked by specially trained units in the first wave.[1]

Goering's response contained the same flaw as his first plan, although neither Hitler nor the Luftwaffe chiefs seemed to notice. Apart from the contribution of OKW, there was no strategic guidance given to the Luftwaffe. They were not told, for example, to give absolute priority to the destruction of Fighter Command and then to concentrate on ports and imports. The implication was that every target listed was as important as every other target. Yet if the Luftwaffe tried to attack them all, the force would be spread very thin. Goering's instructions to his airmen amounted to this: destroy Fighter Command on the ground (which implied an attack on all their major airfields) and at the same time attack the aircraft industry while continuing with current operations against ports and merchant shipping. This multiplicity of objectives ensured that whatever pressure was brought to bear against Fighter Command, it would not be maximum pressure. The great offensive had to some extent dissipated before it had begun.

Goering's immediate problem, however, was to find a period of fine weather in which he could launch Eagle Day. Forecasts for 5 August predicted low cloud and haze, so 10 August was chosen. A low over the Azores made that day problematical as well, but the high that followed finally gave Goering a date. Eagle Day would take place on 13 August; the attack on the radar chain would precede it by a day.

No doubt Goering was impatient to start his offensive, but he was confident of the result. In a widely quoted statement he boasted that if he were given four days of fine weather the RAF would be no more. In the light of the fighting in July this might seem just another of Goering's characteristically bombastic statements. Certainly his confidence was high after the unbroken chain of victories achieved by the Luftwaffe since the beginning of the war. But there was more to his assessment than bombast.

Goering's confidence was based on a series of reports issued by Luftwaffe Intelligence on the state of British defences. The problem for the Germans was that these reports increasingly diverged from reality. The one fact the intelligence section calculated with reasonable accuracy was that Fighter Command had lost 220 to 250 modern fighters in July, when actual losses were about 200.[2] But Luftwaffe Intelligence had then made the assumption that Fighter Command was in crisis because of a catastrophic fall in fighter production. On 1 August the report said:

> According to statements put out by an authoritative British source in mid-July, the effect [on aircraft production by bombing] was achieved at the factories of Boulton and Paul at Norwich (Defiant), Vickers Supermarine at Southampton (Hurricane), Bristol at Filton (Blenheim, Bristol engines) and Gloster at Hucclecote (Hurricane), resulting in a fall in production of at least 50%.[3]

The report also claimed that the Rolls Royce Merlin engine factory at Hillingdon had been hit.[4]

From this report Luftwaffe Intelligence concluded that the number of British fighters received from the factories in July had been 180. This was a major miscalculation based on a 'source' that was either spreading disinformation or was woefully misinformed. It was true that the aircraft plants mentioned had been bombed – or at least had had bombs dropped near them. But whatever happened to production of the Defiant or Blenheim was hardly relevant because, as any Luftwaffe pilot knew, their overwhelming opposition came from Hurricanes and Spitfires. And it was in regard to these types that the report was totally inaccurate. The Supermarine works at Southampton (which anyway made Spitfires not Hurricanes) had not been touched; nor had the Merlin engine factory (which made engines for Hurricanes and Spitfires); nor had the Hucclecote works. In fact, far from declining, the production of Hurricanes and Spitfires in the period discussed by the Luftwaffe report remained steady at a combined total of approximately 100 per week.[5] As for the production of Defiants and Blenheims, the first was being phased out as obsolescent and the second was a light bomber with very marginal relevance to the Battle of Britain.

More faulty intelligence followed. The report went on to quote another 'authoritative source', which to some extent contradicted the first source. This authority stated that British aircraft production had fallen by 20 per cent (i.e. much less than was claimed by the first source). Yet this fall had not been due to bombing but to shortages of raw materials, partly caused by the sinking of 259,000 tons of shipping, mainly in the Channel, and by the refusal of workers to staff night shifts at aircraft factories.[6]

This report too was wide of the mark. Only 62,000 tons of shipping had been sunk in the Channel and despite the best efforts of the U-boats, there were no shortages of raw materials that would have affected the aircraft industry. As for the 'reluctant' workers in the aircraft factories, they were actually working longer hours than they had at the beginning of the war. Moreover, the number of people employed in the aircraft industries increased from 757,000 in the second quarter of 1940 to 866,000 in the third and 964,000 in the fourth quarter.[7] So much for the reluctance of Beaverbrook's workforce to carry on. In addition, the Germans did not seem to notice that their two authorities contradicted each other. Or perhaps they did notice and felt that the discrepancies did not matter because they both pointed in the same direction – to a 'weakening in British fighter defence'.[8] It was with these false impressions that the great air offensive was launched.

While the Luftwaffe waited for favourable weather, operations continued along similar lines to those conducted in July. Two of these are worthy of note because they demonstrate what a fine line there was for the British between success and failure.

The first occurred on 8 August. It began with an attack on a British convoy (Peewit) of 25 ships – not by the Luftwaffe but by German E-boats (fast motor torpedo boats). As the convoy approached Brighton the E-boats struck and sank three ships.[9] The attack scattered the convoy and soon the remaining 22 ships were straggling along the south coast, making them very difficult to defend. Before long a force estimated by radar to be at least 30 German aircraft discovered the ships and prepared to attack. 11 Group immediately scrambled five squadrons to intercept, but for reasons that are unclear only 145 Squadron arrived in time. The enemy was in greater strength than anticipated (80 aircraft, including dive-bombers, bombers and fighters), but the 12 Hurricanes of the squadron went straight for the bombers. The result was that the bombers were prevented from launching a concerted attack on the ships and had to bomb individually. In the melee no ships were hit.[10] Later, 238 Squadron disrupted an attack on the straggling ships by a similar number of aircraft in a similar way.[11] Once more, no ships were sunk.

The overall results for the day were heavily in Fighter Command's favour. They had shot down 25 German aircraft for a loss of seven Hurricanes and four pilots.[12] These incidents demonstrated that even outnumbered by 8:1, the British could thwart bombing attacks on a vulnerable convoy while inflicting significant losses on the Luftwaffe.

However, other days did not go as well for the British. On 11 August the enemy mounted an attack with over 100 aircraft on the Isle of Portland. The radar chain had given 10 and 11 Groups ample warning of the attack and five squadrons were scrambled to meet it. However, the strong German fighter escort managed to lure most of the Hurricanes and Spitfires to the west, which allowed Portland and Weymouth to be bombed at will.[13] In the ensuing fighter dogfight the Germans had the advantage of height and numbers (both underestimated by the radar plots), and so had by far the better of the contest. The British shot down 16 Me 109s, but the Germans destroyed 28 fighters and crippled another 17. Worse still for the British, 25 pilots were killed. This was the first time that pilot losses exceeded the daily replacement number.[14]

So here we have two days of combat. On the first the tenacity of two single British squadrons wreaked havoc among the attackers, disrupting their bombing runs while inflicting heavy losses on them. On the second, clever German diversionary tactics led three British squadrons to attack a much larger German fighter force in disadvantageous circumstances. One squadron (145) was involved in both incidents. In the first encounter its decision to attack the bombers was correct and in the second its decision to follow the fighters was mistaken. Yet if the British were going to come through the battle they had to make correct decisions more often than not. Was it possible that the Battle of Britain could have been lost by a series of incorrect decisions made by squadron leaders in a split second as they closed with the enemy at 500 mph? It was not. Park paid close attention to events such as those on 11 August and he responded. On 19 August he issued an instruction to his Sector controllers, which ordered them to 'despatch a minimum number of squadrons to engage enemy fighters. *Our main object is to engage enemy bombers.*'[15] This instruction was clear enough. No doubt there would still be occasions when British units were lured away from the bombers, but this was unlikely to happen often under the watchful eye of Park.

The overture to Eagle Day was to be an attack on the British radar stations. For this the Germans used a unit specially trained to bomb difficult targets.[16] But, typically, this attack would be confined to a relatively small section of the radar chain. Nor would the radar network be the only German target that day. Airfields at Manston, Hawkinge and Lympne (which was not an operational station) were to be attacked and Portsmouth was to bombed. Thus the effort of the Luftwaffe would be spread from Kent to the West Country.

Nevertheless, the attack on the Kentish radar stations (the main target of the Luftwaffe that day) could have been serious enough had it succeeded. From Fighter Command's point of view the alarming aspect of the attack was that between 9.32 a.m. and 9.45 a.m. the stations at Pevensey, Rye, Dover and Dunkirk (Kent) were all bombed without intervention by a single British fighter. Partly this was due to mischance. Radar had detected a German force assembling across the Channel just after 7.00 a.m. and three squadrons (610, 111 and 54) were sent up to meet it. However, this German force directed its attack against the coastal airfields of Manston and Lympne. Even then, the squadrons failed to engage the bombers, which proceeded to render their airstrips temporarily unserviceable.[17] The force attacking the radar chain (KGr 210) did not leave Calais until 9.15 a.m., by which time the initial three squadrons had landed and their replacements had not taken off. This gave the bombers a free run. They managed to hit all four stations but the damage, except to Pevensey, was not serious. The stations at Dunkirk and Dover suffered damage to huts but were never off the air. At Rye, all huts were destroyed but it was back in operation by noon.[18] Pevensey was the hardest hit. The electricity cables were cut with the result that it was out of action for 24 hours.[19]

Meanwhile, in the west another station – Ventnor on the Isle of Wight – had been severely damaged. In this attack the main target was Portsmouth, but a number of Ju 88s, operating as dive-bombers, peeled off and struck Ventnor. All buildings were destroyed and all cables – electricity and communication – were severed. It was to be off the air for 11 days.[20]

For their first effort against the radar chain, the Luftwaffe had achieved good results. One station had been crippled and four others damaged.

Further raids might have dealt the system a mortal blow. But further raids, as part of a systematic attempt to deprive Fighter Command of its eyes in the air, did not follow. Goering apparently questioned the value of the attacks and they were stopped.[21] Certainly, Ventnor was hit again on 17 August and the station at Poling was put out of action on the next day. But this was collateral damage arising from operations against quite different targets, not from a sustained attempt to eliminate the radar system. These few operations constituted the only German attacks on the radar chain for the entire period of the Battle of Britain. To some extent the Germans, although they had radar of their own, failed to realise how the British used it and how it formed the vital link between Fighter Command headquarters, Group headquarters and the Sector airfields. Partly, it was a matter of the targets being so hard to hit. The dive-bombers aimed at the towers and hit none of them. Moreover, as they could detect signal emissions from all stations on 13 August (the British sent a dummy signal from Ventnor), they assumed that all were in working order.[22]

It is hard to explain why the radar chain did not attract a more concerted attack. Even if the Germans had not realised the importance of radar, they were aware that it constituted some form of early-warning system. While the radar towers had not been hit, aerial reconnaissance revealed to the Luftwaffe that they had inflicted some damage on the stations attacked. The Intelligence section noted that during the bombing of Ventnor 'sheets of flame, intense fires and thick smoke were observed'. And the next day a reconnaissance patrol reported: 'Craters in vicinity of wireless station masts. Station quarters on fire.'[23] To commanders with fixity of purpose and with a determination to pursue their objectives, these results would have provided encouragement to continue. But Goering could not see the importance of the radar stations and there is no evidence that Kesselring or Sperrle could either. Hitler's staff had recognised their importance and had advised the Luftwaffe commanders that attacks on the radar chain should precede the intensification of the air war against other targets, but except for the initial attack this advice had been ignored. Not for the last time, the lack of a well-thought-out plan gave a reprieve to the British.

Eagle Day was finally implemented on 13 August. It did not live up to Goering's expectations. When the weather turned bad, he attempted to cancel the operation but this misfired. The first waves of bombers did not receive the signal and flew to their targets unescorted by the fighters that *had* received the cancellation message. A massacre was averted when Fighter Command failed to find the bombers, but the farcical aspect of the day continued when the bombers proceeded to bomb Eastchurch airfield heavily – a Coastal Command station only used by fighters for emergency landings. More concerted action followed in the afternoon. Southampton was badly bombed, but there was redemption for Park's men when 609 Squadron came across a group of 12 Stukas and downed nine of them. Altogether the 12 Spitfires shot a total of 19,665 rounds at the Stukas, attacking them from 250 yards astern to point-blank range.[24] This was the beginning of the end for the machines that had caused such terror in the campaign in the west. After further heavy losses, on 18 August most were withdrawn from the battle.

At the end of Eagle Day the British had lost just 14 Spitfires and Hurricanes and destroyed 43 German machines, comprising 9 Stukas, 12 Me 110s, 16 bombers and 6 fighters.[25] This was a poor return for the 1,400 sorties flown by the Luftwaffe.[26] Moreover, although substantial damage had been inflicted on the Southampton docks, only one fighter airfield had been attacked (Middle Wallop) and that yielded no result.[27]

Despite the fiasco of Eagle Day, the Luftwaffe would, during the next month, make a concerted effort against RAF aerodromes. The next 24 days saw the Luftwaffe target airfields right across southern England. The pattern of attack raises a number of questions. The first concerns targeting. The Luftwaffe made a total of 67 airfield attacks in this period. Yet 27, or 40 per cent, of them were against stations that were not Fighter Command airfields. This misdirected effort was partly the result of faulty intelligence. For example, on 12 August German photographic reconnaissance identified 18 Spitfires at the Gosport Coastal Command station when in fact there were none.[28] Similarly, 16 Hurricanes were noted at Thorney Island and 10 Spitfires at Ford when neither airfield had any single-engine fighters.[29] Mistakes of a similar nature were made by the Luftwaffe throughout the period, leading to many wasted missions.

This also reveals that the Luftwaffe was relying, at least to some extent, on reconnaissance missions to establish the whereabouts of the British fighter force. This either means that they thought the British could move squadrons at will to any airfield without loss of control, or that they had no real grip on the location of Fighter Command's airfields.

That Fighter Command's organisation remained a mystery to the Luftwaffe chiefs is reaffirmed when we turn to the attacks made against those airfields that actually belonged to Fighter Command. Clearly, it was the Sector airfields that were the vital cog in the British system. It was these airfields that received the radar and Observer Corps information from Group headquarters and passed it on to the squadrons on its own airfield and those satellite airfields under its control. To disrupt Fighter Command it was crucial that these Sector airfields be destroyed. That only 50 per cent of the raids on fighter airfields were made against the Sectors confirms that the Germans had little understanding of their role. The concentrated attention given by the Germans to Biggin Hill might be thought to run counter to this point. However, the repeated assaults on it probably came about because it was easy to see, was obviously a large airfield and, being just south of London, was frequently flown over. Kenley, Hornchurch, North Weald, Tangmere and others were just as important and yet were only sporadically attacked.

Another weakness in this approach is that, with one or two exceptions, the Germans failed to bomb a Sector airfield systematically to the point where it could no longer operate. An attack on Kenley on 18 August provides a good example of this. On that day the airfield was heavily bombed. All hangers were demolished, six Hurricanes destroyed or damaged on the ground, and telephone cables cut. The Sector operations room had to be closed and an emergency system brought into use. From then on Kenley could only operate two squadrons instead of its usual complement of three, with a consequent loss of efficiency. Follow-up raids might have put the airfield out of operation altogether, yet Kenley was not bombed again during this period. In the interval, huts were repaired, communications restored, and business as usual was resumed.[30]

Indeed, the only Sector airfield to suffer a sustained assault was Biggin Hill, which was bombed on six occasions in eight days during late August and early September.[31] The assault on Biggin Hill started on the morning of 30 August but no vital targets were hit. In the afternoon the story was different. Then a group of Ju 88s eluded the defence and bombed the workshops, the stores depot and the armoury. More importantly, they cut the power and telephone communications to part of the station. Thirty-nine personnel were killed and 26 wounded. On 31 August the raiders returned

216

and achieved a direct hit on the operations room. Temporary telephone communications, rigged up the day before, were also hit. After another raid on 1 September the station could only control one of its three squadrons. The other two were dispersed to satellite airfields because of the large number of craters in the runway and from fear that buildings might fall on the aircraft.[32]

Three consecutive days of bombing had reduced Biggin Hill to a shambles and the dispersal of squadrons certainly reduced its operational efficiency, but subsequent events demonstrated how difficult it was to put a fighter station out of commission. On 2 September a temporary operations room was set up in a nearby shop and the GPO soon restored cable and telephone communications. The station could then pass on radar and Observer Corps information to its dispersed squadrons. Craters were also filled in and a degree of normality was restored.

The other Sector airfield that was heavily bombed on 31 August was Hornchurch, where dispersal huts, petrol dumps and barrack blocks were hit. However, within 24 hours the airfield was serviceable again. Most damage had been repaired and the operations rooms and hangers had not been affected by the raid. In addition, Hornchurch was a grass airfield with no runways to crater.[33]

The experience of Biggin Hill is proof that the Luftwaffe could make life extremely difficult for Fighter Command, but to inflict serious damage they needed to identify the Sector airfields, realise that the operations rooms and the communications cables were the crucial targets, hit them and keep them out of action by repeated raids. It is clear that the Germans lacked the information needed to identify the airfields and the crucial targets on them, and the accuracy to hit these targets with any regularity.

Their difficulties were compounded by the multiplicity of targets they attempted to destroy. At the same time as the Luftwaffe attacked the airfields, it was also required to attack ports, convoys and other pre-invasion targets. During this period the following non-RAF targets were bombed: Portland, Chichester, convoys off Flamborough Head, Brighton, Sandwich, shipping in the Thames Estuary, Dover, Portsmouth, Exmouth, Yarmouth, Ipswich and many more locations.[34]

Admittedly, some of these targets such as Southampton, which contained the Spitfire works, could be regarded as targets of vital concern to Fighter

Command. However, the overall pattern indicates that once again the Luftwaffe was dispersing its efforts. There was clearly no single-minded purpose behind these attacks. Perhaps the Germans thought that they had the power to destroy a whole range of targets simultaneously. What they actually achieved, in trying to destroy everything, was to destroy nothing. Some airfields were badly damaged, some ports grievously affected. But neither the RAF nor Britain's coastal shipping nor its export trade was disastrously disrupted.

There was a temporary change in the German tactics when the Luftwaffe decided to attack not just the south of England but the Midlands and Scotland as well. For this purpose they mobilised Luftflotte 5 under Generaloberst Hans-Jurgen Stumpff, flying from aerodromes in Norway and Denmark. The main problem with this plan (apart from the dispersal of effort it represented) was that because of the great distances involved, the bombers would have to fly without single-engine fighter escort. They would have to rely instead on the slow and vulnerable Me 110s. All told, about 130 bombers, escorted by the twin-engine fighters, mounted raids in the north-east. The radar chain located the enemy formations well out to sea and fighter squadrons were scrambled in ample time to meet them. The result was a massacre, as evidenced by the combat report from just one of the intercepting squadrons. The 605 Squadron was south of Newcastle when it was vectored in on a group of about 60 to 70 Heinkel 111s. In all the squadron mounted 16 attacks on the Germans. Their reports make sobering reading:

Attack No. 1 – 200–50 yards – no deflection – 7 bursts of 3 seconds – engine put out of action.

Attack No. 2 – 300–50 yards – no deflection – 1 burst of 2–3 seconds – e/a destroyed.

Attack No. 3 – Astern attack – no deflection – 1 burst of 2 seconds – e/a destroyed.

Attack No. 4 – Astern attack – 150–50 yards – no deflection – 1 burst of 2–3 seconds – no result.

Attack No. 5 – Beam attack – 200–100 yards – slight deflection – 1 burst of 3 seconds – e/a destroyed.

Attack No. 6 – Astern attack – 150–70 yards – oil blinded fighter pilot – e/a probably destroyed.

Attack No. 7 – Quarter attack from port side – 1 burst of 3 seconds – e/a damaged.

Attack No. 8 – Dive attack 250–25 yards – 1 burst of 5 seconds – oil on windscreen prevented observation.

Attack No. 9 – Dive attack – 1 burst of 3 seconds – e/a destroyed.

Attack No. 10 – Beam attack of 3 seconds – e/a destroyed.

Attack No. 11 – Dive attack 400–100 yards – 1 burst of 7 seconds – e/a damaged.

Attack No. 12 – Beam attack – 250–100 yards – 4-second burst – e/a destroyed.

Attack No. 13 – Beam attack – 300–200 yards – ammunition ran out – no result.

Attack No. 14 – Attack on 2 e/a. Engines of both on fire – probably destroyed.

Attack No. 15 – Attack 100–20 yards – 1 burst of 3 seconds – e/a probably destroyed.

Attack No. 16 – Attack on straggler – e/a destroyed.[35]

And so the slaughter continued. By the end of the day the two Luftwaffe units involved in the north-east had lost eight Heinkel 111s, nine Junkers 88s and ten Me 110s. Fighter Command lost no aircraft.[36] The experiment was never repeated and many of the planes from Luftflotte 5 were transferred to France.

It must also be kept in mind that throughout this period the German bombers were also active at night – not against airfields, which could not be accurately identified during hours of darkness – but against industrial targets such as Liverpool, Bristol, the Midlands, South Wales and others. The importance of these raids as far as the Battle of Britain is concerned is that bombers used at night were not bombing airfields. Nor could they be used in any capacity the following day as their crews had to be rested.

As a consequence, on any given day the Luftwaffe could attack Fighter Command *only* with aircraft not involved with pre-invasion bombing *and* those not used in operations on the previous night. While the intensification of the air attack caused Fighter Command considerable grief and inconvenience, it did not represent an all-out assault by the forces at the Luftwaffe's command.

It is hardly surprising that there were many in Fighter Command (both pilots and commanders) who nevertheless felt that the whole weight of the Luftwaffe had been turned against them. By 6 September southern British airfields had been under attack for a month. Although, as noted, there was little system in the German approach, Sector airfields at Middle Wallop, Kenley, Biggin Hill, Hornchurch, North Weald, Debden and Tangmere had been hit. The condition of this last station, although it was not put out of action even for an hour, could make a powerful impression. P. O. Wissler, who had just been posted there, noted: 'Tangmere is in a shocking state. The buildings being in an awful shambles. Several 1000lb bombs having fallen.'[37]

The most anguished reaction to the state of 11 Group airfields, however, came from the man in charge of them, Sir Keith Park. In a report to Dowding he stated:

36. Contrary to general belief and official reports, the enemy's bombing attacks by day did extensive damage to five of our forward aerodromes, and also to six of our seven Sector Stations. The damage to forward aerodromes was so severe that Manston and Lympne were on several occasions for days quite unfit for operating fighters.

37. Biggin Hill was so severely damaged that only one squadron could operate from there, and the remaining two squadrons had to be placed under the control of adjacent Sectors for over a week. Had the enemy continued his heavy attacks against the adjacent Sectors and knocked out their Operations Rooms or telephone communications, the fighter defences of London would have been in a parlous state . . .

38. Sector Operations Rooms have on three occasions been put out of action, either by direct hits or by damage to G.P.O. cables, and all Sectors took into use their Emergency Operations Rooms, which were not only too small to house the essential personnel, but had never been provided with the proper scale of G.P.O. landlines to enable normal operation of three squadrons per Sector. In view of this grave deficiency, arrangements were made to establish alternative Sector Operations Rooms within five miles of each Sector aerodrome, and this work is now proceeding with the highest priority . . .

40. The attacks on our fighter aerodromes soon proved that the Air Ministry's arrangements for labour and equipment quickly to repair aerodrome surfaces were absolutely inadequate, and this has been made the subject of numerous signals and letters during the past four weeks.[38]

41. There was a critical period between 29th August and 5th September when the damage to Sector Stations and our ground organisation was having a serious effect on the fighting efficiency of the fighter squadrons, who could not be given the same good technical and administrative service as previously.

Luckily, Park concluded, the enemy then turned its attention to other targets (London) and this gave the Sectors and other airfields time to recover.[39]

Park's report has been quoted at length because it is probably the origin of the view that if the Luftwaffe had not turned its attention to London on 7 September, Fighter Command might well have been doomed. Park certainly makes some cogent points in the report about the damage done to his Sector airfields, the inadequacy of repair facilities, and the drop in efficiency caused by the dispersal of squadrons. However, it is not hindsight to see in this report the response of a commander under the utmost pressure. It bears repeating that to a large extent Park's 11 Group fought the Battle of Britain. Park was required, day after day, to make the critical decisions on which squadrons to send up and when and where to send them. He had to get these decisions right to give his squadron leaders a chance to engage the enemy on favourable terms. Park, in short, could have lost the battle. Dowding was well aware of the pressure on Park, so when he passed his report on to the Air Ministry he added a few comments to give perspective to the situation that faced the embattled commander of 11 Group. In particular he selected Paragraph 40 for detailed comment:

Paragraph 40 reads very pessimistically and in it I think A.O.C. No. 11 Group has done justice neither to himself or to the units of his command. The fact is that the battle of August and September was very fierce and sustained . . . [In these conditions] it was inevitable . . . that the efficiency of the Fighter squadrons should fall off in a marked manner; but the point to remember is that the losses sustained by the enemy were so great that heavy day attacks by bombers [on airfields] were brought to a standstill.[40]

It is apparent that Dowding, while conceding Park's difficulties, did not think that Fighter Command was at the end of its tether. In this he was surely correct. Five of the six Sector stations had indeed been hit, but few remained out of action for more than a few hours. Operating squadrons from adjacent Sectors or from satellite airfields was indeed less efficient than operating them from home base, but they could still be deployed in time to meet enemy attacks. Temporary Operations Rooms were no doubt crowded and less efficient than the originals, but they were well able to function away from the Sector airfield, receive the radar and Observer Corps plots, and send their squadrons up. As for Park's remarks about the forward aerodromes, it was inevitable that as soon as the Germans gained possession of the Channel coast in France, airfields such as Manston and Lympne (which anyway was only an emergency landing strip) would become untenable. In short, there seems no reason that Fighter Command could not have absorbed yet more punishment to its airfields while remaining a going concern. This is not to say that Park's worries were not understandable or that the turn of the Luftwaffe against London did not give his stations a respite. Whether such a respite extended to the pilots and aircraft of Fighter Command is another matter.

CHAPTER 11

THE BATTLE OF BRITAIN
THE BATTLE WON
7 SEPTEMBER–31 OCTOBER 1940

THE DECISION TO BOMB London constituted the third plan formulated by the Germans. First, there had been a 'reconnaissance in force' to test the strength of Fighter Command. Then there had been the more intense period with fighter airfields as the main, but by no means only, target. Now it was to be London's turn.

The origin of this plan is often portrayed as a reprisal raid for the British bombing of Berlin. On 25 August a number of bombs had fallen on London. Churchill ordered an immediate reprisal and an ineffectual raid was mounted against Berlin. In retaliation, it is claimed, a furious Hitler and Goering decided that London would become the major target of future Luftwaffe operations.[1] That bombs fell first on London and then on Berlin is not in doubt, but that bombing Berlin caused the Luftwaffe to change policy can be questioned.

In late August Luftwaffe Intelligence estimated that between 12 and 19 August 644 British aircraft had been destroyed (that is, almost all of Fighter Command's serviceable strength), and 11 airfields (Eastchurch, Gosport, Lee-on-Solent, Lympne, Manston, Tangmere, Hawkinge, Portsmouth, Rochester, Driffield, Martlesham) had been put permanently out of action.[2] The actual figures were 139 aircraft destroyed and two airfields out of action, but at a meeting of the Luftwaffe high command at The Hague in early September, Kesselring declared that on the basis of the intelligence figures the RAF was finished. Goering, always anxious to declare a victory in the west so that he could reorient the Luftwaffe towards Russia, agreed, and despite a warning from Sperrle that the British still possessed 1,000 fighters, Kesselring's view prevailed. It was decided to finish off what little remained of Fighter Command by selecting a target that its few fighters were bound to defend – London. Without fighter defence civilian morale was bound to collapse and peace terms be sought. It would be victory without invasion.[3] London must be attacked.

If Luftwaffe intelligence on the state of Fighter Command was deluded, their thinking about the importance of London was accurate enough. Fighter Command was bound to defend the capital. But when the first mass attack was made on 7 September, Park was not yet certain that London had become the main target. So when 300 German bombers escorted by 600 fighters crossed the coast just after 4.00 p.m., 11 Group expected the mass of aircraft to split into disparate raids and make for the fighter airfields, as had been the case for the last month. As a result the 11 Group controller dispatched many squadrons to patrol their own airfields, which gave the German bombers converging on London almost a free passage. In particular, the third wave of bombers penetrated to the capital unharried. It is clear from the combat reports that most British squadrons only intercepted the enemy after they had delivered their bombs. But even when a squadron managed to intercept enemy aircraft advancing on London, they were often unable to stop them. In this regard the experience of 54 Squadron was typical:

> Twelve aircraft of 54 squadron engaged the enemy over Maidstone . . .
> Our fighters went in to attack the bombers in separate sections but were
> soon harassed by the fighters. Our pilots were unable to break the
> enemy bomber formations or to inflict much damage.[4]

There could be no doubting the effort put in by Fighter Command. That day 25 squadrons from 10, 11 and 12 Groups were sent up, some on more than once. A total of 817 sorties were flown and over 200 aircraft actually engaged the enemy. But when the locations of the combats are analysed, few of them took place over London. The most common location was Kent and the most common time after 6.15 p.m., that is after the last German bomber had dropped its bombs on the East End.[5] In all, on 7 September the Germans dropped over 600 tons of high explosive and 13,000 incendiaries on the capital, killing over 400 civilians and seriously wounding about 1,400 others.[6] The Luftwaffe paid a price. They lost 16 fighters, 15 bombers and 8 fighter-bombers – a total of 39 aircraft. In addition another 18 were damaged. But Fighter Command lost 25 Hurricanes and Spitfires, with another 29 damaged. This was the fourth highest loss for any day of the Battle of Britain, only exceeded on 15, 18 and 31 August. The attrition rate on Fighter Command had not been lessened by the change of targets.[7]

In the light of this heavy and concentrated raid, Park changed tactics. He noted that three or four hundred German aircraft in two or three waves had made the raid on London in rapid succession – the whole battle lasting only 45 to 60 minutes. To counter these tactics he divided his squadrons into three groups. 'Readiness Squadrons' would be dispatched in pairs against the first enemy wave, the Spitfire squadrons attacking the fighters and the Hurricane squadrons going straight for the bombers. The next group of squadrons would also operate in pairs and be at 15 minutes' readiness. The third group would act as single squadrons and be used as a reserve against the second and third wave of bombers should they come in.[8]

That these tactics required honing is evidenced by the results of combat on 11 and 14 September, the next two days when the Germans mounted major raids on London. On 11 September, Fighter Command lost the same number of aircraft (28) as the Luftwaffe and on 14 September it lost 13 compared to the Germans' 10.[9] In addition, on these two days, 28 pilots were killed or so severely wounded that they would take no further part in the battle.[10] It was no doubt some consolation to Park that London was not severely hit, but the attrition rate on his pilots and aircraft was unacceptable.

All that was to change on the day now celebrated as Battle of Britain Day, 15 September. German manoeuvres over the Channel had been observed by British radar since 9.00 a.m. By 11.00 a.m. it was clear that a large force was assembling near Calais. London, it was adjudged, would be their target. Immediately, 12 squadrons from 11 Group and the Duxford Wing of five squadrons from 12 Group were alerted. Between 11.05 a.m. and 11.25 a.m. they took off. The result was that between the coast and

London the German force of about 50 bombers and probably 100 fighters was attacked by 12 squadrons (about 100 planes) from Fighter Command, many of them acting in pairs following Park's instructions. These formations launched six separate attacks against the Germans, who finally struck by the Duxford force over London. The result was a decisive defeat for the Luftwaffe. Most bombers failed to reach the capital and those that did dropped their bombs at random and turned for home. Even then, they were harried by three squadrons from the reserve which struck them over Brooklands and inflicted many casualties.[11]

Then, at 2.00 p.m., a time that allowed Fighter Command a period of recovery after the first raid, a second large force was detected by the radar chain. This time 15 squadrons from 11 Group and the five from Duxford were scrambled to meet them. In all eight attacks were delivered against the enemy – most in the area Canterbury–Dartford. Once more a concerted German bombing attack on the capital was thwarted. The experience of 213 Squadron (Hurricanes) from Tangmere is worth noting in detail:

Twelve Hurricanes of No. 213 Squadron took off from Tangmere at 1410 hours ... The enemy aircraft were met at 1450 hours flying towards London at 13,000 feet. They consisted of about 80 Do. 17's flying in two formations of 40 each ... 213 Squadron carried out a head-on attack on the Do. 17's. The Leader of the Squadron (F/Lt. Sing) singled out one enemy aircraft and shot away the whole of the nose, including the pilot's cockpit. The a/c went into a steep dive and a probable [!] is claimed. Sub/Lieut Jeram (Green 2 and F/O Duryang) (Polish) Red 2 both went right through the enemy formation and then, turning back, attacked astern an enemy aircraft each and both claim one Do. 17 each destroyed, as they followed their opponents down through the clouds and saw them blazing on the ground. Green 1 (F/Sgt Grayson) carried out an astern attack on another and after several bursts saw e/a go down in an absolute vertical dive out of control ... Sgt. Bushell carried out an astern attack on a Do. 17 and damaged it. Blue 2 (F/O Cottam) dived vertically onto a Do. 17, damaged it, and having lost it, proceeded to Dungeness where he saw a Spitfire attacking an Me. 110. He joined in and helped to shoot it down into the sea. Green 3 (Sgt. Snowdon) never had a chance of attacking a Do. 17 so he also proceeded to Dungeness on the look out for stragglers, and, having found an Me. 110 he attacked it, and using deflection, shot it down into the sea . . .

The enemy attack was completely broken up. Many e/a were seen to jettison their bombs as they were attacked and then turned back.[12]

The report reveals the absolute terror that must have been experienced by German bomber crew, in their Perspex cockpits, as a fighter approached them at 350 mph; the value of a head-on attack in breaking the bomber formation; the tenacity of the British (and Polish) pilots in seeking out a target; in this case the absence of any fighter protection for the bombers; and the ability of a force outnumbered 6:1 to thwart a large attack.

In the event, Fighter Command could not prevent some bombs falling on London. Targets in south London, including Tooting, and some in the West End, including Buckingham Palace, were hit, but the bombing was sporadic and no vital centres were irreparably damaged.

At the end of the day, Fighter Command had shot down far fewer than the 185 aircraft claimed at the time, but the actual result was still highly favourable to Park's men. For the loss of 30 Hurricanes and Spitfires they shot down 56 German aircraft, comprising 23 fighters and 33 bombers, the second highest bomber loss for the entire Battle of Britain.[13]

Indeed, the turn to London placed the pilots of the short-range Me 109s in an impossible position. Their limited range meant that the Me 109s could spend little time protecting the bombers over the capital. In some cases a head wind forced the Me 109s to turn for home early and leave the bombers unescorted. This left the slow-moving Dornier 17 particularly vulnerable to the British fighters and many were picked off over London with the greatest of ease.[14]

The decision to bomb London did lessen the pressure on Fighter Command in several respects. The diminution of the mass attacks on their airfields enabled runways and buildings to be repaired and communications restored. Moreover, the defence of London actually cost Fighter Command fewer losses in aircraft in September than the losses suffered in August in defence of its airfields. From 11 August to 6 September, Fighter Command had lost from all causes about 800 Spitfires and Hurricanes.[15] At the same time it received almost exactly the same number of new and repaired aircraft. During the intense phase of attacks on airfields Fighter Command was holding its own, but only just. From 7 to 30 September its losses from all causes were 440 aircraft while Fighter Command gained 534 from new production and the repair depots. In the two most intense months of the battle 1,240 front-line fighters had been lost. These were prodigious losses but over the same period 1,330 fighters had been gained.[16] Some of this came from running down the number of aircraft in store, but it was always the case that more aircraft could have been flown into 11 Group from other areas of the country. Park noted in his report to Dowding in October that the position of Fighter Command had improved both in regards to the efficiency of their airfields and in the growth in numbers. The pessimism of his earlier report had gone.[17]

The one factor that caused great concern to Park and Dowding in this period was the attrition of their fighter pilots. Table 5 gives the weekly available pilots compared with the weekly available serviceable aircraft. The dates for serviceable aircraft and available pilots do not exactly coincide but are close enough to make reasonable comparisons. The final figure in Table 5 expresses the number of available pilots per serviceable aircraft.[18]

Table 5: Fighter Command Aircraft and Pilot Availability.

Date	Serviceable aircraft	Available pilots	Pilots per plane
8 July	749	1,259	1.68
15 July	828	1,341	1.62
22 July	771	1,365	1.78
30 July	828	1,377	1.67
4 August	879	1,434	1.63
12 August	811	1,396	1.72
16 August	793	1,379	1.74
26 August	888	1,377	1.55
2 September	864	1,422	1.65
10 September	762	1,381	1.81
17 September	737	1,492	2.02
22 September	791	1,509	1.91
29 September	755	1,581	2.09

If a squadron is taken as consisting of 12 aircraft and 18 pilots, Table 5 reveals that at no point during the Battle of Britain was there a pilot shortage.[19] So the constant worry expressed by Dowding and Park during the battle, that they were facing an acute pilot shortage, requires explanation. Partly, as Stephen Bungay explains, Dowding had created the shortage in May 1940 when he increased the establishment of a squadron from 18 pilots to 26.[20] No doubt this was a prudent step, designed to give pilots sufficient rest between sorties to remain at peak efficiency, but it meant that from then on Fighter Command figures always showed a deficiency of pilots to establishment.

Nevertheless, Table 5 should be read bearing in mind that it relates to Fighter Command as a whole. There were days in August when the pilot availability in front-line squadrons fell alarmingly. For example, in August, Spitfire squadrons had only 16 operational pilots for their 12 aircraft.[21] Douglas Evill (Senior Air Staff Officer to Dowding) noted that in just two weeks in August, Fighter Command lost 114 front-line pilots killed, wounded or missing. Replacement pilots from the Operational Training Units (the penultimate training establishment for pilots before release to combat squadrons) only made up for 60 per cent of these losses. The situation was particularly serious regarding Hurricane pilots, where replacements would only account for 16 per cent of losses. He concluded that 'the period under discussion is very short but it does look as though we shall have to do something to boost up the production of Hurricane pilots in particular'.[22]

In early September, Dowding called a meeting between his staff, Park and Sholto Douglas from the Air Ministry to discuss the pilot shortage. Various expedients were adopted, including taking pilots from Lysander and Fairey Battle squadrons and retraining them in modern types. In addition, pilots from Poland and Czechoslovakia in particular were to be trained in Hurricanes, adding another 40 pilots to the total. This was a very bad-tempered meeting with Douglas rather sanguine about the position but with Dowding insisting that 'I want you to take away from this meeting the feeling that the situation is very grave'. The key remark, however, was probably made by Park, usually (with good reason) the most pessimistic of the group. He assured the others that in his opinion the Luftwaffe could not keep up the pressure on Fighter Command for more than three weeks and that they would probably get through.[23] And so they did. Table 5 shows that while the pilot position did indeed weaken in August, it soon improved and by 17 September was as strong as it was to be for the entire battle. Certainly Dowding never attained the comfortable reserve that he had sought in May, but the fact remained that the British had a sufficiency of pilots to win the battle.

On the other side of the Channel attrition had also been at work on the Luftwaffe and the state of its operational aircraft bore out Park's suspicions. On 10 August the Luftwaffe had 2,651 serviceable aircraft. In the weeks that followed there was a downward trend as indicated in Table 6.[24]

Table 6: Luftwaffe: Serviceable Aircraft, 10 August–5 October 1940.

Date	SE fighters	TE fighters	Bombers	Dive-bombers	Total
10 August	933	357	1,015	346	2,651
17 August	853	254	1,038	307	2,452
24 August	839	266	1,038	328	2,471
31 August	692	215	866	354	2,127
7 September	762	175	876	344	2,157
14 September	755	154	915	340	2,164
21 September	727	136	846	352	2,061
28 September	721	114	818	375	2,028
5 October	667	99	836	379	1,981

These figures reveal that the Luftwaffe suffered an overall decline in aircraft numbers of 25 per cent during the intensive phase of the Battle of Britain. The numbers of serviceable, single-engine fighters declined by 28.5 per cent and bombers by 18 per cent. The decline in twin-engine fighters was a catastrophic 72 per cent. The figures for dive-bombers actually indicate an increase, but this was only because they had largely been withdrawn from the battle around 18 August. Indeed, the figure for the dive-bombers should actually be removed from the Luftwaffe total altogether, and if this is done it shows that the number of usable German aircraft available to the Luftwaffe suffered a 40 per cent overall decline.

What is the explanation for this precipitate decline? The first part of the equation is the fearful losses inflicted on the Luftwaffe by Fighter Command during this phase of the battle. It will be recalled that from 12 August to 30 September the British suffered 1,240 aircraft lost and damaged. In the same period, however, the Germans lost 1,760 aircraft to the British Hurricanes and Spitfires. These losses consisted of 565 fighters, 812 bombers, 291 twin-engine fighters and 92 dive-bombers. The vulnerability of the Me 110 is demonstrated by the fact that in just four days of combat 78 were shot down or damaged. In the case of the dive-bombers, on 18 August the Germans lost 18 aircraft or 6 per cent of their total force, which was why they were rapidly withdrawn. As for bombers, the Luftwaffe lost 10 per cent of its force in the week of 12–18 August, another 10 per cent from 24 to 31 August, and 6 per cent of the force from 1 to 7 September. The losses of the fighter force are just as drastic. Between 12–18 August they lost about 10 per cent of their force, from 24 to 31 August close to 15 per cent, and from 1 to 7 September another 15 per cent.

The second part of this equation is the German aircraft production effort. Here the figures are indeed stark. While losing 565 fighters the Germans produced only 250, for bombers the figures are 812 lost and 350 produced, for twin-engine fighters 291 and 147. Only with dive-bombers are losses and production about equal (92 and 88), but as noted the losses are low because the Ju 87s were withdrawn from the battle after 18 August. As for the numbers of damaged aircraft returned to service by the Germans, there are no available figures, but Table 6 reveals that they were insufficient to prevent the decline of the force.

In short, during this phase of the Battle of Britain the Luftwaffe was a wasting asset, whose position was only likely to worsen as British production continued to outstrip German.

The Germans were well aware of the decline of the Luftwaffe and Goering was certainly conscious of the planned attack on the Soviet Union in the spring of 1941. This meant that there would have to be a radical change in Luftwaffe policy if the air force was to play a meaningful role in the eastern campaign. Goering decided therefore to persist with the night bombing of London but to use the bomber force sparingly by day. Instead he would equip his single-engine fighters with bomb racks (250 or 500kg bomb loads) and direct them to make tip-and-run sweeps over southern England while flying at heights of 30,000 feet to make interception difficult.

Ironically, at the very moment the new tactics were implemented, the Luftwaffe bombers scored their most telling blow against Fighter Command. On 24 September the Supermarine works at Southampton was raided. Forty-two people were killed and 161 wounded but the aircraft production line was hardly touched. Then a lucky blow was struck on 26 September. Two waves of bombers hit the Spitfire factory with 70 tons of high explosive. The plant was wrecked to such an extent that it was never rebuilt. Although Castle Bromwich in the Midlands, beyond the range where bombers could be escorted, was entering full production, it could not make up for the loss of the Southampton works. Emergency measures were put in place, which saw the dispersal of production of Spitfires to dozens of sites across southern England. This masterpiece of improvisation did not fully solve the problem, however. In early 1941 Spitfire production had been reduced to 30 per cent of its September 1940 figure.[25] But by then the Luftwaffe was largely confining itself to night-bombing operations.

Goering's change of tactics was in effect a tacit recognition that the battle against Fighter Command had been lost, because even if the German fighters penetrated to vital targets, the constraints on their bombing capacity would strictly limit any damage they might do. For example, even a direct hit by a 250kg bomb on a concrete control room on a Sector airfield would not materially damage it. Nevertheless, during October the Germans kept coming and Park found it particularly difficult to intercept the sweeps. Radar could not give accurate information on very high raids and it was found that large numbers of fighters were being dispatched without sighting or engaging the enemy.[26] In mid-October he issued revised instructions to his controllers to take account of the new situation. Spitfire squadrons were to be assembled in pairs and given fixed patrol lines near the coast, from where they could intercept high-flying enemy fighter raids. Behind these forward patrols mixed wings of Hurricanes and Spitfires would engage the enemy in the usual way – the Spitfires tackling the fighters while the Hurricanes went for the bombers. If the enemy appeared to be in great strength, squadrons based to the north of London would converge on the capital.[27]

Even so it proved difficult to inflict great damage on this sort of raid:

9 a/c from 41 squadron left Hornchurch . . . to patrol Maidstone . . . When at 31,000 feet 'A' Flight in the rear of the squadron sighted a large number of widely dispersed Me 109's at 30,500 feet. A few Me 110's accompanied by Me 109's were also seen. 'A' Flight dived on the enemy who immediately fled, diving for cloud at such speed that the Spitfires could not overtake. They were last seen dodging in and out of the 9/10 cloud.[28]

However, a bomb-carrying Me 109 was no match for a determined Spitfire pilot:

The Squadron [74] was given various vectors for single high raiders but did not connect. They were then ordered to join No. 92 Squadron at 30,000 feet over Maidstone. The Squadron Leader (S/Ldr. A. G. Malan) remained at 30,000 feet in order to push out exhaust condensation to frighten the Messerschmitt bomb carriers. No. 92 Squadron gave a 'Tally Ho' and No. 74 Squadron dropped to 28,000 feet. The enemy, consisting of 6 plus Me 109's were seen steering S. E. over Ashford at 26,000 feet and were attacked.

Squadron Leader Malan attacked the leading enemy aircraft in a fast dive and fired bursts from 200 to 50 yards range. The enemy aircraft smoked heavily after the second burst, but carried on. Malan continued to fire but had to break away momentarily to wipe ice off the windscreen. He then followed the Me 109 to the coast, and saw the enemy aircraft crash into the sea five miles out from Hastings – the Dungeness area.[29]

The main point to note is that compared with August and September these were minor skirmishes. In all of October, Fighter Command lost just 161 Hurricanes and Spitfires, less than half those lost in August and September, and with production figures averaging over 100 per week British fighter defences gained markedly in strength. German fighter losses were also down from 225 in September to 129 in October, but production still struggled to keep pace. German bomber losses decreased but only from 258 to 182, still well above replacement levels.

In this way the Battle of Britain rather fizzled out, but there is no doubt that Fighter Command had won the day. The Germans just could not risk large losses of fighters or bombers by day and so bombed at night.

How did the British achieve this victory? In war, casualty statistics can often illustrate the decline of one side as against the other. Here the statistics tell only part of the story. In terms of pilots Fighter Command suffered significant losses. Between 10 July and 31 October 1940, of its 2,228 pilots, 537 were killed and a somewhat larger number wounded. This amounts to an overall casualty rate of about 50 per cent. Yet because the training of new pilots proceeded throughout the battle, Fighter Command had more pilots available to it in November than it had in July.

The Luftwaffe lost many more personnel simply because most of their casualties were bombers with crews of two, three or four. The total German aircrew killed was 2,262. Attrition rates of aircraft add another dimension to the picture of decline. Although the Germans still possessed 836 bombers in October, this was 25 per cent fewer than they had started with in July. The numbers for single-engine fighters tell a similar story. There were over 900 available in July – just 650 in October, a decline of almost 30 per cent. No force could continue to suffer losses at this rate, especially when the aircraft were being insufficiently supplemented by new production. These German statistics reveal two things. First, the reduced number of available fighters meant that fewer bombers could be safely escorted. Second, because of the losses, the pilots of both bombers and fighters were much less experienced in October than those in July.

These figures reveal another factor that is a major part of the explanation for the defeat of the Luftwaffe – it was just too small to mount a constant series of raids over Britain. If we examine those days during the battle when the Germans managed to fly over 1,000 sorties, we find they only amounted to eight days out of 113 – on 13, 14, 15, 16, 30 August and 7, 18, 30 September. What is doubly notable about these figures is that only in one period (13–16 August) did the Luftwaffe mount *consecutive* attacks on this scale. On most occasions, therefore, a massive raid would be followed by a pause while pilots were rested and aircraft repaired. The Germans just did not have the capacity to maintain constant heavy pressure on Fighter Command.

One feature of the battle is seldom dealt with. Because the British won it, the manner of its winning is seldom questioned. But was there a better way? One of the great historians of the battle, T. C. G. James, thought there was. In his official narrative of the battle, written in 1944, he said:

It is at least debatable whether the Commander-in-Chief's policy [of retaining so many squadrons in the north] was correct. If, for example, he had packed additional squadrons into No. 11 group early in the battle so powerful a blow might have been struck at the attacking forces that the daylight offensive might conceivably have been abandoned.[30]

Certainly Dowding was parsimonious in the number of squadrons he maintained in the front line. 11 Group never had more than 43 per cent of Fighter Command's serviceable Spitfires and Hurricanes at any period of the battle. No doubt Dowding wanted to keep a reserve of his modern fighters distant enough from enemy aerodromes in France so that escorted German bombers could not attack them. But could Dowding not have done more to reinforce Park? Would not an additional 100 fighters have dealt the Luftwaffe such a blow that they might have called off the battle? After all, 15 September demonstrated that Goering was not prepared to take losses of that scale as a regular occurrence.

In Dowding's defence it is said that there was a limit to the number of squadrons that a single Group could handle. Let us examine this situation more closely. When battle commenced 11 Group had 18 squadrons of Hurricanes and Spitfires, two squadrons of Defiants and three squadrons of Blenheims. The location of the Defiants and Blenheims in the front line does raise some questions about Dowding's strategy. Both types had been used in the French campaign where they were found to be entirely outclassed by the Me 109 and even by the Me 110 fighter-bomber. They had no place, therefore, in the front line of British air defence. Yet Dowding only moved two of them (141 Defiant Squadron and 604 Blenheim Squadron) to the north during the first month of battle. If all five of these obsolescent squadrons had been moved, Park's group could have been provided with five modern squadrons – about 60 additional Hurricanes and Spitfires – without being required to handle more squadrons than he began with. The remaining two Blenheim squadrons stayed with Park throughout the battle and, more amazingly, a squadron of Defiants was moved back into 11 Group on 22 August. (These did not last long. The squadron was so knocked about that it was removed a week later.)

Park certainly thought that 11 Group could handle additional squadrons. In early September he wrote to Dowding drawing his attention to the movement of German aircraft from Scandinavia (as a result of the disaster they suffered on 15 August) to the Pas de Calais. He asked for two additional squadrons, one to be based at Hendon under the control of the North Weald Sector and the other at Red Hill to operate under the control of the Kenley Sector.[31] So Park foresaw no difficulty in handling two new squadrons and there seems little doubt that yet more could have been brought into 11 Group along the lines he suggested.

The fact that Dowding stuck to his strategy was not of course a matter of pure stubbornness. Dowding, it will be recalled, had overestimated the strength of the Luftwaffe bomber force by about 100 per cent. Air Ministry estimates were similarly astray and Lindemann, Churchill's scientific adviser, had pointed this out to them as early as July. However, there is no evidence that they passed these revised figures on to Dowding. Perhaps they themselves placed no credibility on Lindemann's figures. The result of this lamentable situation was that the head of Fighter Command considered he was confronting a force twice as strong as it actually was. In this position no doubt he thought it prudent to hold back a considerable proportion of his fighter force to meet an onslaught that never came.

In fact, it is not the case that Dowding did nothing in the face of the intensification of the German effort in late August and early September. As the fighting approached London, he strengthened that section of 12 Group that lay just to the north of the capital. Thus we can see that the percentage of fighters allocated to 12 Group increased from just fewer than 20 per cent to 26 per cent in the first week of September. So while Dowding kept 11 Group at about the same strength throughout the battle, this move enabled 12 Group to take a larger percentage of the fighting.

Moreover, if Dowding refused Park's request to strengthen his group, at least he ensured that Park received the best pilots. At a meeting with Park and Air Ministry officials on 7 September, Dowding decided to stop rotating squadrons into 11 Group but instead to rotate pilots. These were divided into three categories, A, B and C. Only A pilots – that is, the most experienced – would be sent to Park. The next most experienced – the B group – would be sent to 12 Group, and C pilots would be sent to 13 Group for training until they reached B or A standard. A nucleus of A pilots would remain in 12 and 13 Group for training purposes.[32] There was a justification for this policy of which Dowding was aware at the time. There was a very small number of pilots in Fighter Command who could shoot well enough to destroy an enemy aircraft. These men had to be placed in the front line to ensure that the attrition rate on the Luftwaffe would be maintained.

Of course, for the pilots, Dowding's policy was a two-edged sword. It actually increased the attrition rate on Fighter Command's best pilots. In the event, however, this did not affect the battle. By the time the scheme was operational, the Luftwaffe was turning to night bombing. If the battle had continued during the latter half of September and October at an intense level, it remains a serious question as to how long the experienced fighters in 11 Group would have lasted.

Did, then, 'the few' prevail over the many? Some commentators have pointed out that on most days of the Battle of Britain the British had more serviceable fighters than the Germans and more pilots. This might well be true but it misses the way in which the battle was fought. Because of Dowding's cautious disposition of squadrons and because Park had limited time in which to scramble his squadrons, there was always the probability that any British force engaging the enemy would be outnumbered. Some of the examples given earlier suggest that the ratio could be as high as 8:1 in favour of the Luftwaffe. Indeed, if we calculate the number of British aircraft actually in combat on any particular day, we find that they were almost always outnumbered by the Luftwaffe. To take just two examples, on 18 August just 328 aircraft from Fighter Command fought 560 German aircraft, and on Battle of Britain Day (15 September) 392 British aircraft were in combat against over 600 from the Luftwaffe.[33] Similar figures or ones even more favourable to the Germans can be found for almost all days of the battle.

The other point to be made about the 'few' is that it was usually the same squadrons from 11 Group that confronted the Germans day after day. While it is true that for most of the battle squadrons were rotated, many of them stayed in the battle zone for considerable periods of time. Thus 56, 1, 43, 54 Squadrons stayed in the south from 10 July until early September, and 17 Squadron remained in the Group throughout the battle. These squadrons therefore experienced all the major battles in August and many in the first week of September. Later in the battle these figures disguise the effect on particularly experienced pilots who, under Dowding's 'stabilisation' scheme, would have found themselves rotated back into the combat areas even when their squadrons were located in the north.

There was an even smaller group who inflicted a very high percentage of casualties on the Germans. As noted above, there were very few British pilots who had mastered the art of deflection shooting or who were just good shots. It has been calculated that 3.5 per cent of pilots in Fighter Command accounted for about 30 per cent of German casualties. Other pilots did their bit in disrupting the German bombers, but for the battle to be won German aircraft had to be destroyed. Most of them were destroyed by just a handful of men.

Overall we can conclude that Fighter Command won the battle by a considerable margin. However, it must always be remembered that this was not obvious at the time. Few then seem to have been aware of the actual combat strength of their opponent or the feeble effort of the German aircraft industry compared to the British. Moreover, it could not be known how long the battle would last or whether the strain on the British pilots might prove too much. During the battle, day after day after day three or four hundred men from Fighter Command were obliged to risk their lives – often several times on the same day. They proved capable of the task. They were the few. And they won the battle.

CHAPTER 12

TERROR BY NIGHT
BRITAIN SURVIVES THE BLITZ,
SEPTEMBER 1940–MAY 1941

THE WAR ON THE civilian population of Britain began on 7 September 1940 when London was subjected to mass bombardment from the air. The British people had endured many shocks in the course of 1940 – the Norway fiasco, the retreat to Dunkirk, the desperate days of the evacuation, the collapse of France, the invasion threat, and the uncertainty about the outcome of the great air battles that raged above them. Could they endure a direct assault? How robust was the mood of the country on the eve of the Blitz? Public mood is notoriously difficult to assess but there are some guides through this minefield. In 1940 the measurement of public opinion was in its infancy but the authorities considered the matter important enough in wartime to make an attempt. From May 1940 the Home Intelligence Department of the Ministry of Information (MOI) and a private organisation later hired by the Ministry (Mass Observation or MO) compiled daily or weekly 'morale' reports. The information in these reports came from a variety of sources – the Regional Information Officers of the MOI, postal censorship, bookshop owners, cinema proprietors, and a group of investigators who listened in on the private conversations of people whom they considered to be a representative sample of the population. At their peak, however, only about 2,000 investigators were employed in these organisations. Moreover, most of the staff were middle class, male and well educated, factors that at least had the potential to skew the

239

reported views of women, the working class and groups outside the social milieu of the investigators.

By focusing on 'morale' the government hoped to obtain some measure of the civilian population's willingness to continue working.[1] But the definition of morale for survey purposes was open to wide interpretation. Both the MOI and MO thought they knew what was meant by this most slippery of terms. To them, more often than not, high morale was equated with 'cheerfulness', a commodity in pretty short supply in Britain after recent events in Europe. Nevertheless, cheerfulness was considered crucial by the investigators, who assumed that only the cheerful could contribute effectively to the war effort.[2] But even when circumstances were grim (and in MOI or MO terms morale had slipped) it was possible that those with so-called low morale could still do a decent day's work, as suggested by this comment made at the end of a raid: 'there was little time for grief, for after all the next raid was imminent and every air-raid warning in the night was followed by a new day when people had to work'.[3]

Without a correlation between cheerfulness and the performance of the war economy the daily fluctuations in morale detected by the MOI and MO are virtually worthless as an indication of how the population might respond to the Blitz. Nevertheless, the MOI/MO reports can be instructive – not to track fluctuations in morale – but to identify frequently occurring themes that indicated ongoing concerns and attitudes.

The most constant of these themes is approval for any action taken by the Churchill government to prosecute the war more vigorously and a corresponding disapproval of any policy that seemed inadequate to the situation or harked back to the bad old days of appeasement. So the Emergency Powers Bill of May 1940 had 'an excellent reception',[4] even though this bill stated that all persons might be called upon to 'place themselves, their services and their property' at the disposal of the government.[5] It was an indication of the stern temper of the times that this measure was greeted with satisfaction among all regions in Britain. It was 'well received' in Northern Ireland, 'welcomed' in Birmingham and Leeds, 'excellently received' in Manchester, and met with a more sober 'general approval' in Cambridge.[6]

In contrast was the public response to a broadcast by the Minister of Information, Duff Cooper, urging the public to show the courage now that they had displayed in past crises. The reply the MOI conveyed to the minister was that the people had no doubt about their own courage but considerable doubt about the resolve of the government of which Duff Cooper was a part.[7]

This concern was most often expressed over the extent of unemployment in Britain. This figure had stood at over 1 million at the beginning of the war and due to the lethargy of the Chamberlain government was taking some time to reduce. In June the MOI noted that whereas the French were said to be 'staking all' in their battles, Britain still had 500,000 unemployed.[8] In particular, the high levels of unemployment in Belfast drew the ire of the Northern Irish – why did the government not place more war orders in the area to soak up the jobless?[9]

Perhaps the most forthright comment on the government's perceived tardiness to mobilise the economy came in response to one of Churchill's most famous speeches. The MOI noted that in some quarters it had been said that 'Phrases like "We will never surrender", "We will fight in the streets, on the hills" are being criticised in the light of the inadequate mobilisation of men and materials.'[10] Even the finest of phrases was deemed no substitute for action.

The Chancellor of the Exchequer, Sir Kingsley Wood, was never thought to be adequate for his position. His interim budget in July 1940 raised taxation from 7s 6d to 8s 6d in the pound, increased taxes on cigarettes, alcohol and entertainment, and foreshadowed a purchase tax.[11] All the comments the budget brought forth were critical of its feebleness. The opinion that it 'did not go far enough to carry the tremendous burdens of expenditure needed to win the war' was typical.[12] Leeds, Cardiff and Reading all thought the budget 'too timid'.[13] General criticism of the budget continued into August: 'Not nearly drastic enough' was the usual comment.[14]

There were other indications of the resolute mood in the country after the shock of Dunkirk. On 3 July Churchill ordered that the French Fleet at Mers-el-Kebir in Algeria be sunk to prevent it falling into German hands. The French command was given the options of joining Britain or of sailing to a neutral port, but rejected both. Churchill gave the order with great reluctance and the British admirals carried it out with even greater reluctance. But the move proved highly popular with the public. Home Intelligence reported that the news of the action was 'received in all

Regions with satisfaction and relief', the only criticism being that some French ships escaped.[15]

This incident highlights the high approval given by the public to Churchill and his policy of victory at all costs. His great speeches were 'much appreciated' or held to have had a 'steadying effect'. His determination to defend London 'street by street' was taken as an indicator that 'we shall not be sold out as the French were by their government'. Generally his messages were well regarded even (or perhaps especially) when they painted the strategic picture exactly as he saw it without glossing over the peril in which the country found itself. It was said that 'if he [Churchill] says things are all right . . . people know they are all right; if he says things are bad, we know they are bad'.[16] His warnings against complacency in the invasion period were 'widely welcomed'.[17] His speech on the 'few' was thought to be 'the most forceful and heartening he has yet made' and 'created a strong feeling of confidence'.[18] Even critics who thought that he might have to be voted out after the war considered 'he's the man for us now'.[19]

The most frequently mentioned members of the government apart from Churchill were Neville Chamberlain and the Foreign Secretary, Lord Halifax. The attitude of the public towards these men was almost universally hostile. The adverse remarks began just after Churchill had seen off efforts by Halifax (sometimes supported by Chamberlain) to seek some kind of compromise peace with Hitler. On 12 June the MOI reported that the most that could be said about Chamberlain was that the view that he should resign from the War Cabinet was not increasing strongly.[20] A week later there were reports from Newcastle, Scarborough, Brighton and London that both appeasers should go. The Ministry reports reveal that the public was 'angry' that they remained in power and even prepared to accuse them of treachery.[21] These feelings did not diminish as the year went on. There was 'puzzlement' that Chamberlain in particular was still in office.[22] 'Demands' were expressed that members of the previous government (with the exception of Churchill) 'should be removed'.[23] Criticisms such as these were almost a weekly occurrence throughout the year. Even after the Blitz had started, people found time to observe that Chamberlain should be dismissed.[24] In October when Chamberlain finally resigned due to ill-health, he got scant sympathy. One remark was that 'I think it is a damned good thing . . . We're going to win the war now.'[25] Only when he died of cancer in November was 'some' sympathy expressed, but that emotion was far from universal.[26]

Halifax did not escape censure either. His reply to Hitler's 'peace' overture in June was a public relations disaster that brought down some criticism on Churchill's head for giving him the job. But that criticism was mild compared to what was said about the Foreign Secretary. Home Intelligence felt moved to give the replies verbatim: 'Too much like a bishop', 'Depressing', 'Disappointing', 'Unsatisfactory', 'What about the Burma Road?', 'A statesman has to be a fighter these days', 'He didn't explain anything', 'Old-fashioned diplomacy', 'Too much like the Chamberlain days', 'It was a dull speech: I switched off . . . It's no use treating a mad dog like that.' Someone commented that he liked the 'high moral tone' in which the speech was delivered, but that was drowned out by the chorus of disapproval.[27] The MOI tried to put the best gloss on this that they could. Perhaps, they reasoned, what Halifax said went over the heads of a large section of the public.[28] Reading the comments, however, it seems that the public understood Halifax only too well.

Nor did Halifax's image improve. In October hope was expressed that he would soon join Chamberlain in retirement, 'as he has been living in a fool's paradise for years'.[29] Later in the month the view that he was only fit to be a bishop resurfaced in what Home Intelligence reported as a 'growing feeling' against him. This negative view remained. Churchill eventually shipped Halifax off to be ambassador in Washington in December. As far as the British people were concerned the Prime Minister could have acted earlier and not necessarily rewarded him with a plum job.

Another indication of the mood of the people was shown by attitudes towards feeding those in Europe under German occupation. Ex-President Herbert Hoover warned Britain that its blockade was threatening millions in Europe with starvation. The government's policy was to maintain the blockade, as any food sent would be seized by the Germans. The MOI found that 82 per cent of the population supported the policy whereas only 3 per cent disapproved.[30]

Finally there was the attitude to bombing the enemy. Bombs had fallen on London (by accident as it happened) in late August. Even before Churchill could respond, the public were calling for reprisal raids on

Berlin.[31] When the enemy capital was eventually bombed on 25 August, the raid caused 'great satisfaction' and evoked a 'wide expression of approval'.[32] Among the public there were 'no scruples' about the fact that some of the bombs might fall on civilians. On the contrary the only criticism of the raids was that they were not heavier.[33] Later there was a another criticism – that 'further accounts of the damage done by our raids on Germany' should be published.[34]

To sum up, the attitude of the British public (mobilise more rapidly, sink the French Fleet, remove the appeasers from office, call for victory at all costs, maintain the blockade of Europe, bomb Berlin and don't mind the civilians) pointed in one direction. On the eve of the Blitz there was a remarkable unanimity in Britain around the general proposition of waging vigorous war. The arrival of the Blitz found the British people in good heart.

* * * * *

It is conventional to think of the Blitz on London as commencing on 7 September. Certainly, that date saw the first day of concentrated bombing of the capital. But bombs had been falling on Britain consistently since late May. After Dunkirk, Goering had ordered the Luftwaffe, as well as preparing the way for invasion and destroying the RAF, to carry out 'dislocation and nuisance raids on Britain'.[35] Such raids commenced in some strength in late June. Many of them were made at night by (usually) small numbers of aircraft. The idea was to dislocate British industry by forcing factories to cease work while the bombers were in range or by bombing factories that could be definitely identified. The method was for small flights to range far and wide across Britain so that no area could be considered safe. For example, on the night of 6–7 July bombs were dropped on the North and West Ridings of Yorkshire, Lincolnshire and Norfolk. On the following night Peterborough was overflown, while on the night of 10–11 June bombers were in the vicinity of Portsmouth, Brighton, Horsham, Ipswich, Colchester, Grimsby, Hull, Lincoln, Boston, Canterbury, Norwich and King's Lynn, causing sirens to be sounded and work in factories to cease for some hours.[36]

From late August the attacks against industrial cities such as Birmingham, Coventry, Liverpool and Swansea were stepped up – on some nights over

100 tons of bombs being dropped.[37] Little lasting damage was done to industry by these raids. The only vital target damaged in this period was the Spitfire factory at Castle Bromwich, which was hit on 27 August. Some machine tools were destroyed but the overall effect on Spitfire production was slight.[38]

However, there is no doubt that these raids did cause dislocation. The siren policy adopted by the government meant that on most occasions when the sirens sounded, work would stop. Later the siren policy was changed and tools were only downed when raiders, identified by spotters on the roofs, were immediately overhead. But even in this period the production indices of most war materials increased, indicating that the greater numbers entering war production offset the dislocation or that workers went on working unless in immediate danger.

There is also no doubt that despite the lack of damage, these raids assisted the Luftwaffe in honing their night-flying skills. In addition the raids killed or maimed about 4,000 people – 6 to 7 per cent of the total bombing casualties for the entire war.[39] However, there is another side to this story. Most raids were small scale so the damage they could do was limited. And the wide-ranging nature of the raids meant that a high proportion of the British population acquired some experience of air raids and sleeping in shelters before being subjected to ferocious bombing. This experience would prove useful preparation for the much sterner ordeal that was to follow.

That ordeal began for London on 7 September. In the afternoon a mass of German bombers crossed the coast and instead of following their past practice of peeling off to attack airfields or ports, they continued on to London. This wrongfooted Fighter Command which had scrambled its squadrons to protect its airfields, leaving the way to the capital fairly clear. This raid, it needs to be emphasised, was not in retaliation for the bombing of Berlin by the RAF. The leader of Luftflotte 2 (Kesselring) had always wanted to bomb London. Now he was convinced that the RAF was down to its last few aircraft, which would have to come up to defend the capital.

There were two main raids that day. The first was between 5.00 a.m. and 6.15 p.m.; the second lasted much longer – from 8.10 p.m. to 4.30 a.m. the following day.[40] The statistics of the raids paint a formidable picture. In all the Luftwaffe dropped 649 tons of high explosive and 27 tons of incendiary bombs on London. The bombing was concentrated on the East End, especially on the docks around Stepney, Rotherhithe, Woolwich and Bermondsey, although 45 other London boroughs were also hit. Over 1,000 fires were started, nine of which were categorised as 'conflagrations' requiring the attendance of at least 100 fire engines. An area to the north of the Thames for a distance of about one a half miles was obliterated. Many from Silvertown, which lay in this area, had to be evacuated by river. Fifteen large factories were hit and three of these were totally destroyed. Five docks were put out of action. The Royal Arsenal at Woolwich was damaged, severely restricting its output of ordnance. Three power stations were crippled and the Beckton Gas Works, the largest in Europe, was badly damaged. Transport along the river halted and almost 30,000 tons of shipping was sunk in the Thames while an additional 170,000 tons suffered damage. Over 400 people were killed and 1,600 severely injured.[41]

The effect of this raid on London and Londoners was severe. A fireman attempting to fight the conflagration on the wharves thought of the destruction of Pompeii. Another fireman in West Ham was 'frightened out of my life'. To him the bombs seemed to be saying 'here comes death'. The docks to the south of the river were 'a square mile of fire'. At night the scene at the Beckton Gas Works was chaotic: 'Gasometers were punctured and were blazing away', shrapnel rained down from destroyers firing (in vain) at the raiders. Many residents near the north Woolwich docks were trapped and were rowed to safety along the Thames.[42]

Shortly after the bombing, the Isle of Dogs, one of the worst affected areas, was visited by a Mass Observation investigator. He found considerable damage in the area, with a bomb having fallen about every 50 or 60 yards. Many shops were shut or destroyed, although all the pubs were open. Transport was chaotic, with the main routes out of the area (the Blackwall Tunnel and the Greenwich foot subway) closed. The only way out was to walk or wade through mud to an improvised ferry. Gas and electricity supply was non-existent, which meant that most food had to be consumed cold. Immediately after the raid there had been no water for 12 hours. Telephone services were only available from the police station and postal deliveries were unreliable. After the raid there had apparently been a certain amount of panic and many had left with the few belongings they could muster. Some had decamped to Greenwich Park but others had trekked into the country. All told, the MO investigator estimated that two-thirds of the population of 5,000 had gone, with the caveat that most of the men seemed to be at work. He added apprehensively that there 'was very little smiling and few jokes'.[43] We will return to this theme later.

For London this was just the beginning. During the remainder of September the capital was bombed on most days and every night, the emphasis gradually shifting to night bombing because of the toll taken on the bombers by the RAF. That month on average 238 tons of high explosive and 14.5 tons of incendiary bombs were dropped on London every 24 hours. About 7,000 people were killed in the raids and about 10,000 seriously wounded. In all 15,000 fires were started, the worst night being 19 September when there were 1,142 fires.[44]

Bad weather reduced the number of large raids in October. The days when more than 100 tons of high explosive were dropped decreased to 19 out of 31. However, London suffered some form of raid on every day and the total tonnage dropped was approximately 5,000. The number of incendiaries is not known with any accuracy but the Germans, for reasons that are obscure, seemed to use fewer per raid than in September. About 4,300 people were killed in these raids and 6,500 seriously wounded. Some 8,200 fires were started, the worst night being that of 14 October when there were over 1,000.[45]

In November, London was raided on most nights but on a much reduced scale. Bad weather often kept German incursions to a minimum. In all there were just eight occasions when over 100 tons of high explosive were dropped and only four occasions on which more than 100 people were killed.

This was not the end of London's ordeal. It was heavily bombed on 28–29 December, 11 January, 8 March, 17 and 19 April and, finally, on 10 May 1941. Nevertheless these were sporadic raids and it is the experience of the concentrated raids that will be dealt with in depth here. By the time that bad weather in November 1940 limited the raids, London had been bombed for 56 consecutive days. This was unprecedented in the history of aerial bombing. Before the war, the small town of Guernica had been destroyed in an afternoon, Rotterdam had been bombed on just one occasion and Warsaw for eight days. The civilian population of London had therefore undergone an unparalleled and shocking experience – 13,000 had been killed, 18,000 severely wounded and about 24,000 fires started. Homes were damaged or destroyed at the rate of 40,000 per week in September and October 1940 but the severe raid on 19 April 1941 in itself affected 178,000 houses. The number of homeless in rest centres was never much less than 20,000 on any given night in the first months of the Blitz. A total of 200,000 people were made homeless from September 1940 to June 1941.[46]

How did this onslaught further the German aims of breaking the morale of the country and crippling its industry? There are a number of factors that have to be considered. The first is the sheer size of London. In 1939 it encompassed 1,156 square miles of territory and had a population of 8,500,000. It was the largest city in the world.[47] However, it has been estimated that just over 1 million people (evacuated women and children, and men moving into the armed forces) had left London in 1939 and they were followed by another 900,000 during the period of the bombing. Offsetting this was a considerable drift back to London from evacuation points during the whole period. Perhaps it would be conservative to estimate the population at about 7 million during the Blitz. If, taking the figures already cited, we estimate that about 12,000 people were killed in the concentrated bombing period, this amounts to 0.17 per cent of the population. If the seriously wounded are added in we have a figure of about 30,000 or 0.43 per cent. This means that the vast majority of Londoners came through the Blitz unscathed so far as major injury or death is concerned. The Luftwaffe had a long way to go before it could kill or maim widely across the capital. In this sense London was just too big a target for the Luftwaffe.

Some light is shed on this by examining the composition of the force that was attempting to reduce London to ruins. The Luftwaffe had about 1,400 bombers operational during the period of the Blitz.[48] But in order to conserve aircraft and rest crews it was usually impossible for the Germans to send more than 300 or 400 bombers over London on any given night. When they occasionally exceeded this number, as they did on 7 September 1940 and on 17 April and 10 May 1941 (to select just three examples), they were not able to match this effort again for some days. And it must be remembered that in the pre-war years the Germans had built up a force of tactical bombers, well designed to aid the army but unable to carry the heavy bombloads of the later Allied aircraft such as the Lancaster and the B17. Most German bombers could carry approximately 1 ton of bombs and in a large raid drop 300 or 400 tons of high explosive.[49] With the introduction of the Max, a bomb of 2,500 kilograms, the Luftwaffe was occasionally able to deliver a heavier load, but their efforts never matched the raids on Hamburg when Bomber Command was able to deliver 10,000 tons of bombs on just four nights.[50]

Of course some areas of London were bombed much more heavily than average figures indicate. We have noted that after the raid of 7 September two-thirds of the population of the Isle of Dogs decamped. Although Chelsea was not a prime target for the Germans, the vagaries of bombing in 1940 meant that because it was on the river and proximate to Westminster it was hit hard. One air-raid warden in the area (Jo Oakman) noted every 'event', as bombings were called, which she attended. Between 4 September and 29 December she was called out on over 400 occasions. If these are plotted on a map of an area bounded by Sloane Street, Cheyne Walk and the Brompton Road, the detail on the map disappears under a mass of red dots. And some of the 'incidents' she attended had multiple victims. On 11 September she visited 57 Cadogan Square, only to find that a shelter had been hit and some occupants 'crushed beyond recognition'. Her comment 'heaven help us all' summed up the helplessness of those in the Air Raid protection squads.[51] Almost every diary from the period contains the words 'frightened', 'terrified' or something similar. One account was entitled 'Journal Under The Terror', a reference to the period under Maximilien Robespierre during the French Revolution. The diarist described the night of 8 September as 'a night of horror, a hell on earth'.[52] The proprietor of a cinema in East Ham, one of the worst affected areas, wrote:

> This week has turned us into a very frightened and a very desperate crowd of people . . . Men on my staff that were in the last war show their misery in the present situation more openly than the rest . . . Stranded in the theatre all night with half a dozen of them it was very pathetic . . . These old sweats are very defeatist in their views and keep rubbing in the terrible future they think we have in store for us. All my friends and acquaintances are quite sure they 'can't stand much more of this night after night'.[53]

Nevertheless, despite the anxiety and fear, we know that even in areas that were badly bombed the Germans failed in their attempt to induce mass panic. Certainly some left the city. There were 25,000 'unauthorised evacuees' to various towns and villages in Berkshire, Buckinghamshire and Oxfordshire by 15 September.[54] Others trekked out to areas such as Epping Forest and the Chislehurst Caves at night, but many came back to work during the day. Indeed, special trains were laid on to assist them.[55] In this regard it is worth noting the MO finding that of the 301 inhabitants of one street, 23 per cent of the women and children had gone but just 3 per cent of the men – no doubt because most of the men had to remain in reasonable proximity to their work.[56]

How did people cope with the Blitz and carry on with their normal lives? Many factors seemed to have helped. Some are quite mundane. Most people simply had to go to work, for without work there was no pay and without pay there was no sustenance. And for most people work was an ingrained habit. This factor is often overlooked in analyses of the Blitz but it cannot be emphasised too strongly. Work was the bedrock of industrial society then as it is now. Many diarists mention this. Phyllis Warner made much of the fact that the horror was mixed with everyday routine. She picked her way to work past bomb craters and still did her job although there was a large hole in the roof.[57] Even in the most difficult of circumstances people would stick to their jobs. One bank employee walked to and from work, although it was a journey of 12 miles and it took him three and a half hours each way.[58] Only unexploded bombs kept him away.[59] Others were just too busy or were in such key areas that stopping work never occurred to them. A sister on a children's hospital ward records the daily terror, regularly notes her lack of sleep, but is only concerned about the babies and children under her care and their screams of terror when the bombs fall.[60] There are innumerable other examples, but work and the routine of work should not be underestimated as providing the spur to continue.

Another factor was the sheer difficulty of leaving. Those who left either had a relative in the country or trekked back during the day. But for most, their support network in the form of family and friends was nearby. And the services they needed to sustain them if their house was demolished were also local. There were rest centres, mobile canteens and other facilities run by the local council. Few had the resources to move away from this network. Indeed, the majority of people did not own a car, the most immediate and personal means of transport. There was always the railway and some availed themselves of it, but the question remained of where to go and to whom to appeal for support on arrival. At other times it was German bombing that prevented this particular escape route from functioning. In short, there were powerful reasons to remain in the familiar surroundings of street and suburb.

It is in this context that statements to the effect that 'over the first weekend, the nerve and spirit of those in the East End came close to breaking' should be taken.[61] That there was some panic is beyond doubt. That some of these people fled to safer areas is unquestionable. It also seems unquestionable that for many, removing themselves from where the bombs were falling was not so much a panic reaction as a sensible precaution. But most remained – either because they had no alternative or to utilise the local support networks. How many of these 'came close to breaking' can never be known. All we can observe is what actually happened. Most stayed in place and went to work when they could, hardly indicative of broken morale or mass panic. Perhaps the last word should be that of a keen observer of Britain (and of human nature). Before the Blitz had even started, Raymond Chandler predicted its outcome. He wrote to a friend, 'as for bombing it will be bad but . . . the English civilian is the least hysterical in the world'.[62]

It is even possible that the bombing stiffened the resolve of Londoners. Certainly they developed, unsurprisingly, a deep antipathy for the people bombing them. Most diarists record this fact. Vere Hodgson, that most sane and broad-minded of Londoners, thought she might never bother with Germans again.[63] Ida Naish hoped to see Hitler in Hell.[64] Winifred Bowman spoke of 'those swines of Jerries'.[65] Mrs Brinton-Lee compared British soldiers with the 'bombastic' or 'craven' German prisoners she had met.[66] Finally a survey taken by Home Intelligence recorded that after three months of bombing 68 per cent of the people were in favour of subjecting Germany to a harsher peace settlement than Versailles. The diaries certainly show no overwhelming desire by Londoners to come to any kind of settlement with the country that was bombing them.

And even in these circumstances people displayed that normal tendency to come to terms with their situation. Phyllis Warner, who found the first days of the Blitz an appalling experience, reported on 18 September 'that I'm glad to say that I'm not as frightened as I was. Last week I couldn't sleep at all, and found the greatest difficulty in getting through my day's work, but this week I feel much stronger ... It's just a case of getting over the first shock.'[67] Others felt the same. G. Thomas reported that by 15 September 'we seem to be getting used to these battles',[68] while Ann Shepperd, although near an anti-aircraft battery, was sleeping well by 17 September.[69] These individual impressions are supported by the statistics. Mass Observation noted that those getting no sleep decreased from 31 per cent on 12 September to 9 per cent on 22 September and 3 per cent on 3 October.[70] And the numbers recorded by Home Security as sheltering in Underground stations reached a peak of 178,000 on the night of 27–28 September, but decreased to 105,000 on 5 December, 84,000 on 15 January, and just 63,000 on 11 March as more and more people decided to sleep at home.[71] As the head of Mass Observation put it:

> For the first few days of the London blitz, social life was shocked almost to a standstill: one left work in the evening to go home to an air-raid. One emerged from the air-raid in the morning to go back to work, maybe late, that was all; and while it was new, exciting, overwhelming, it was enough. Few had the time or the emotional energy for anything else – at first. Gradually, as the nights went by, priorities began to shift. Home life began to acquire some patterns again. New infrastructures were evolved, suited to the new conditions. Routines were established – going to the shelter or not going to the shelter; eating early before the sirens or packing up a picnic. The repetition of bombing on London, every night, helped give such routines both urgency and rhythm.[72]

A comment is needed at this point on the shelters, both public and private, that were made available by the government. Mass Observation reports are highly critical of public shelters.[73] They were unsanitary, there were too few of them, and some of the surface shelters were shoddily built and in effect little more than death traps. The government, including the new Minister of Home Security, Herbert Morrison, who had replaced the rather ineffectual Sir John Anderson in October, was reluctant to allow the Underground stations to be used as deep shelters.[74] Why, given this situation, was there not some kind of rebellion? There was of course anger – after specific incidents – and many local authorities suffered a backlash due to the inadequacy of the shelters provided. The fact is, however, that most people did not repair to shelters during the Blitz. At its peak only 15 per cent of the population of London used a public shelter and this figure declined from late October to under 10 per cent.[75] Hence the dissatisfaction that did exist had no widespread implications for the war effort.

The final factor to thwart the Germans was Churchill. It is easy now to adopt a cynical attitude to politicians touring disaster areas. But this was 1940 and Churchill's visits to bomb-damaged areas fulfilled a number of needs. He was often moved to tears at the sight of the homeless and he developed an instant empathy with those whose houses and lives would never be the same. But he also represented something else. He had come to power at a desperate time when a fear was expressed that a British government might go the way of the French. A common call to him as he toured the devastated areas was 'Give it 'em back'[76] or 'when are we going to bomb Berlin?'[77] His resolute responses were invariably described as 'reassuring'. In the course of the Blitz, Churchill toured most of Britain's major cities, cheering people with his obvious concern but also letting them see that as long as he was in charge the war would be fought to the end.

This symbiotic relationship between Churchill and the people is often overlooked. He was seeking to comfort them and assess the response of the local authorities to their plight, but they were also assessing him as an indicator that there was no defeatism in the higher ranks of the government.

He made other interventions as well. It was his minute of 21 September in favour of allowing people to shelter in the Underground that broke the paralysis on the issue that had developed in Cabinet.[78] And it was his experience of destroyed homes on the south coast that resulted in the War Damages Act that saw compensation paid to people for bomb damage.[79]

If the German bombing did not cause a breakdown of society in London, to what extent did it achieve its other aim, that of stifling the capital's war effort? During the war the 'key points' in the city were identified. These were facilities that, if hit or destroyed, could substantially damage the functioning of London as part of the war economy.[80] They encompassed transport facilities, water storage, telecommunications, factories, radar, government buildings and docks. In 1940, 840 such points had been identified in London, a number that increased to 1,109 in 1941.[81] One half to two-thirds of these were factories, 35 were electricity power stations, 23 were gas works, 15 ordnance factories and so on.

Let us examine two nights of heavy bombing to investigate what damage the Luftwaffe could inflict on these targets in London. On the nights of 14–15 and 15–16 October, London was repeatedly bombed. On the first night five factories were hit, including one that made instruments for aircraft. In addition six gas works, three electricity supply substations and a water main were damaged, two telephone exchanges were put out of action and six hospitals. No. 10 Downing Street and the Treasury were hit, 10 major roads blocked and five Underground lines affected. Railway services had to be suspended from Broad Street, Fenchurch Street, Marylebone, Charing Cross and London Bridge. Only restricted services could run from Euston, St Pancras and Waterloo.[82]

The next evening the Luftwaffe returned in equal strength. On this night seven factories, two gas works, four electricity supply substations and three water supply facilities were hit, and five docks put out of action. One water culvert at New Bridge Road, Edmonton, supplied London with 46 million gallons of water per day. Fifteen million gallons were restored within 24 hours, but it took 2,000 workers some time to excavate the 2,000 cubic yards of soil to get to the source of the problem. Meanwhile many London suburbs had no running water. Also that night, railway services were again hit badly and the position deteriorated further from the previous bombing. Damage was inflicted on four additional Underground lines, and services from three telephone exchanges were suspended. Finally Marlborough House, the BBC and four hospitals were hit.[83]

This amounted to substantial damage. It made everyday life difficult, getting to work inconvenient, and it did affect the efficient running of the capital. But what the bombing did not do was radically affect the war effort. A total of twelve factories were hit but over 600 were not. The docks were back in operation in short order. The railway lines could be repaired. Buses could replace damaged Underground lines. Routes could be found around blocked roads. Interruptions to electricity and gas supplies were usually short. Couriers could be used by some firms instead of the telephone. The

Home Security Report on electricity supply was an indicator of a more general trend:

London suffered the most [of any city in this area]. 30 power stations and three transformer stations were hit, while 1,393 main and secondary transmission cables and 8,590 distribution cables were involved in the general damage. Despite all this it was unusual for stoppages of supply to last longer than an hour. The most seriously affected generating station was that at Fulham, where a 190,000kw plant was not in full operation for a year. The load, however, was taken over by the grid system and the supply was only interrupted for a matter of hours.[84]

This situation applied generally to all of London's facilities. As for its output of war materiel, it was just too widely spread for the Luftwaffe to make much of an impact. Overall just 35 factories were totally destroyed. Damaged factories were usually soon back in operation and a sophisticated system of sub-contracting provided many alternative sources of supply.[85]

* * * * *

So far we have dealt only with the Blitz on London. But there was another aspect of the German air assault – the assault on British provincial cities. These phases of the Blitz are not discrete events – there was much overlap between the raids on London and those on the provinces. As we have seen, the Luftwaffe never gave up on attacking the capital. And some heavy raids on the provinces took place while London was being bombed. However, as a generalisation and with one notable exception, London bore the brunt of the enemy attacks from September to December 1940, whereas the Germans concentrated more on the provinces in the early months of 1941. And in this case we cannot stop the story on the last day of December 1940. The campaign to break the British people and the industrial capacity of the country was just as severe in the New Year as it had been in 1940.

The main problem for the Luftwaffe was that provincial Britain was what would now be called a target-rich environment. In the north there were the industrial cities of Birmingham, Manchester, Coventry, Sheffield and Leeds. South Wales also had a concentration of industry around

Cardiff and Swansea. Along the south coast lay the major ports of Plymouth, Portsmouth and Southampton. In the north-east were major shipbuilding and industrial areas around Hull and Newcastle. Major ship-building centres were located at Clydeside and Belfast. Each group of cities could be given a high priority. Spitfires were made around Southampton and at Castle Bromwich near Birmingham. The south coast ports commanded the Channel. The west coast ports saw vital supplies of oil and raw materials arrive from the United States. The ships that kept the trans-Atlantic trade flowing were built and based at Liverpool, the Clyde, the Tyne and Belfast.

Given the plethora of targets and given the fact that the Luftwaffe was hard pressed to assemble many more than 400 bombers per night, it was vital to the fulfilment of their objectives that a plan be developed to maximise the effectiveness of their bombing. No such plan eventuated or even formed in the minds of Goering, Kesselring or Sperrle. All they knew was that the attack on London had neither reduced the RAF to manageable proportions nor collapsed morale. Nor had the capital's industry and infra-structure been reduced to rubble. Yet they would continue to attack London, while at the same time sending small packets of bombers to a variety of targets around Britain and mounting major raids on a selection of provincial cities. This was the opposite of a concentration of effort, but it was what the Germans would carry through from November 1940 until March 1941.

In that period heavy raids (defined as the dropping of over 100 tons of bombs) would be carried out on London on 12 occasions. Cities such as Southampton, Liverpool, Bristol, Portsmouth, Manchester and many others would be visited by small numbers of bombers and occasionally attacked in force.

The limitations of such methods can be demonstrated by examining one of the best-known provincial raids, the attack on Coventry on 14–15 November 1940. In many ways the city was an ideal target for the Luftwaffe. Coventry was small (a population of just under 250,000 in 1940) but it had many factories making such warlike goods as aero engines, motor vehicles and munitions. Some of these works (such as Daimler) were large, but there was a great number of smaller factories clustered with houses in the city centre around the medieval cathedral. The raid was carefully planned by the Germans. The special pathfinder group (Kg 100) led the way, guided by radio beams that the British failed to jam.[86] Around 7.00 p.m. they dropped a mixture of high explosive with some accuracy on the city centre. The fires started guided the main force of about 440 bombers to the city. Around 11.45 p.m. the raid reached its height but bombing continued until 6.15 a.m., some German aircraft returning to France to refuel and then bombing a second time. In all over 500 tons of high explosive and 30,000 incendiary bombs were dropped. The havoc caused was considerable. The medieval cathedral of St Michael was destroyed beyond repair. A total of 41,500 houses (three-quarters of all houses in the city) suffered some damage. Of these 2,300 were totally destroyed and 6,000 rendered unlive-able. In addition 624 shops and 121 offices were destroyed. The war economy was badly hit. Overall 111 out of 180 factories were damaged and 75 of them completely destroyed. The casualties (570 dead and 1,100 wounded) would have been more severe had not a proportion of the popu-lation been out of the city on their nightly trek.[87]

Mass Observation rushed a team to Coventry and they reported on 18 November. The investigators found the damage greater than in any other city including London. They found a feeling of 'helplessness' among the population, many of whom had no idea what to do. There were signs of hysteria, terror and neurosis.[88] It would indeed be surprising had there not been such feelings in a city small enough for almost everyone to know one of the dead or injured and with such widespread property damage. The mood soon improved, however. The army was drafted in to help clear rubble and essential services slowly returned. Two days after the raid, arrangements had been made to transport 10,000 people out of the centre, but only 300 actually left.[89]

Nevertheless, considerable damage had been done to the war economy. One of the Daimler aero-engine factories was completely wrecked. It was estimated that it would take a month to restore production. A further 14 factories making engines or components for aircraft had suffered damage, as had such firms as Triumph that made parts for tanks and armoured cars.[90]

Coventry, if not quite 'finished' as one observer put it, was certainly on its knees.[91] Further raids of this nature by the Luftwaffe were greatly feared. Home Security concluded that 'Another such raid might well have put

Coventry beyond the possibility of repair.'[92] But the Luftwaffe did not return. In subsequent days and weeks it turned its attention back to London, then to Birmingham, then Bristol and then to other cities. Coventry did not suffer another major raid for some five months, when 100 aircraft dropped 100 tons of high explosive and incendiaries on it. Casualties were high – some 281 killed and 525 severely wounded. The Daimler works was again put out of operation for several weeks. On the night of 10–11 April there was a further major raid but on this occasion no important target suffered significant damage.[93] These raids were certainly intense, but the five-month interval had allowed Coventry to recover – both in spirit and in productive capacity. By repeated bombing the Germans probably could have obliterated Coventry and that would have slowed British aircraft production significantly. This was a lesson that its citizens were happy for the Luftwaffe not to learn.[94]

This pattern of dreadful destruction and then neglect was repeated by the Luftwaffe throughout the Blitz. Bad weather drastically curtailed their operations in January and February 1941, but by then some in the German High Command were becoming disturbed by the lack of results. On 4 February Admiral Raeder, General Jodl and Field Marshal Keitel expressed their concerns to Hitler. Raeder emphasised the importance of British dependence on imports and its need to continually build escort and merchant ships for the trans-Atlantic trade. As a result Hitler issued a new directive that gave the Luftwaffe at least some direction. He ordered that major raids be concentrated on the western ports that either built ships or received imports.[95] Accordingly, when the weather cleared the Luftwaffe launched a major raid on Clydebank, which contained some of Britain's largest shipbuilding yards. On the night of 13–14 March over 400 bombers dropped 1,100 tons of high explosive and incendiary bombs on Clydebank. The loss of life was massive because many workers lived close to the ship-yards – over 1,200 were killed and 1,000 injured. Clydebank was a rather self-contained area just to the west of Glasgow. Of its 60,000 inhabitants, just 3,000 remained after the raids – the rest had fled to safety. Indeed, there was not much to return to – only seven houses out of a total of 12,000 remained undamaged.[96] The damage to the actual shipyards was not exten-sive, but the dispersal of the population had serious repercussions for the industry. John Brown's shipyard normally employed 10,000 workers, yet a week after the raids just 6,500 had reported for work. Another week was to pass before the yard was 75 per cent effective.[97]

For one of the very few occasions during the Blitz the deductions drawn by Home Security were alarming:

There is a real danger that continued and concentrated attacks on the residential areas of the ports will lead to a large-scale movement of the population, as a result of damage to houses and public services. These attacks may prove more effective in hampering the work of the ports than accurate bombing of the port facilities themselves. Undoubtedly provision of relief for the homeless and facilities to enable the workers to get back to work is of vital importance.[98]

Home Security was no doubt correct. Many more raids on this scale would have seen vital works such as John Brown's shut down through lack of labour. Yet once again the Luftwaffe did not follow up the attack. Over time the workers were rehoused and returned to their tasks.

In keeping with Hitler's directive, Belfast suffered a major raid in mid-April. The shipbuilders Shorts and Harlands were out of production for three weeks. Some 20,000 people were made homeless by this single raid.[99] Yet there was again no follow-up and shipbuilding in Northern Ireland was soon back to normal.

If we follow the pattern of bombing during February, March and April 1941, we can see that the Luftwaffe attempted to follow Hitler's directive. There were raids on Swansea, Hull, Bristol, Portsmouth, Plymouth, Barrow and the Tyne in this period. But the pattern of one or two night raids repeated itself. Plymouth was hit particularly hard in April to the extent that civil administration almost broke down. Mass Observation reported much dissatisfaction with the local authorities.[100] Yet Plymouth survived. This time there would be no more raids because Hitler had begun to regroup the Luftwaffe for operations against Russia.

The last period of the Blitz presents one of the great question marks over German strategy. Liverpool was the port through which flowed most supplies from America. Before May 1941 the weekly tonnage handled by the docks was 181,562 tons.[101] It was an obvious target for the Luftwaffe. Indeed, Liverpool was raided on over 60 occasions between the outbreak of war and May 1941. Yet many of these raids were flights by just one or two aircraft and most did not attain the status of a major raid.[102] The main exceptions were the nights of 12–13, 13–14 and 14–15 March. In these three nights over 450 tons of high explosive were dropped, causing damage to the docks and to commercial and residential buildings.[103]

Despite these three nights it could be reasonably stated that before May 1941 Liverpool had not received from the Germans the attention warranted by its importance. That all changed in the first week of May. From 1 May the city was bombed for seven consecutive nights. In all 839 tons of high explosive were dropped along with hundreds of thousand incendiaries. The raids killed 1,900 people and seriously injured 1,450. At one stage four miles of docks were engulfed in flames.[104] On the night of 3–4 May the SS *Malakand*, which had 1,000 tons of ammunition on board, was hit and exploded, virtually destroying the Huskisson Dock.[105] A total of 70,000 people, almost 10 per cent of the total population, were made homeless and trekking became a way of life for many. Mass Observation reported widespread dissatisfaction with the local authorities and described an atmosphere of ineptitude, lack of energy and drive on their part. A strong rumour circulated that martial law had been declared. It had not but this was probably a comment on the population's view of the local leadership.[106]

By the end of the week the capacity of the docks had been reduced to just 25 per cent, a potentially disastrous situation for Britain. Yet even during the Merseyside Blitz the Germans could not concentrate on just one target. In the middle of their campaign against Liverpool they diverted major forces of bombers to Barrow, Belfast, Glasgow and Hull. Thus the number of bombers over Merseyside dropped from 293 on the night of 3–4 May to 55 on the following night, to 27 on the following two nights, then back up to 166 on the final night.[107]

But the surpassing folly from the German point of view was that this series of devastating raids came at the very end of the Blitz. After one more massive attack on London on the night of 10–11 May, the bombers were gradually withdrawn to the east for the impending attack on the Soviet Union. Slowly Liverpool returned to some kind of normality. By mid-May the docks were unloading just less than half their normal tonnage and by mid-June they had returned to full capacity. The thousands of trekkers also returned. In fact most of the dock workers who trekked only did so at night and returned to their jobs during the day, so the same everyday imperatives that acted to keep London going through the Blitz applied at Liverpool as well. For the remainder of the war Liverpool continued to be the main destination for American imports. Any chance that the Germans might have had to cut this lifeline had gone.

* * * * *

The Blitz failed in its objectives. The Germans could neither cow the British people into surrender nor destroy the fundamentals of their war economy. The Luftwaffe, which was never developed as a strategic weapon, proved inadequate to the task. It had too few aircraft that carried inadequate bomb loads, had too many targets to hit and lacked a coherent overall plan. Civilians, it was proved, could stand up to bombing over a prolonged period without cracking, despite the rather feeble defences the British could deploy against the night Blitz and the government's ramshackle shelter policy.

However, this is much more apparent now than it was then. When they put their minds to it the Luftwaffe could deliver concentrated blows – against London, Coventry, Glasgow, Belfast, Plymouth, Birmingham and other centres – that caused havoc and destruction to an extent never witnessed in Britain before. To those under the bombs this certainly did not seem like an air force too feeble to prevail. No city or country had ever been subjected to the level of aerial bombardment experienced by Britain in these months. In this sense those in charge of Home Security were only being prudent in their attempts to test the daily 'morale' of the people. Their methods might appear amateurish today but there seems little doubt that the overall tenor of the reports must have given some comfort to those in authority. Panic at times was reported; there was some looting; defeatist talk was occasionally expressed. But the solidarity of the population was no myth. Most carried on with their lives as best they could. After the constant series of reverses that marked the first part of the year, the ordeal suffered by the British might have been the last straw. That it came nowhere close to delivering a knock-out blow says much about the resolution of a determined people. They had accepted Churchill's proposition that this war had to be fought to the end. Indeed, there was some concern that the government might fall below this level of resolve. Churchill's presence in the bombed cities reassured them that this would not be the case, as did his assurances that when the time came Nazi Germany would receive a greater measure of destruction than had been meted out to Britain. He was as good as his word.

CHAPTER 13

A LITTLE HELP FROM OUR FRIENDS
BRITAIN AND AMERICA, 1940–1941

WHAT WAS THE STATE of Europe after the fall of France? The Czechs, the Poles, the Danes, the Norwegians, the Dutch, the Belgians, the Luxembourgers were totally under the German heel. The Atlantic and Channel coasts of France and most of its industry were German occupied. The rump state of Vichy France existed at the whim of the Führer and was in any case busy introducing its own slightly milder form of Fascism. Fascist Italy was allied with Germany. Spain, Hungary and Romania all had their own variants of Fascism that disposed them to lean towards Germany. The Soviet Union was not yet in the anti-fascist camp either. In fact it was doing very nicely supplying Hitler with war materials of all kinds. Only Switzerland and Sweden – impotent, isolated, weak – remained as independent states.

Britain was secure for the moment, protected by the Royal Navy and the RAF, and with the industrial strength to at least prosecute a defensive war. Assistance was arriving from Canada, Australia, New Zealand, South Africa and other parts of the Empire, but this assistance was not in the main industrial. And it was not at all clear that British naval and air power could keep the Germans at bay indefinitely. With the industrial resources of Europe at his disposal, Hitler could eventually build the Luftwaffe and the Kriegsmarine to a size that outmatched Britain, should a government willing to endure for years the trials of war continue in power. In June and

WHEN BRITAIN SAVED THE WEST

July 1940 Churchill had a good grip on the levers of power, but he had been challenged by Chamberlain and Halifax as recently as the end of May, and in June the spectre of a Halifax–Butler axis had emerged again.

In 1940 it seemed that only one state had the industrial power to tilt the balance against Nazism and that was the United States. No one in Britain expected America to declare war immediately after the fall of France, but given Roosevelt's impeccable anti-Nazi sentiments and his frequent statements condemning German aggression there was the possibility that a declaration of war against Hitler might eventually be forthcoming. In the meantime the US could provide aid to Britain and it could help carry that aid across the Atlantic.

Churchill rapidly put the issue of aid to the test. On 15 May 1940 – the same day that he received the telephone call from Premier Reynaud claiming that the French were defeated – Churchill wrote to Roosevelt:

> I trust you realize Mr. President, that the voice and force of the United States may count for nothing if they are withheld too long. You may have a completely subjugated and Nazified Europe established with astonishing swiftness, and the weight may be more than we can bear . . . Immediate needs are: first the loan of forty or fifty of your older destroyers to bridge the gap between what we have now and the large new construction we put in hand at the beginning of the war.[1]

He went on to ask for several hundred aircraft, anti-aircraft guns and ammunition and steel, and ended by saying: 'We shall go on paying dollars for as long as we can, but I should like to think when we can pay no more, you will give us the stuff all the same.'[2]

Roosevelt did not respond to the request for aid positively. In answer to Churchill he claimed that the destroyers could not be transferred to Britain without Congressional approval, which he was uncertain of obtaining. As for Churchill's other requests, he would do what he could about aircraft, anti-aircraft equipment and steel. On the wider points of a Nazified Europe and a Britain sagging under a heavy defence burden, and on the matter of British payments to the US, he was silent.[3]

Churchill was distressed by this reply. Only an essential visit to France prevented him from an immediate riposte. But on the night of 19 May he told his Private Secretary that he had drafted a telegram 'for those bloody Yankees' and that he was to send it off at once.[4]

The telegram was couched in more diplomatic terms but it contained an ominous warning to Roosevelt. After expressing his disappointment about the destroyers, Churchill said:

> Our intention is whatever happens to fight on to the end in this Island and, provided we can get the help for which we ask, we hope to run them very close in the air battles in view of individual superiority. Members of the present administration would likely go down during this process should it result adversely, but in no conceivable circumstances would we consent to surrender. If members of the present administration were finished and others came in to parley amid the ruins, you must not be blind to the fact that the sole remaining bargaining counter with Germany would be the fleet, and if this country was left by the United Sates to its fate no one would have the right to blame those then responsible if they made the best terms they could for the surviving inhabitants. Excuse me, Mr. President, putting this nightmare bluntly.[5]

This was putting it very bluntly indeed. Roosevelt had not raised the fate of the British fleet; Churchill was just making sure that its acquisition did not enter American calculations. A government led by an appeaser would certainly have used it as a bargaining chip, and Roosevelt knew that there were members of Churchill's Cabinet who were attempting to set up mediation through Mussolini for a compromise peace.[6] In that sense he was well aware of the nightmare of which Churchill spoke.

In any case Churchill thought that his messages had had some effect on FDR. On 10 June, at the University of Virginia, the President made a rousing speech on foreign policy, in the course of which he said of the Italian declaration of war against France, 'the hand that held the dagger has struck it into the back of its neighbor'. He then went on:

> We will extend to the opponents of force the material resources of this nation; and at the same time, we will harness and speed up the use of those resources in order that we ourselves in the Americas may have

equipment and training equal to the task of any emergency and every defense. All roads leading to the accomplishment of these objectives must be kept clear of obstructions. We will not slow down or detour. Signs and signals call for full speed ahead.[7]

Churchill had listened to this speech and told Roosevelt that he was much 'fortified by the grand scope of your declaration'. He particularly noted the reference about material aid to the Allies and renewed his request for 50 destroyers, particularly needed now that Britain had an additional foe in the Mediterranean.[8] Privately, Churchill thought that an American declaration of war must shortly follow such a speech.[9]

He was to be disappointed. Not for the first time a rousing speech by Roosevelt was followed by inaction. No more 'material resources' were made available to the Allies, nor was there any sign of the US economy moving into 'full speed ahead' mode.[10] Indeed, some members of Roosevelt's own Cabinet were becoming alarmed at his inaction. Henry Morgenthau, the Secretary of the Treasury, told Roosevelt that after reading Churchill's letter he thought 'unless we do something to give the English additional destroyers, it seems to me absolutely hopeless to expect them to keep going'.[11] Harold Ickes, the Secretary of Labor, was also putting pressure on Roosevelt. On 5 July he told the President that 'by hook or by crook, we ought to accede to England's request [for the destroyers]', but to no effect.[12] Roosevelt would not act.

As inaction from the Americans continued, Churchill became more and more impatient with them. He pressed Lord Lothian, the British ambassador in Washington, to reiterate to the President that he could not rely on getting the British fleet because a quisling government might use it to bargain with Hitler. He told Lothian, no doubt to be repeated to Roosevelt, that 'we have really not had any help worth speaking of from the United States so far', and that what mattered was whether Hitler was in command of Great Britain in three months or not.[13] On the same day he wrote to his friend the American financier Bernard Baruch that 'your people are not doing much. If things go wrong with us it will be bad for them.'[14] Beyond that he could do little.

In fact, although he could hardly say so in public, Churchill was despairing that any substantial help would flow from the Great Republic.

He cooled towards them to the extent that, against the advice of his scientific experts, he withheld some British wartime secrets such as ASDIC and radar from the Americans until they were more forthcoming on the destroyer issue. He instructed the Defence Committee not 'to give our secrets until the United States is much nearer to the war than she is now'.[15]

Eventually, in July, he was persuaded to draft yet another letter to Roosevelt concerning destroyers. Churchill put his message bluntly:

> I know you will do all in your power, but when the consequences to the United States of our being overwhelmed are so grievous, it seems to me very hard to understand why this modest aid is not given <u>now</u> at the time when it could be perhaps decisively effective. Pray let me know if there is no hope.[16]

But this part of his letter was so heavily amended by the Foreign Secretary, Lord Halifax, and Ambassador Joseph Kennedy that Churchill in the end decided to send no message at all. He was not to contact Roosevelt on any subject for almost another month.

Finally, on 31 July, with the Battle of Britain in full swing and invasion by Germany thought to be imminent, Churchill tried again. He told Roosevelt that Britain must now have the destroyers, motor boats and flying boats which it had requested, and he noted that in the last 10 days, 10 destroyers had been sunk or damaged:

> We could not keep up the present rate of casualties for long, and if we cannot get a substantial reinforcement, the whole fate of the war may be decided by this minor and easily remediable factor. I cannot understand why, with the position as it is, you do not send me at least 50 or 60 of your oldest destroyers ... Mr. President, with great respect, I must tell you that in the long history of the world this is a thing to do now.[17]

In the US those who had been pressing Roosevelt for a decision were alarmed by Churchill's message. They developed a compromise that they thought the President might accept which did not involve an outright gift of the ships to Britain. The Secretary of the Navy, Frank Knox, suggested to Lothian that Britain might lease bases on its Caribbean islands and along the Atlantic coast in such areas as Newfoundland to the United States in return for the destroyers. The whole transaction could then be presented as a quid pro quo – the United States would help defend Britain in return for bases which would help defend the United States.[18] This proposition was put to the US Cabinet by Knox and approved providing Britain promised to send its fleet to America in the event of a successful German invasion.[19]

This last proviso infuriated Churchill, who declared that such a promise would amount to defeatism.[20] He railed against it to the War Cabinet but in the end accepted that it must form part of the deal. At last Britain was to have the destroyers. After protracted negotiations and exchanges of notes, the deal was signed on 2 September.[21] The Americans made much of the assurances given about the British fleet, but in London this side of the deal was not published, the War Cabinet noting that the agreement could hardly be binding on a new government.[22]

In the end, Britain obtained little from the destroyers deal. By the end of 1940 just nine were in service. In fact many had been so badly stored that they had practically to be rebuilt before they were fit for combat. Even by May 1941 only 30 were in service and they were described by many who were unfortunate to have to serve in them as the 'worst destroyers they had ever seen'. Moreover, the deal had not been agreed with sufficient celerity to ensure that the ships were on hand to help thwart a German invasion attempt. In the dangerous months of August and September 1940, while the invasion barges were being collected in the Channel ports opposite Britain, the Americans proved unwilling to expedite the transfer. Britain probably had sufficient of its own more modern destroyers and other ships as well to force the Germans into paying an unacceptable price in any invasion. But the British and the Americans could not be certain that this was the case. An additional 50 second-rate craft would have avoided the need to take so many small warships away from convoy duties and assign them to anti-invasion roles. At the very least the US destroyers might have helped mitigate the number of sinkings of merchant ships in the Atlantic. But Roosevelt in particular did not feel able to take any leadership in this matter either with Congress or with the wider population. And so the invasion season came and went without Britain obtaining the assistance of any American ships.

Churchill, however, portrayed the deal as another kind of victory – that of enticing the United States closer to war. He stated that selling Britain destroyers was 'not a neutral action' and that when the proposal went through 'the United States would have made a long step towards coming into the war on our side'.[23] No doubt he did not anticipate such a move until after the presidential election in November. But because the Republican candidate, Wendell Willkie, had approved the deal the re-election of Roosevelt would not be vital for the British cause. Only time would tell whether the American election on 6 November 1940 would make the British supply position any easier or lead the United States closer to belligerency.

The destroyers at least had not cost the British any hard currency. But most British war materiel bought from the United Sates in this period had to be paid for. The British had benefited from the repeal of the Neutrality Act in November 1939, which enabled the US to sell to any belligerent country war materiel on a cash and carry basis. Although theoretically this might have meant that American goods also flowed to the Axis powers, in practice it is doubtful whether the US would have sold goods to Nazi Germany and in any case the British blockade prevented such transactions from taking place. Needless to say, these large Allied orders also assisted the US – in fact they were the factor that finally pulled them out of the second recession which had hit the country very hard from 1937.

The British orders (which incorporated previous orders made by France) were considerable. The main war materials purchased were aircraft, tanks, motor vehicles, ammunition, ships and machine tools. By 1 November 1940 the value of orders placed amounted to almost $2 thousand million, while an estimate of goods to be ordered in the near future totalled $3.2 thousand million.[24] Britain was still in 1940 a wealthy country with overseas investments of $12.8 thousand million[25] and gold reserves of $1.8 thousand million.[26] Yet a quick calculation reveals that well over one-third of that total had already been committed to orders in the US. And it was the fact that many of the assets held by Britain (such as Indian railways) could not be readily sold or indeed sold at all to realise dollars. The moment that Churchill had foreshadowed to the President – that the US would have to start giving Britain the 'stuff' it needed – was fast approaching.

And for the British, 'carry' was becoming almost as large a problem as 'cash'. Losses to U-boats in the North Atlantic had averaged a manageable 40,000 tons per month in the North Atlantic from January to May 1940.[27] But from June to November the monthly total increased to over 200,000 tons.[28] The time was rapidly approaching when Britain could not replace lost merchant ships from its own building programme. Either the Americans were going to send goods to Britain in their own ships or Britain would have to purchase many more ships in the US to make up the deficit. Moreover, the extension of the war by the outbreak of large-scale fighting in North Africa and the invasion of Greece by Italy in October meant that the British would require even more equipment to assist its offensive in the desert and to aid its new ally.

However, FDR had by no means put the American economy on a war footing. Indeed, despite his speech to the University of Virginia, his actual policy in June 1940 was to use only idle resources for wartime production.[29] This is reflected in the national account figures that show only 3 per cent of the American economy geared to war in 1940.[30] Moreover, some of that wartime production reflected British government expenditure in America on buildings, machine tools and land. By January 1941 this spending amounted to $800 million.[31]

Meanwhile on 5 November, Roosevelt won the presidential election with increased majorities in both the House and the Senate.[32] This caused much excitement in Britain. Even the Foreign Office, notoriously sceptical about US intentions, thought that the US would now enter the war as soon as possible.[33] But silence followed Roosevelt's victory. He did not even see fit to reply to a letter of congratulations sent to him by Churchill.[34]

It was Lothian who applied a good dose of realism to British hopes. He had been in Britain since 20 October for discussions and he told the Foreign Office to put aside any thought that America would soon enter the war. In his opinion the United States would not take this step until its re-armament was fully under way in 1942. Meanwhile he advised Churchill to set out for Roosevelt Britain's economic situation in great detail, opening the books to demonstrate that Britain was indeed running out of dollars.[35]

Churchill took the advice but struggled to strike the right tone in the letter. His irritation with the President's inaction was evident in one of his first drafts, which contained the following paragraph:

While we will do our utmost, and shrink from no proper sacrifice to make payments across the Exchange, I should not myself be willing, even in the height of the struggle, to divest Great Britain of every conceivable saleable asset, so that after the victory was won by our blood and sweat, and civilization saved and the time gained for the United States to be fully armed against all eventualities, we should stand stripped to the bone. Such a course would not be in the moral or economic interests of either of our countries.[36]

Finally, a more suitable document was drafted and sent to Roosevelt on 7 December. By then Britain's position regarding dollars was desperate and Lothian decided on his own initiative to bring the crisis to the attention of the American public via the press. When he arrived in New York he summoned a group of reporters and allegedly said: 'Well, boys, Britain's broke; it's your money we want.'[37] Whatever words he used the message was clear. The press reported that Britain's gold and securities had been used up and that England would need help if orders for more equipment were to be made in the United States.[38]

Morgenthau and Churchill were furious with Lothian for this calculated indiscretion. Morgenthau worried that Congress might be less likely to extend help if they thought the situation irredeemable;[39] Churchill worried that Lothian had given the impression that Britain was bankrupt rather than just running out of dollars.[40]

Nevertheless, the Lothian interview concentrated minds in America on what was becoming an urgent problem and this was useful preparatory work for Roosevelt's consideration of Churchill's letter. As it happened the President, exhausted by months of campaigning, was about to take a holiday on the presidential yacht when Churchill's plea for help arrived. In the letter Churchill stressed the shipping crisis that Britain was facing in the Atlantic and the desperate need for more aircraft, munitions and machine tools. In the revised wording the crunch came towards the end:

The moment approaches when we shall no longer be able to pay cash for shipping and other supplies. While we will do our utmost and shrink from no proper sacrifice to make payments across the exchange, I believe that you will agree that it would be wrong in principle and mutually disadvantageous in effect, if at the height of the struggle, Great Britain were to be divested of all saleable assets.[41]

The letter then went on to make many of the same points as in Churchill's earlier drafts and concluded with a table of British shipping losses in the Atlantic. Nowhere in the letter did Churchill appeal for the Americans to enter the war. The appeal was rather couched in terms that the best way to defend the United States was to keep Britain in the war.[42]

In Washington, the hawks in the Cabinet, led by Ickes, Morgenthau, Knox and Stimson, agreed with Churchill. While Roosevelt was relaxing in the Caribbean they met as a group to discuss the whole matter of British debt. Knox put the situation plainly. He saw 'no choice . . . but to pay for the war from now on'.[43] The others agreed but all were worried about the reaction in Congress and the mechanism by which the war would be financed.[44] When he returned from his cruise on 17 December the President provided the answer. At lunch that day he told Morgenthau:

> I have been thinking very hard on this trip about what we should do for England, and it seems to me that the thing to do is to get away from the dollar sign . . . I don't want to put the thing in terms of dollars or loans, and I think the thing to do is to say that we will manufacture what we need, and the first thing we will do is to increase our productivity, and then we will say to England, we will give you the guns and ships that you need, provided when the war is over you will return to us in kind the guns and ships that we have loaned to you, or you will return to us the ships repaired and pay us, always in kind, to make up the depreciation.[45]

Later in the afternoon he explained to the press that if your neighbour's house was on fire you would not haggle over the price of the hose you were about to lend him. The main thing you wanted was the fire put out and the hose returned.[46] What emboldened Roosevelt to take this step was never revealed. Perhaps he feared that without such help Britain might conclude a compromise peace and the fate of the British fleet on which American safety would then depend was too uncertain to risk. Perhaps he felt strengthened by the election result. Perhaps he had seen opinion polls which showed that by December 1940 over 60 per cent of Americans favoured sending all help possible to Britain.[47]

For whatever reason, this was Roosevelt's contribution to what became known as Lend-Lease, called by Churchill 'the most un-sordid act in history'. It did come with a few strings, however. The Americans never really took to heart Churchill's point that Britain was fighting against Nazism not only to maintain its own independence but on behalf of the wider cause of those democratic values which Roosevelt repeatedly proclaimed were vital for the future of mankind. So until the bill wended its way through Congress, a process that was bound to take months, the British found themselves in exactly the same position as they had been before Roosevelt had taken his cruise. They had little money with which to pay for the orders already placed and for some of the goods already delivered. They were in dollar terms broke and they had not got the money they wanted, for Roosevelt, in a manner that was typical of him, had not provided any detail about what arrangements Britain was to operate under until the act became law.

In fact Roosevelt saw no reason to fill in any detail. He thought the British still had 'plenty of exchange' to pay for existing orders.[48] In any case Roosevelt had thought of several ways in which the British could pay until Lend-Lease was passed. The first was to dispatch a destroyer to Cape Town to collect £50 million in gold from British gold reserves held there to cover immediate purchases. This was cash and carry with a vengeance. Churchill (who had not been told until the destroyer was on its way) was furious. He drafted a letter to the President complaining that the act might produce 'embarrassing effects' when it became known. He continued: 'It would wear the aspect of a sheriff collecting the last assets of a helpless debtor', but he then crossed this through and contented himself with saying that it would look like 'you are sending for our last reserves'.[49] He then went on to try to clarify exactly where Britain stood in regard to finance:

We do not know how long Congress will debate your proposals and how we should be enabled to place orders for armaments and pay our way if this time became protracted. Remember, Mr President, we do not know what you have in mind, or exactly what the United States is going to do, and we are fighting for our lives. What would be the effect upon the world situation if we had to default in payments to your contractors, who have workmen to pay? Would not this be exploited by the enemy as a complete breakdown in Anglo-American co-operation? . . . [Also] what is to be done about the immense heavy payments still to be made under existing orders before delivery is completed? Substantial advance payments on these same orders have already denuded our resources.[50]

Churchill's irritation with the vagueness of Roosevelt's proposals is evident from the many stinging sentences he deleted from this letter. Originally he had said 'It is not fitting that any nation should put itself wholly in the hands of another, least of all a nation which is fighting under increasingly severe conditions for what is proclaimed to be a cause of general concern.'[51] His general plea that Britain's fight against Nazism was also America's fight still fell on deaf ears. Roosevelt sent no reply to this message. This left the British purchasing mission in the US in an impossible position. Should they place orders for war materiel based on the fact that Lend-Lease (whatever its details) would take care of the payments? Eventually Morgenthau told the Treasury representative in Washington, Sir Frederick Phillips, that Britain should go ahead and place the orders. But even then there was ambiguity. Phillips assumed this meant that these commitments would be covered by Lend-Lease.[52] But Roosevelt defined Morgenthau's commitment as meaning that the British could place orders for 'anything they wanted if they said they had the money to pay for it'.[53] And to make matters worse, when the head of the British Purchasing Mission in the US, Arthur Purvis, asked Roosevelt for clarification, 'he gave Purvis no satisfactory answer'.[54]

Moreover, Morgenthau had decided that the best way he could sell Lend-Lease to Congress was to stress to them that Britain for its part was divesting itself of every asset that could be realised in return for American aid. So when the Lend-Lease Act was passed on 11 March, the British to their considerable shock finally grasped the fact that the Americans did indeed intend that they should pay for all goods ordered before its passage. So another destroyer arrived in South Africa in mid-March to collect a further £35 million in gold and there would be yet another in April to collect a similar amount.[55] And that was not all. On 10 March Morgenthau insisted to the new ambassador (Lord Halifax) that the British-owned

American Viscose (Courtaulds) be sold 'by the end of the week' to American interests.[56] The British felt that they had no option – the company was sold for the knock-down price of $54 million, about half its actual value.[57]

But the sale of Viscose and the movement of gold still left Britain with a deficit of about $400 million. Keynes was dispatched to the United States to negotiate a deal. The best he could do was to arrange for a loan of $425 million against British-owned investments in the United States at an interest rate of 3 per cent. The British completed loan and interest payments in 1951.[58]

The Act (actually called 'An Act to Promote the Defense of the United States' and given the symbolic number of 1776) was passed on 11 March 1941, after three long months of debate by Congress. It did not produce in the immediate future the bonanza of production for the British that had been anticipated. In the first place, the American economy was still far from being on a war footing and the needs of the glacial, but steady rearmament of the US military had to be met first. Eventually the British received around $900 million in Lend-Lease aid by the end of 1941.[59] This figure may be compared with the $3.2 thousand million that Britain had spent in the US by the year's end.[60] In fact purchases covered by Lend-Lease represented just 1 per cent of Britain's war supplies.[61] In stark contrast was the aid provided by Canada, which announced in December 1941 that all munitions, war supplies and food produced in Canada for Britain would be *given* to Britain to the extent of $1 billion.[62] To all intents and purposes, economically as well as militarily, Britain and its Empire in the period 1940–41 stood alone.

It had occurred to the Americans early in the war that goods made in the US would be useless if they were sunk before they arrived in Britain. Initially, the depredations of German submarines in the Atlantic were minimal but in the second half of 1940 sinkings increased to 200,000 tons per month and in the first six months of 1941 they amounted to 300,000 tons per month.[63] The greater scale of losses had several causes. In the first place Britain had to deploy many potential escorts around its coasts for anti-invasion purposes and the absence of the American destroyers was keenly felt in this regard. Second, the number of U-boats on operational duty steadily rose from just over 50 at the beginning of the war to over 150 by mid-1941.

But even before the U-boat depredations made a significant impact on British imports, Churchill sought American aid in convoying goods across the Atlantic. The course of the discussions over convoy had (from a British point of view) a depressing aspect in that they paralleled the manner of the discussions already detailed over war materiel.

The first request by Churchill for US help in convoying came in a letter to Roosevelt just after FDR's victory in the November 1940 election:

> Is it possible for you in some way to make available the greater part of the 140 ships, which I understand you now have in the Atlantic, to convoy merchant ships across the Atlantic and protect them against illegal [U-boat] methods of warfare.[64]

In the end this was one of a series of draft letters that Churchill did not send to the President. But in the 'Lend-Lease' letter of 7 December, Churchill finally laid bare his concerns:

> It would, I suggest, follow that protection should be given to this lawful trading by the United States forces i.e. escorting battleships, cruisers, destroyers and air flotillas. Protection would be <u>immediately</u> more effective if you were able to obtain bases in Eire.[65]

Churchill was potentially muddying the convoy issue by suggesting that the Americans or British coerce Southern Ireland into letting Allied warships use its western ports. Certainly the use of these ports would have extended the range of escort craft, but it was never practical politics and could only risk alienating an important section of American public opinion. Yet it was only a theoretical risk because Roosevelt never intended using US warships for convoy at this point in the war anyway.

Roosevelt did not directly reply to Churchill's letter, but some help came Britain's way in early 1941. In February a United States Atlantic Fleet was formed which contained a support group of three destroyer flotillas and five flying-boat squadrons.[66] Then, in March, Churchill asked whether a stricken British battleship could be repaired in an American port (at British expense).[67] Roosevelt agreed. The battleship could use an American dockyard, although this was in contravention of international law.[68]

And in other ways, US actions became more amenable to Britain. They transferred 10 coastguard cutters to Britain, which excited all concerned at the time but seems pretty small beer now.[69] More importantly, some cargoes now sailing the Atlantic consisted of goods transferred to Britain under Lend-Lease. Churchill pointed out to Roosevelt in early April that U-boat attacks were now sinking 'cargoes produced by American labour' and that these attacks were extending closer and closer to the American coast.[70]

In Washington the hawks were well aware that U-boats might soon threaten US commerce. Knox in particular regarded the situation in the Atlantic as desperate and along with Stimson concocted a scheme to extend the American security zone from a narrow strip along the American, Caribbean and South American coasts far into the Atlantic. In addition they considered that if waters around the Red Sea were removed from the war zone, American ships could supply the British armies in the Middle East directly.[71] The announcements, when they came, were quite dramatic, especially the extension of the war zone to 25 degrees west because this encompassed the greater part of the Atlantic. But once again appearances were deceptive. Roosevelt told Morgenthau that 'public opinion was not ready for the United States to convoy ships'.[72] This statement requires careful analysis. The supposed lack of public support for a more vigorous war policy has long been used to explain Roosevelt's inaction. The reality is not this simple. It is correct to say that when the American people were asked the bald question, 'Should the United States declare war on Germany?', the answer was always no. However, if the question was framed differently, 'Should the United States enter the war if there was no other way of defeating Germany and Italy?', no fewer than 72 per cent of respondents said yes. And concerning Britain, when the public was asked whether more help should be given 'even at the risk of us getting in to a war', the majority (which rose from 60 per cent to 70 per cent by April 1941) also said yes.[73] In short, there was always a solid base of opinion on which a President committed to action rather than speeches against Nazism could have built. Public opinion, as Ickes and the hawks in Cabinet knew, was there to be led.[74] In the end Roosevelt took no lead. There would be no convoying of ships. The Americans would patrol the area with aircraft and warships, but no orders were given to fire on any U-boats observed, nor would any public announcement be made that these patrols had commenced.

The announcements about the Red Sea and the extension of the war zone were made in early April, but the British were to see no more action from FDR until June. Apparently the President spent most of the month of May in bed because of ill-health. But Ickes, for one, was more concerned about a deeper malaise:

> I do know in every direction I find a growing discontent with the President's lack of leadership. He still has the country if he will take it and lead it. But he won't have it much longer unless he does something. It won't be sufficient for him to make another speech and then go into a state of innocuous desuetude again. People are beginning to say: I am tired of words; I want action . . . if I could have looked this far ahead and seen an inactive and uninspiring President, I would not have supported Roosevelt for a third term. My desire for him was due almost entirely to the fact that I believed he would prove to be a great leader in the time of grave crisis that I saw approaching.[75]

For the British May 1941 was a bad month. They had rushed reinforcements from the Western Desert to Greece in April to try to stem the German attack. These had proved ineffective and Greece was evacuated by Allied troops on 30 April. Meanwhile Field Marshal Rommel had seized the opportunity and driven back British forces in the Desert almost to the border of Egypt. Then in May the Germans invaded Crete, where the British had sheltered after the disastrous Greek campaign. By the end of the month that force too had to be evacuated. And meanwhile sinkings of merchant ships increased in the Atlantic.

On 23 May, Churchill felt desperate enough to send FDR a detailed list of sinkings, which even included map coordinates to show exactly where each ship had been sunk. He also accompanied his message with a map to indicate the area in the Atlantic where US assistance would be most helpful.[76]

Once more Roosevelt offered no direct response to Churchill's cry for help. Instead he made a radio broadcast in which he declared a state of 'unlimited national emergency'.[77] But he went into no detail as to what this might mean for the war effort, and Ickes sourly commented 'that without acts to follow it up [it] means little'.[78] In the days that followed this seemingly dramatic announcement no one in FDR's closest circle could detect any change in policy.

But there were signs that the President was becoming increasingly worried. He thought the reverses in the Mediterranean might encourage Portugal or Spain to allow the Germans to base U-boats in the Azores and Cape Verde Islands, from where they could reach American shores. While he was not prepared to contribute to a projected British-led expedition to occupy the islands, he was prepared to free up British troops by relieving their garrison that had been occupying Iceland since the fall of Denmark in April 1940.[79] Churchill jumped at this offer. Clearly he hoped that US ships would become involved with U-boats during the process of convoy and that this would lead the Americans closer to war.

Most of the Iceland scenario played out as Churchill had anticipated. An American garrison occupied the island on 7 July. This led to US warships escorting the ships of any nation that plied between the US and Iceland. And this measure was extended after the meeting between Roosevelt and Churchill at Argentia, Newfoundland, in August when the President decided to allow the US to escort the ships of any nation across the Atlantic. Soon this led to the kind of result Churchill had hoped for. On 4 September the USS *Greer* was attacked by a U-boat and responded by depth-charging the German vessel. Then on 17 October the USS *Kearny* was sunk while escorting a convoy and two weeks later the USS *Reuben James* was sunk in similar circumstances.[80]

The President broadcast after the *Greer* incident, calling the German attack 'legal and moral piracy'.[81] Then after the *Kearny* was sunk he broadcast again, noting that 'history has recorded who fired the first shot'.[82] After the *Reuben James* went down there was no presidential comment and it was left to Churchill to express his grief at its loss.[83]

These incidents, it might be thought, provided FDR with a scenario he had often articulated – that if there was an overt incident caused by Germany the US would enter the war. He had told Ickes as early as April 1941 that 'probably we would have to wait for a German "incident"'.[84] And in June he told Bill Bullitt (previously American ambassador to France) that he was waiting for an 'incident' before he came in.[85]

Yet he did not come in. Churchill might rail at him – he told the Cabinet in August that he wondered 'if the President realized the risk the United

States were running by keeping out of the war'.[86] He might tell Harry Hopkins that 'a wave of depression' had swept over the Cabinet 'about the President's many assurances and no closer to war'.[87] He might tell his Private Secretary that after the joint declaration of war aims by Roosevelt, himself and Stalin (on 12 August), 'America could not honourably stay out'.[88]

But in all likelihood Roosevelt had never intended to become an ally of Britain in the formal sense. Each of the tiny steps he took was designed to keep the US out of the war. The destroyers were intended to ward off invasion and help with convoys so that US waters could remain safe. The leased bases made the American mainland easier to defend. Lend-Lease was designed to help Britain continue the war alone. It also had the desirable side effect of keeping intact the large British investment in American industry. And while Lend-Lease was being negotiated, FDR and others took the opportunity to strip Britain of gold and assets – perhaps in the spirit of cash and carry but also in the spirit of reducing a post-war Britain to modest economic status. The extension of the American zone into the Atlantic was a measure to protect goods that the US was now paying for. The sinking of American warships in the Atlantic could have provided Roosevelt with a reason to go to war but did not. As it happened, the only prominent statesman who was confident that Roosevelt was inching towards war was Hitler. After the Japanese attack on Pearl Harbor on 7 December 1941 he thought an American declaration of war against Germany inevitable, and so on 11 December he declared war on the United States. In a sense Britain was bailed out not by Roosevelt, Ickes or Knox, but by the Führer.

The only conclusion to be reached is that Britain in 1940 and in 1941 survived with no significant outside help except that freely given by the Dominions, especially Canada. That the great majority of the American people hated Nazism and that this view was shared by Roosevelt is beyond question. That Roosevelt refused to show any leadership in this matter is also beyond question. The defender of liberal democracy in 1940–41 was not Britain along with the United States; it was Britain and the Dominions. They fought freedom's battle while the largest democracy on earth occasionally threw them some crumbs.

CONCLUSION

THE YEAR 1940 COULD have been disastrous for Britain and for the West. Any number of events that occurred during that year might have seen Germany victorious over Britain. As Churchill said of another series of crises in another war, 'The terrible "If's" accumulate.'[1]

If the government of Neville Chamberlain had not been overthrown in early May, a compromise peace might have followed the military disaster in France. Chamberlain had no stomach for war. On 3 September he reluctantly declared war but he hardly prosecuted it, apparently relying on an internal revolt in Germany to get him out of his difficulties. This explains why he was reluctant fully to mobilise the country for war or to attack Germany directly. It is difficult to see his resolve for even this partial effort surviving the setbacks in France. It is not difficult to imagine Chamberlain joining the defeatist elements in the French government to seek a settlement with Hitler.

That such a settlement would have been to Germany's advantage goes without saying. This was the only kind of settlement Hitler made. That the war would have been resumed in short order against the weakened Allies also goes without saying. Nazism could not stand still. Chamberlain's ultimate act would have been to preside over the destruction of his country.

If Churchill had not come to power on 10 May it is difficult to see the year ending well for Britain. Churchill had taken the measure of Hitler. He knew that negotiations with 'that man', as he called him, were futile. He had grasped, long before the Holocaust, the evil and aggression that had to be fought. In seeing the struggle in Manichean terms, black versus white, he was surely correct. Against Hitler, victory had to be at 'all costs', it had to be 'in spite of all terror' – for the alternative was unthinkable. At this moment, Britain needed more than an anti-appeaser as Prime Minister; it needed someone with the perception, the courage and the deadliness to see the fight against Germany through to the end.

If Halifax had succeeded in his challenge to Churchill during the Cabinet crisis of late May, he would have followed a path similar to Chamberlain's. Once the British sat down at the table with Mussolini or Hitler or both, there would have been no going back. The slippery slope, as Churchill called it, would have grown more precipitate as home morale plummeted. Moreover, the peace that Halifax sought entailed a guarantee only of Britain's independence. There were two dangers inherent in this approach. The first was that, as already noted, Hitler never honoured agreements of this kind with states he considered a threat. Second, on no occasion did Halifax ever mention the independence of other states. The security of France, Belgium, the Netherlands, Denmark, Norway and Poland was never his concern. He might fight to keep the grouse moors of Yorkshire safe for the aristocracy but not much more. The second danger was that under Halifax's peace terms Europe and all its resources would have fallen under the Nazi yoke. Exactly how he thought a Europe organised by Hitler for aggression would not represent a danger to Britain was not specified. But it is well for Britain and for Europe that Halifax did not prevail.

If the British army had not survived the German onslaught and had been trapped in Europe, the consequences, both militarily and politically, would have been dire. Thanks to Gort's actions to shore up the British position and his determination to ignore Churchill and retreat to the coast, the steadiness of Brooke, Alexander and lower-order commanders such as Montgomery, Franklyn and others, the retreat was managed reasonably well. The fighting quality of the troops and indecisiveness on the German side ensured that the BEF arrived at Dunkirk in a state where a systematic evacuation could be undertaken. The strength and efficiency of the navy and the intervention of the RAF enabled such an operation to be carried out and the vast bulk of the army returned to Britain.

If these events had played out differently, if Britain had lost 300,000 men and most of the officer corps of the Regular Army, its role in the subsequent years of the Second World War would necessarily have been diminished. Whether Britain could have maintained campaigns in the Western Desert, Italy and the Far East, as well as playing a major role in the invasion of north-western Europe, is doubtful.

If Churchill had been unable to portray Dunkirk at least as some form of success, there is no doubt that his position politically would have been weakened. In this situation Halifax might have returned to the charge, pointing out the necessity, now that Britain was without an army, to open talks with the dictators. Churchill had to use all his political skill to fight off Halifax's first challenge. It was as well for Britain that a second was never made.

If the German army had been able to cross to Britain and land in sufficient numbers in 1940, the outlook would have been grim. The British army had to some extent recovered from Dunkirk but whether it was equipped to fight Panzer divisions is another matter. Fortunately for Britain the strength of the Royal Navy and the RAF acted as a sufficient deterrent to Hitler. It must, however, be said that in this instance the hesitations shown by Hitler were well founded. An invasion along the lines of that planned by the Germans would almost certainly have come to grief.

If Fighter Command had been defeated in the Battle of Britain, invasion would have been an easier prospect for Germany. However, the power of the navy would still have acted as a considerable deterrent. In any case a close examination of the air battles in the summer of 1940 indicates that Park and Dowding had the conflict under control. Nevertheless, in war everything is in flux. Park was still required to make the correct decisions during the battle; the pilots had to be prepared to risk their lives daily; the factories had to retain the capacity to produce new aircraft. We can see in retrospect that all these things happened. At the time the picture was not quite so clear, and the decision to fight on was accordingly more debatable in some quarters at least.

If the night bombing of Britain in the last few months of the year had succeeded in crippling industry or breaking civilian morale, Britain may have been forced to seek terms. The Luftwaffe did not remotely have the power to succeed in its attack on industry. The bomb loads it could carry were too small, the targets too numerous. The effect of the attack on the civilian population was more difficult to assess. The fact was that no people had ever before been subjected to bombardment from the air for such a sustained period. The terror and helplessness experienced by people threatened by the bombs are captured in every diary and letter from the period. The casualties suffered during the Blitz of about 40,000 dead may seem small in comparison to later aerial campaigns but they were unprecedented at the time. In the event, the mood of the country was resolute.

So Britain would survive. But Britain in 1940 was fighting for more than its own survival. Churchill's efforts to keep the French in the war were clearly partly dictated by Britain's national interest. It was better to have a continental ally than not. But while Dunkirk was in progress Churchill ordered that the French be evacuated in equal numbers. As it happened they were not, but 150,000 French troops were lifted to safety during the evacuation. During May and June he offered the French a steady supply of fighters over and above what his own experts told him Britain must keep at home for its own safety. During the last few visits Churchill made to France he assured the leadership that Britain would see their country restored. And the most dramatic of Churchill's gestures in this direction – the offer of Union – was made *after* the French army had collapsed and *after* the French government had been driven from Paris to Bordeaux. The offer of Union would have been of little benefit to Britain. It might have gained a proportion of the French Fleet but that would have depended on whether the offer of Union forestalled the formation of a defeatist administration under Pétain. The overwhelming likelihood was that it would not.

Churchill, then, was appealing to something beyond material assistance to Britain when he offered the Union to France. He was appealing to the French to stay in the fight as part of a larger unity that we can call the West and that he sometimes categorised as Christian civilisation. When he spoke to the French people in October 1940 in his broken French he assured them that they were not forgotten and that France would resume its place among 'the greatest nations of the world' when Britain emerged victorious.[2] Churchill would have no truck with the Pétain regime and, as we saw, he was implacable in his determination to neutralise their fleet by whatever means. However, his attitude to France was always tempered by the fact that it had fought the Germans and that many of its troops had fought very hard.

When it came to the Americans in 1940, Churchill showed no such understanding. His appeals to Roosevelt for aid were often coupled with an appeal for the United States to join the fight for civilised values. What infuriated Churchill during this period was that Roosevelt made frequent speeches in which he seemed to take Churchill's point. He spoke of the barbaric policies being pursued by Nazi Germany, the many atrocities committed by them in Occupied Europe, and how America would assist the free world to thwart Hitler. But none of this led Roosevelt to take America into the war. Sympathy with Britain's cause did not mean participation. Even economic aid came at the highest price it was thought Britain could afford. And Lend-Lease was only enacted when the administration realised that Britain was running out of dollars, that it might default on contracts to American suppliers, and that it might be forced out of the war. Roosevelt did not want Britain to leave the war but he was willing to risk it, hence his constant badgering of Churchill on the fate of the British fleet. He was never willing to accept Churchill's warning that a completely Nazified Europe would represent a deadly threat to American security. In the end Roosevelt was not even willing to follow public opinion. When 70 per cent of his countrymen thought America should even risk war to aid the British, Roosevelt remained resolute for inaction. There seems no doubt from Churchill's responses to this inaction that he thought the President had fallen far below the level of events. There was no meeting of minds between the two statesmen in this period, no hint of a special relationship. Somewhat ironically, the popular view that Churchill and Roosevelt were of one mind in 1940–41 was largely created by Churchill. In his morale-raising wartime speeches he often held out the hope of immediate American intervention and made much of the aid Britain was receiving from the US. And his war memoirs, which might have taken a different line, were written during the Cold War when the friendship and aid of America to Britain and Europe were vital.[3]

For Roosevelt there was no conception that America should join Britain in the fight for something larger than survival. For Roosevelt the survival of Fortress America seemed to be sufficient. For Churchill this was never the case. From the moment Britain entered the war and he held high office, his speeches made constant reference to the fact that the war was being waged to ensure the survival of the West. In his first speech as First Lord of the Admiralty he emphasised that this was not just a war for Danzig and Poland but for the rights of the individual.[4] Later he said that the fate of Holland, Belgium, Czechoslovakia, Poland and Austria would be decided by Britain's victory, for 'if we are not destroyed, all these countries will be rescued and restored to life and freedom'.[5]

When Churchill became Prime Minister he continued with this theme. He clearly saw the French and British as being in the vanguard of freedom. His first broadcast was notable for its mention of the enslaved states of Europe and the duty of the Allies to rescue them from the 'long night of barbarism'.[6] When Britain was 'alone' (always a concept that for Churchill included the Empire and Dominions), in perhaps his most famous speech ('Their Finest Hour') and just before he reached the peroration he said:

> However matters go in France or with the French Government or other French Governments, we in this Island and in the British Empire will never lose our sense of comradeship with the French people. If we are now called on to endure what they have been suffering, we shall emulate their courage, and if final victory rewards our toils they shall share the gains, aye, and freedom shall be restored to all. We abate nothing of our just demands; not one jot or tittle do we recede. Czechs, Poles, Norwegians, Dutch, Belgians have joined their causes to our own. All these shall be restored.[7]

Later, in a Mansion House speech, he said:

> We have not abandoned ... any of our obligations or undertakings towards the captive and enslaved countries of Europe or towards any of those countries which still act with us. On the contrary, since we have been left alone in this world struggle we have reaffirmed or defined more precisely all the causes of all the countries with whom and for whom we drew the sword – Austria, Czechoslovakia, Poland, Norway, Holland, Belgium; greatest of all France; latest of all Greece. For all these we will toil and strive, and our victory will supply the liberation of them all.[8]

Churchill's whole policy was in fact encapsulated in his speech of 14 July 1940 when he reminded the people that 'we are fighting *by* ourselves alone but not *for* ourselves alone'.[9] It was a theme that he would return to until the end of the war.

Any survey of Churchill's pronouncements must conclude that he had a broader concept of what was at stake in the war than many of his political colleagues. The deluded Vichyites thought that they would be left in peace. Roosevelt was willing to risk the prospect of a Nazified Europe. Churchill was different. He knew that a British victory was essential if the West was to survive. He knew that Britain had to endure during the dark hours of 1940 and beyond until it was joined by a major ally. In 1945 when the end of the war came and Churchill addressed the crowds in Whitehall, he told them 'This is your Victory'. They shouted back, 'No, it's yours'. They were both right. And the origins of that victory lay in 1940 when Churchill and the British people saved the West.

NOTES

Introduction

1. Stephen Bungay, *The Most Dangerous Enemy: A History of the Battle of Britain* (London: Aurum, 2001); Juliet Gardiner, *The Blitz: The British Under Attack* (London: Harper, 2011); John Lukacs, *The Duel: 10 May–31 July 1940; Five Days in London; Blood, Toil, Tears and Sweat* (all published by Yale University Press, London, in 1991, 2001 and 2009 respectively). The publisher missed an opportunity with the last of these volumes. It could have been called *Five Minutes in London*.
2. Lawrence Thompson, *1940: Year of Legend, Year of History* (London: Fontana, 1968).
3. Clive Ponting, *1940: Myth and Reality* (London: Cardinal, 1990).
4. Malcolm Smith, *Britain and 1940: History, Myth and Popular Memory* (London: Routledge, 2000).

1. Half-Hearted War

1. War Cabinet Conclusions 4/9/39, CAB 65/1/2. The conclusions are abbreviated minutes of the War Cabinet meetings.
2. Ibid., 5/9/39, CAB 65/1/3.
3. Ibid.
4. See N. H. Gibbs, *Grand Strategy, vol. 1* (London: HMSO, 1976), pp. 229–64, for a discussion of this issue. For Chamberlain's veto see Robert Self, *Chamberlain: A Biography* (Farnham: Ashgate, 2006), p. 254.
5. Michael Howard, *The Continental Commitment* (London: Penguin, 1971), p. 117.
6. Talbot Imlay, *Facing the Second World War: Strategy, Politics and Economics in Britain and France, 1938–1940* (Oxford: Oxford University Press, 2003), p. 86; Gibbs, *Grand Strategy, vol. 1*, pp. 510–13. The Territorials were part-time soldiers who trained on weekends and at annual camps but on the positive side were officered by Regular soldiers and in many cases had exactly the same equipment as the Regulars.
7. War Cabinet Conclusions 6/9/39, CAB 65/1/5.
8. Malcolm Smith, *British Air Strategy between the Wars* (Oxford: Oxford University Press, 1984), pp. 253–7. Smith's extensive account of the development of the Fairey Battle is well worth reading.

288

9. Ibid., pp. 257–8.
10. The British air staff realised that their bomber force hardly amounted to a strategic weapon. In 1936 they began a programme of designing four-engine bombers, which would result in the Halifax, the Stirling and the Lancaster bombers. None would be ready in numbers until 1943. The Germans, however, never reached this conclusion.
11. Richard Overy, *The Bombing War* (London: Allen Lane, 2013), p. 246.
12. J. R. M. Butler, *Grand Strategy, vol. 2* (London: HMSO, 1954), Appendix 1, 'Bombing Policy', p. 567.
13. Ibid.
14. War Cabinet Confidential Annex 9/9/39, CAB 65/3/2. The Confidential Annexes of the War Cabinet consist of those sections of the meetings that were deemed too secret for wider circulation. Although they have a different TNA number, they should be read in conjunction with the War Cabinet Conclusions because they are continuations of the same meeting.
15. Ibid.
16. War Cabinet Confidential Annex 14/9/39, CAB 65/4/13.
17. Ibid., 14/12/39, CAB 65/3/26.
18. Ibid.
19. See War Cabinet Conclusions 16/11/39, CAB 65/2/19, for a discussion of German atrocities in Poland.
20. So said Chamberlain in the War Cabinet 3/9/39, CAB 65/1/1.
21. Ibid.
22. Ibid., 8/9/39, CAB 65/1/8.
23. War Cabinet Conclusions 16/9/39, CAB 65/1/17.
24. War Cabinet Confidential Annex 29/1/40, CAB 65/11/22.
25. M. Middlebrook and C. Everett, *The Bomber Command War Diaries* (London: Penguin, 1980), pp. 22–4, 28.
26. The quotation is the title of Uri Bialer's important book. See *The Shadow of the Bomber: The Fear of Air Attack and British Politics* (London: Royal Historical Society, 1980).
27. George Peden, *Arms, Economics and British Strategy: From Dreadnoughts to the Hydrogen Bomb* (Cambridge: Cambridge University Press, 2007), Table 3.9, p. 152.
28. Stephen Roskill, *The War at Sea, vol. 1* (London: HMSO, 1954), Appendix E, pp. 583–4. There were many other warships in the nearby Mediterranean Fleet.
29. Ibid., Appendix D, p. 577.
30. Ibid., Table 3.6, p. 141.
31. Winston S. Churchill, *The Gathering Storm* (London: Cassell, 1951), pp. 550–2.
32. W. N. Medlicott, *The Economic Blockade, vol. 1* (London: HMSO, 1952), p. 51.
33. Imlay, *Facing the Second World War*, pp. 113–14; Adam Tooze, *The Wages of Destruction: The Making and Breaking of the Nazi Economy* (London: Allen Lane, 2006), p. 309.
34. Medlicott, *Economic Blockade, vol. 1*, p. 254. A bizarre Buchanesque plan was hatched by a committee under Hankey to sabotage the Romanian oilfields and to block the Danube so as to prevent any remaining supplies from reaching Germany via this route. The one snag was that Romania would have to cooperate in destroying its own oilfields. To the consternation of the British they refused to have anything to do with the scheme. See Medlicott, *Economic Blockade, vol. 1*, pp. 254–9.
35. Tooze, *Wages of Destruction*, p. 321.
36. Imlay, *Facing the Second World War*, pp. 315–16.
37. Minister of Supply Speech to the House of Commons 19/5/39, quoted in ibid., p. 325.
38. W. Hancock and M. Gowing, *British War Economy* (London: HMSO, 1949), p. 85.
39. War Cabinet Conclusions 19/10/39, CAB 65/1/20.
40. The source of the table is Hancock and Gowing, *British War Economy*, p. 136.
41. War Cabinet Conclusions 9/9/39, CAB 65/1/9.
42. H. M. D. Parker, *Manpower: A Study of War-time Policy and Administration* (London: HMSO, 1957), pp. 62–3.

43. Hancock and Gowing, *British War Economy*, p. 122; Parker, *Manpower*, pp. 62–3.
44. War Cabinet Conclusions 22/9/39, CAB 65/1/23.
45. Indicated by his reference to total outlays possibly exceeding £2,000 million. See Simon in Hansard 27/9/39, vol. 351, Columns 1362–80.
46. Ibid.
47. For those unfamiliar with the British taxation system in this period, the 'standard' rate of tax was the amount paid on the bulk of a taxpayer's income. That is, a person earning £500 per annum would pay 2/4d on the first £135 and 5/6d on the remainder. Those with incomes of say £2,000 would pay a surtax over and above the standard rate on the last £500 of that income. For these details see B. E. V. Sabine, *British Budgets in Peace and War, 1932–1945* (London: Allen & Unwin, 1970), Appendices A and B, pp. 304–5.
48. Hansard 27/9/29, vol. 351, Columns 1372–3.
49. Ibid., Column 1377.
50. Keynes to *The Times*, 28/9/39, quoted in Donald Moggridge (ed.), *The Collected Writings of John Maynard Keynes, vol. XXII: Activities 1939–1945: Internal War Finance* (Cambridge: Cambridge University Press, 1978), pp. 30–1.
51. Ibid., p. 31.
52. Sabine, *British Budgets in Peace and War*, pp. 162–3.
53. Simon in Hansard 23/4/40, vol. 360, Columns 74–86.
54. J. M. Keynes, *How to Pay for the War* (London: Macmillan, 1940), p. 10.
55. Amery in Hansard 24/4/40, vol. 360, Columns 290–5.
56. Dalton in Hansard 25/4/40, vol. 360, Columns 411–12.
57. Crookshank in Hansard 25/4/40, vol. 360, Columns 411–12.
58. Davies in Hansard 25/4/40, vol. 360, Column 412.
59. Ibid., Column 423.
60. Chamberlain in Hansard 3/9/39, vol. 351, Column 292.
61. The quotation is from Compton Mackenzie. See Terry Charman (ed.), *Outbreak 1939: The World Goes to War* (London: Imperial War Museum, 2009), p. 166. Many other listeners that day agreed with Mackenzie.
62. Quoted in Keith Feiling, *The Life of Neville Chamberlain* (London: Macmillan, 1946), p. 419.
63. Chamberlain to Hilda 10/9/39, quoted in Robert Self, *The Neville Chamberlain Diary Letters, vol. 4* (Farnham: Ashgate, 2005), p. 445.
64. Chamberlain to the Archbishop of Canterbury 25?/12/39, quoted in Feiling, *Chamberlain*, p. 430.
65. Chamberlain to Hilda 8/10/39, in Self, *Chamberlain Diary Letters, vol. 4*, pp. 455–6.
66. Chamberlain to Ida 5/11/39, in ibid., p. 466. In can be said with some confidence that Chamberlain was not afflicted in this way.
67. Chamberlain to Hilda 9/2/40, in ibid., p. 498.
68. War Cabinet Conclusions 30/9/39, CAB 65/1/32.
69. Chamberlain to Hilda 9/2/40, in Self, *Chamberlain Diary Letters, vol. 4*, p. 498.
70. War Cabinet Conclusions 16/11/39, CAB 65/2/19.
71. Ibid., 28/11/39, CAB 65/2/31.
72. War Cabinet Confidential Annex 23/10/39, CAB 65/3/32.
73. Ibid., 27/10/39, CAB 65/3/34.
74. Chamberlain to Hilda 19/11/39, in Self, *Chamberlain Diary Letters, vol. 4*, p. 472.
75. War Cabinet Conclusions 29/9/39, CAB 65/3/17.
76. Christopher Hill, *Cabinet Decisions on Foreign Policy: The British Experience* (Cambridge: Cambridge University Press, 2002), p. 111.
77. War Cabinet Confidential Annex, 5/10/39, CAB 65/1/43.
78. Ibid.
79. Ibid.; Hill, *Cabinet Decisions*, p. 112. Hill's dissection of this episode is a model of forensic analysis.
80. War Cabinet Conclusions 9/10/39, CAB 65/1/43.

81. See Churchill's note on 9 October (in effect a draft reply to Hitler) and his covering letter to Chamberlain in Chartwell 19/2.
82. War Cabinet Confidential Annex 12/10/39, CAB 65/3/24.
83. War Cabinet Confidential Annex 25/10/39, CAB 65/3/27; Hill, *Cabinet Decisions*, p. 140.
84. Ibid.; War Cabinet Confidential Annex 17/1/40, CAB 65/11/16.

2. The Parliamentary Crisis

1. A. R. Peters, *Anthony Eden at the Foreign Office* (Aldershot: Gower, 1986), p. 359.
2. N. Crowther, *Facing Fascism: The Conservative Party and the European Dictators* (London: Taylor & Francis, 2002), p. 84.
3. David Dutton, *Anthony Eden: A Life and Reputation* (London: Edward Arnold, 1997), p. 127.
4. Lynne Olson, *Troublesome Young Men: The Rebels who Brought Churchill to Power in 1940 and Helped Save Britain* (London: Bloomsbury, 2007), p. 177.
5. Larry L. Witherell, 'Lord Salisbury's "Watching Committee" and the Fall of Neville Chamberlain', *English Historical Review*, 116, November 2001, pp. 1,139 and 1,136.
6. Olson, *Troublesome Young Men*, p. 178.
7. Both Robert Rhodes James in *Bob Boothby: A Portrait* (London: Hodder & Stoughton, 1991), p. 185, and Martin Gilbert, *Winston S. Churchill, vol. 5: 1922–39* (London: Heinemann, 1976), p. 1002, put the size of the group at 30. Crowther in *Facing Fascism*, p. 100, says that the consensus figure is 25 but his estimate is 40. He lists some members outside the Eden or Churchill groups such as John Gretton, Ernest Makins, Victor Raikes and J. J. Stanton as abstainers. These are credible names.
8. Salisbury to the *Daily Telegraph* and the *Morning Post* 8/7/39, quoted in Witherell, 'Lord Salisbury's "Watching Committee"', p. 1139.
9. See Witherell, 'Lord Salisbury's "Watching Committee"', for these details. He has a list of members on pp. 1,165–6.
10. Ibid.
11. See John Barnes and David Nicholson (eds), *The Empire at Bay: The Leo Amery Diaries, 1929–1945* (London: Hutchinson, 1980), p. 585, for the details. Hereafter, *Amery Diaries*.
12. Quoted in Olson, *Troublesome Young Men*, p. 286. The delegation member was Paul Emrys-Evans.
13. Witherell, 'Lord Salisbury's "Watching Committee"', p. 1,153.
14. James, *Boothby*, p. 238.
15. Paul Addison, *The Road to 1945: British Politics and the Second World War* (London: Hodder & Stoughton, 1975), p. 69. See also Robert Rhodes James, *Victor Cazalet: A Portrait* (London: Hamish Hamilton, 1976), p. 213, for Cazalet's ambivalent attitude towards Chamberlain.
16. Lord Croft, *My Life of Strife* (London: Hutchinson, n.d). See in particular chapter 37, 'Peril Through Weakness'.
17. This section is based on the excellent article, 'The Old Tories and British War Policy 1939–40', by Aaron Krishtulka in Brian Farrell (ed.), *Leadership and Responsibility in the Second World War, 1939–1940* (Quebec: McGill-Queens University Press, 2004).
18. Nicklaus Thomas-Symonds, *Attlee: A Life in Politics* (London: I. B. Tauris, 2010), p. 82.
19. Ben Pimlott, *The Second World War Diary of Hugh Dalton* (London: Jonathan Cape, 1986), p. 269.
20. Ibid., pp. 272–3.
21. All references to the debate come from the House of Commons Debates (Hansard) 5th Series, vol. 360, May 1940. The column numbers in Hansard are given after particular references.

22. Robert Rhodes James (ed.), 'Chips': The Diaries of Sir Henry Channon (London: Weidenfeld & Nicolson, 1967), p. 244.
23. Hansard 7/5/40, Columns 1074–5.
24. Ibid., Column 1082.
25. Christopher Tomlin Diary 7/5/40, quoted in Simon Garfield (ed.), We Are At War: The Diaries of Five Ordinary People in Extraordinary Times (London: Ebury Press, 2005), p. 212.
26. Tilly Rice Diary 7/5/40, quoted in ibid., p. 212.
27. Hansard 7/5/40, Column 1084.
28. Pimlott, Dalton Diary 8/5/40, p. 340; James, 'Chips' Diary, 7/5/40, p. 245.
29. Hansard 7/5/40, Column 1189.
30. Ibid., Column 1189.
31. For Jones see Hansard 7/5/40, Columns 1130–35, and for Southby, Columns 1151–60.
32. Harold Nicolson Diary 7/5/40, Balliol College, Oxford.
33. Hansard 7/5/40, Column 1116.
34. Ibid., Columns 1191–6.
35. Harold Nicolson Diary 7/5/40.
36. Hansard 7/5/40, Columns 1093–4.
37. Hansard 7/5/40, Columns 1094–1106.
38. Ibid., Column 1172.
39. Ibid.
40. For Wedgewood see ibid., Column 1124, and for Bellinger, Columns 1136 and 1139.
41. Hansard 7/5/40, Columns 1126–30.
42. Harold Nicolson Diary 7/5/40.
43. Pimlott, Dalton Diary, p. 341; James, 'Chips' Diary, p. 245.
44. Harold Nicolson Diary 7/5/40.
45. Hansard 7/5/40, Columns 1140–1150.
46. Bernard Donoughue and George Jones, Herbert Morrison: Portrait of a Politician (London: Weidenfeld & Nicolson, 1973), p. 272; Thomas-Symonds, Attlee, p. 93.
47. Hansard 8/5/40, Column 1263.
48. Ibid., Column 1265.
49. Ibid., Columns 1265–66.
50. Ibid., Columns 1261–76.
51. For Lambert see ibid., Column 1286. For the interjection, see Column 1321.
52. Ibid., Column 1301.
53. Ibid., Columns 1322–23.
54. Ibid., Column 1298.
55. Ibid.
56. Harold Nicolson Diary 8/5/40.
57. James, 'Chips' Diary, 8/5/40, p. 246.
58. Hansard 8/5/40, Column 1349.
59. Hansard 8/5/40, Column 1351.
60. Ross McKibbon, Parties and People: England 1914–1951 (Oxford University Press, 2010), pp. 121–2. As far as I am aware Mr McKibbon is the first historian to draw attention to this important passage in Churchill's speech. This remarkable book gives an excellent exposition of the Norway debate from the left, a perspective much needed.
61. Major General Sir Edward Spears, Assignment to Catastrophe (London: Reprint Society, 1956), pp. 132–3.
62. N. Smart, 'Four Days in May: The Norway Debate and the Downfall of Neville Chamberlain', Parliamentary History, 17, no. 2, 1998, p. 221. The actual majority enjoyed by the government is not easy to calculate. After the 1935 election the National Government (Conservatives, National Liberals, National Labour and Nationals) enjoyed a majority of 254 over all other parties. Between 1935 and 1940 there were 99 by-elections. But of these only 20 had resulted in a change from one party to another.

In all the Conservatives lost 14 by-elections, the National Liberals 5 and the Nationals 1. Labour had gained 13 seats, Independent Conservatives 2, Nationals 2, Independent Progressive 1, Independent 1 and National Liberals 1. Probably this reduced the government majority to 213, but because the voting behaviour of the independents was variable this is only an approximation.

63. The numbers given by various authorities are: Harold Macmillan, *The Blast of War, 1939–1945* (London: Macmillan, 1967), 43; Herbert Morrison, *Autobiography* (London: Odhams, 1960), 43; Clement Attlee, *As It Happened* (London: Heinemann, 1954), 40; Ronald Tree, *When the Moon Was High: Memoirs of Peace and War, 1897–1942* (London: Macmillan, 1975), 44; *The Times* 10/5/40, 21; Smart, Four Days in May, 38; Nicolson Diary 8/4//40, 44; Jorgen Rasmussen, 'Party Loyalty in War-Time: The Downfall of the Chamberlain Government', *Journal of Politics*, 32, no. 2, May 1970, 42.

64. For non-voters see Smart, 'Four Days in May', p. 226, and Rasmussen, 'Party Loyalty', p. 384. On abstentions Smart's calculations are on p. 226 and Rasmussen's on pp. 384–5.

65. This is the figure given by Harold Nicolson in his diary on 8/5/40. A note in the diary by his son and editor reduced it to 30. However, Nigel Nicolson seems to be following A. J. P. Taylor's *English History 1914–1945* (Oxford: Oxford University Press, 1965), not the most reliable source.

66. James, *'Chips' Diary*, p. 247.

67. W. S. Churchill, *The Gathering Storm* (London: Cassell, 1951), p. 233.

68. Nicolson Diary 8/5/40.

69. Andrew Roberts, *Eminent Churchillians* (London: Weidenfeld & Nicolson, 1994), p. 145.

70. Churchill, *Gathering Storm*, p. 233.

71. Anthony Eden, *The Reckoning* (London: Cassell, 1965), p. 96. Eden says that the time of this meeting was 9.30 a.m. This was early for Churchill, who to arise at this hour must have been aware that large events were to be played out that day.

72. Halifax Diary 9/5/40, Churchill College, Cambridge.

73. R. A. Butler, *The Art of the Possible* (London: Hamish Hamilton, 1971), p. 94.

74. A. J. P. Taylor, *Beaverbrook* (New York: Simon & Schuster, 1972), p. 409.

75. Olson, *Troublesome Young Men*, p. 309.

76. Eden, *The Reckoning*, pp. 96–7. According to Lord Moran, Bracken had given Churchill the same advice on the evening of 8 May. See Lord Moran, *Churchill: The Struggle for Survival* (London: Constable, 1966), p. 323.

77. *Amery Diary* 9/5/40, p. 611.

78. Note by Lord Salisbury 9/5/40, quoted in Witherell, 'Lord Salisbury's "Watching Committee"', p. 1162.

79. David Dilks (ed.), *The Diaries of Sir Alexander Cadogan, 1938–1945* (London: Cassell, 1971), 9/5/40, p. 280.

80. Halifax Diary 9/5/40.

81. Ibid.

82. Lawrence Thompson, *1940: Year of Legend, Year of History* (London: Fontana, 1968), p. 88.

83. Churchill, *Gathering Storm*, pp. 522–3. This account may have been massaged in keeping with Churchill's decision in his memoirs to play down party divisions during the crisis.

84. *Amery Diary* 9/5/40, p. 612. Halifax, Dalton and Cadogan confirm the questions to be put to the Labour Executive, but Cadogan has Chamberlain posing the questions. The crisp directness of the questions, however, suggests Attlee's style rather than the Prime Minister's.

85. Dalton told Butler (if the latter, who was implacably hostile to Churchill, can be believed) that Labour would prefer Halifax. But Dalton was not on the Labour Executive. Attlee and Greenwood gave no indications during the Norway debate that they would not serve under the First Lord.

86. *Amery Diary* 10/5/40, p. 612.

3. The Cabinet Crisis

1. Churchill to Chamberlain 11/5/40, Chartwell 20/11.
2. Handwritten note on Admiralty paper in ibid. I have been unable to decipher the portfolio offered to Greenwood. Minister without Portfolio seems a reasonable guess.
3. Undated list in ibid.
4. Chamberlain to Mary Chamberlain 11/5/40, Chamberlain Papers NC1/20/1/198.
5. *Amery Diary* 11/5/40, p. 615.
6. Ibid., 12/5/40, pp. 616–17.
7. Andrew Roberts, *The Holy Fox: The Life of Lord Halifax* (London: Phoenix, 1997), p. 210.
8. Robert Self, *Neville Chamberlain: A Biography* (Farnham: Ashgate, 2010), p. 432.
9. Churchill to Chamberlain 10/5/40, Chartwell 19/2.
10. Churchill to Halifax 10/5/40 in ibid.
11. See the exchange of letters between Churchill and Chamberlain in Chartwell 20/11.
12. Harold Nicolson Diary 13/5/40.
13. Davidson's remarks are quoted by Martin Gilbert in *Winston S. Churchill, vol. 6: 1939–41* (London: Heinemann, 1983), p. 332.
14. John Colville, *The Fringes of Power: Downing Street Diaries 1939–1955* (London: Weidenfeld & Nicolson, 1985), 10/5/40. Hereafter, *Colville Diaries*.
15. Hankey to Hoare 12/5/40, quoted in Martin Gilbert, *The Churchill War Papers, vol. 2: Never Surrender, May 1940–December 1940* (New York: Norton, 1995), pp. 14–15.
16. 'Crooks' comes from Davidson and is quoted in Roberts, *Holy Fox*, p. 208. 'Gangsters' is Halifax's contribution and is quoted in the same source, p. 209. 'Despicable jackals' etcetera comes from Self (*Neville Chamberlain*, p. 431).
17. Hansard, 13/5/40, vol. 360, Column 1502.
18. The meetings of the War Cabinet are to be found for this period in the series CAB 65/7 in the National Archives. The meetings of the five permanent members, which were usually continuations of these meetings, are to be found in the series War Cabinet Confidential Annex in CAB 65/13.
19. War Cabinet Conclusions 12/5/40, CAB 65/7/14.
20. Ibid., 15/5/40, CAB 65/7/18.
21. Churchill to Mussolini 16/5/40 in Gilbert, *Churchill War Papers, vol. 2*, p. 50.
22. W. S. Churchill, *Their Finest Hour* (London: Cassell, 1955), pp. 107–8.
23. Churchill to Chamberlain 17/5/40 in Gilbert, *Churchill War Papers, vol. 2*, p. 68.
24. War Cabinet Confidential Annex 18/5/40, CAB 65/13/10.
25. War Cabinet Conclusions 19/5/40, CAB 65/7/24.
26. Ibid., 24/5/40, CAB 65/7/32.
27. Ibid., 25/5/40, CAB 65/7/33.
28. Ibid.
29. Defence Committee Minutes 25/5/40, CAB 69/1.
30. 'British Strategy in a Certain Eventuality', COS Paper 25/5/40, CAB 80/11.
31. War Cabinet Confidential Annex 26/5/40, CAB 65/13/20. The discussion that follows comes from this meeting except where indicated.
32. War Cabinet Confidential Annex 26/5/40, CAB 65/13/20.
33. This section owes much to the excellent account of these events by Christopher Hill in *Cabinet Decisions on Foreign Policy: The British Experience* (Cambridge: Cambridge University Press, 2002). See p. 155.
34. War Cabinet Confidential Annex 26/5/40, CAB 65/13/20.
35. Ibid.
36. The full document can be found in CAB 80/11.

37. This is my interpretation of the minutes, which appear to contain a contradiction. They state that after the circulation of the Aide-Memoire, Halifax said that 'as he read the Chiefs of Staff paper' Britain's ability to continue the war hinged on air superiority'. However, at the end of the meeting the minutes note that the report of the Chiefs of Staff 'was being circulated'. To which paper was Halifax then referring? It could not have been the Aide-Memoire, which made no reference to air superiority. The only other paper was 'British Strategy in a Certain Eventuality'. I can only assume that Halifax had already obtained a copy of this paper. It is possible that Halifax's pessimistic demeanour at this meeting derived in part from his having read the Chiefs' gloomy assessment. No authority (Lukacs, Roberts, Bell or Hill) has noted this apparent paradox in the minutes.

38. Eleanor M. Gates, *End of the Affair: The Collapse of the Anglo-French Alliance, 1939–40* (Berkeley: University of California Press, 1981), p. 144. Reynaud told his Under-Secretary of State, Paul Baudouin, when he returned to France that he found himself unable to put the question of France leaving the war to Churchill.

39. War Cabinet Confidential Annex 26/5/40, CAB 65/13/21. All subsequent quotations are taken from this meeting.

40. *Cadogan Diary* 26/5/40, p. 290. Cadogan says he was 'summoned to the Admiralty at 5'.

41. These notes have the same Cabinet file number as that above.

42. The Halifax–Bastianini discussions are attached to the War Cabinet Confidential Annex of 26/5/40.

43. Ibid.

44. The usually precise John Lukacs suggests this. See *Five Days in London* (London: Yale University Press, 2001), pp. 113, 116–17.

45. War Cabinet Confidential Annex 27/5/40, CAB 65/13/22.

46. COS, 'British Strategy in the Near Future', 26/5/40, CAB 80/11.

47. War Cabinet Confidential Annex 27/5/40, CAB 65/13/22.

48. Quoted in Roberts, *Holy Fox*, p. 218. Roberts claims that the document is to be found in the War Cabinet's Confidential Annex of 26 May. I cannot find it. A copy is to be found, however, in the War Cabinet Papers in CAB 66.

49. War Cabinet Confidential Annex 27/5/40, CAB 65/13/23.

50. Ibid.

51. John Lukacs has 'falling ally' (*Five Days in London*, p. 147), which certainly conveys the sense of the situation.

52. War Cabinet Confidential Annex 27/5/40, CAB 65/13/23. Emphasis added.

53. Ibid. Emphasis added.

54. Ibid. Emphasis added.

55. Ibid.

56. *Cadogan Diary* 27/5/40.

57. Halifax Diary 27/5/40.

58. War Cabinet Confidential Annex 27/5/40, CAB 65/13/23.

59. John Lukacs states that David Dilks said the following in an article in the *Transactions of the Royal Historical Society*: 'Here was Churchill, of all people, prepared to think of a peace which would inevitably leave Germany master of Europe and would also involve the loss of some British territory. The traditional belief that Churchill, from the moment of his accession as Prime Minister, was determined to fight until the whole of Europe was liberated can no longer be sustained in pure form.' Lukacs does not give an exact reference and I cannot find this quotation in the article.

60. War Cabinet Confidential Annex 27/5/40, CAB 65/13/23.

61. Ibid.

62. Ibid.

63. *Cadogan Diary* 27/5/40; Halifax Diary 27/5/40.

64. War Cabinet Conclusions 28/5/40, CAB 65/7/39.

65. Ibid.

66. War Cabinet Confidential Annex 28/5/40, CAB 65/13/24.

67. Ibid.
68. Ibid.
69. Ibid.
70. Churchill, *Finest Hour*, p. 88.
71. Ben Pimlott, *The Second World War Diary of Hugh Dalton* (London: Jonathan Cape, 1986), 28/5/40, p. 28.
72. *Amery Diary* 28/5/40.
73. Churchill to Reynaud 28/5/40, War Cabinet Confidential Annex 28/5/40, CAB 65/13/24.

4. A Close-Run Thing

1. Major L. F. Ellis, *The War in France and Flanders, 1939–1940* (London: HMSO, 1953), p. 77. The British Official History.
2. Ibid., p. 7.
3. Field Marshal Lord Alanbrooke, *War Diaries 1939–1945*, ed. Alex Danchev and David Todman (London: Phoenix Press, 2002). Entries for 21 and 22 November 1939, p. 19. Hereafter *Brooke Diaries*.
4. Meeting at Chateau Casteau 12/5/40, in GHQ War Diary 12/5/40, WO 167/5.
5. War Cabinet Confidential Annex 9/11/39, CAB 65/4/8, statement by the Chief of the Imperial General Staff.
6. Ellis, *France and Flanders*, p. 23.
7. Many thought the Germans had changed their plan because the original plan had been compromised by a German aircraft crash in Belgium in January 1940, from which Belgian intelligence retrieved its main outline. Gamelin thought the Germans would persist with this plan. He was wrong, but the crash was not the reason for the German decision. Manstein and eventually Hitler thought the new plan superior. Halifax was one on the British side who thought the plan a ruse, but he did not draw the obvious conclusion that if the Germans were not to attack across Belgium they must attack elsewhere.
8. For these details see Karl-Heinz Freiser, *The Blitzkrieg Legend: The 1940 Campaign in the West* (Annapolis: Naval Institute Press, 2005), p. 86, and K. Maier et al., *Germany and the Second World War, vol. 2* (Oxford: Clarendon Press, 1991), pp. 247–9.
9. Montgomery Diary 14/5/40, Montgomery Papers, BLM 19, Australian Defence Force Academy Library.
10. GHQ War Diary 15/5/40, WO 167/5.
11. Ibid.
12. For the whole sorry story of the brief Dutch resistance to the Germans see P. L. G. Doorman, *Military Operations in the Netherlands from 10th–17th May, 1940* (London: Allen & Unwin, 1944).
13. GHQ War Diary 16/5/40, WO 167/40 and Advanced Brassard War Diary for the same date, WO 167/82. Advanced Brassard was the rather weird name given by Gort to his forward headquarters.
14. *Brooke Diaries* 16/5/40.
15. Montgomery Diary 16/5/40; 3 Division War Diary 16/5/40, WO 167/218.
16. 4 Division War Diary 17/5/40, WO 167/230.
17. 12 Lancers War Diary 16–18/5/40, WO 167/452.
18. Brian Bond (ed.), *Chief of Staff: The Diaries of Lieutenant-General Sir Henry Pownall, vol. 1* (London: Leo Cooper, 1972). Hereafter *Pownall Diaries*. The locations of Gort's Command Post can be found on pp. 307–50.
19. I Corps Telephone Log and War Diary 16/5/40, WO 167/124.
20. *Pownall Diaries*, 14/5/40, p. 315.
21. *Brooke Diaries*, 21/11/39, p. 18.
22. GHQ War Diary 16/5/40, WO 167/5.
23. Ibid. 17/5/40.

24. Ibid.
25. 'Account of Operations of Petre Force in the Area of Arras 18th–25th May, 1940', WO 197/118.
26. 50 Division War Diary 19/5/40, WO 167/300.
27. Ellis, *France and Flanders*, p. 72.
28. GHQ War Diary 19/5/40, WO 167/5.
29. Ibid., night of 18–19 May 1940.
30. *Pownall Diaries* 19/5/40, p. 323.
31. War Cabinet Conclusions 16 and 17 May 1940, CAB 65/7/19–21; Churchill to the War Cabinet 16/5/40, Chartwell 4/149.
32. War Cabinet Confidential Annex 19/5/40, CAB 65/13/12.
33. GHQ War Diary 20/5/40, WO 167/5.
34. R. Macleod and D. Kelly (eds), *The Ironside Diaries 1937–1940* (London: Constable, 1962), 20/5/40. The editors have done their best to make these diaries unusable by splitting them into subject areas and by providing commentary that is often intermixed with the diary entries.
35. Command Post War Diary 20/5/40, WO 167/29.
36. Ellis, *France and Flanders*, pp. 103–5.
37. Gort to Eden 20/5/40, GHQ War Diary WO 167/5; Dill to Churchill 20/5/40 in Anglo-French Liaison Folder, CAB 21/1289.
38. Command Post War Diary 21/5/40, WO 167/29.
39. Ibid.
40. Gregory Blaxland, *Destination Dunkirk* (London: Kimber, 1973), pp. 136–7.
41. Command Post War Diary 21/5/40, WO 167/29.
42. 12 Lancers War Diary 21/5/40, WO 167/452.
43. Rommel Diary 21/5/40, in B. H. Liddell Hart (ed.), *The Rommel Papers* (London: Collins, 1953), pp. 32–3.
44. This account has been taken from 'Summary of Events May–June 1940' in CAB 106/284. This folder contains summaries of the actions of the 4th and 7th Royal Tank Regiments that took part in the Arras counter-attack.
45. See the Report of the 4th RTR in ibid.
46. 6 Panzer Division War Diary 21/5/40 in CAB 146/452.
47. XXXIX Corps War Diary 21/5/40 in ibid.
48. Army Group A War Diary 21/5/40 in IWM 19757 M.I.I.T.
49. Ibid.
50. Ibid. Underlining in the original.
51. Ibid., 22/5/40.
52. Ibid.
53. Churchill to Keyes 21/5/40, Chartwell 20/14.
54. Transcripts of the various meetings at Ypres on 21 May are to be found in CAB 106/862.
55. Churchill to Gort 22/5/40, Chartwell 22/14.
56. *Pownall Diaries* 22/5/40, p. 325.
57. For these moves see GHQ War Diary entries between 21 and 23 May 1940, WO 167/5.
58. Ibid.
59. Ellis, *France and Flanders*, pp. 121 and 123.
60. Major General Franklyn, 'Report on Operations of Frank Force 20th–24th May 1940', WO 197/118.
61. These dispositions have been gleaned from the German Corps War Diaries in CAB 146/452 for 23 May and from the folder 'Maps of German Divisions in the West', CAB 146/453.
62. Extract from Kleist Group War Diary in CAB 146/452.
63. See XXXIX Corps War Diary in ibid.
64. Fourth Army War Diary 23/5/40 in ibid.
65. Army Group A War Diary 23/5/40.

66. Ibid.
67. Ibid., 24/5/40.
68. H. R. Trevor-Roper, *Hitler's War Directives, 1939–1945* (London: Pan, 1966), p. 67.
69. GHQ War Diary 24/5/40, WO 167/5.
70. XIX Corps War Diary 24/5/40, CAB 146/452.
71. Ibid.
72. Ellis, *France and Flanders*, p. 159.
73. Ibid., p. 161.
74. XIX Corps War Diary 26/5/40, CAB 146/452.
75. Churchill to Ironside and Eden 25/5/40, Chartwell 4/150; Churchill to Ironside 25/5/40 in ibid.
76. See Airey Neave, *The Flames of Calais* (London: Hodder & Stoughton, 1972), chapter 21. Neave was in Calais and subsequently taken prisoner. However, writing 30 years after the event he had no doubt as to the usefulness of its defence.
77. 2 Division War Diary 24/5/40, WO 167/203.
78. XXXIX Corps War Diary 24/5/40, CAB 146/452.
79. 'Report on the Operations of Polforce 20–25 May and of 46 Div 25 May–1 June 1940', WO 167/286.
80. XXXIX Corps War Diary 24/5/40, CAB 146/452.
81. See the 6th Army Order No. 12, 24/5/40, in Battle Post War Diary WO 167/27.
82. See Battle Post War Diary 25/5/40, WO 167/27, and the 12 Lancers report 25/5/40 in ibid.
83. Battle Post War Diary entry for 1800 hours, 24/5/40, WO 167/27.
84. Dill to Churchill and Eden 25/5/40 in ibid.
85. Battle Post War Diary 26/5/40.
86. Eden to Gort 26/5/40 in 'Telegrams: Secretary of State–BEF' in WO 106/1689.
87. Eden to Gort 26/5/40 in ibid.
88. 'Operations of II Corps during the Retreat from Louvain to Dunkirk' (written by Brooke) in CAB 106/252.
89. Ibid.
90. M. H. R. Piercy, 'The Manoeuvre that Saved the Field Force', in Brian Bond and Michael Taylor, *The Battle for France and Flanders: Sixty Years On* (Barnsley: Leo Cooper, 2001), p. 57.
91. 13 Brigade War Diary 28/5/40, WO 167/372.
92. 150 Brigade War Diary 26/5/40, WO 167/402. The Germans commented on the ferocity of the British counter-attacks. See 'Experiences Gained in Action against English Troops', in CAB 106/281.
93. Gort to Eden 26/5/40 in CAB 106/1689.
94. Brooke, 'Operations of II Corps', CAB 106/252.
95. Keyes to Gort, GHQ War Diary 27/5/40, WO 167/5.
96. Defence Committee Minutes 27/5/40, CAB 69/1.
97. Army Group B War Diary 27/5/40. It is interesting to reflect that it was Hitler who first used the term 'unconditional surrender' in this war. He would not be the last.
98. 12 Lancers War Diary 28 and 29/5/40, WO 167/452.
99. Brooke, 'Operations of II Corps'.
100. 4 Division War Diary 28 and 29/5/40, WO 167/230.
101. XXXIX Corps War Diary 27/5/40, CAB 146/452.
102. See the 4, 5 and 6 Brigade War Diaries for this day. It is obvious from the scanty nature of the entries that headquarters had little idea of what was unfolding at the front. The diaries are to be found in WO 167/352, 354 and 356 respectively.
103. 2 Division War Diary 27/5/40, WO 167/203.
104. Ibid.
105. XXXIX Corps War Diary 27/5/40, CAB 146/452.

106. 'Note on the 61st [2 Gloucesters] in France with Sketch Map, May 1940, collated by Captain E. Jones – adj 2 Bn Glosters', in CAB 106/292.
107. Ibid.
108. Army Group A War Diary 27/5/40.
109. XIX Corps War Diary 23/5/40, CAB 146/452.
110. Ibid., 26/5/40.
111. XXXXI Corps War Diary 27/5/40, in ibid.
112. Ibid., 28/5/40.
113. Ibid.
114. XIX Corps War Diary 28/5/40 in ibid.
115. Ibid.
116. XXXXI Corps War Diary 28/5/40, CAB 146/452.
117. XXXIX Corps War Diary 28/5/40 in ibid.
118. XXXXI Corps War Diary 29/5/40 in ibid.
119. Ibid.

5. The Great Escape

1. An account of Adamforce 20/6/40, WO 197/19.
2. Ibid. Adam's report claims that the 15 Grenadier Guards occupied the Canal Line to the east of Bergues. There is no such unit and it is not clear which unit is meant.
3. Colonel Whitfield Report 8/6/40, WO 197/118.
4. John Colville, *Gort: Man of Valour* (London: Collins, 1972), p. 204.
5. War Cabinet Conclusions 20/5/40, CAB 65/7.
6. 'Notes on Conference Held at Dover, 20 May, and at War Office, 21 May', WO 167/5.
7. Stephen Roskill, *The War at Sea, vol. 1* (London: HMSO, 1954), p. 216. Oddly, a call had been made via the BBC on 14 May for the owners of small craft to send particulars of them to the navy. Perhaps someone in the navy was taking a gloomier (or more realistic) view of the military campaign in France than most. See Robert Jackson, *Dunkirk: The British Evacuation 1940* (London: Cassell, 1976), p. 73.
8. 'Operation Dynamo – Narrative of Events', ADM 199/792.
9. Ibid.
10. Captain Tennant, 'Evacuation of the British Expeditionary Force', ADM 199/789.
11. Ibid. Signal sent at 8.05 p.m.
12. Williamson Murray, *Luftwaffe* (London: Allen & Unwin, 1985), p. 42.
13. Vincent Orange, *Dowding of Fighter Command: Victor of the Battle of Britain* (London: Grub Street, 2008), p. 169.
14. T. C. G. James, *The Growth of Fighter Command, 1936–1940,* ed. Sebastian Cox (London: Frank Cass, 2002), pp. 94–6.
15. Air Historical Branch, 'The Campaign in France and the Low Countries', AIR 41/21.
16. 'Dunkirk Evacuation Figures', CAB 106/271.
17. These details have been taken from 'Dynamo – Narrative of Events'.
18. AHB, 'Campaign in France and Low Countries'.
19. 'Dynamo – Narrative of Events'; Dunkirk Evacuation Figures.
20. Roskill, *The War at Sea, vol. 1*, p. 219.
21. Patrick Wilson, *Dunkirk: From Disaster to Deliverance* (Barnsley: Leo Cooper, 1999), p. 142.
22. Major L. F. Ellis, *The War in France and Flanders, 1939–1940* (London: HMSO, 1953), pp. 216–19.
23. See, for example, the account of the 4/7 Dragoons in CAB 106/231.
24. Ellis, *France and Flanders*, pp. 210–11.
25. Quoted in Jackson, *Dunkirk*, pp. 102–3.
26. 'Extract from the Diary of Maj-Gen R. A. Osborne' – attached to 44 Division War Diary, WO 167/275.

27. 44 Division War Diary 29/30 May, WO 167/275.
28. Adam Report, WO 197/19.
29. Julian Thompson, *Dunkirk: Retreat to Victory* (London: Sidgwick & Jackson, 2008), p. 233.
30. 3 Division War Diary 29/5/40, WO 167/218.
31. Army Group B War Diary 29/5/40 states that these were the Luftwaffe priorities.
32. 'Dynamo - Narrative of Events'.
33. Commander Ellwood Beach Report in 'Evacuation of Troops from Dunkirk - Various Beach Party Reports', ADM 199/788A.
34. Tennant Report 29/5/40, ADM 199/789.
35. 'Dynamo - Narrative of Events'.
36. Ibid.
37. Tennant Report 29/5/40.
38. Ibid.
39. 'AHB Narrative - France and Flanders 29/5/40', AIR 41/21.
40. 'Dynamo - Narrative of Events'.
41. Ibid.
42. Ibid.
43. Ibid.
44. 'Dunkirk - Evacuation Figures'.
45. 'Dynamo - Narrative of Events'.
46. Lecture by Brigadier W. Robb on Operations in Belgium, May 1940, 3 Division War Diary 30/5/40, WO 167/218; Army Group B War Diary 30/5/40.
47. 4th Army War Diary 30/5/40, CAB 146/452.
48. Ibid.
49. Ibid.
50. Ibid.
51. 6th Army War Diary 30/5/40, in ibid.
52. 4th Army War Diary 30/5/40 in ibid.
53. Ibid.
54. Army Group B War Diary 30/5/40. Underlining in the original.
55. Ibid.
56. Commander Richardson, 'Situation on the Beaches', in Beach Party Reports, ADM 199/788A.
57. Dover War Diary 29/5/40, ADM 199/360.
58. Tennant Report 30/5/40.
59. 'Dynamo - Narrative of Events'.
60. Tennant Report 30/5/40.
61. 1 Division War Diary 30/5/40, WO 167/190.
62. Ellwood Report, in Beach Party Reports, ADM 199/788A.
63. Dunkirk - Evacuation Figures.
64. 'AHB Narrative - France and Flanders'.
65. War Office to British Liaison Missions 30/5/40, in Dunkirk Telegrams, WO 106/1478.
66. Thompson, *Dunkirk*, p. 241.
67. Churchill to Ismay 29/5/40, Chartwell 20/14.
68. Telephone conversation between Gort and Dill 30/5/40, in Dunkirk Telegrams, WO 106/1478.
69. There is some controversy surrounding the choice of Alexander. Montgomery stated that Gort had chosen Barker and had to be taken aside and told that the I Corps Commander was on the brink of collapse, and it was after this conversation that Alexander got the command. However, in a telephone conversation between Gort and Ironside on the night of 30/31 May, the CIGS made the point that there was no need to leave a Corps Commander in charge of the dwindling BEF - a divisional commander would be sufficient and he suggested Alexander because he had seniority over the others. For Monty's version see Nigel Nicolson, *Alex: The Life of Field Marshal Earl Alexander of Tunis* (London: Weidenfeld & Nicolson, 1973), p. 103. For the telephone conversation see GHQ War Diary 30/31/5/40, WO 167/5.

70. GHQ War Diary 31/5/40, WO 167/5.
71. For the best discussion of these events see Nicolson, *Alex*, pp. 105–8.
72. 'Arm in Arm'. Supreme War Council Minutes 31/5/40, CAB 99/3.
73. War Office to Alexander, in Dunkirk Telegrams, WO 106/1478. It took a second telegram from Alexander to clarify the issue about when the 50:50 evacuation should commence.
74. Nicolson, *Alex*, pp. 108–9.
75. 4 Division War Diary 31/5/40, WO 167/230.
76. 'AHB Narrative – France and Flanders'.
77. Thompson, *Dunkirk*, p. 249.
78. Wilson, *Dunkirk*, pp. 85–6.
79. Wake-Walker Report 31/5/40, ADM 199/792.
80. 'Narrative of Events 28th May 1940 to 5th June 1940, Evacuation of the British Expeditionary Force from Dunkirk and Beaches to the Eastward by H. M. S. Sutton, Fourth Minesweeping Flotilla' in 'Various Ships' Reports', ADM 199/786.
81. 'Dynamo – Narrative of Events'.
82. Ibid.
83. Dunkirk – Evacuation Figures.
84. These are rough estimates gleaned from the War Diaries. It is often not clear which troops remained and which had gone in the confused conditions under which the war diaries were written.
85. Army Group B War Diary 1/6/40.
86. Ibid.
87. Ellis, *France and Flanders*, p. 242.
88. 'Dynamo – Narrative of Events'.
89. Ibid.
90. Wake-Walker Report 1/6/40, ADM 199/792.
91. 'Dynamo – Narrative of Events'.
92. Dunkirk Evacuation Figures.
93. 'AHB Narrative – France and Flanders'.
94. 'Dynamo – Narrative of Events'.
95. Ibid.
96. Army Group B War Diary for these dates.
97. See Ellis, *France and Flanders*, pp. 244–5; Tennant Report and Dunkirk Evacuation Figures.
98. Ibid., p. 246.
99. See Defence Committee Minutes 14/6/40, CAB 69/1, and Brooke's much more colourful account in his diary for 14 June. The whole episode of the Breton Redoubt is dealt with in a report by Brooke in WO 167/4.
100. Dunkirk – Evacuation Figures.
101. Ellis, *France and Flanders*, p. 327.
102. Orange, *Dowding*, p. 168.

6. Alone

1. Churchill: Telephone conversation with Paul Reynaud 15/5/40, Prem [Premier] 3/188/1.
2. Ibid.
3. Chief of Staff Committee Minutes 15/5/40, CAB 79/4.
4. War Cabinet Conclusions 15/5/40, CAB 65/7/18.
5. Chiefs of Staff [COS] Committee Minutes 16/5/40, CAB 79/4; War Cabinet Confidential Annex 16/5/40, CAB 65/13/10.
6. Ismay recollection, Chartwell 4/44.
7. Supreme War Council Minutes 16/5/40, CAB 99/3.

8. Lord Ismay, *Memoirs* (London: Heinemann, 1960), p. 126; Winston S. Churchill, *Their Finest Hour* (London: Cassell, 1955), pp. 42–3.
9. War Cabinet Conclusions 16/5/40, CAB 65/7/19.
10. Eleanor M. Gates, *End of the Affair: The Collapse of the Anglo-French Alliance, 1939–40* (Berkeley: University of California Press, 1981), p. 79.
11. War Cabinet Conclusions 20/5/40, CAB 65/7/26.
12. Supreme War Council Minutes 22/5/40, CAB 99/3.
13. Churchill to Reynaud 23/5/40, Chartwell 20/14.
14. War Council Confidential Annex 26/5/40, CAB 65/13/21.
15. Supreme War Council Minutes 31/5/40, CAB 99/3.
16. War Cabinet Confidential Annex 2/6/40, CAB 65/13/30.
17. COS Appreciation 3/6/40, Cabinet Papers, CAB 66/8.
18. 'Support for France': General Sir H. L. Ismay's Correspondence, CAB 21/1488.
19. Only fighter aircraft will be discussed here because those were the type of aircraft the French constantly sought from the British.
20. François Fonville-Alquier, *The French and the Phoney War, 1939–40* (London: Tom Stacey, 1973), pp. 197–8.
21. Most of the information about the French Air Force has been taken from an extremely useful article, 'The French Air Force in 1940', by Lt-Col. Faris B. Kirkland in *Air University Review*, September–October 1985, pp. 1–14.
22. Patrick Facon, *L'Armée de l'air dans la tourmente: La bataille de France, 1939–1940* (Paris: Economica, 1997), p. 259.
23. Churchill to Reynaud and Weygand 5/6/40, Chartwell 20/14.
24. Campbell to Halifax 5/6/40, War Cabinet Confidential Annex 65/13/33.
25. Churchill to Reynaud and Weygand 5/6/40, Chartwell 20/14.
26. Gates, *End of the Affair*, pp. 165–6.
27. Churchill to Reynaud and Weygand 7/6/40, Prem 3/188/1.
28. Churchill to Roosevelt 11/6/40, Prem 3/468/1.
29. Churchill to Roosevelt 11/6/40, Chartwell 20/14.
30. Major General Sir Edward Spears, *Assignment to Catastrophe* (London: Reprint Society, 1956), p. 444.
31. Ibid., p. 449.
32. Ismay, *Memoirs*, pp. 138–9.
33. It is certainly more readable than the Supreme War Council Minutes from which the gist of this meeting has been taken. See the minutes for 11/6/40 in CAB 99/3.
34. Supreme War Council Minutes 12/6/40, CAB 99/3.
35. War Cabinet Conclusions 12/6/40, CAB 65/7/57.
36. Churchill to Roosevelt 12/6/40, Prem 3/468/1.
37. Gates, *End of the Affair*, p. 190.
38. Supreme War Council Minutes 13/6/40, CAB 99/3.
39. Warren F. Kimball, *Churchill & Roosevelt: The Complete Correspondence, vol. 1* (Princeton, NJ: Princeton University Press, 1984), pp. 45–6. The whole matter of Anglo-American relations in this period will be discussed in another chapter.
40. War Cabinet Conclusions 13/6/40, CAB 65/7/59.
41. Churchill to Roosevelt 13/6/40, Kimball, *Complete Correspondence, vol. 1*, p. 47.
42. Roosevelt to Churchill 14/6/40, in ibid., p. 48.
43. War Cabinet Conclusions (12.30) 14/6/40, CAB 65/7/61.
44. Churchill to Roosevelt 15/6/40, Kimball, *Complete Correspondence, vol. 1*, pp. 49–51.
45. Avi Shlaim, 'Prelude to Downfall: The British offer of Union to France, June 1940', *Journal of Contemporary History*, 9, no. 3, July 1974, pp. 40–1. The pre-history of the union, which goes back to the beginning of the war, can be found in this lucid exposition.
46. Ibid., p. 41.

47. War Cabinet Confidential Annex 16/6/40, CAB 65/13/45; Churchill to Reynaud 16/6/40, Chartwell 20/14.
48. Quoted in ibid., p. 50.
49. Spears, *Assignment to Catastrophe*, p. 589.
50. Ibid.
51. The name of the minister should be recorded; it was Ybarnegaray.
52. Shlaim, 'Prelude to Downfall', p. 53.
53. Gates, *End of the Affair*, p. 247.
54. 'Record of Conversation Held at Bordeaux on 18th June, 1940, Between First Lord, First Sea Lord and Admiral Darlan, First Sea Lord's Records 1939–1945', ADM 205/4.
55. Quoted in Gates, *End of the Affair*, pp. 278–9.
56. Ibid., pp. 288–92.
57. War Cabinet Confidential Annex 24/6/40, CAB 65/13/48 and 49.
58. War Cabinet Conclusions 23/6/40, CAB 65/7/30; *Cadogan Diary* 23/6/40, p. 314.
59. Hansard 25/5/40, vol. 362, Column 304–5.
60. Ibid.
61. The terms to be offered to the French regarding the fleet were discussed many times by the War Cabinet. A useful summary of the alternatives to be offered to Darlan can be found in the Conclusions for 27/6/40, CAB 65/13/53.
62. Andrew Roberts, *The Holy Fox: The Life of Lord Halifax* (London: Phoenix, 1997), p. 231. Roberts has by far the best account of this affair. I am afraid, however, I take his view that this was a chance meeting with a grain of salt.
63. Churchill to Halifax 25/6/40, quoted in Martin Gilbert, *The Churchill War Papers, vol. 2: Never Surrender, May 1940–December 1940* (New York: Norton, 1995), pp. 419–20.
64. Roberts, *Holy Fox*, pp. 232–6. Ironically, Butler's move to Education would rehabilitate his reputation.
65. Joint Planners Report on French Fleet 29/6/40, COS Papers, CAB 80/14.
66. COS Report on French Fleet 30/6/40, CAB 79/5.
67. The details of French naval dispositions can be found in A. J. Marder, 'Oran, 3 July 1940', in his *From the Dardanelles to Oran* (London: Oxford University Press, 1974), pp. 200–5.
68. Marder, *Oran*, p. 228.
69. War Cabinet Confidential Annex 30/6/40, CAB 65/13/56.
70. These instructions are attached to the COS paper of 30th June. See CAB 80/14.
71. Marder, *Oran*, pp. 231–2.
72. See ADM 1/10321.
73. The details can be found in Marder, *Oran*, pp. 230–68.

7. Hitler at the Door

1. Chiefs of Staff Committee, 'Invasion of the United Kingdom', 25/5/40, CAB 80/12.
2. German Naval Staff (Operations Division) War Diary 15/11/39, vol. 9. The copy used here is a microfilm edition published by Scholarly Publications. The volumes refer to those used by the publishers. Hereafter this source will be referred to as German Naval Staff War Diary.
3. German Naval Staff War Diary 21/5/40, vol. 10.
4. Ibid., 20/6/40.
5. OKW Directive 2/7/40 in *Führer Directives and Other Top-Level Directives of the German Armed Forces, 1939–1941* (United States and British Intelligence Services: Washington and London, 1948; republished by Partizan Press, Nottingham), pp. 105–6. Hereafter *Führer and Other Top-Level Directives*.
6. German Naval Staff War Diary 9/7/40, vol. 11.
7. OKW, 'Artillery Protection for Transports to Britain', 10/7/40, in *Führer and Other Top-Level Directives*, pp. 106–7.

8. German Naval Staff War Diary 2/7/40, vol. 11.
9. J. P. Mallmann Showall (ed.), *Führer Conferences on Naval Affairs, 1939-1945* (London: Chatham Publishing, 2005), p. 114. Hereafter *Führer Naval Conferences.*
10. Ibid., p. 115.
11. *Führer and Other Top-Level Directives*, pp. 107-11. The directive was issued on 19/7/40.
12. Ibid.
13. German Naval Staff War Diary 16/7/40, vol. 11.
14. Ibid. 17/7/40. See also the account by Admiral Assmann, 'German Plans for the Invasion of England 1940: Operation Sea Lion', in ADM 223/484. Assmann wrote this account for the British while a prisoner of war. He had access to a wide range of documents from military and political sources as well as naval.
15. Ibid.
16. German Naval Staff War Diary 19/7/40, vol. 11.
17. Stephen Roskill, *The War at Sea, vol. 1* (London: HMSO, 1954), p. 249.
18. Jodl's notes in Martin Marix Evans, *Invasion! Operation Sea Lion, 1940* (London: Longman, 2004), p. 84.
19. *Führer Naval Conferences* 21/7/40, p. 119, emphasis added.
20. Ibid., p. 120.
21. German Naval Staff War Diary 22/7/40, vol. 11.
22. Ibid., 25/7/40.
23. Ibid.
24. Ibid.
25. *Führer Naval Conferences*, 26/7/40, p. 121.
26. German Naval Staff War Diary 29/7/40.
27. *Führer Naval Conferences*, 31/7/40, p. 122.
28. Ibid.
29. Ibid.
30. German Naval Staff War Diary, vol. 12 5/8/40.
31. *Führer Naval Conferences*, 13/8/40, p. 125.
32. Führer Directives, 'Operation Seelöwe', 16/8/40, in ibid., p. 113.
33. 'Army Group Operation Order No. 1', 14/9/40, quoted in Marix Evans, *Invasion!*, pp. 129-36.
34. Ronald Wheatley, *Operation Sea Lion: German Plans for the Invasion of England, 1939-1942* (Oxford: Clarendon Press, 1958), pp. 158-9.
35. Walter Schellenberg, *Invasion 1940: The Nazi Plan for Britain* (London: St Ermine's, 2001). The title is a contemporary one.
36. For the number of soldiers in Britain see 'Manpower in the Army' – Memorandum by the Adjutant General 17/6/40 in WO 163/48.
37. Memorandum by the C-in-C Home Forces (Ironside), 'Forces for the Defence of the United Kingdom', 31/5/40, CAB 80/12.
38. Army Council Minutes 19/7/40, WO 163/48.
39. Admiralty to C-in-C Home Fleet 13/6/40, ADM 116/4469.
40. GHQ Home Forces, 'Preparations for Defence', 4/6/40 in Invasion – General Policy, ADM 116/4469.
41. Basil Collier, *The Defence of the United Kingdom* (London: HMSO, 1957), p. 129.
42. Army Council Minutes 17/6/40, WO 163/48.
43. *Brooke Diaries*, p. 93.
44. Ibid., entries for 26 and 27 July respectively.
45. Churchill to Brooke 15/7/40, COS Papers, CAB 80/14.
46. War Office Progress Report July 1940 in the Army Council Minutes, WO 163/48.
47. War Office Progress Report August 1940 in ibid.
48. Selected Equipment numbers 16/8/40, Army Council Minutes, in ibid.

49. For the exact locations of these forces see Map 15, which is taken from Map 17 of Collier, *Defence of the United Kingdom*, facing p. 219.
50. *Brooke Diaries* 15/9/40.
51. 'The State of the Army in England', 1/9/40, WO 106/2795B.
52. Ibid.
53. Roskill, *War at Sea*, Appendix L, p. 603.
54. See the weekly Pink Lists, which show the distribution of warships in home waters in ADM 187/8, and Roskill, *War at Sea*, p. 242.
55. For a short account of the Dakar expedition (Operation Menace) see Roskill, *War at Sea*, pp. 308–20.
56. Note by Assistant Chief of the Naval Staff (ACNS) 29/8/40 in ADM 223/484.
57. 'Possible Invasion of the U.K. by Germany', C-in-C's Appreciation, 27/5/40, ADM 1/10566.
58. Notes on the above paper 27/5/40.
59. See the correspondence between Forbes and the Admiralty in ADM 1/10566. The order to Forbes was issued on 4 June.
60. Ibid.
61. Note by ACNS in ADM 1/10566.
62. Note by Vice Chief of the Naval Staff 24/6/40 in ibid.
63. Note in ibid.
64. Admiralty Training and Staff Duties Division, 'The Navy and the Threat of Invasion 1940', ADM 234/436.
65. Ibid.
66. Ibid.
67. The Pink List 21/8/40, ADM 187/9.
68. Collier, *Defence of the United Kingdom*, p. 132.
69. Home Fleet War Diary 13/8/40, ADM 199/361.
70. Ibid. 7/9/40.
71. F. H. Hinsley, *British Intelligence in the Second World War: Its Influence on Strategy and Operations, vol. 1* (London: HMSO, 1979), p. 185.
72. Home Fleet War Diary 13/9/40, ADM 199/361.
73. 'Invasion – The Role of the RAF', Draft Minutes of the Meeting to Discuss Inter-Service Co-operation, 3/7/40, ADM 199/1202.
74. Ibid.
75. Drax to Dowding in ibid.
76. Dowding to Drax 5/7/40 in ibid.
77. COS Committee Paper 15/7/40.
78. Brooke note on diary 29/7/40.
79. Churchill to Ismay 30/6/40, Chartwell 20/13.
80. All these letters can be found in the Ismay file of correspondence, Chartwell 20/13.
81. Churchill to A. V. Alexander (First Lord of the Admiralty) 8/8/40; Churchill to A. V. Alexander and Pound 25/8/40, both in Chartwell 20/13.
82. Churchill to A. V. Alexander and Pound 1/9/40, Chartwell 20/13.
83. Roskill, *War at Sea*, p. 256.
84. Churchill to Ismay 30/6/40, Chartwell 20/13.
85. Ibid.
86. War Cabinet Confidential Annex 2/7/40, CAB 65/14/2.
87. Ibid.
88. Churchill to Eden 7/7/40, Chartwell 20/13.
89. Churchill to Eden 3/7/40, Chartwell 20/13.
90. Most of these matters can be found in Churchill's correspondence with Ismay in Chartwell 20/13.
91. Churchill to Ismay 30/6/40, Chartwell 20/13.
92. 'Gas Policy', WO 199/328.

8. The Battle of Britain: The Antagonists

1. Air Defence Research: Radio Direction Finding, CAB 21/1099. The method was called Radio Direction Finding (RDF) because that was a suitably opaque name for a scientific breakthrough. Radar was the name given to it by the Americans and this name came into such popular use that RDF will be shortened to Radar in this account.
2. Air Defence of Great Britain, Night Operations, AIR 41/17. This long document gives an excellent summary of Fighter Command intelligence methods.
3. Ibid.
4. Ibid. Thousands of miles of this cable were laid by the GPO from 1936 to 1940.
5. Vincent Orange, *Dowding of Fighter Command: Victor of the Battle of Britain* (London: Grub Street, 2008), p. 102.
6. This information is largely taken from the document mentioned in footnote 635 in AIR41/17.
7. Orange, *Dowding*, p. 153.
8. Tangmere was an exception. Its operation room was made of concrete. See Stephen Bungay, *The Most Dangerous Enemy: A History of the Battle of Britain* (London: Aurum, 2001), p.67.
9. This information has been taken from the excellent biography by Vincent Orange, *Park: The Biography of Air Chief Marshal Sir Keith Park* (London: Grub Street, 2000). There is as yet still no statue of Park in London.
10. This discussion of Schmid relies on Nigel Dempster and Derek Wood, *The Narrow Margin: The Battle of Britain and the Rise of Air Power, 1930–1940* (London: Hutchinson, 1961), pp. 103–8.
11. There are many sources for the capabilities of the aircraft in the Battle of Britain. I have relied on Richard Townshend Bickers, *The Battle of Britain: The Greatest Battle in the History of Air Warfare* (London: Salamander, 1999), chs 3–5, and the excellent Bungay, *The Most Dangerous Enemy*, chs 5 and 6. Also note the diagram in Bungay, chapter 30, for the turning circles of the Me 109 and Spitfire and Hurricane. These have been calculated by engineers and must supersede all other figures for this crucial measurement of performance. In particular, Bungay's figures must render obsolete those used by Len Deighton in *Fighter: The True Story of the Battle of Britain* (London: Pan, 1979), p. 83, where it is claimed that the Messerschmidt had the smaller turning circle.
12. Luftwaffe Strength and Serviceability Tables, compiled from the records of VI Abteilung Quartermaster General Department of the German Air Ministry and translated by the Air Historical Branch, AIR 20/7706.
13. These figures are based on an unreferenced source in Dempster and Wood, *Narrow Margin*, p. 229, where they give the German air strength actually deployed against Britain on 10/8/40. Unfortunately, there does not seem to be a series of these figures.
14. States of Aircraft in Fighter Command, AIR 16/943. The serviceability rates for British fighters were about 90 per cent, so there were about 75 additional Hurricanes and Spitfires ready within seven days.
15. Ibid.
16. Comparative Study of RAF and Luftwaffe Striking Power, 16/7/40, quoted in Dempster and Wood *Narrow Margin*, pp. 106–8.
17. Hinsley, *British Intelligence*, p. 177.
18. German Quartermaster General's Return.
19. Hinsley, *British Intelligence*, p. 177.
20. Ibid., p. 178.
21. Orange, *Dowding*, p. 147.
22. Size of German Air Threat 1/8/40, AIR 25/197 (11 Group Appendices September 1939–September 1940.) The paper also overestimated the number of German fighters available, but only by about 20 per cent.

23. Peter Dye, 'Logistics and the Battle of Britain', *Air Power Review*, 3, no. 4, Winter 2000, p. 29.
24. Ibid., pp. 22-4.
25. Ibid., p. 28.

9. The Battle of Britain: Overture

1. Interview with Goering by an American journalist Mr von Wiegand 28/7/40, reproduced in the *West Australian* 29/7/40.
2. Goering memorandum 30/6/40 quoted in Nigel Dempster and Derek Wood, *The Narrow Margin: The Battle of Britain and the Rise of Air Power, 1930-1940* (London: Hutchinson, 1961), pp. 220-2. The italics are mine.
3. Many German accounts do not accept this date. They mark the commencement of the battle from the date that they first sent over 1,000 aircraft against Britain on 13 August. However, the British had been enduring raids of up to 200 aircraft since 10 July and this represented intensification from earlier German efforts. Perhaps the battle began on different days for the two air forces.
4. The figures are from 'State of Aircraft in Fighter Command', AIR 16/943. I have decided to use the figures for *serviceable* aircraft only, on the grounds that Fighter Command was open to attack in force on any day of the battle and that therefore only those aircraft immediately airworthy might count.
5. Ibid.
6. 'Record of Enemy Air Activity Over the United Kingdom', AIR 40/1642.
7. Fighter Command HQ Record Book, AIR 24/525.
8. Richard Townshend Bickers, *The Battle of Britain: The Greatest Battle in the History of Air Warfare* (London: Salamander, 1999), p. 43.
9. 11 Group Record Book 10/7/40, AIR 25/193.
10. Fighter Command Combat Report, 66 Squadron, 10/7/49, AIR 16/955.
11. See the combat reports from 74, 111 and 609 Squadrons, and in addition T. C. G. James, *The Battle of Britain*, ed. Sebastian Cox (London: Frank Cass, 2002), pp. 26-7, and Dempster and Wood, *Narrow Margin*, pp. 239-40.
12. James, *Battle of Britain*, p. 27.
13. This is probably an overestimate. Reports of numbers of enemy aircraft in combat reports are not always reliable. Other figures suggest that there were 20 Dorniers, 30 Me 110s and 30 Me 109s present that day (Dempster and Wood, *Narrow Margin*, p. 239). The fact that the British were heavily outnumbered is unaltered, however.
14. De Wilde ammunition was an incendiary bullet that left no flame trace or smoke. 'As Al Deere explained, its greatest value lay in the fact that it produced a small flash on impact thus providing confirmation to the attacking pilot that his aim was good.' Quoted in Leo McKinstry, *Spitfire: Portrait of a Legend* (London: John Murray, 2007), p. 173.
15. 74 Squadron Intelligence Report 10/7/40, AIR 16/955. The language of the original report has been kept.
16. AIR 16 contains the overwhelming number of combat reports filed during the Battle of Britain. The consolidated reports were compiled by the Group and were designated Form F. Some reports are obviously missing because squadrons with no reports are sometimes noted as being in combat by the official narrative or other sources. Where I have come across reliable reports of combat I have added them to those in AIR 16. While the totals given in this account may not be 100 per cent accurate, I am satisfied that I have obtained as close an approximation of the number of combats on any given day of battle as is reasonably possible.

    One statistic, often used in accounts of the battle, can cause confusion about the intensity of the fighting. That statistic is the sortie, which may be defined as one flight by one aircraft but not necessarily a flight that results in combat. On 10 July Fighter

Command flew between 600 and 650 sorties but most of these were routine patrols, or practice flights where skills such as formation flying and gunnery might be developed.

17. The most accurate figures for lost and damaged aircraft have been compiled from the daily lists in Winston G. Ramsey (ed.), *The Battle of Britain: Then and Now* (London: Battle of Britain International, 1989). The claims made by each side will be dealt with later.
18. Karl Maier et al., *Germany and the Second World War, vol. 2* (Oxford: Clarendon Press, 1991), p. 378.
19. The statistics have been compiled from combat reports in AIR 16. The numbers represent the number of days that the Luftwaffe was brought to battle in the area indicated.
20. Ibid.
21. T. C. G. James, *The Growth of Fighter Command, 1936–1940*, ed. Sebastian Cox (London: Frank Cass, 2002), p. 43.
22. Ibid., p. 44.
23. 11 Group Instructions to Controllers No. 4, AIR 16/842.
24. Compiled from Fighter Command combat reports in AIR 16/955.
25. See State of Aircraft in Fighter Command, AIR 16/943.
26. Pilot Officer Wissler Diary 29/7/40, Imperial War Museum (IWM) 91/41/1.
27. Ibid., 21/7/40.
28. Ibid., 27/8/40 and 7/8/40.
29. See Wissler's Diary for the period 12 July to 7 August for these incidents.
30. All figures for aircraft casualties are taken from Ramsey, *Battle of Britain: Then and Now*.
31. 'Weekly Output of Aircraft', AIR 22/293.
32. 'German Aircraft Production During WW2', http://members.aol.com/for country/ ww2/gma.htm Accessed 26/8/2011. For other aircraft the Germans lost 189 bombers and added 238, lost 31 Me 110s and added 90, and lost 36 dive-bombers for 50 gained.
33. Air Commodore Alan Deere (72 Squadron) quoted in Richard Townshend Bickers, *The Battle of Britain: The Greatest Battle in the History of Air Warfare* (London: Salamander, 1999), p. 97.
34. 'Air Fighting Tactics', HQ 13 Group, 7/7/40, AIR 16/281; "Single Seater Fighter Tactics, 19 Squadron, Duxford', 22/6/40. AIR 16/281.
35. These figures have been compiled from the lists in Ramsey, *Battle of Britain: Then and Now*.

10. The Battle of Britain: The Crisis

1. Karl Maier et al., *Germany and the Second World War, vol. 2* (Oxford: Clarendon Press, 1991), p. 380.
2. 'Situation Reports Issued by Luftwaffe Fuhrungsstab 1C', Part 3, 1 August–15 August 1940 (translated by Air Ministry, A.H.B.6, April 1953, AIR 20/7708).
3. 'Appreciation of the Effect of Air Attacks', 1/8/40 in ibid.
4. Ibid.
5. Weekly Output of Aircraft, AIR 22/293.
6. Luftwaffe Situation Report 1/8/40.
7. 'Total and Regional Employment by M.A.P (Ministry of Aircraft Production) in the Munitions Industries in Great Britain', AVIA 10/311.
8. Ibid.
9. Stephen Roskill, *The War at Sea, vol. 1* (London: HMSO, 1954), p. 325.
10. 145 Squadron Intelligence Report 8/8/40, AIR 16/956.
11. 238 Squadron Intelligence Report in ibid.
12. The statistics have been compiled from Winston G. Ramsey (ed.), *The Battle of Britain: Then and Now* (London: Battle of Britain International, 1989).

13. It is clear from the combat reports of 145, 601 and 609 Squadrons that they attacked a purely fighter force. See their reports in AIR 16/956.
14. T. C. G. James, *The Battle of Britain*, ed. Sebastian Cox (London: Frank Cass, 2002), p. 62.
15. 11 Group, 'Instructions to Controllers No. 4', 19/8/40, AIR 16/842. Emphasis added.
16. Stephen Bungay, *The Most Dangerous Enemy: A History of the Battle of Britain* (London: Aurum, 2001), has a useful discussion of KGr 210. See pp. 203–4.
17. The combat reports of 610 and 54 Squadrons make it clear that they engaged no bombers. See AIR 16/954. For the airfields see James, *Battle of Britain*, ed. Cox, Appendix VIII, part III, p. 347.
18. James, *Battle of Britain*, ed. Cox, p. 347.
19. Bungay, *Most Dangerous Enemy*, p. 203.
20. Ibid., p. 206, states that Ventnor was out of action for three days, but other authorities are agreed on 11 days. See James, *Battle of Britain*, ed. Cox, p. 70.
21. Williamson Murray, *Luftwaffe* (London: Allen & Unwin, 1985), p. 52.
22. Cajus Bekker, *The Luftwaffe War Diaries* (New York: Doubleday, 1966), pp. 146–7.
23. Luftwaffe Situation Reports 12/8/40, AIR 20/7708.
24. 609 Squadron Combat Report 13/8/40, AIR 19/956.
25. Figures from the combat reports and Ramsey (ed.), *Battle of Britain: Then and Now*.
26. Bekker, *Luftwaffe War Diaries*, pp. 154–5.
27. Nigel Dempster and Derek Wood, *The Narrow Margin: The Battle of Britain and the Rise of Air Power, 1930–1940* (London: Hutchinson, 1961), pp. 276–7.
28. 'Final Evaluation of Photographic Reconnaissance Carried out on 12 August', in Luftwaffe Situation Reports, AIR 20/7708.
29. Ibid.
30. James, *Battle of Britain*, ed. Cox, p. 111. Surprisingly, James does not list Kenley in his table of airfields attacked in Appendix VIII of his book.
31. There were other smaller attacks on Biggin Hill, but I am only dealing with assaults which caused damage to the fabric of the station.
32. This account has been compiled from James, *Battle of Britain* ed. Cox, Dempster and Wood, *Narrow Margin*, and the article in Ramsey (ed.), *Battle of Britain: Then and Now*, by Peter Halliday.
33. David Ross with Bruce Blanche and William Simpson, *The Greatest Squadron of Them All: The Definitive History of the 603 (City of Edinburgh) Squadron, vol. 1* (London: Grub Street, 2003), p. 212.
34. The combat reports in AIR 16 are the vital source for Luftwaffe targets.
35. 605 Squadron Combat Report 15/8/40, AIR 16/ 956.
36. Figures from Ramsey (ed.), *The Battle of Britain: Then and Now*.
37. Wissler Diary 20/8/40.
38. It might be thought that the cratering of runways would have been given some thought by Fighter Command as well as the Air Ministry. The fact that eventually this matter was easily dealt with owed little to either of them. On 28 August Churchill visited Manston, which had been cratered so often that it had been abandoned. The Prime Minister was shocked to learn that just 150 staff were available to fill in craters. He immediately ordered that four crater-filling companies be established, with 250 personnel, the latest equipment and motor transport to make them highly mobile. In addition he insisted that airfields have on hand dumps of gravel and other filling material sufficient to fill 100 craters.
39. Park, 'German Attacks on England – 6th Aug–10th Sept', 12/9/40, AIR 16/635.
40. Dowding to the Air Ministry 13/11/40, AIR 16/667.

11. The Battle of Britain: The Battle Won

1. Nigel Dempster and Derek Wood, *The Narrow Margin: The Battle of Britain and the Rise of Air Power, 1930–1940* (London: Hutchinson, 1961), p. 330.

2. Schmid Report, quoted in ibid., p. 115.
3. Ibid., p. 116.
4. 54 Squadron Combat Report 7/9/40, AIR 16/943.
5. These statistics are derived from the total number of combat reports on 7/9/40, in ibid.
6. See T. C. G. James, *The Battle of Britain*, ed. Sebastian Cox (London: Frank Cass, 2002), p. 238, and Dempster and Wood, *Narrow Margin*, p. 339.
7. Losses have been calculated from Winston G. Ramsey (ed.), *The Battle of Britain: Then and Now* (London: Battle of Britain International, 1989).
8. Park, Instructions to Controllers No. 16, 11/9/40, AIR 25/198.
9. Figures are compiled from Ramsey (ed.), *The Battle of Britain: Then and Now*.
10. Ibid.
11. This account largely relies upon the combat reports from the squadrons in AIR 16/943, supplemented by James, *Battle of Britain*, ed. Cox, pp. 258–60.
12. Combat Report 213 Squadron 15/9/40, AIR 16/943.
13. Figures calculated from Ramsey (ed.), *The Battle of Britain: Then and Now*.
14. Memoir of Feldwebel Rolf Heitsch, quoted in Chris Gross, *The Luftwaffe Bombers' Battle of Britain* (Manchester: Crecy, 2000), p. 151.
15. Hurricane, Spitfire, Strength, Production, Wastage, AIR 20/2307.
16. Ibid. All the above figures come from this source. Other tables list slightly different losses and production rates but the tendency is the same.
17. Park to Dowding 7/11/40, 'First Phase (September 11th–October 5th)', AIR 16/635.
18. Ibid.
19. Certainly at times the ratios were high only because the number of serviceable aircraft had dropped at a faster rate than the number of available pilots. That was the case in the weeks ending 10 and 17 September. The converse could also be the case – serviceable aircraft could increase faster than pilot replacement. This happened in the weeks ending 12 and 26 August.
20. Stephen Bungay, *The Most Dangerous Enemy: A History of the Battle of Britain* (London: Aurum, 2001), p. 103.
21. These and other statistics for pilots come from AIR 16/903, a document which records many conferences and statistics on pilots during the Battle of Britain.
22. Evill to Dowding 17/8/40, AIR 16/490.
23. Minutes of a meeting HQFC 7/9/40, AIR 16/330.
24. Figures taken from the Quartermaster General's Return.
25. For a lucid and detailed account of this incident see Leo McKinstry, *Spitfire: Portrait of a Legend* (London: John Murray, 2007), pp. 248–55.
26. 'Conference on Fighter Tactics – held at Uxbridge 21st September 1940', AIR 25/197.
27. Park, 'Instructions to Controllers No. 31', AIR 16/198.
28. 41 Squadron Combat Report 1/10/40, AIR 16/943.
29. 74 Squadron Combat Report 22/10/40, AIR 16/943.
30. James, *The Battle of Britain*, ed. Cox., p. 322.
31. Park to Dowding ?/9/40, AIR 16/330.
32. 'Policy of Maintenance of Fighter Squadrons in Pilots', 8/9/40, AIR 16/903.
33. The number of British aircraft in combat has been calculated from the combat reports of squadrons plus additional sources such as Ramsey (ed.), *The Battle of Britain: Then and Now*. The number of German aircraft over Britain has been taken from James or Dempster and Wood, *The Narrow Margin*. While the figures may not be precise down to the last plane, I am confident that the overall picture they provide is accurate.

12. Terror by Night

1. Dietmar Suss, *Death from the Skies: How the British and Germans Survived Bombing in World War II* (Oxford: Oxford University Press, 2014), p. 48.
2. Tom Harrisson, *Living Through the Blitz* (London: Collins, 1976), p. 282.

3. Suss, *Death from the Skies*, p. 382.
4. Ministry of Information Daily Morale Report 23/5/40, INF 1/264. These reports have been conveniently published by the excellent Paul Addison and Jeremy Craig. See their *Listening to Britain* (London: Vintage, 2010). The reports used here are the originals in The National Archives, but there are no discrepancies between them and those published. The quotation above comes from the General Introduction to such reports, which were written by the head of the Home Intelligence Department, Mary Adams.
5. W. Hancock and M. Gowing, *British War Economy* (London: HMSO, 1949), p. 85. It has been pointed out that the act was in practice less draconian than it seemed. See W. I. Jennings, 'The Emergency Powers (Defence) (No. 2) Act 1940', in *Modern Law Review*, 132, 1940, pp. 132-6. This was not how it was viewed by the general public at the time.
6. MOI Morale Report 23/5/40, INF 1/264.
7. MOI Morale Report 20/6/40 in ibid.
8. MOI Morale Report 14/6/40 in ibid.
9. MOI Morale Report 19/6/40 and 29/6/40 in ibid.
10. MOI Morale Report 14/6/40 in ibid.
11. Hancock and Gowing, *British War Economy*, p. 327.
12. MOI Morale Report 24/7/40, INF 1/264.
13. MOI Morale Report 25/7/40 in ibid.
14. MOI Morale Report 1/8/40 in ibid.
15. MOI Morale Report 6/7/40 in ibid.
16. MOI Morale Report 21/8/40 in ibid.
17. MOI Morale Report 5/8/40 in ibid.
18. MOI Morale Report 21/8/40 in ibid.
19. MOI Morale Report 31/5/40 in ibid. On the evidence before me I am unable to agree with Richard Toye's more downbeat assessment of the reception of Churchill's speeches. See his *The Roar of the Lion: The Untold Story of Churchill's World War II Speeches* (Oxford: Oxford University Press, 2013) for his interpretation.
20. MOI Morale Report 12/6/40, INF 1/264.
21. MOI Morale Report 18/6/40 in ibid.
22. MOI Morale Report 8/7/40 in ibid.
23. MOI Morale Report 9/7/40 in ibid.
24. MOI Morale Report 24/9/40 in ibid.
25. Mass Observation, Second Weekly Report for Home Intelligence 18/10/40, File 459, Mass Observation Archive. The online version of this archive published by Adam Matthew and held by the University of Adelaide Library has been accessed.
26. Mass Observation, Seventh Weekly Report for Home Intelligence 15/11/40, File 493.
27. MOI Morale Report 23/7/40, INF 1/264. There is some irony in the reference to the Burma Road. It was closed by a War Cabinet decision to appease Japan. Halifax had spoken against its closure.
28. Ibid.
29. Weekly Home Intelligence Report, INF 1/292.
30. MOI Morale Report 22/8/40, INF 1/264.
31. MOI Morale Report 23/8/40 in ibid.
32. MOI Morale Report 26/8/40 in ibid.
33. MOI Morale Report 27/8/40 and 28/8/40 in ibid.
34. MOI Morale Report 4/9/40 in ibid.
35. John Ray, *The Night Blitz* (London: Arms and Armour, 1996), pp. 28-9.
36. 'Record of Enemy Air Activity Over the United Kingdom', AIR 40/1642.
37. 'Air Defence of the United Kingdom', AIR 41/17.
38. Leo McKinstry, *Spitfire: Portrait of a Legend* (London: John Murray, 2007), p. 246.
39. Ray, *Night Blitz*, p. 80.
40. Peter Stansky, *The First Day of the Blitz: September 7, 1940* (Melbourne: Scribe, 2007), pp. 32, 38 and 48.

41. 'Chronicle of Main Air Attacks on Great Britain and Northern Ireland and of their Effects on the Vital National War Effort (1939–1945)', HO 201/42.
42. The above paragraph is taken from the incomparable account in Juliet Gardiner's *The Blitz: The British Under Attack* (London: Harper, 2011), pp. 13–24. The human side of the Blitz has never been better described than in this superb book.
43. Mass Observation, 'The Isle of Dogs: Effect of Air Raid' 12/9/40, File 403.
44. The information in this paragraph has been compiled from 'Chronicle of Main Air Attacks on Great Britain and Northern Ireland', HO 201/42; Home Security Weekly Appreciations, HO 202/8; Home Security Daily Appreciations, September–October, HO 202/1. Occasionally the above sources have been supplemented from Winston G. Ramsey (ed.), *The Blitz: Then and Now, vol. 1* (London: Battle of Britain International, 1987).
45. See the sources listed above.
46. Richard Titmus, *Problems of Social Policy* (London: HMSO, 1950), pp. 270–2.
47. Jerry White, *London in the 20th Century* (London: Viking, 2007), p. 26.
48. Williamson Murray, *Luftwaffe* (London: Allen & Unwin, 1985), p. 53, Table XI.
49. Ramsey (ed.), *The Blitz: Then and Now*, pp. 147–9.
50. Martin Middlebrook and C. Everett, *The Bomber Command War Diaries* (London: Penguin, 1990), p. 410.
51. Jo Oakman, Diary and Incident Book, Imperial War Museum, 91/20/1.
52. Phyllis Warner's account in the Imperial War Museum, 95/14/1.
53. Sidney Bernstein Reports for Home Intelligence, Imperial War Museum SLB MOI.
54. Titmus, *Problems of Social Policy*, p. 271, note 2.
55. Gardiner, *The Blitz*, p. 71; Harrisson, *Living Through The Blitz*, p. 131.
56. Mass Observation, Fourth Weekly Report for Home Intelligence 24/10/40, File 406.
57. Warner, 'Journal Under the Terror', 19/9/40.
58. Queenie (Anne) Shepperd, Blitz Diary, Imperial War Museum, 95/13/1.
59. Ibid.
60. G. Thomas Diary, Imperial War Museum, 90/30/1.
61. Stansky, *First Day of the Blitz*, p. 181. See also p. 81. It is not my intention to criticise this excellent book in any other way. It is the best book written on this subject.
62. Chandler to a friend 27/6/40 quoted in *A Mysterious Something in the Light: Raymond Chandler: A Life* by Tom Williams (London: Aurum, 2012), p. 166.
63. Vere Hodgson, *Few Eggs and No Oranges: A Diary* (London: Dennis Dobson, 1976), p. 96.
64. Naish letter 8/9/40, Imperial War Museum, 99/66/1.
65. Bowman Letters, Imperial War Museum, Misc.
66. Brinton-Lee Diary P178, Imperial War Museum.
67. Phyllis Warner, 'Journal Under the Terror', Imperial War Museum, 95/14/1.
68. G. Thomas Diary 15/9/40, Imperial War Museum, 90/30/1.
69. Ann Shepperd Diary 17/9/40.
70. MO, 'Weekly Report for Home Intelligence', 4/10/40, File 439.
71. See daily reports from Home Security for these nights in HO 202-1-4.
72. Harrisson, *Living Through the Blitz*, p. 74.
73. See, for example, 'Shelter in London', 3/10/40, File 436.
74. Gardiner, *The Blitz*, p. 88.
75. Winston G. Ramsey (ed.), *The Blitz: Then and Now, vol. 2* (London: Battle of Britain International, 1988), pp. 120–1; see also Home Intelligence Daily Reports for October to see the gradual decline in those using the Underground as shelters.
76. Ismay to Churchill 1948, Chartwell 4/198.
77. Samuel Battersby to Martin Gilbert 6/4/77 in Martin Gilbert, *The Churchill War Papers, vol. 2: Never Surrender, May 1940–December 1940* (New York: Norton, 1995), p. 788.

78. Churchill to Bridges, Anderson and Reith 21/9/40, CAB 21/773, 'Air Raid Precautions: Use of the Tube Railway System as Shelters'. The whole file is an interesting study of bureaucrats at work on a matter which required instant decision.
79. Winston S. Churchill, *Their Finest Hour* (London: Cassell, 1955), pp. 308–9. Churchill introduced the scheme in Parliament on 5 September.
80. 'Chronicle of Main Air Attacks', HO 201/42.
81. Ibid.
82. Home Security Daily Report, 14–15 October, HO 202/1.
83. Ibid., 15–16 October.
84. 'Chronicle of Main Air Attacks', HO 201/42.
85. Ibid.
86. Ray, *Night Blitz*, pp. 152–3.
87. Ibid., pp. 153–7; The Coventry Blitz: Some Blitz Statistics; http://www.historiccoventry.co.uk/blitz/stats.php. Accessed 11/11/2013.
88. MO, 'Coventry', 18/11/40, File 495.
89. Home Security, 'Air Raid On Coventry', in Home Security Weekly Reports, HO 202/8.
90. Ibid.
91. Ray, *Night Blitz*, p. 157.
92. Air Defence of Great Britain Narrative, AIR 41/17. Also quoted in Ray, *Night Blitz*, p. 157.
93. Home Security, 'Daily Appreciations', April 1941, HO 201/4.
94. The British authorities did learn from Coventry. Operational researchers descended on the city and rapidly established that high-explosive bombs to blast openings in buildings, then incendiaries to burn them out, and then more high explosive for total destruction was the best pattern. They also developed the idea of dropping bombs in such a way as to create high winds or firestorms. The lessons of Coventry were to be visited on many a German city, most notably Hamburg, in the years to come.
95. Dudley Seward, *Victory Denied: The Rise of German Air Power and the Defeat of Germany, 1920–45* (London: Buchan & Enright, 1985), pp. 207–8.
96. Jerry Curtis, Humanities360.com: The Clydebank Blitz, online site accessed 11/11/13.
97. Home Security Daily Report 15/3/41, HO/201/4.
98. Ibid.
99. Home Security Daily Report 15–16 March, HO 201/4.
100. Mass Observation, 'Report on Plymouth', 1/4/41, File 626.
101. Neil Holmes, *Liverpool Blitzed: Seventy Years On* (Wellington, Somerset: Halsgrove, 2011), p. 96.
102. Ibid., pp. 8–13.
103. See the Home Security Daily Reports for these nights, HO 202/3.
104. These statistics are taken from the Home Security Daily Reports, HO 202/6.
105. Holmes, *Liverpool Blitzed*, p. 104.
106. Mass Observation, 'Report on Liverpool', 22/5/41, File 706.
107. Ramsey (ed.), *The Blitz, vol. 2*, pp. 579–602, for these statistics.

13. A Little Help from Our Friends

1. Churchill to Roosevelt 15/5/40, Warren F. Kimball, *Churchill & Roosevelt: The Complete Correspondence, vol. 1* (Princeton, NJ: Princeton University Press, 1984), p. 37. I have read all the Roosevelt–Churchill letters in the Roosevelt Presidential Papers and in the Churchill Papers. Where possible, however, I have used the excellent edition of the letters edited by Warren Kimball to enable readers to check the references with ease.
2. Ibid.
3. Roosevelt to Churchill 16/5/40, Kimball, *Complete Correspondence, vol. 1*, pp. 38–9.
4. *Colville Diary* 19/5/40, p. 136.
5. Churchill to Roosevelt, Kimball, *Complete Correspondence, vol. 1*, p. 40.

6. David Reynolds, *The Creation of the Anglo-American Alliance: A Study in Competitive Co-operation* (London: Europa, 1981), p. 115. This is the definitive account of the establishment of this alliance.
7. The Presidential Papers of Franklin D. Roosevelt, BACM Research, Disc 1. Speech 10/6/40.
8. Churchill to Roosevelt 11/6/40, Kimball, *Complete Correspondence, vol. 1*, p. 43.
9. *Colville Diary* 12/6/40, p. 153.
10. Reynolds, *Creation of the Anglo-American Alliance*, p. 146.
11. Morgenthau Note 18/6/40, Presidential Papers of FDR, Disc 1.
12. Harold L. Ickes, *The Secret Diary of Harold L. Ickes, vol. 3: The Lowering Clouds, 1939–1941* (New York: Simon & Schuster, 1955), p. 233. Hereafter Ickes, *Secret Diary*.
13. Churchill to Lothian 28/6/40, Chartwell 20/14.
14. Churchill to Baruch 28/6/40, Martin Gilbert, *The Churchill War Papers, vol. 2: Never Surrender, May 1940–December 1940* (New York: Norton, 1995), p. 436.
15. Churchill to Ismay 17/7/40, Prem 3/475/1.
16. Churchill to Roosevelt 5/7/40, Kimball, *Complete Correspondence, vol. 1*, p. 54.
17. Churchill to Roosevelt 30/7/40, Prem 3/462/2. There is a different and toned-down version in Kimball, *Complete Correspondence, vol. 1*, pp. 56–7. The version quoted was sent through the Foreign Office and it is possible that Halifax and Lothian toned it down to match the Kimball version. There is no evidence that this was the case and so I have preferred to use the cable in the Prem Papers. Kimball is usually assiduous in noting amendments such as this, but there is nothing in this volume to indicate that he is quoting a toned-down version.
18. Ickes, *Secret Diary, vol. 3*, 4/8/40, p. 283, reporting a meeting between Knox and Lothian.
19. Ibid., p. 292.
20. *Colville Diary* 6/8/40, p. 210.
21. Reynolds, *Creation of the Anglo-American Alliance*, p. 131.
22. *The New York Times* headline on its front page for 4 September 1940 included 'Britain Pledges Never to Yield or Sink Fleet'; War Cabinet Conclusions 2/9/40, CAB 65/9/1.
23. War Cabinet Conclusions 14/8/40, CAB 65/8/39.
24. H. Duncan Hall, *North American Supply* (London: HMSO, 1955), p. 212.
25. W. Hancock and M. Gowing, *British War Economy* (London: HMSO, 1949), p. 107.
26. Ibid., p. 117.
27. Stephen Roskill, *The War at Sea, vol. 1* (London: HMSO, 1954), Appendix R, p. 617.
28. Ibid.
29. Duncan Hall, *North American Supply*, p. 305.
30. Mark Harrison, 'Resource Mobilisation for World War II: The U.S.A., U.K., USSR and Germany, 1938–1945', Paper given at the Department of Economics, University of Warwick, 1988, p. 16.
31. Duncan Hall, *North American Supply*, p. 289.
32. Reynolds, *Creation of the Anglo-American Alliance*, pp. 148–50. The margins were 268 to 167 in the House and 66 to 30 in the Senate.
33. Ibid.
34. Churchill to Roosevelt 6/1/40, Kimball, *Complete Correspondence, vol. 1*, p. 81.
35. *Colville Diary* 12/11/40, pp. 291–2.
36. Churchill to Roosevelt 29/11/40 (not sent), Colville Papers, quoted in Gilbert, *Churchill War Papers, vol. 2*, p. 1,157.
37. Robert Skidelsky in *John Maynard Keynes: Fighting for Britain, 1937–1946* (London: Macmillan, 2000), p. 96, seems in no doubt. Reynolds in his book on Lothian is not so sure. See *Lord Lothian and Anglo-American Relations* (New York: American Philosophical Society, 2007), p. 50.
38. *The New York Times*, 24/11/40, p. 1.

39. John Morton Blum (ed.), *From the Morgenthau Diaries, vol. 3: Years of Urgency, 1938–1941* (Boston: Houghton Mifflin, 1965), p. 199. Hereafter *Morgenthau Diaries*.
40. Churchill to Lothian 26/11/40, Prem 4/17/1.
41. Churchill to Roosevelt 7/12/40, Kimball, *Complete Correspondence, vol. 1*, pp. 102–9.
42. Ibid.
43. *Morgenthau Diaries, vol. 3*, 3/12/40, p. 202.
44. Ibid., pp. 202–3.
45. Ibid., pp. 28–9.
46. Skidelsky, *Keynes*, p. 100.
47. Adam Berinsky et al., 'Revisiting Public Opinion in the 1930s and 1940s', *Political Science*, July 2011, Fig. 5, p. 519.
48. Reynolds, *Creation of the Anglo-American Alliance*, p. 158.
49. Prem 4/17/1 has several drafts of this letter.
50. Churchill to Roosevelt 31/12/40, Prem 4/17/1.
51. Ibid. Deleted paragraphs.
52. Skidelsky, *Keynes, vol. 3*, p. 103.
53. *Morgenthau Diaries, vol. 3*, p. 210.
54. Ibid.
55. Duncan Hall, *North American Supply*, p. 262.
56. *Morgenthau Diaries, vol. 3*, p. 237. Lord Lothian had died in December of an easily treatable complaint. As a Christian Scientist, however, he had refused all medical treatment.
57. Duncan Hall, *North American Supply*, p. 275, note 1.
58. Ibid., p. 276.
59. Hancock and Gowing, *British War Economy*, p. 237.
60. Duncan Hall, *North American Supply*, p. 288.
61. Ibid., p. 39.
62. Ibid., p. 240.
63. Roskill, *War at Sea, vol. 1*, Table II, Appendix R, pp. 617–18.
64. Churchill to Roosevelt 1/12/40, Kimball, *Complete Correspondence, vol. 1*, p. 92.
65. Churchill to Roosevelt 7/12/40 in ibid., p. 106.
66. Roskill, *War at Sea, vol. 1*, p. 455.
67. Churchill to Roosevelt 23/3/41, Kimball, *Complete Correspondence, vol. 1*, p. 151.
68. Roosevelt to Churchill 25/3/41, in ibid., p. 151. Roosevelt asked the press not to publicise this or to take pictures of the British ship. The press complied. See Ickes, *Secret Diary, vol. 3*, p. 474.
69. Roskill, *War at Sea, vol. 1*, pp. 454–5.
70. Churchill to Roosevelt 6/4/41, Kimball, *Complete Correspondence, vol. 1*, p. 164.
71. *Morgenthau Diary*, 10/4/41, p. 252.
72. Ibid., p. 251.
73. This information is taken from a huge compilation of American public opinion polls; see Hadley Cantrill (ed.), *Public Opinion 1935–1946* (Princeton, NJ: Princeton University Press, 1951). The straightforward question about the US immediately entering the war can be found in Poll 60, p. 971. The series of polls on entering the war if there was no other way of defeating the Axis powers is in Poll 70, p. 974. Helping Britain at the risk of war is in Poll 69 on the same page. In a recent book on the Bretton Woods Agreement, *The Summit* (New York: Little Brown, 2014), the author (Ed Conway) uses this compilation to show that Roosevelt was hobbled by public opinion. On p. 104 he quotes an opinion poll in the above compilation (p. 973) taken in September 1940, which he says shows that 80 per cent of Americans did not wish to enter the war. In fact the only poll with that date on p. 973 indicates that American opinion on entering the war shows that 53 per cent were for keeping out of the war and 47 per cent were for helping England at the risk of war. Where the 80 per cent figure comes from is a mystery. In any case, in an area such as public opinion it is safer to use a variety of polls as I have done above.

74. Ickes, *Secret Diary, vol. 3*, pp. 481–2.
75. Ibid., 10/5/41, p. 511.
76. Churchill to Roosevelt 23/5/41, Kimball, *Complete Correspondence, vol. 1*, pp. 192–5.
77. See Kimball's comment in ibid., p. 196.
78. Ickes, *Secret Diary, vol. 3*, 30/5/41, p. 526.
79. Churchill to Roosevelt 29/4/41, Kimball, *Complete Correspondence, vol. 1*, p. 201.
80. Roskill, *War at Sea, vol. 1*, p. 613. An American merchantman, the *Robin Moor* had been torpedoed on 21 May in the South Atlantic. No one seems to count this ship as a sinking because it was not a warship. See Reynolds, *Creation of the Anglo-American Alliance*, pp. 203–4, who does count it.
81. Kimball, Note in *Complete Correspondence, vol. 1*, p. 236.
82. Kimball, Note in ibid., p. 264.
83. Churchill to Roosevelt 2/11/40 in ibid., p. 265.
84. Ickes, *Secret Diary, vol. 3*, 12/4/41, p. 470.
85. Ibid., 8/6/40, p. 538.
86. War Cabinet Conclusions 25/8/41, CAB 65/19/22.
87. Churchill to Hopkins 28/8/41, Chartwell 20/42.
88. *Colville Diary* 30/8/41, p. 434.

Conclusion

1. Winston S. Churchill, *The World Crisis, vol. 1* (London: Thornton Butterworth, 1923), p. 255.
2. Robert Rhodes James, *Winston S. Churchill: His Complete Speeches, vol. 6* (New York: Chelsea House, 1974), includes this speech. However, I have not used this edition for Churchill's 1940 speeches. It is littered with errors and I have where possible preferred Hansard. See Hansard 13/5/40, vol. 360, Column 1502.
3. David Reynolds, *In Command of History: Churchill Fighting and Writing the Second World War* (London: Allen Lane, 2004), pp. 259–64.
4. Speech to the House of Commons 3/9/39, Hansard vol. 351, Columns 295–6. These rights did not extend, in Churchill's view, to the right to express the wish to leave the British Empire.
5. Ibid., Broadcast 12/11/39, quoted in Charles Eade (ed.), *The War Speeches of the Rt. Hon. Winston S. Churchill, vol. 1* (London: Cassell, 1951), p. 119.
6. Ibid., Broadcast 19/5/40, pp. 184–5.
7. Speech to the House of Commons (later broadcast) 18/6/40, Hansard vol. 362, Column 57–60.
8. Speech at the Mansion House 9/11/40, in Eade (ed.), *War Speeches, vol. 1*, p. 296.
9. Broadcast 14/7/40, in ibid., p. 230.

BIBLIOGRAPHY

Primary Sources

Australian Defence Force Academy Library

General Montgomery Papers

Australian National University Library

German Naval War Staff Diary

Imperial War Museum

Army Group A War Diary
Army Group B War Diary
Lt Col. O. A. Archdale Papers 78/52/1
D. Brinton-Lee Papers P178
I. H. Grainger Papers 94/45/1
Major T. E. B. Howarth Diary 84/7/1
Ministry of Information: Theatre Managers' Reports on the morale of audiences
I. Naish Papers 99/66/1
Jo Oakman Papers 91/20/1
Major Reid Papers 83/37/1
Anne Sheppard Papers 95/13/1
Joan Thompson Papers 90/30/1
P. Warner Papers 95/14/1
Flying Officer Wissler Papers 91/41/1

The National Archives, Kew

Admiralty Papers

ADM 1 Admiralty and Secretariat Papers
ADM 116 Case Papers on Special Subjects

ADM 187 The Pink List – Ships' Locations
ADM 199 War History Cases and Papers
ADM 205 First Sea Lord Papers
ADM 234 Battle Summaries
ADM 267 Damage Reports

Air Ministry Papers

AIR 16 Fighter Command Files
AIR 20 Unregistered Papers
AIR 22 Daily Summaries of Operations
AIR 24 Operations Record Books: Commands
AIR 25 Operations Record Books: Groups
AIR 40 Reports on Operations
AIR 41 Air Historical Branch Narratives
AIR 50 Combat Reports

Cabinet Records

CAB 21 Registered Files on Specific Topics
CAB 44 Historical Section Narratives
CAB 45 Historical Section Correspondence
CAB 65 War Cabinet Conclusions and Confidential Annexes
CAB 66 War Cabinet Memoranda WP and CP Series
CAB 67 War Cabinet Memoranda WP (G) Series
CAB 68 War Cabinet Memoranda (WP) (R) Series
CAB 69 Defence Committee
CAB 79 War Cabinet Chiefs of Staff Committee Minutes
CAB 80 War Cabinet Chiefs of Staff Committee Memoranda
CAB 81 War Cabinet Chiefs of Staff Committees and Sub-Committees
CAB 99 Supreme War Council Minutes
CAB 106 Cabinet Office: Historical Section
CAB 146 Cabinet Office: Enemy Documents Section

Ministry of Aircraft Production

AVIA 9 Private Office Papers
AVIA 10 Unregistered Papers

Ministry of Home Security

HO 201 Key Points Intelligence Directorate: Daily Reports
HO 202 Home Security War Room Reports
HO 203 Home Security Daily Intelligence Reports

Ministry of Information

INF 1 Files of Correspondence

War Office Files

WO 32 Registered Files
WO 106 Directorate of Military Operations and Intelligence
WO 163 War Council Minutes
WO 166 War Diaries – Home Forces
WO 167 War Diaries – BEF

WO 197 BEF Files and Various Narratives 1939–1940
WO 199 Military Headquarters Files: Home Forces
WO 208 Directorate of Military Intelligence Papers
WO 216 Chief of the Imperial General Staff Papers
WO 217 Private War Diaries

University of Adelaide Library

Neville Chamberlain Papers
Winston S. Churchill Papers (online)
Hansard
Mass Observation Archive (online)

Books and Articles

Paul Addison, *The Road to 1945: British Politics and the Second World* War (London: Hodder & Stoughton, 1975).

Paul Addison and Jeremy Craig, *Listening to Britain* (London: Vintage, 2010).

—(eds), *The Burning Blue* (London: Pimlico, 2000).

A. Agar, *Britain Alone, June 1940–June 1941* (London: Bodley Head, 1972).

Field Marshal Lord Alanbrooke, *War Diaries 1939–1945*, ed. Alex Danchev and David Todman (London: Phoenix, 2002).

H. Allen, *Who Won the Battle of Britain?* (London: Arthur Barker, 1974).

Clement Attlee, *As It Happened* (London: Heinemann, 1954).

John Barnes and David Nicholson (eds), *The Empire at Bay: The Leo Amery Diaries, 1939–1945* (London: Hutchinson, 1980).

Cajus Bekker, *The Luftwaffe War Diaries* (New York: Doubleday, 1966).

Amy Helen Bell, *London Was Ours: Diaries and Memoirs of the London Blitz* (London: I. B. Tauris, 2008).

P. M. H. Bell, *A Certain Eventuality: Britain and the Fall of France* (London: Saxon House, 1974).

Adam Berinsky et al., 'Revisiting Public Opinion in the 1930s and 1940s', *Political Science*, July 2011, pp. 516–21.

Isaiah Berlin, *Mr Churchill in 1940* (London: John Murray, 1964).

Uri Bialer, *The Shadow of the Bomber: The Fear of Air Attack and British Politics* (London: Royal Historical Society, 1980).

Richard Townshend Bickers, *The Battle of Britain: The Greatest Battle in the History of Air Warfare* (London: Salamander, 1999).

The Earl of Birkenhead, *Halifax* (London: Hamish Hamilton, 1965).

Gregory Blaxland, *Destination Dunkirk* (London: Kimber, 1973).

John Morton Blum (ed.), *From the Morgenthau Diaries, vol. 3: Years of Urgency, 1938–1941* (Boston: Houghton Mifflin, 1965).

Brian Bond (ed.), *Chief of Staff: The Diaries of Lieutenant-General Sir Henry Pownall, vol. 1* (London: Leo Cooper, 1972).

Brian Bond and Michael Taylor, *France and Belgium, 1939–1940* (London: Davis Poynter, 1975).

—*The Battle for France and Flanders: Sixty Years On* (Barnsley: Leo Cooper, 2001).

Stephen Bungay, *The Most Dangerous Enemy: A History of the Battle of Britain* (London: Aurum, 2001).

J. R. M. Butler, *Grand Strategy, vol. 2* (London: HMSO, 1954).

R. A. Butler, *The Art of the Possible* (London: Hamish Hamilton, 1971).

Angus Calder, *The Myth of the Blitz* (London: Pimlico, 1992).

—*The People's War* (London: Jonathan Cape, 1969).

Angus Calder and D. Sheridan, *Speak For Yourself: A Mass-Observation Anthology, 1937–1940* (London: Jonathan Cape, 1984).

Garry Campion, *The Good Fight: Battle of Britain Propaganda and The Few* (London: Palgrave Macmillan, 2009).

Hadley Cantrill (ed.), *Public Opinion 1935–1946* (Princeton, NJ: Princeton University Press, 1951).

David Carlton, *Anthony Eden* (London: Allen Lane, 1981).

Central Statistical Office, *Statistical Digest of the War* (London: HMSO, 1951).

Terry Charman (ed.), *Outbreak 1939: The World Goes to War* (London: Imperial War Museum, 2009).

Winston S. Churchill, *The Gathering Storm* (London: Cassell, 1951).

—*The World Crisis, vol. 1* (London: Thornton Butterworth, 1923).

—*Their Finest Hour* (London: Cassell, 1955).

Basil Collier, The Defence of the United Kingdom (London: HMSO, 1957).

John Colville, *Gort: Man of Valour* (London: Collins, 1972).

—*The Fringes of Power: Downing Street Diaries, 1939–1955* (London: Weidenfeld & Nicolson, 1985).

Ed Conway, *The Summit* (New York: Little Brown, 2014).

M. Cooper, *The German Army, 1933–1945: Its Political and Military Failure* (London: Macdonald, 1978).

Lord Croft, *My Life of Strife* (London: Hutchinson, n.d.).

N. Crowther, *Facing Fascism: The Conservative Party and the European Dictators* (London: Taylor & Francis, 2002).

Robert Dallek, *Franklin D. Roosevelt and American Foreign Policy, 1932–1945* (New York: Oxford University Press, 1979).

Len Deighton, *Fighter: The True Story of the Battle of Britain* (London: Pan, 1979).

Nigel Dempster and Derek Wood, *The Narrow Margin: The Battle of Britain and the Rise of Air Power, 1930–1940* (London: Hutchinson, 1961).

David Dilks (ed.), *The Diaries of Sir Alexander Cadogan, 1938–1945* (London: Cassell, 1971).

Alan P. Dobson, *US Wartime Aid to Britain, 1940–1946* (London: Croom Helm, 1986).

Bernard Donoughue and George Jones, *Herbert Morrison: Portrait of a Politician* (London: Weidenfeld & Nicolson, 1973).

P. L. G. Doorman, *Military Operations in the Netherlands from 10th–17th May, 1940* (London: Allen & Unwin, 1944).

David Dutton, *Anthony Eden: A Life and Reputation* (London: Edward Arnold, 1997).

Peter Dye, 'Logistics and the Battle of Britain', *Air Power Review*, 3, no. 4, Winter 2000, pp. 16–36.

Charles Eade (ed.), *The War Speeches of the Rt. Hon. Winston S. Churchill vol. 1* (London: Cassell, 1951).

Anthony Eden, *The Reckoning* (London: Cassell, 1965).

Major L. F. Ellis, *The War in France and Flanders, 1939–1940* (London: HMSO, 1953).

Martin Marix Evans, *Invasion! Operation Sea Lion, 1940* (London: Longman, 2004).

Patrick Facon, *L'Armée de l'air dans la tourmente: La bataille de France, 1939–1940* (Paris: Economica, 1997).

Brian Farrell (ed.), *Leadership and Responsibility in the Second World War, 1939–1940* (Quebec: McGill-Queens University Press, 2004).

Keith Feiling, *The Life of Neville Chamberlain* (London: Macmillan, 1946).

Peter Fleming, *Invasion 1940* (London: Hart Davis, 1957).

François Fonville-Alquier, *The French and the Phoney War, 1939–40* (London: Tom Stacey, 1973).

John Foreman, *Fighter Command War Diaries, vol. 1: September 1939–September 1940* (Walton-on-Thames: Air Research Publications, 1996).

—*Fighter Command War Diaries, vol. 2: September 1940–December 1941* (Walton-on-Thames: Air Research Publications, 1998).

Karl-Heinz Freiser, *The Blitzkrieg Legend: The 1940 Campaign in the West* (Annapolis: Naval Institute Press, 2005).

Juliet Gardiner, *The Blitz: The British Under Attack* (London: Harper, 2011).

Simon Garfield (ed.), *We Are at War: The Diaries of Five Ordinary People in Extraordinary Times* (London: Ebury Press, 2005).

Eleanor M. Gates, *End of the Affair: The Collapse of the Anglo-French Alliance, 1939–40* (Berkeley: University of California Press, 1981).

N. H. Gibbs, *Grand Strategy, vol. 1* (London: HMSO, 1976).

Martin Gilbert, *The Churchill War Papers, vol. 1: At the Admiralty September 1939–May 1940* (New York: Norton, 1993).

—*The Churchill War Papers, vol. 2: Never Surrender, May 1940–December 1940* (New York: Norton, 1995).

—*The Churchill War Papers, vol. 3: The Ever-Widening War 1941* (New York: Norton, 2000).

—*Winston S. Churchill, vol. 5: 1922–39* (London: Heinemann, 1976).

—*Winston S. Churchill, vol. 6: 1939–41* (London: Heinemann, 1983).

Midge Gillies, *Waiting For Hitler: Voices from Britain on the Brink of Invasion* (London: Hodder & Stoughton, 2007).

Chris Gross, *The Luftwaffe Bombers' Battle of Britain* (Manchester: Crecy, 2000).

Heinz Guderian, *Panzer Leader* (London: Futura, 1974).

Franz Halder, *The Halder War Diary*, ed. Charles Burdick and Hans-Adolf Jacobsen (London: Greenhill, 1988).

H. Duncan Hall, *North American Supply* (London: HMSO, 1955).

W. Hancock and M. Gowing, *British War Economy* (London: HMSO, 1949).

Nicholas Harman, *Dunkirk: The Necessary Myth* (London: Coronet, 1981).

Mark Harrison, 'Resource Mobilisation for World War II: The USA, UK, USSR and Germany, 1938–1945', Paper given at the Department of Economics, University of Warwick, 1988.

Tom Harrisson, *Living Through the Blitz* (London: Collins, 1976).

Tom Harrisson and Charles Madge, *War Begins At Home* (London: Chatto & Windus, 1940).

Max Hastings, *Finest Years: Churchill as Warlord, 1940–45* (London: Harper, 2009).

Geoff Hewitt, *Hitler's Armada: The Royal Navy and the Defence of Great Britain, April–October 1940* (Barnsley: Pen & Sword, 2008).

Christopher Hill, *Cabinet Decisions on Foreign Policy: The British Experience* (Cambridge: Cambridge University Press, 2002).

F. H. Hinsley, *British Intelligence in the Second World War: Its Influence on Strategy and Operations, vol. 1* (London: HMSO, 1979).

James Hinton, *Nine Wartime Lives* (Oxford: Oxford University Press, 2010).

—*The Mass Observers: A History, 1937–1940* (Oxford: Oxford University Press, 2013).

Vere Hodgson, *Few Eggs and No Oranges: A Diary* (London: Dennis Dobson, 1976).

Neil Holmes, *Liverpool Blitzed: Seventy Years On* (Wellington, Somerset: Halsgrove, 2011).

Alistair Horne, *To Lose a Battle: France 1940* (London: Macmillan, 1969).

Michael Howard, *The Continental Commitment* (London: Penguin, 1971).

Harold Ickes, *The Secret Diary of Harold L. Ickes, vol. 3: The Lowering Clouds, 1939–1941* (New York: Simon & Schuster, 1955).

Talbot Imlay, *Facing the Second World War: Politics and Economics in Britain and France, 1938–1940* (Oxford: Oxford University Press, 2003).

Lord Ismay, *Memoirs* (London: Heinemann, 1960).

Julian Jackson, *The Fall of France: The Nazi Invasion of 1940* (Oxford: Oxford University Press, 2003).

Robert Jackson, *Dunkirk: The British Evacuation of 1940* (London: Cassell, 1976).

Robert Rhodes James, *Bob Boothby: A Portrait* (London: Hodder & Stoughton, 1991).

— 'Chips': The Diaries of Sir Henry Channon (London: Weidenfeld & Nicolson, 1967).

— Victor Cazalet: A Portrait (London: Hamish Hamilton, 1976).

— Winston S. Churchill: His Complete Speeches, vol. 6, 1935–42 (New York: Chelsea House, 1974).

T. C. G. James, The Growth of Fighter Command, 1936–1940, ed. Sebastian Cox (London: Frank Cass, 2002).

— The Battle of Britain, ed. Sebastian Cox (London: Frank Cass, 2002).

Kevin Jeffreys, The Churchill Wartime Coalition and Wartime Politics (Manchester: Manchester University Press, 1991).

W. I. Jennings, 'The Emergency Powers (Defence) (No. 2) Act 1940', Modern Law Review, 132, 1940, pp. 123–36.

J. M. Keynes, How to Pay for the War (London: Macmillan, 1940).

Warren F. Kimball, Churchill & Roosevelt: The Complete Correspondence, vol. 1 (Princeton, NJ: Princeton University Press, 1984).

— The Most Un-Sordid Act: Lend-Lease, 1939–1941 (Baltimore, MD: Johns Hopkins University Press, 1969).

Lt-Col. Faris B. Kirkland, 'The French Air Force in 1940', Air University Review, September–October 1985, pp. 1–14.

R. Langhorne (ed.), Diplomacy and Intelligence in the Second World War (Cambridge: Cambridge University Press, 1985).

Eric Larrabee, The Commander in Chief: Franklin Delano Roosevelt, his Lieutenants and their War (New York: Harper & Row, 1987).

Herbert Levy and Henry Morgenthau Jr.: The Remarkable Life of FDR's Secretary of the Treasury (New York: Skyhorse Publishing, 2010).

B. H. Liddell Hart (ed.), The Rommel Papers (London: Collins, 1953).

John Lukacs, Blood, Toil, Tears and Sweat (London: Yale University Press, 2009).

— Five Days in London (London: Yale University Press, 2001).

— The Duel: 10 May–31 July 1940 (London: Yale University Press, 1991).

Ross McKibbon, Parties and People: England 1914–1951 (Oxford: Oxford University Press, 2010).

Leo McKinstry, Spitfire: Portrait of a Legend (London: John Murray, 2007).

Ian McLaine, Ministry of Morale (London: Allen & Unwin, 1979).

R. Macleod and D. Kelly (eds), The Ironside Diaries, 1937–1940 (London: Constable, 1962).

Harold Macmillan, The Blast of War, 1939–1945 (London: Macmillan, 1967).

Karl Maier et al., Germany and the Second World War, vol. 2 (Oxford: Clarendon Press, 1991).

Joe Maiolo, Cry Havoc: The Arms Race and the Second World War, 1931–1941 (London: John Murray, 2011).

J. P. Mallmann-Showall (ed.), Führer Conferences on Naval Affairs 1939–1945 (London: Chatham Publishing, 2005).

Arthur J. Marder, From the Dardanelles to Oran (London: Oxford University Press, 1974).

Ernest R. May, Strange Victory: Hitler's Conquest of France (London: I. B. Tauris, 2000).

W. N. Medlicott, The Economic Blockade, vol. 1 (London: HMSO, 1952).

Martin Middlebrook and C. Everett, The Bomber Command War Diaries (London: Penguin, 1990).

Donald Moggridge, The Collected Writings of John Maynard Keynes, vol. XXII: Activities 1939–1945: Internal War Finance (Cambridge: Cambridge University Press, 1978).

Lord Moran, Churchill: The Struggle for Survival (London: Constable, 1966).

Herbert Morrison, Autobiography (London: Odhams, 1960).

Williamson Murray, Luftwaffe (London: Allen & Unwin, 1985).

Airey Neave, The Flames of Calais (London: Hodder & Stoughton, 1972).

Nigel Nicolson, Alex: The Life of Field Marshal Earl Alexander of Tunis (London: Weidenfeld & Nicolson, 1973).

Lynne Olson, *Troublesome Young Men: The Rebels who Brought Churchill to Power in 1940 and Helped Save Britain* (London: Bloomsbury, 2007).

Vincent Orange, *Dowding of Fighter Command: Victor of the Battle of Britain* (London: Grub Street, 2008).

—*Park: The Biography of Air Chief Marshal Sir Keith Park* (London: Grub Street, 2000).

Richard Overy, *The Bombing War* (London: Allen Lane, 2013).

H. M. D. Parker, *Manpower: A Study of War-time Policy and Administration* (London: HMSO, 1957).

R. A. C. Parker, *Chamberlain and Appeasement* (London: Macmillan, 1993).

—(ed.), *Winston Churchill: Studies in Statesmanship* (London: Brassey's, 1995).

George Peden, *Arms, Economics and British Strategy: From Dreadnoughts to the Hydrogen Bomb* (Cambridge: Cambridge University Press, 2007).

A. R. Peters, *Anthony Eden at the Foreign Office* (Aldershot: Gower, 1986).

Ben Pimlott, *Hugh Dalton* (London: Jonathan Cape, 1985).

—*The Second World War Diary of Hugh Dalton* (London: Jonathan Cape, 1986).

Clive Ponting, *1940: Myth and Reality* (London: Cardinal, 1990).

Alfred Price, *Battle of Britain: The Hardest Day: 18 August 1940* (London: Macdonald and Jane's, 1979).

Winston G. Ramsey (ed.), *The Battle of Britain: Then and Now* (London: Battle of Britain International, 1989).

—*The Blitz: Then and Now, vol. 1* (London: Battle of Britain International, 1987).

—*The Blitz: Then and Now, vol. 2* (London: Battle of Britain International, 1988).

—*The East End: Then and Now* (Battle of Britain International, 1997).

Jorgen Rasmussen, 'Party Loyalty in Wartime: The Downfall of the Chamberlain Government', *Journal of Politics*, 32, 2, May 1970, pp. 379–406.

John Ray, *The Night Blitz* (London: Arms and Armour, 1996).

David Reynolds, *In Command of History: Churchill Writing and Fighting the Second World War* (London: Allen Lane, 2004).

—*Lord Lothian and Anglo-American Relations* (New York: American Philosophical Society, 2007).

—*The Creation of the Anglo-American Alliance: A Study in Competitive Co-operation* (London: Europa, 1981).

Denis Richards, *The Royal Air Force, 1939–1945, vol. 1: The Fight At Odds* (London: HMSO, 1974).

Andrew Roberts, *Eminent Churchillians* (London: Weidenfeld & Nicolson, 1994).

—*The Holy Fox: The Life of Lord Halifax* (London: Phoenix, 1997).

Anthony Robinson, *R.A.F. Fighter Squadrons in the Battle of Britain* (London: Brockhampton, 1999).

Derek Robinson, *Invasion 1940: The Truth about the Battle of Britain and what Stopped Hitler* (London: Constable, 2005).

Stephen Roskill, *The War at Sea, vol. 1* (London: HMSO, 1954).

David Ross with Bruce Blanche and William Simpson, *The Greatest Squadron of Them All: The Definitive History of the 603 (City of Edinburgh) Squadron, vol. 1* (London: Grub Street, 2003).

B. E. V. Sabine, *British Budgets in Peace and War, 1932–1945* (London: Allen & Unwin, 1970).

Walter Schellenberg, *Invasion 1940: The Nazi Plan for Britain* (London: St Ermine's, 2001).

Maxwell Philip Schoenfeld, *The War Ministry of Winston Churchill* (Ames: Iowa State University Press, 1972).

Philip Selb, *Broadcasts from The Blitz: How Edward R. Murrow Helped Lead America into War* (Washington, DC: Potomac, 2006).

Robert Self, *Neville Chamberlain: A Biography* (Farnham: Ashgate, 2010).

—*The Neville Chamberlain Diary Letters, vol. 4* (Farnham: Ashgate, 2005).

Dudley Seward, *Victory Denied: The Rise of German Air Power and the Defeat of Germany, 1920–45* (London: Buchan & Enright, 1985).

Avi Shlaim, 'Prelude to Downfall: The British Offer of Union to France, June 1940', *Journal of Contemporary History*, 9, July 1974, pp. 27–63.

J. P. Mallmann Showell, *Führer Conferences on Naval Affairs* (London: Chatham Publishing, 2005).

Robert Skidelsky, *John Maynard Keynes: Fighting for Britain, 1937–1946* (London: Macmillan, 2000).

Nick Smart, 'Four Days in May: The Norway Debate and the Downfall of Neville Chamberlain', *Parliamentary History*, 17, 2, 1998, pp. 215–43.

—*Neville Chamberlain* (London: Routledge, 2010).

Malcolm Smith, *Britain and 1940: History, Myth and Popular Memory* (London: Routledge, 2000).

— *British Air Strategy between the Wars* (Oxford: Oxford University Press, 1984).

Major General Sir Edward Spears, *Assignment to Catastrophe* (London: Reprint Society, 1956).

Peter Stansky, *The First Day of the Blitz: September 7, 1940* (Melbourne: Scribe, 2007).

Dietmar Suss, *Death from the Skies: How the British and Germans Survived Bombing in World War II* (Oxford: Oxford University Press, 2014).

A. J. P. Taylor, *Beaverbrook* (New York: Simon & Schuster, 1972).

—*English History, 1914–1945* (Oxford: Oxford University Press, 1965).

Telford Taylor, *The Breaking Wave: The German Defeat in the Summer of 1940* (London: Weidenfeld & Nicolson, 1967).

John Terraine, *The Right of the Line: The Royal Air Force in the European War, 1939–1945* (London: Hodder & Stoughton, 1985).

Nicklaus Thomas-Symonds, *Attlee: A Life in Politics* (London: I. B. Tauris, 2010).

Julian Thompson, *Dunkirk: Retreat to Victory* (London: Sidgwick & Jackson, 2008).

Lawrence Thompson, *1940: Year of Legend, Year of History* (London: Fontana, 1968).

Richard Titmus, *Problems of Social Policy* (London: HMSO, 1950).

Adam Tooze, *The Wages of Destruction: The Making and the Breaking of the Nazi Economy* (London: Allen Lane, 2006).

Richard Toye, *The Roar of the Lion: The Untold Story of Churchill's World War II Speeches* (Oxford: Oxford University Press, 2013).

Ronald Tree, *When The Moon Was High: Memoirs of Peace and War, 1897–1942* (London: Macmillan, 1975).

H. R. Trevor-Roper, *Hitler's War Directives, 1939–1945* (London: Pan, 1966).

United States and British Intelligence Services, *The Führer Directives and Other Top-Level Directives of the German Armed Forces, 1939–1941* (Washington and London, 1948; reprinted by Partizan Press, Nottingham, n.d.).

Ronald Wheatley, *Operation Sea Lion: German Plans for the Invasion of England, 1939–1942* (Oxford: Clarendon Press, 1958).

Jerry White, *London in the 20th Century* (London: Viking, 2007).

Tom Williams, *A Mysterious Something in the Light: Raymond Chandler—A Life* (London: Aurum, 2012).

Patrick Wilson, *Dunkirk: From Disaster to Deliverance* (Barnsley: Leo Cooper, 1999).

Larry L. Witherell, 'Lord Salisbury's "Watching Committee" and the Fall of Neville Chamberlain', *English Historical Review*, 116, November 2001.

R. Wright, *Dowding and the Battle of Britain* (London: Penguin, 1969).

Philip Ziegler, *London at War, 1939–45* (New York: Knopf, 1995).

INDEX